# Royal Rebels

$\blacklozenge$

## Princess Louise
### &
### the Marquis of Lorne

by
Robert M. Stamp

# Royal Rebels

◆

## Princess Louise
## &
## the Marquis of Lorne

by
Robert M. Stamp

Toronto & Oxford
Dundurn Press
1988

Design and Production:Andy Tong
Printing and Binding:Gagné Printing Ltd., Louiseville, Quebec, Canada


The writing of this manuscript and the publication of this book were made possible by support from several sources. The publisher wishes to acknowledge the generous assistance and ongoing support of **The Canada Council, The Book Publishing Industry Development Programme** of the **Department of Communications** and **The Ontario Arts Council.**

*J. Kirk Howard, Publisher*

**Dundurn Press Limited**
2181 Queen Street East
Toronto, Canada
M4E 1E5

**Dundurn Distribution Limited**
Athol Brose, School Hill,
Wargrave, Reading
England RG10 8DY


**Canadian Cataloguing in Publication Data**

Stamp, Robert M., 1937-
 Royal Rebels

Bibliography: p.
Includes Index.
ISBN 1-55002-039-0 (bound) ISBN 1-55002-041-2 (pbk.)

1. Louise, Princess, Duchess of Argyll, 1848-1939.
2. Argyll, John Douglas Sutherland Campell, Duke of,
1845-1914. 3. Governors general - Canada - Biography.
4. Governors general - Canada - Spouses - Biography.
I. Title.

FC521.A74S73 1988          971.05'4'0922    C88-093627-4
F1033.A74S73 1988

# CONTENTS

# FOREWORD

My interest in the Marquis of Lorne began when I first read of his 1881 expedition across the Canadian prairies — one of the last great trans-prairie treks prior to the completion of the Canadian Pacific Railway. How romantic and how aventurous it seemed! A little more reading, some superficial research, and I produced an article for the Calgary *Herald's* travel section of September 12, 1981 — the hundredth anniversary of Lorne's arrival at old Fort Calgary.

Reaction to that article was surprising. Through letters to the editor and personal conversations, *Herald* readers pointed out the errors I had made in my story. People seemed interested in Lorne — and in his wife, Princess Louise — and knew quite a bit about them. Perhaps they were worth more than a travel article. More reading and more research were necessary.

I lived with Lorne and Louise for the next seven years, moving them between front burner and back burner as other writing projects demanded attention. My "Royal Rebels" survived a permanent move from Calgary to Toronto, gained a new dimension after a summer's research in Britain, and flowered during a temporary residency in Vancouver.

At first this book was meant to be a solo biography of the Marquis of Lorne, later Ninth Duke of Argyll. As a Canadian Governor General, Scottish aristocrat, and prolific writer during Victorian and Edwardian times, surely he merited a biography. Yet it was soon evident that his wife, Princess Louise, was equally interesting. She was the most talented of Queen Victoria's daughters, and would have pursued a life as a professional sculptress had she not been trapped by her royal birth.

The result is a dual biography of husband and wife — a married couple torn apart by conflicting sexual inclinations, yet always reconciled through mutual interests in the arts and in travel. The story follows their lives from early Victorian days to the upheavals produced by the First and Second World Wars, and from Scotland through England to Canada and across Europe. It spotlights a most unusual, multi-talented couple who would have been more at home in the twentieth than the nineteenth century.

I am indebted to a host of librarians and archivists, all of whom invariably answered my research questions with courtesy and interest. Thanks first of all to those who pointed the way in Calgary — staff members at the Glenbow-Alberta Institute, University of Calgary Library, and Calgary Public Library. In Toronto I must thank their counterparts at the Metropolitan Toronto Reference Library, Royal Ontario Museum, and the libraries at York University and the University of Toronto. Also the National Gallery and the Public Archives of Canada in Ottawa; Provincial Archives of British Columbia in Victoria; and Vancouver City Archives, Vancouver Public Library, and the University of British Columbia Library in Vancouver.

In London, England, I wish to thank staff members of the British Library, the Newspaper Library of the British Library, Public Record Office, Kensington Palace Archives, St. Paul's Cathedral, borough libraries in Westminster and Kensington, Mary Evans Picture Library, and the National Portrait Gallery. Elsewhere in Britain: Berkshire Record Office, Reading; Trinity College Library, Cambridge; Bodleian Library, Oxford; St. George's Chapel, Windsor; Eton College, Eton; and the National Library of Scotland in Edinburgh.

Special thanks to Hugh Dempsey and Carol Fullerton of Calgary, Dr. Stanley Frost of McGill University, Montreal, and Douglas and Janet Fetherling of Toronto, for sharing their knowledge and research materials with me. Finally, the enthusiastic and efficient group at Dundurn Press turned the chores of editing and publishing into pleasurable experiences; thanks to publisher Kirk Howard and staff for bringing "Royal Rebels" into print.


Robert M. Stamp
March 1988

**PRINCESS LOUISE**     **MARQUIS OF LORNE**

# CHAPTER ONE

# YOUNG IAN CAMPBELL, 1845-1856

*S*tafford House, the birthplace of Ian Campbell, Marquis of Lorne and later Ninth Duke of Argyll, can easily be found by the contemporary visitor to London. It is but a short stroll from Canada House and Trafalgar Square, through Admiralty Arch and along The Mall. The structure commands the west end of The Mall, along its north side, within sight of Buckingham Palace across Green Park to the west. Today the building is known as Lancaster House, and serves as the major centre for official dinners and receptions hosted by the British government. A century and a half ago, as Stafford House, it was the London residence of Ian Campbell's maternal grandparents, the Duke and Duchess of Sutherland.

The exterior of the building strikes the casual observer as comparatively plain. Like most aristocratic London homes of the second quarter of the nineteenth century, Stafford House/ Lancaster House shuns external decoration and depends for its effect on a sense of proportion and the emphasis given by its great columns and pilasters.

Privileged visitors, however, encounter one of the most ornate and magnificent interiors in all of London. Prime Minister Benjamin Disraeli considered its splendours "not unworthy of Vicenza" (the Italian city famous for the architectural works of Andrea Palladio), while Lord Greville likened the central hall — with its double staircase, gilded balustrade, and white marble columns — to one of Veronese's paintings. Off this main hall lay ante-rooms, a grand dining room and a magnificent library. Above were bedrooms and sitting rooms. The walls proudly displayed the Sutherlands' superb collection of English, French and Italian paintings.

During the early years of Queen Victoria's reign, Stafford House exercised a strong political, social and moral influence over Court and society. The Duke of Sutherland's extensive English and Scottish holdings made him one of the largest landowners in the entire kingdom. His wife, Duchess Harriet, was the foremost Whig lady of the land, and the close confidante of Queen Victoria as Mistress of the Robes.

At Stafford House the Duke and Duchess gave the most splendid parties in town. But they also used their residence as a rallying point for many of the great social reforms of the day. Here Italian patriot Giuseppe Garibaldi received a hero's welcome during his 1864 London visit; here Lord Shaftesbury advocated the reforms which led to the Factory Act, Florence Nightingale received support for her nursing work during the Crimean War, and Charles Sumner and William Lloyd Garrison pleaded for the abolition of slavery in America. Being part of the Stafford House set, claimed Disraeli, was being at the "innermost circle of initiation" both in politics and social affairs.

During the summer of 1845, however, Stafford House was popularly known as the "lying-in hospital." During August it produced three Sutherland babies. Duchess Harriet led the way on the second day of the month by giving birth to her youngest child, Ronald. Four days later, on the sixth, Harriet's eldest daughter Elizabeth Campbell gave birth to her first child, Ian, while another daughter, Evelyn Blantyre, produced the third infant at the end of the month.

Our focus is on the middle baby of these three, the infant son of Elizabeth and her husband, George Campbell, heir to the dukedom of Argyll. "Baby has an angel's little face," wrote Elizabeth, a face she thought looked "exactly like" his father's. [1]

Baby was christened John George Edward Henry Douglas Sutherland Campbell. Within his immediate family, he was always called Ian, the Scottish equivalent of John. Formal photographs from later years identify him as John Campbell. Colleagues in the House of Commons called him Johnny Lorne. In 1900 he succeeded his father as Duke of Argyll. Like all Campbell lairds he was called Mac Cailein Mhor (Great Son of Colin) in honour of an illustrious ancestor. But he is best known as the Marquis of Lorne, a courtesy title he held as eldest son of the Duke of Argyll from twenty-one months to fifty-four years of age.

The Campbells of Argyll advanced down the centuries to a powerful position among the clans of Scotland, chiefly through their hereditary flare for identifying themselves with the winning side. In the sixteenth century they were among the first Highland clans to commit themselves to the Protestant cause. They were leaders of the Scottish forces against King Charles I in the Civil War of the 1640s. They backed William of Orange in the Revolution of 1688-89. Archibald Campbell, Earl of Argyll, was one of the lords who brought William over from The Hague and administered the oath of kingship to him in London. As a reward, the earldom was raised to a dukedom, and Archibald became the First Duke

Lorne's father, George Campell, 8th Duke of Argyll.

of Argyll. His son John, the second Duke, led Scottish support for the union of the English and Scottish parliaments in 1707, and the Hanoverian succession to the British throne in 1714-15.

Such was the Anglo-Scottish, pro-Hanoverian heritage into which Ian Campbell was born in August 1845. But Ian's own memories barely stretched back to his paternal grandfather, John Campbell (1777-1847), Seventh Duke of Argyll. Duke John spent most of his life in the Highlands where he pursued a vigorous, outdoor life. His hobbies were fishing and shooting, while his scholarly interests lay in the natural sciences. Like his grandson and namesake in the 1860s, Duke John had been bored by the musty atmosphere of university learning, and withdrew from Oxford before graduating. Again like his grandson in later years, John learned much about life while travelling through continental Europe as a young man. In Paris in 1803 he met both Bonaparte and Talleyrand; Madame de Stael helped him escape Geneva when Anglo-French hostilities resumed.

Ian's grandfather spent sixteen years in an unhappy and childless marriage. After his first wife's death in 1818, he married for a second and much happier time, fathering two sons and a daughter. Yet the dukedom seemed far from secure. The elder son died while still in his teens; only the frail younger son George blocked the prospect of the Argyll estates passing into the hands of distant and hated cousins. Happily, young George survived the usual round of childhood illnesses, and blossomed into a promising young man with interests in politics, literature, religion and the natural sciences.

Like so many of his mediaeval ancestors, George Campbell made a brilliant marriage. His young bride of 1844 was Elizabeth Leveson-Gower, daughter of the powerful Duke and Duchess of Sutherland. Elizabeth was a beautiful young woman, extremely well read, with an "enthusiasm for every great and good cause" inherited from her mother. George acquired a large family of in-laws as well as a wife. "My wife's family connections were unusually numerous," he wrote. "In the fullest sense of the word, my wife's mother became like a mother to me, and her sisters like my own." The Leveson-Gowers introduced George Campbell to the larger world of London society and English country weekends. Finally, their Whig outlook was a healthy antidote to George's Toryism — "an immense advantage to me." [2]

A Whig daughter-in-law mattered less than a healthy grandson to old John Campbell at this stage in his life. The sixty-eight year-old Duke was understandably ecstatic when George and Elizabeth produced baby Ian in the summer of 1845. His anxiety and protectiveness were expressed in frequent admonitions that this precious baby "be kept in cotton wool," safe from the ravages of the external world. [3]

Young Ian's earliest memory focussed on the death-bed of his grandfather at Inverary Castle, the family seat of the Campbells in

Argyllshire, in the spring of 1847 — "the picture of a dark head on a white bed." The old man enjoyed having his grandson lifted onto his bed during his last few days, and listening to Ian imitate the noise of a steam engine. "But of this there is no recollection," lamented the grandson in later life, "only the head on the white pillow." [4]

With John Campbell's death in May 1847, his son George succeeded as Eighth Duke of Argyll, and his twenty-one month-old grandson became the new Marquis of Lorne.

\* \* \* \* \*

George and Elizabeth Campbell produced a large family, even by Victorian standards. After Ian's birth in 1845, at twelve to eighteen month intervals, came four more boys — Archie, Walter, George and Colin. They were followed, in turn, by seven girls — Edith, Elizabeth, Victoria, Evelyn, Frances, Mary and Constance. Any fears of the Argyll dukedom passing into alien hands were quickly dispelled, as all twelve children survived till adulthood.

Among the boys, Ian was closest in age and merriment to Archie and Walter. Archie was the family wit, a born mimic and caricaturist, and Ian was his frequent subject. "Archie parodied his verses, imitated his absent ways," recalled their sister Frances, "with an exactness which reduced the whole family, including the victim himself, to helpless laughter." Brother Walter added the gift of ventriloquism to that of mimicry, often imitating a cat, apparently up the chimney of the drawing room, while the children sat with their parents at tea. [5]

The Campbell household was noisy and active, particularly in late afternoons when children, tutors and governesses put down their books and took tea together. "I still see the living tide of golden-headed seniors coming in at the door, and settling to amuse themselves," recalled Frances. Taunts flew between brothers and sisters, tutors teased governesses, while the older boys tormented their tutors. Tea-time, concluded Frances, was "a pretty argumentative repast." [6]

The Campbells were typical Victorians in their faithful observance of family rituals — gathering of the household for prayers, high teas and formal dinners, reading aloud in the evenings before a blazing fire. Duchess Elizabeth was the familiar mother-figure, dispensing generous doses of comfort and affection to her large brood of children. Duke George was the archetypal family patriarch who commanded automatic respect and made the important decisions. Temperance accompanied his stern demeanour. "My father never smoked, and never drank wine or spirits," Ian wrote. "He had a great horror of any excess, and used to teach us how absurd it made men to lose their wits." [7]

Ian and his siblings grew up in a stimulating political environment. On the death of his own father in 1847, George Campbell took his hereditary seat in the House of Lords as the Eighth Duke of Argyll. He was a Peelite and a convinced free trader, prepared to give his independent support to the ministry of Lord John Russell. In January 1853, though not yet thirty years old, the Duke became Lord Privy Seal in a coalition ministry of Whigs and Peelites formed by Lord Aberdeen. From then until 1866, with the exception of one sixteen-month period in opposition, the Duke held office either as Privy Seal or Postmaster-General in a succession of Whig ministries under Aberdeen and Palmerston. Not an exceptionally gifted administrator, Argyll proved most valuable to his party as a brilliant parliamentary debater and orator.

Duke George attracted as much public attention through his religious and scientific writing as he did through politics. His first publication, *Letters to the Peers from a Peer's Son*, a pamphlet on Scottish Church matters, appeared before he was twenty years old. This marked the beginning of a profusion of pamphlets and articles, reviews and books, spanning the fields of religion and philosophy, domestic politics and foreign affairs, and the geology and biology of his native Argyllshire. In 1851 his scientific writings won him election as a Fellow of the Royal Society and Chancellor of the University of St. Andrews. Later he served as Lord Rector of the University of Glasgow and President of the Royal Society.

Elizabeth Campbell was devoted to her husband and his work. "She never tired of sitting in the room where my father wrote," recalled Ian, "or of having him read what he had written for her criticism and approval."[8] She also shared her husband's love for the Argyllshire estates. Ian remembered the two of them frequently walking through the woods at Inverary Castle, taking a forester along for a discussion of planting, pruning and thinning. She introduced new varieties of flowers and shrubs into the castle gardens. In everything she did, Elizabeth won the love of Inverary's domestic staff and tenant farmers for her kindness and generosity; they called her the "Good Duchess."

Elizabeth was small and slight of figure, much like her husband, but with the added feature of a soft, radiant face that drew instant attention. Her character seems to have been impeccable. "Nothing of the grosser elements of the earth could have found room in her," eulogized her daughter Frances. Acquaintances spoke of her as moving in regions aloof from the world. "She lived on mountain tops," one friend commented. "Very woman of woman" wrote family friend Alfred Tennyson at the time of her premature death in 1878.[9]

Yet Elizabeth Campbell was much more than the other-worldly, beautiful and dutiful, seen-but-not-heard wife of a Duke and cabinet minister. She was, after all, the daughter of Harriet, Duchess of Sutherland, and from her famous mother she inherited a brand of liberalism that influenced her views and demanded expression. She supported publicly such reformers as Elizabeth Fry, Florence Nightingale, Lord Shaftesbury, and the American abolitionist writer Harriet Beecher Stowe. For a number of years she poured forth her political views in correspondence with Prussian diplomat George von Bunsen and American senator Charles Sumner. Ian believed his mother's correspondence with Sumner, chairman of the Senate Committee on Foreign Relations, contributed much towards "pressing our friendship with the United States" when the North was "much exasperated against England" during and after the American Civil War. [10]

But her children always came first, and among them her first-born Ian enjoyed a special pride of place. Elizabeth was an anxious mother, fretting needlessly over Ian's every word and gesture. On one visit with family friends, she worried of "Ian's shyness being taken for pride." On another occasion, however, Ian "was marvellously at ease," whispering to Lady Sarah Cholmondeley, whom he had never seen before, that he thought "the strawberries would make her 'ick." [11]

\* \* \* \* \*

In the early years of their marriage the Duke and Duchess of Argyll spent most of the time at their Highland homes of Inverary and Rosneath, staying with Elizabeth's parents at Stafford House during short visits to London. But such an arrangement was bound to be short-lived as the Duke's entry into the House of Lords and then the cabinet necessitated longer stays in the capital. Besides, the increasing number of Campbell infants imposed a burden on the ageing Sutherland grandparents.

Rental accommodation provided an interim solution. Ian remembered a leased home in Hamilton Place, close to the Duke of Wellington's, where his little-boy eyes gazed on the "iron shutters the Duke insisted on keeping on his windows, to remind the London mob of how they had smashed them in the Reform Bill demonstrations." Another year the Argylls rented 15 Park Lane, "a narrow house and very noisy", but near the Duchess of Gloucester, who delighted the Campbell youngsters by holding "a crowded ball for children in a large upper room." [12]

With increasing political and social obligations it was just a matter of time before George and Elizabeth purchased a London home of their own. Their ultimate choice in 1854 was Bedford Lodge, soon renamed Argyll Lodge, a suburban Regency villa on the east side of Holland Park. Though Argyll Lodge was demolished in 1955 for the building of Holland Park School, its site is easily accessible to the inquisitive visitor. From Kensington High Street, proceed north on Campden Hill Road, past the

Lorne's mother, Elizabeth Campell, Duchess of Argyll.

modern Kensington Town Hall, then west on a short cul-de-sac simply called Campden Hill. On the south side of this tree-lined lane, just at the edge of Holland Park, Argyll Lodge stood on the crest of a hill amid four acres of idyllic beauty.

The Duke was delighted with the rural setting and abundant bird life, as if deep in an English woodland. "When we took possession of this villa, there were fields and orchards all round it, with the exception of four other villas in a line with us, each having a large garden," Ian recalled in later years. "There was high grass in summer by the roadside. There were green fields down to Kensington High Street, one row of buildings only blocking the view of that road."[13]

The children remembered Argyll Lodge with great affection. "The Lodge was no mere place in which to sleep, and from which to rush in an unending round of social engagements," wrote Frances. "It was the centre where the Duke lived surrounded by his family, and where he carried on all his work, literary and public, and the spreading trees and wide verandah gave shade and air to his colleagues and friends, who sought the society of himself and the Duchess." The young ones were always underfoot. "They were brought up in the best of all schools, with a hearing ear to the conversation of the men and women who were filling the stage of life, and working in their day and generation." [14]

Next door neighbour Thomas Macaulay was a heroic figure for the Campbell youngsters. "We boys used to climb a tree and sit reading in its branches, and see the great historian reading as he walked up and down on his verandah," recalled Ian. Often Macaulay would visit the Campbells and impress the children with his vast store of knowledge. "We looked upon him as almost supernatural, especially after we had to repeat the whole of the *Lays of Ancient Rome*, the fine verses that we knew had come from him." [15]

From an early age, however, literary heroes such as Macaulay and Tennyson competed for Ian's attention with various political and military figures. A bout of chickenpox, followed by a long convalescence during the winter of 1852-53, introduced the seven year-old boy to Emperor Louis Napoleon of France. Propped up in bed, Ian eagerly scanned each week's *Illustrated London News*, which graphically portrayed events in Paris as Louis Napoleon transformed himself from elected president to emperor-for-life. "Many people disapproved of these proceedings," Ian wrote, "but they made me distinctly better, and gave me an interest in the movements of the world." [16]

Ian's Whig mother and grandmother found it difficult to sympathize with this subverter of democratic institutions. During Louis Napoleon's visit to England in 1855 Elizabeth Campbell "held out stoutly" against "showing him any attention". So Ian and his brothers decided to have a bit of fun. They obtained a photograph of the Emperor, sent it to their mother, and imitating his handwriting, wrote underneath "With the homage of Louis Napoleon". Now Elizabeth, who felt she was obliged to respond to such politeness, was in an absolute panic. "What shall I do?" she cried. "How can I write my name in his book? Why should he wish to be civil to me?" Panic continued until the boys confessed their prank, then normalcy was restored. [17]

The Crimean War provided further learning experiences and additional heroes. Through 1854 Ian avidly studied the military news in the London papers. His father took him to Portsmouth to cheer the troops as they left for Crimea. Elizabeth thought it quite "bold to let Ian go, for he was not quite well, but I could not resist his violent wish." [18] He came to know the British and French regiments in Crimea through playing with his sets of model soldiers. With his father he watched the parading troops on their return home — "a wonderful scene of enthusiasm, women rushing now and then into the ranks to greet their sweethearts or husbands." [19]

The decade of the 1850s also gave Ian a military hero in Sir Colin Campbell, later Lord Clyde, a distant kinsman, and one of the few British generals to distinguish himself in the Crimea. Hearing of Sir Colin's 1857 appointment to command an expedition to suppress the Indian Mutiny, Ian and his brother Archie mounted their ponies at Argyll Lodge to "go and say good-bye to our old friend." Luckily Sir Colin was at his Knightsbridge home, engaged with a military aide in "multitudinous affairs, writing, ordering, despatching, with a constant stream of officers and others arriving and departing." When the elderly general saw his two small visitors, he came out, invited them to dismount, and took them inside to witness the flurry of activity. For ten minutes they stayed, then the general helped them re-mount their ponies. "God bless you, my boys," he called out, and two small voices called back, "God bless you, Sir Colin" as they rode away. [20] It was no surprise to Ian that Sir Colin quelled the uprising in India and returned to Britain two years later a national hero. "Ian and Archie in great excitement," wrote their mother, "about a little illumination in the garden" in honour of their military idol.[21]

Given such memories of the Crimean War and the Indian Mutiny, the Duke of Wellington, Emperor Louis Napoleon, and Sir Colin Campbell, it was not surprising that Ian Campbell's most "fervent desire" was to become a soldier. But his parents were adamantly opposed. Duke George might take Ian to watch the great military parades of the day, but neither he nor Elizabeth could bear the thought of their eldest son, heir to the Argyll dukedom and its vast landed estates, risking his life. There could be no thought of a military career; at an early age Ian "abandoned it in deference to their wishes."[22] He would have to find other career outlets for his energies and his patriotism.

\* \* \* \* \*

The Campbell family was often on the move, shuffling back and forth between Argyll Lodge and their many ancestral and family homes spread through the English and Scottish countrysides. Christmas was usually spent at Trentham, the Staffordshire seat of Ian's maternal grandparents, the Duke and Duchess of Sutherland. "It was the frosty time we boys liked best, and frost at Christmas-time seldom disappointed us." Outside on the estate's frozen lake, Uncle Hugh Leveson-Gower organized family hockey games. Inside, presiding over a multitude of aunts and uncles, cousins and friends, plus a vast army of servants, was the great Duchess Harriet. Ian and his brothers liked to creep into their grandmother's private rooms where "we could see the beautiful lady and keep her all to ourselves." [23]

Once a year the Campbells visited their maternal kinfolk at Dunrobin, the largest estate in the entire kingdom, encompassing some 1.3 million acres of land in northeastern Scotland's Sutherlandshire. Here Ian's grandfather had built a huge French chateau, high up over the Moray Firth. Here the Campbell children rode their ponies over the hills, listened to scary tales of the firth's legendary sea-serpent, and on at least one occasion took part in a mock jousting tournament organized by family friend Lord Dufferin.

Despite the charms of Trentham and Dunrobin, — plus Cliveden, another Sutherland home overlooking the Thames near Maidenhead — the Campbells' own ancestral homes at Rosneath and Inverary loomed larger in the consciousness of young Ian. These were the Scottish homes of his father and his grandfather, the seats of the dukedom of Argyll, and his own inheritance.

On their way to Rosneath, the Campbells detrained at Helensburgh and were rowed across the Gare Loch, an arm of the Firth of Clyde leading north into the Highlands, on the Duke's colorfully emblazoned personal barge. This barge was signalled by an elaborate system of smokes or fires — three separate fires if the Duke or Duchess were to be transported, two for relatives and close friends, one for "those in a humbler position in life." [24]

One of Ian's favourite sights was north along the Gare Loch towards the mountains of Argyllshire. "From sunrise to sunset the lovely colouring is ever changing on their rugged forms, and evening brings them out in blues and purples against the reddened skies." Yet the Gare Loch's beauty and tranquility were not as strategicly important as its depth and sheltered location, offering a "war harbour unrivalled on any part of the coast." [25] Today, true to his prediction, the Gare Loch serves as a military installation, providing anchorage for nuclear-powered submarines of the British and American navies.

Rosneath Castle was begun in 1803 as an extravagant Italian villa by the Sixth Duke of Argyll, Ian's great-uncle, "on a scale which no available money could have finished." The old Duke died suddenly "in the midst of his spendthrift life", leaving the castle half-finished. Little was done over the next few years, and when Ian's father took possession in 1847 Rosneath was in deplorable condition. But this did not distress the frugal George and the good-spirited Elizabeth, "who would have found it easy to make an encampment in any barrack, however big or small." [26] Not wishing to divert large sums of money to finishing Rosneath, Duke George and family took possession only of the completed central tower and one wing.

More remote than Rosneath, and almost uncomfortably large, stood the eighteenth century ducal castle at Inverary on Loch Fyne. Approaching it by land the family travelled by train as far as Balloch on Loch Lomond, then by carriage over the delightfully named Rest-And-Be-Thankful Pass. Only at spacious Inverary, with its large staff and grounds, did the Duke and Duchess feel they could entertain their "great variety of friends" in comfort and style. Inverary also demanded the Duke's presence for administering the vast Argyll estates that spread over so much of the southwestern Highlands.

For young Ian Campbell, Inverary meant wild, untamed lands to explore, constant streams of visitors, frequent hunting and shooting parties — all played out against a brilliant background of autumn colours in the Highlands. Here the young Marquis of Lorne drank deeply of his Highland heritage; here he acquired the patience and skills of marksmanship and angling. Here, too, he first turned his sensitive observation of the natural landscape into rhyming prose:

### FIRST MEMORIES

*In the rapids that cover the River,*
*Almost in the heart of the foam,*
*I have seen a calm pool, that for ever*
*Welled dark from the depths of its home.*

*So now, in the rush of the present,*
*The pools of the memory glow;*
*Today's haste and hurry incessant*
*O'erwhelms ne'er the calm "Long Ago."*

*Like canoes flying fast on the spindrift,*
*We seem but the sport of the spray,*
*When a turn of the paddle and wrist lift*
*The boat, to float free of the fray!*

*So now, from the strife evanescent,*
*We turn — from Today to the Past,*
*And Age, by our memory chastened,*
*Recalls our first Home at the last!* [27]

* * * * *

On 18 August 1847, Inverary Castle witnessed the first "meeting" between future husband and wife — Ian Campbell, Marquis of Lorne, and Her Royal Highness Princess Louise Caroline Alberta. Young Ian was all of two years old, while Louise was but an embryo in her mother's womb.

For Queen Victoria and Prince Albert, the summer of 1847 featured a leisurely cruise up the west coast of Scotland. No part of the trip could be too strenuous for the Queen was once again pregnant; her sixth child and fourth daughter, the future Princess Louise, had been conceived in June.

As they sailed north, the royal couple decided to stop at Inverary on Loch Fyne. A short visit to the Duke and Duchess of Argyll would provide a nice break from shipboard routine. The Queen could pay her respects to the new duke, George Campbell, and renew her friendship with his young wife, Elizabeth, daughter of her longtime friend, the Duchess of Sutherland. Since the Argylls had been strong supporters of the British crown for generations, the visit might silence those who saw pro-Jacobite overtones in the Queen's growing love affair with the Highlands.

At eight o'clock in the morning of August 18 the royal party transferred from their yacht *Victoria and Albert* to the smaller vessel *Fairy* for the journey up the loch to Inverary. "I only came on deck when we were within an hour of Inverary," noted the Queen, "where the lake widens, and the hills on either side are very green and undulating, but not very high. The approach to Inverary is splendid; the loch is very wide; straight before you a fine range of mountains splendidly lit up — green, pink, and lilac; to the left, the little town of Inverary; above it, surrounded by pine woods, stands the Castle of Inverary, square, with turrets at the corners." [28]

Apprehension and nervousness prevailed on shore. Duke George had received news of the royal visit while sailing off Skye, nearly 300 kilometres to the north. It could not have come at a worse time, as he and Elizabeth were breaking up the large household establishment at Inverary, following the death of George's father in April. They were looking forward to a holiday with Elizabeth's parents at Dunrobin.

But now the Queen was coming, and plans had to be altered. Argyll rose to the occasion. His mother-in-law, the Duchess of Sutherland, brought down her staff from Dunrobin. Nearby lairds helped round up assorted kinsmen and clansmen. A field battery was obtained to provide

Lorne's grandmother, Hariett, Duchess of Sutherland.

the royal salute. All was ready when the *Fairy* docked at Inverary quayside.

"Our reception was in true Highland fashion," the Queen noted in her journal. "The Duke and Duchess of Argyll, the Duchess of Sutherland, Lord Stafford, Lady Caroline Leveson-Gower, and the Blantyres received us at the landing place, which was all ornamented with heather." From quayside to castle Campbell clansmen "formed a living avenue, clad in their dark tartans with broad red facings, and all the Highland accoutrements." [29]

The royal party drove up Glen Shira to view the Highland panorama. "The weather was particularly fine," observed the Queen, "and we were struck much by the extreme beauty of Inverary — presenting as it does such a combination of magnificent timber, with high mountains, and a noble lake." [30] Back at the castle by two o'clock, the royal visitors sat down to a luncheon feast ringed by an honour guard of 200 Campbell clansmen in full Highland dress. But there was little time to dally in this eighteenth century fairyland castle. By late afternoon the royal party was on its way, bound for Fort William and the Grampians.

Ian's only lasting memory of the day was a vivid image of a "number of tents pitched on a grass field, and men in Highland dress coming out of one of the tents." [31] Of the Queen, the Prince Consort, and other members of the royal family, the two year-old child had no recollection.

But the sight of young Ian at the castle, as the party went inside for lunch, stayed in the Queen's memory. "Outside stood the Marquis of Lorne, just two years old, a dear, white, fat, fair little fellow with reddish hair, but very delicate features, like both his father and mother: he is such a merry, independent little child. He had a black velvet dress and jacket, with a sporran, scarf and Highland bonnet." [32]

Young Ian also amused the Queen when, as the party said their goodbyes at the quayside, he declined to kiss the hand of her daughter Vicky, the Princess Royal, then eight years old. The youngster was simply overwhelmed by all the pomp and ceremony surrounding the occasion. How was he to know that Princess Vicky would one day be his sister-in-law! How was Queen Victoria to know that young Ian Campbell would one day marry the two-month old embryo she carried in her womb, the future Princess Louise!

# CHAPTER TWO

# YOUNG PRINCESS LOUISE, 1848-1861

*U*nlike Stafford House/Lancaster House, Buckingham Palace requires no special directions for the contemporary visitor to London. It sits in all its majestic splendour, at the west end of The Mall, drawing tens of thousands of curious onlookers every day. But note its proximity to Stafford House, just across Green Park on the north side of The Mall. Today the distance is but a short walk; in the 1840s, when the trees of Green Park were much younger, the two grand residences were within easy waving distance from upper windows.

Here at Buckingham Palace at eight o'clock in the morning of 18 March 1848, Queen Victoria gave birth to Princess Louise Caroline Alberta. Despite a long and difficult labour, there were no undue complications. The Queen was attended by Sir James Cook, the royal physician; Charles Locock, London's leading obstetrician, known as "The Great Deliverer of His Country;" and by Mrs. Lilly of Camberwell, the midwife who ushered all of Victoria's children into the world. The baby was vigorous and healthy and mother and daughter were soon doing very well.

The birth announcement appeared later that day in *The Times* and the London *Gazette*; the Privy Council was convened at 2:30 in the afternoon to receive the news; the Archbishop of Canterbury prepared a thanksgiving prayer; congratulatory addresses were duly moved and seconded in the Lords and Commons; batteries in Hyde Park and at the Tower of London fired royal salutes.

This sixth pregnancy of Queen Victoria had begun on a happy and tranquil note. Victoria and Albert seemed in the best of spirits through the summer and early autumn of 1847. During the Scottish trip that included their stop at Inverary, a reporter wrote that the Prince Consort "looked pleased with everything and everybody, and with himself too." Albert passed on the comment in a letter to his mother-in-law, the Duchess of

Kent, adding: "I must confess the reporter was right." [1] Victoria also seemed at ease. During her confinement she relaxed by reading *Letters of W. von Humboldt to a Female Friend*, a book recommended by Baron Stockmar, her husband's advisor and mentor, as "admirably fitted for the Queen's reading." [2]

Yet all this was somewhat deceiving, for Princess Louise could hardly have chosen a worse time to be born than the spring of 1848. An influenza epidemic swept through England early in the year, followed by the threat of cholera that finally reached London in October. Anti-English outbursts were nastier than usual in Ireland that spring, while at home the Chartist agitation for parliamentary reform struck terror in the hearts of the well-to-do classes. News from across the Channel was even worse. Revolutionary mobs were at the palace gates, threatening European dynasties and the very lives of kings and queens.

The Campbells of Argyll sheltered themselves from the worst of these upheavals by spending most of the year at Rosneath. "It was difficult in the peacefulness of its woods and waters, and in sight of the calm outlines of its everlasting hills," recalled Lorne's father, "to realize the noise of the voices outside and the tumults of the people." [3]

Victoria and Albert were denied such luxury. From their vantage points of Windsor Castle and Buckingham Palace they alternatively grieved as assorted royal friends and relatives fled their European capitals, and rejoiced as they landed safely as refugees on Britain's shores. At the last moment the Queen was kept so busy organizing their temporary accommodation that her labour was well advanced before she took to bed. Admitting her own troubled state, Victoria predicted the new baby might well grow into "something peculiar."

Prince Albert was mildly disappointed the new arrival was a girl. "If a little boy had come," he wrote his brother Ernest, "our children would have been quite symmetrical. Now there are four [girls] against two [boys]." Still, even "though it be a daughter," Albert confessed to Stockmar that "my joy and gratitude are very great as I was often full of misgivings because of the many moral shocks which have crowded upon Victoria of late." To his mother he confessed the safe birth "brings quite a spot of light for us," at a time when "one is so completely surrounded by what is perplexing and painful." [4]

There were more shocks to come as British authorities faced the increasingly troublesome Chartist movement. The Chartists demanded votes for all men, a secret ballot, equal electoral districts, annual general elections, abolition of property qualifications for members of parliament, and payment for those members once elected. Twice before they had petitioned parliament for action on these demands. Now in April 1848, as revolution swept the Continent and riots were a daily occurrence throughout Britain and Ireland, they proposed to march through London and present a third petition— rumoured to contain over five million signatures!

Prince Albert was apprehensive about the security of Buckingham Palace with the approach of the April 10 Chartist rally at Kennington Common. How to protect a new baby, a host of anxious women and children, even the very throne itself, against a rampaging mob? The old Duke of Wellington, as commander-in-chief, suggested the task would be easier if Buckingham Palace were empty. So on April 8 the entire royal family, baby Louise and all, made a strategic exit from London by train. Their destination was Osborne, their private summer home on the Isle of Wight.

Louise thrived in Osborne's moist seaside air. "The finest child I ever saw," exclaimed the visiting Duchess of Teck, "very large beautiful eyes, a sweet little mouth, and a very pretty good-humoured expression." [5] Lady Sarah Lyttelton, the royal governess, detailed Louise's features at the end of April — "very large; extremely fair, with white satin hair; large, long blue eyes and regular features; a most perfect form from head to foot. She is as placid and happy as possible, cries very little, and begins to laugh and even crow, which at six weeks old is early." [6]

In early May, after Chartist agitation sputtered to a halt, the royal family returned to London for the infant's christening. Prince Albert composed a special christening anthem while Queen Victoria chose the name — Louisa Caroline Alberta. Louisa came naturally from the baby's two grandmothers, the Duchess of Kent and the Duchess of Saxe-Coburg; Caroline acknowledged a great-grandmother, the Duchess of Gotha, who had died two months earlier; Alberta honoured her father. Although the young princess was formally christened Louisa, she was immediately and always referred to as Louise, both in private circles and in official communications.

The christening took place in the private chapel of Buckingham Palace as twilight descended on the evening of May 13. The royal infant was dressed in a robe of Honiton lace over white satin, and lay in the arms of the palace's head nurse. The sacrament was performed by Archbishop Sumner of Canterbury, who broke all tradition by not wearing a wig. Clutches of royal relatives, members of the British aristocracy, and representatives of the diplomatic community looked on. Due to the troubled state of Europe, however, none of the baby's sponsors could be present. So the Duchess of Cambridge stood proxy for the Grand Duchess of Mecklenburg-Strelitz, Dowager Queen Adelaide for the Duchess of Saxe-Meiningen, and Prince Albert for the Duke of Mecklenburg–Schwerin.

Princess Louise's christening on the thirteenth day of the month, in the absence of all her God-parents, caused the superstitious to shake their heads and whisper of bad luck. As it happened there was just one

Royal family at Osborne, 1857.

embarrassing moment during the ceremony. The ageing Duchess of Gloucester, an aunt of Queen Victoria, had one of her periodic mental lapses. When the service was at its climax the duchess became muddled as to the nature of the gathering, rose from her seat, advanced towards the Queen and knelt before her. "Imagine our horror!" exclaimed Victoria. [7]

Princess Louise's birth and christening did not excite the same level of public interest as had been the case with the five older royal children. In the spring of 1848 public attention was too engrossed in Chartist agitation at home and revolutions on the Continent. With more time on their hands the editorial cartoonists of the London newspapers might have had a field day over the birth of yet another royal infant, especially a fourth daughter. Could husbands be found for all these princesses? How much royal dowry money would the national treasury have to produce at some later date?

* * * * *

Princess Louise was the sixth of nine children born to Queen Victoria and Prince Albert. Now there was one youngster for each day of the week, omitting Sunday, as the older children said, "as a day of rest." Like her siblings before her, Louise surrendered her proper name for one or more pet names within nursery and family circles. Princess Victoria was Vicky or Pussy or Pussette, Albert Edward was Bertie or Princey, Alice was Alee, Alfred was Affie, and Helena was Lenchen. Baby Louise began life as La Nouvelle, then was variously called Louisechen, Loozey, Loosey, or Loo-Loo.

The royal family seemed a happy family during the years of Louise's childhood. Parents and children lived in close intimacy, sharing much in the way of daily routines and special pleasures. Each child's morning lessons were usually inspected by one or both parents. The elder ones normally ate lunch with Mama and Papa. During the afternoon Victoria often played with the children or supervised their music lessons. In the evening the parents heard prayers and tucked the wee ones into bed before going in to their own dinner.

Each season of the year brought its special amusements as the family moved about on an almost regular timetable from Buckingham Palace to Windsor Castle, to Osborne and Balmoral. Christmas was usually spent at Windsor, with skating parties and sleigh rides during the day and family games around the fire in the long evenings. The children received their presents on Christmas Eve in the Queen's private sitting rooms. Chandeliers in these rooms were taken down and huge Christmas trees lighted with candles — the scene resembling a brilliant bazaar. "Vraiment," exclaimed Louise, demonstrating her proficiency in French at age twelve, "c'est un peu trop extravagant." [8]

Osborne in the summer months was a particular favourite of the children. Albert and Victoria purchased Osborne as a private rather than a state residence, and re-built it along Italianate lines in the mid-1840s. Succeeding summers at this idyllic retreat on the Isle of Wight saw endless family fun. Albert taught the children to swim and fly kites. Victoria seemed more relaxed, more fun for the children to be with. Here Louise and her siblings had fewer formal lessons, and more time to romp outdoors in the fresh air.

When Osborne proved too accessible to London's politicians, Victoria and Albert looked north to the Scottish Highlands for a more secluded family holiday spot. They first vacationed at Balmoral the year Louise was born, purchased the estate shortly afterwards, and within five years constructed their own grand residence. Here they were more remote from the bothersome world of politics. They cut out the pomp and ceremony of monarchy and played husband and wife, mother and father, often travelling incognito on expeditions through the countryside.

Besides the regularity of Osborne and Balmoral, the older children could look forward to periodic family and holiday visits to the Continent. On 18 August 1857 the royal yacht *Victoria and Albert* sailed into Cherbourg harbour with the Queen, Prince Albert, seven year-old Princess Louise, and six other royal youngsters aboard. This was not a state visit, but a grandiose family excursion from Osborne. The family went ashore and bundled themselves into a rickety open coach for an "incognito" trip along the coast to the village of Bricquebec. They were eventually recognized, of course, but that was half the fun.

In later years Louise would derive just as much pleasure from incognito travel as did Queen Victoria herself. In fact Louise proved to have much in common with her formidable mother. From Victoria she received a zest for life, a strong sense of self-reliance, an indomitable will, a fiery temper, and an insistence on putting her own needs ahead of others. From her father, Louise inherited an intellectual and inquisitive turn of mind, plus a scarcely concealed belief that artificial social functions were a great waste of time.

Through the 1850s, however, Louise acted more the unknown and undiscovered "middle child" than anything else. She apparently received far less parental attention than the two eldest problem children — Vicky and Bertie — or the three youngest favourites who followed her — Arthur, Leopold, and Beatrice. She was inclined to be withdrawn and less communicative than the others. Yet she relished attention when it was bestowed. "Louise is so happy to be made a little of," observed Lady Augusta Stanley on one occasion. [9]

"Louise stood somewhat aloof from the others," observed David Duff in his 1940 biography of the Princess. "One can see her in portraits with her head slightly downcast, a shy smile playing round her lips as if she held a secret that she shared with no one, a secret that caused her infinite amusement." [10] What she needed, like any child, was a special talent that would allow her to proclaim her individuality to the world.

\* \* \* \* \*

Just prior to Louise's birth, Victoria and Albert mapped out a thorough and well-organized scheme of education for their growing brood. Phase one consisted of elementary grounding under the guidance of the children's chief governess, Lady Sarah Lyttelton and her successor Lady Caroline Barrington. The chief governess continued to be responsible for the general care of the children even after they passed into the second stage of their education, when they were placed under Miss Hildyard for English, Madame Rollande de Sange for French, Fraulein Gruner for German, Mrs. Anderson for music and Edward Corbould for art. The third and final phase featured specialist instruction for a final polishing before adulthood. For the boys, this might include a term at university, or officer training at a military or naval school. But there was little chance of the girls leaving home for comparable learning experiences.

Louise was usually paired with her sister Helena, two years her senior, for lessons both inside and outside the classroom. These lessons began early in life, and they were serious business, for Prince Albert believed vigorous devotion to formal studies was the key to success in life. Although he concentrated most of his energies on the two eldest children, the younger ones never completely escaped his supervisory eye. Every day he gathered the children around him while he scanned their progress reports. Sometimes praise was given, but more often the youngsters would be advised to take their studies more seriously.

In later life Louise criticized her childhood education. "Luckily the habit of moulding all children to the same pattern has gone out of fashion," she stated when in her eighties. "It was deplorable. I know, because I suffered from it." Yet her father never believed he was forcing them into the same mould. "The education of six different children is a difficult task," he wrote his brother Ernest after Louise's birth, "for they are none of them the least like the other in looks, mind or character." [11]

Though traditional in many respects, the children's education did include examples of advanced pedagogical thinking. Louise and her sisters, for instance, acquired home-making skills in the Swiss Cottage erected on the grounds at Osborne in 1854. This grandiose play house offered a unique learning-by-doing approach two or three generations ahead of its time in the educational world. Inside its small kitchen were miniature stoves and ovens, where the princesses were taught domestic science. They and their brothers had their own garden plots, and the girls were encouraged to cook the produce. Sometimes Victoria and Albert dined at the cottage, witnessing their daughters' progress at first hand. Sometimes the girls baked for sick or elderly folk in the neighbourhood or, after 1858, for their married sister Vicky in Prussia.

Innovation also characterized the learning of great works of drama. The princes and princesses became famous for staging dramatic shows or theatricals for their parents on special birthday and anniversary occasions at Windsor Castle. Putting on plays was a natural extension to the children's language classes and to their mother's love of the theatre.

Louise made her stage debut in January 1853 when she was not yet five years of age. "Louise did not come on when she ought, so that the others had to wait for her," observed her mother. Next year she played a supporting role in a production of James Thomson's *The Seasons* — "Louise in a sort of Russian dress sitting before a fire," observed Queen Victoria, "this was the prettiest almost." A year later it was *Rothkappchen*, a German version of *Red Riding Hood*, with Louise "very droll as the whiskered and moustached gentleman." [12]

Louise was slow to emerge from these group activities in royal classrooms, Swiss Cottage, and Windsor Castle stage as an individual in her own right. She certainly mastered her lessons effectively, though not spectacularly. Yet she seemed to have no preference for any one formal subject over another. Gradually, however, Louise's interests and talents in the visual arts provided the distinctiveness she craved as a middle child.

An artistic bent was certainly present on both sides of the family. Prince Albert enjoyed drawing; his aesthetic tastes ranged widely from mediaeval Italian masters to contemporary German artists; and he kept up to date with the changing vagaries of the British art scene. Queen Victoria was a prolific and proficient artist in her own right. Drawing and painting to chronicle her daily life, she had a gift for capturing a quick, lively likeness of one of her children or her friends, preferring always to work from life. Marina Warner calls her an "unknown example of a marvellous and extinct breed: the Victorian amateur watercolourist." [13]

Mama and Papa were naturally delighted that Louise had inherited this artistic interest, and they encouraged her early drawing and sketching. In 1851, when Louise was just three years old, Edward Henry Corbould was hired as art instructor for the royal children. For the next twenty years he tutored them singly and in small groups on various aspects of drawing, painting and aesthetics. Corbould was a "talented as well as a painstaking master of the craft and a fine teacher," according to one art historian. He "knew all the conventions but seldom encouraged the royal children to copy. They were led by him to be original and observant." [14]

Louise blossomed under Corbould's guidance and instruction. Either a pencil or a paint brush seemed always in her hands. She made endless drawings of scenes and people around her. If no paper were available, she remembered the scene in great detail and reproduced it later. As she grew older she covered reams and reams of paper with swift, vigorous drawings. For Louise, somewhat the odd-girl out, drawing took the place of the stories her sisters wrote for their amusement.

As she matured, Louise added sculpture to her drawing and painting. Her first sculpture teacher was Mary Thorneycroft, who had been commissioned by Queen Victoria to execute a long series of busts and statues, chiefly of the royal children. Louise modelled both for her own sculpture and for an abstract figure emblematic of "Plenty". To Louise, this was not the least bit dull and boring. She was quite taken with the art of modelling and carving, and Thorneycroft was quite willing to give her simple instruction. Here, too, Louise's talents were well above average — perhaps even stronger in sculpture than in painting. Here, too, was a strong female role model for the young princess.

\* \* \* \* \*

Apparently the children of both the royal family and the Campbells of Argyll spent little time with other youngsters. Perhaps Victoria and Albert, both products of isolated childhoods themselves, never admitted the idea of outside friends into their consciousness; or, with nine children of their own, they felt any more friends would be unnecessary. It was the same with the Campbells. Duchess Elizabeth often said it was unnecessary for the twelve youngsters to go to other children's parties, since they were a party in themselves. Looking back on her childhood in later years, Ian's sister Frances concluded that "a little mixture of the world and his wife" would have been most welcome in "mitigating the exclusive self-consciousness" of their own large family. [15]

Occasionally, however, the Campbell children, along with their young Leveson-Gower relatives, were invited into the presence of the royal family. The Duke of Argyll was one of Prince Albert's earliest supporters among the British aristocracy, while the Duchess and her mother Harriet both held the office of Mistress of the Robes in the royal household. Once in the cabinet, Argyll usually served as Minister-in-Attendance to Queen Victoria during her autumn stays at Balmoral. It was not unusual for the Queen to come to tea at Argyll Lodge in London, or for the Duke and Duchess to be invited to dinner at Windsor Castle.

The children were often included in these visits. "Archie chose to be stupid, but Ian was quite comfortable," wrote Elizabeth after taking her two oldest boys to visit the Queen.[16] Ronald Leveson-Gower — Ian's "uncle," just four days his senior in age — fondly remembered occasions when he and the Campbell boys were invited to Buckingham Palace in the 1850s. "If the weather was fine, we used to play in the gardens, where there was a regular gymnasium, or in the beautifully decorated pavilion.

If it was too wet for outdoor games, we would amuse ourselves with our youthful royal hosts indoors." [17]

Ian Campbell remembered the "infantile misfortunes" of these Buckingham Palace playtimes. Once a skipping rope hit him on the head, knocking him to the ground and slightly injuring a knee. Prince Albert picked him up and carried him into the palace. Ian long remembered "the sensation of seeing the grass as we passed over it, from the secure vantage-place of his arms folded around me." [18]

At least once a year the Campbell and Leveson-Gower youngsters were invited to a special "children's dance" hosted by Victoria and Albert. Grandmother Harriet often engaged the royal dancing master, M. Delplanche, for some last minute lessons to make sure each child knew his steps and would not disgrace himself before the Queen. "The boys have been practising Scotch reels for the ball at the Palace," wrote Elizabeth Campbell, adding that "Ian dances very well." [19] Yet, Delplanche, according to Ronny Gower, was an extremely tough task-master:

"When the night of the ball arrived, and when at the Palace, feeling that the terrible eye of the severe Delplanche was upon us, we almost lost all enjoyment, and nearly trembled to think we were insufficiently turning out our toes, or had hopelessly forgotten the next figure in the quadrille. The Palace balls were rather awful festivities. Her Majesty, an excellent dancer herself, was critical; and when dancing with a princess and knowing that Delplanche's eagle gaze and the august eyes of Royalty were following our gyrations, the honour of the dance was hardly compensated for by the dread of failure." [20]

The girls probably looked forward to these evenings with far less trepidation than the boys. Princess Louise, like her mother and her sisters, enjoyed dancing and was quite proficient for her age. She also enjoyed dressing up for these gala affairs. At a ball given by the Duchess of Kent, the royal grandmother, Queen Victoria described the nine year-old Louise and her eleven year-old sister Helena: "The two darling Princesses arrived first, looking like fairies. So merry and so bright. To see these lovely creatures dancing was a treat indeed." [21]

Louise and Ian would quite naturally have come to know one another and to dance together on such occasions, despite the three-year age difference between them. Most of these outdoor games and ballroom dances were group activities, where children of all ages — plus parents and other adults — joined in spontaneously. Louise and Helena, Ian and Archie Campbell, Prince Alfred and Prince Arthur, Ronny and Albert Leveson-Gower, joined the fun with the others.

We do not know whether Louise and Ian took any particular notice of each other at these parties. Certainly they were both attractive to the eye. Though a little on the chubby side, Ian boasted a fine set of facial features, sparkling blue eyes, and a thick shock of blond hair. Louise was by far the prettiest of all five royal princesses. "Her hair was light and fluffy," writes Daphne Bennett, "curling naturally around her small but shapely head, her large eyes were a spectacular shade of deep blue with long lashes, and she had a small nose and chin which did not recede but stuck out determinedly when she wanted her own way." [22]

Nor do we know whether young Ian and Louise especially enjoyed each other's company, whether their temperaments as children were compatible. Ian would likely have been the easier of the two to get along with. From childhood to old age, everyone found him a most personable and pleasant sort of fellow. Louise, it seems, was not so easy. She was certainly lively and alert, but even as a child she showed sudden bursts of moodiness. Her favourite governess, French teacher Madame Rollande, likened these outbursts to English summer weather — "all sunshine one moment, dark as thunder the next." [23]

Probably no one at this time saw anything more than childhood politeness between Lorne and Louise. "Little did any of us dream," wrote Ronny Gower, "that one of us would become the husband of one of them."[24]

❦ CHAPTER THREE

# AT SCHOOL AND COLLEGE, 1858-1865

*I*an Campbell's thirteenth birthday in August 1858 triggered a family decision on formal schooling. Till then, Ian and his brothers had been educated at home by a succession of governesses and tutors, as had their father and grandfather before them. Yet Duke George was anxious that his older boys go away to school, where they might gain "a wise tolerance of the idiosyncrasies of others and broad catholicity of spirit" not possible through home-based instruction.[1]

Had it been just his father's say, Ian might well have left before 1858. But Duchess Elizabeth doted on her eldest son, and held him at home as long as possible. Relations between Ian and his mother remained very strong over the years, perhaps abnormally so. Writing home from the West Indies at the age of twenty, Ian still addressed his mother as "Darling". His sister Frances described this bond between mother and son as a mutual feeling of "deep and sacred affection". More than that; Ian and Elizabeth seemed so close in age and temperament that "they were more like lovers, than mother and son." [2]

The break from home and family occurred in the autumn of 1858. Ian and his eleven-and-a-half year old brother Archie left for Edinburgh Academy. They were accompanied by Ronny and Albert Leveson-Gower — technically uncles to the Campbell boys, but more like cousins in age and interests. Edinburgh Academy was the leading Scottish preparatory school of the day, not too far removed from Roseneath and Inverary, yet eminently respectable for the sons of the aristocracy.

Just outside Edinburgh, in nearby Cramond, the four boys lived under close supervision at Lauriston Castle, rented for the 1858-59 school year by the Duke of Sutherland. "Lauriston is a pleasant old castle with a fine old-fashioned garden round it," Ronny Gower recalled. "An old and large bowling-green served for our small matches of cricket." From the castle

37

the boys "made pleasant excursions about the somewhat tame neighbourhood," and rode to the Academy each day on their ponies.[3] Edinburgh Academy seemed a success; at Christmas the Duke of Argyll reported both Ian and Archie as "getting on well." [4]

Elizabeth Campbell's letters to Ian at Lauriston Castle that winter reveal the affection and protectiveness she felt towards her first-born child. She sympathized with Ian over mild colds and sore throats. "Remember about the cold sponging of the throat, and take care of your stomach." Was he getting enough rest? "Remember to go to bed at 1/4 to 10 at latest and to be in bed at 10." How were his lessons? "Did you manage to do the thirty lines well?" It was good of Ian to write regular letters, but Elizabeth confessed she "should like them better if you told me what you are reading or thinking about." Most of all, she missed her son terribly. "I am thirsty for you my own boy." [5]

Edinburgh Academy served as a mere transitional year between home and the larger world of British public schooling, for the Duke had earlier decided to send Ian and Archie on to Eton College. Eton promised a continuation of many Edinburgh experiences — the brothers would be joined by their Leveson-Gower relations, and all four boys would again live off campus in a private residence. Yet Ian did not look forward to the change.

"I wish you would tell me a little why you fancy you would not like Eton when you know that every boy you know likes it," implored his mother. "It may be right to do it even if you do not like it, but I ask you not to fancy you would dislike it, unless you have good reasons. I think if you did go, you and Archie would both be liked by other boys, which is the thing to make it pleasant, but we must all think of doing what is best, not only of what is pleasant." [6]

\* \* \* \* \*

Like it or not, Ian was packed off to Eton in the summer of 1859. "Arrived late," he wrote the folks at home, describing his first twenty-four hours in the new environment. "We were not in bed till 2:30 a.m. Next morning we were told there were only two schools on Saturday, and that we need not go to any of them till our exam be over. Worked at my tutor's house from 11 to 2 o'clock, when we had dinner, and then worked all the afternoon. Went to chapel and had great difficulty in finding a place. Boys all round called out, 'Hullo, fellar, what's your name?' and when one asked where one was to sit, it was either 'I don't know' or 'In your skin.' I believe I shall like Eton very much (this for his mother's benefit?), though there is such a lot of chapel and lessons." [7]

The boys settled into a rented town house with their personal tutor, George Howard. It was a snug, two-storey brick house on the east side of the town's High Street, Number 31 and 32, about half way between the river and the college, directly opposite the well-known Christopher Inn. Living outside the college, however, was not entirely satisfactory. "We were at Eton, but not of Eton," wrote Ronny Gower, "and the other lads felt, with some justice, that we were treated as if the usual manner of living at Eton — in one of the masters' houses — was not good enough for us; and among boys, as among men, anything that appears to be exclusive is not popular." [8]

Ian's academic progress at Eton can be glimpsed through the printed lists of scholars in the college archives, lists that give boys' surnames and relative places in the school order, with a few lettered notes about prizes. For the 1859 summer term, Ian is listed as "unplaced" or just entered, not quite at the bottom of the school. Three years later, under the direction of his college tutor, Rev. Leigh Joynes, and his personal tutor, George Howard, he is about halfway up the lists. "Neither startlingly fast nor discreditably slow progress," in the words of a later college archivist. [9]

In later life Ian dismissed his academic experiences at Eton as a grand waste of time. Heavy doses of Greek and Latin simply did not agree with him. "The only thing I cared for in Greek was the song 'Eros pot in rodoisy;' the only thing I cared for in Latin were some of Horace's songs." Why, he wondered, were Latin verses regarded as the "all-in-all necessity for after life."

He remembered only one master who talked to the boys of the contemporary world. Occasionally over holiday periods they were encouraged to read a little British history. "But the living Britain, her Colonies and dependencies, the living action in European and other states, we were not taught to know." With the experience of imperial service behind him, he argued in later life that information on Canada and Australia, for example, "would have been of far more use than much of the obsolete erudition still retailed in our public schools." [10]

But Eton meant more than classroom lessons in Greek and Latin. The boys played football and croquet on the lawn behind their rented home. On warm days they swam at Cuckoo Weir along the Thames. Ian won a place on the school rifle team. And on Eton's famous playing fields, a well-hit cricket ball broke the bridge of his nose. This accident destroyed his near-perfect profile, caused his mother to "nearly weep herself blind," and left Ian speaking for the rest of his life with a strong and annoying nasal twang. [11]

Beyond the classrooms and the playing fields, the world of British society invited the Campbell and Leveson-Gower boys. It was a short trip from Eton to Cliveden, where Ian's beloved grandmother, the Duchess of Sutherland, lived in widowhood through the 1860s. At Cliveden the boys were introduced to William Gladstone, historian John Acton, and Anthony Panizzi, Keeper of the British Museum Library. Best of all, the children and grandchildren of the Duchess of Sutherland were warmly welcomed at nearby Windsor Castle. "We went to see the Queen," Ian wrote home at one point. "She was very kind to us, and laughed a good deal at what we said." [12]

Early in 1861 the boys were invited to a children's ball given by the Queen's aged mother, the Duchess of Kent, at Frogmore. Victoria and Albert "danced a great deal" and "laughed much at us" as the youngsters joined the fun. Ian undoubtedly danced with Princess Louise and her sisters; he probably traded quips with Prince Alfred and Prince Arthur. But other aspects of the evening remained firmer in his memory.

"We stayed till the dancing was over, because if we were late we were to have no morning school," he wrote. This schoolboy prank caused trouble, for Queen Victoria discovered the plan. "A day or two afterwards, we found to our horror and surprise that H.M. had caused inquiries to be made of our masters if it was indeed true that Eton boys had overstayed their time in order to escape their duties of the following morning. Confession did not make things better." [13]

* * * * *

Eton College also introduced young Ian Campbell to the world of homosexuality. The all-male atmosphere of the nineteenth century English boarding school, with its dormitory life, team sports, corporal punishment, ingrained "fagging" practices — where junior boys carried out both mundane and exceptional duties for their seniors — provided fertile ground for homosexual thoughts and activities. Even the curriculum contributed its share. "Intelligent boys," claims A.L. Rowse, "were introduced to the all-round facts of sex life, between the sexes or between persons of the same sex, in Plato or Theocritus, Virgil or Juvenal, or whatever." [14]

Strong homoerotic bonds frequently developed between schoolmasters and schoolboys. Forty-five years after leaving Eton, Ian Campbell — by then the Ninth Duke of Argyll — makes no mention in the text of his 1907 autobiography, *Passages From the Past*, of any Eton tutor or master. But facing page 70 of volume one, in the section dealing with schooling, the curious reader notices a full-page photograph of William Johnson Cory.

William Johnson — he later changed his name to William Cory — was one of the most prominent and popular Eton masters from the time of his arrival at the school in 1845. He authored a number of supplementary Latin texts, wrote poetry, composed the still-popular "Eton Boating Song," and became a beloved character and an inspired teacher of individual boys. Then in 1872, Johnson was suddenly dismissed. No reasons were given publicly, though gossips whispered of incidents between Johnson and his male pupils. In any case, he felt obliged to change his name and seek other means of livelihood.

Johnson, one old Etonian tells us, was "averse to the company of women," while "among men he was attracted by the bold, gay, confident, alert and beautiful." His youngest pupils were said to "feel in Johnson a wondrous sympathy for their vernal joy and adored him for it." Another oldboy calls him "a doer of odd things" who often invited favoured boys to "breakfast, to picnics, and water-parties." The boys he especially loved — whether in a physical or merely platonic sense, — included such adult acquaintances of Ian Campbell's as Lord Rosebery, prime minister in the 1890s, and Reginald Brett, Viscount Esher, advisor to King Edward VII.[15]

Two of Johnson's favourite pupils during Ian Campbell's years at Eton were Charles Wood, later Lord Halifax, and his younger brother Frederick "Mouse" Wood. Years later, Cory said of Frederick Wood that he had grown "under my eyes from childhood to full manhood without a moment's break in continuity, mere expansion and fructifying. His mind is in beautiful order, a fair product of education and inheritance."[16]

In 1864 Johnson composed "An Epoch in a Sweet Life," written especially for Frederick Wood and referring to Wood's friendship with another pupil. Two of its stanzas invite close scrutiny:

> They came; and one was of a northern race,
> Who bore the island galley on his shield,
> Grand histories on his name, and in his face
> A bright soul's ardour fearlessly revealed.
>
> We trifled, toiled and feasted, far apart
> From churls, who wondered what our friendship meant;
> And in that coy retirement heart to heart
> Drew closer, and our natures were content. [17]

In his own notes Johnson identifies the boy "of a northern race/Who bore the island galley on his shield" as Ian Campbell, the young Marquis of Lorne. The friendship described in the second quoted stanza is between Ian and Frederick Wood. The entire poem reads like a praise of young Wood, with Johnson showing some jealousy over Wood's friendship with Ian Campbell. [18]

Was this but a fantasy existing in William Johnson's sexually active imagination? Had a friendship between Ian Campbell and Frederick Wood blossomed into some sort of homosexual relationship? Had this adolescent attachment interrupted something of substance between master Johnson and student Wood, or Johnson and young Campbell?

Certainly the boys' mutual friendship was strong enough to inspire Johnson to poetic verse. Johnson continued to see Wood long after graduation, and Ian Campbell included a photograph of Johnson in his autobiography. Of interest, too, is Ian Campbell's obituary notice in the 4 May 1914 edition of *The Times*. At Eton, remarks the anonymous writer, "he was remarkable for his manly beauty of a fine Celtic type." Ian Campbell's stay at Eton made him well aware of the world of homosexuality.

* * * * *

After three years of mixed results at Eton, seventeen year-old Ian Campbell enrolled as an arts student at St. Andrews University in the fall of 1862. At this time the Scottish universities were in transition, their former wide-ranging generalist curriculum giving way to a narrower focus on the classics. Proponents of change argued the need to compete with Oxford and Cambridge graduates for the better places in British public life. The older curriculum, with its due attention to philosophy, mathematics and the experimental sciences, might have appealed to Lorne. Now he was forced once more into a concentration on those subjects he had despised at Eton. During the 1862-63 academic at St. Andrews, Latin and Greek were relieved by just one outside course in moral philosophy.

Lorne stayed in College Hall, then called St. Leonard's Hall. This building had been opened a year earlier as part of Principal James David Forbes' attempt to revive residence life, and to attract back to St. Andrews the sons of "persons of higher rank" within Scottish society who chose Oxford or Cambridge. "Whilst a small community during its first years, it was a rather distinguished one," writes one St. Andrews historian of College Hall. [19]

Ian enjoyed St. Andrews much more than Eton, as the new environment offered a variety of outlets for his developing interests and talents. Staff members were prepared to deal with student questions both inside and outside the classroom. He could discuss his curiosity in the psychic phenomena of "second sight" and "table turning" with professors John Veitch and J.C. Shairp. [20] He and Andrew Lang — a friend from Edinburgh Academy and later a prolific writer on Scottish themes — began a student magazine. Ian played cricket on his college eleven, golfed on the famous St. Andrews course, and went fox-hunting with future novelist Whyte Melville. He found himself caught up in campaigns both to maintain traditional student rites —St. Andrews' customs seemed less ridiculous than those at Eton — and to shatter tradition by admitting women students to the university.

The climax in student revelry came after a cricket match, when Ian and his victorious College Hall team-mates paraded wildly through the streets of town, blowing horns and lustily singing "We Are Jolly Good Fellows". Along South Street "windows were thrown open, handkerchiefs were waved, and half the population turned out, cheering us in the most patriotic way." The sensation, he remembered, "was wonderful." But it was over within a year. "We left St. Andrews with regret. The old ruins on the low cliff, wide sandy beaches with blue ocean waves forever breaking on them, wonderful golf links, and the cheery student life we led, were all charming." [21]

> *St. Andrews, love for thee's not dead,*
> *Whate'er thou taugh'st of knowledge,*
> *In days when we, not deeply read,*
> *Were yet red gowned at College . . .*
>
> *So here's, St. Andry, to thy Links,*
> *Thy sands, and ancient story:*
> *Drink forty gills, take forty winks,*
> *And toast her 'gain to-morry.* [22]

His sister Frances claimed Ian "wore the academic red gown" of the college, but "left no other mark on the student world." St. Andrews itself was not at fault, nor was Eton entirely to blame before it. The root of the problem lay with the young man himself. "His education was a little too much of everything," added Frances, doubting "if anything could have made him a student." [23]

His parents tried a different approach during the winter of 1863-64 in their efforts to prepare him for Trinity College, Cambridge. They engaged a young clergyman named Pellew Arthur to give Ian some badly-needed private tutoring in the classics. Rev. Arthur seems to have got on well with his pupil. "He was invariably kind and considerate from the very start," wrote Arthur, "so that he won my heart's love and devotion." But tutor soon discovered that pupil "could not give himself whole-heartedly to the reading of Greek and Latin." This was not through lack of natural ability, concluded Arthur, but due to the "varied nature of his education" which had not provided the "constant and uninterrupted training necessary for proficiency in the classics." [24]

Neither Frances Campbell nor Pellew Arthur were entirely correct in their assessments. Ian Campbell was a true son of his father, and of his Campbell grandfather before him. His natural bent lay away from formal classical learning to the outdoor laboratory of natural science, the intuitive milieu of the arts, and the political world of modern history and modern languages. Edinburgh Academy, Eton College, and St. Andrews University had failed to provide the proper environment for his scholarly talents. Would Cambridge be any better?

* * * * *

Ian Campbell, now at age nineteen more frequently called the Marquis of Lorne, turned up at Trinity College, Cambridge in October 1864. Lorne had first been admitted the previous September. But even before commencing formal studies, tutor Mr. Blore concluded that Lorne's performance in the classics did not bode well. Hence the year with Pellew Arthur as additional preparation. When re-admitted to Trinity in the fall of 1864, Lorne's status was "fellow commoner" rather than "pensioner" — the new category conferring greater social status but involving a less demanding academic program. Classics would dominate once again, of course, relieved only by a little mathematics.

Trinity was the largest and most prestigious of the Cambridge colleges, the only one requiring its students to pass an entrance examination. Its sense of history and aura of scholarship were as pervasive then as today. Guide books proclaimed the grandeur of its architecture, climaxed by a library designed by Christopher Wren. Here Isaac Newton made his breakthroughs in mathematics and science; here came Byron, Thackeray and Tennyson. Here generations of students lounged on "The Backs," the grassy banks of the River Cam.

Lorne took rooms overlooking Great Court, and made the most of Trinity's social life. His circle of friends included Ronny Gower; Gilbert Elliot, Lord Melgund, later Earl of Minto and Governor General of Canada; Cyril Flower, later Lord Battersea; and Arthur Strutt, son of Baron Belper, a Derbyshire lawyer, politician and scientist. Lorne won the Trinity Cup in rifle-shooting; he paraded with the volunteer militia; he joined the Debating Society and the Amateur Dramatic Club; he participated in a seemingly endless round of dinners and college parties and country weekends. "Parties of some kind are perpetual here. You are asked out to breakfast, lunch, tea, or supper, and the latter lasts from nine to twelve very often." [25]

But this was not enough for the young man as he passed from his teens into his twenties. "We had all seen the Newmarket races, we had shot many of the neighbouring squire's pheasants, we had won many of the volunteer silver cups, we had cheered the University crews — all this was comfort, but more we wanted." Principal Whewell often told Trinity students: "If you wish to work, there's nothing to prevent you!" Lorne's comment: "Of course this all depended on the nature of the work one was encouraged to do, and the nature of the work favoured as instruction was not encouraging." [26]

Lorne, age 17.

Lorne turned to verse to express his frustrations at the inadequacies of the curriculum:

*As flattened as the country round*
*Seems here all good ambition,*
*Unless by mathematics crowned,*
*Or classics' worse fruition.*

Cambridge, he concluded, "was only a larger paddock in the classical enclosure which had surrounded us at Eton. When a man is young and has already been dosed by old Greek and Roman doctors, he longs to escape from them." Lorne argued that the classics were a decidedly negative influence on learning, for the time spent mastering the intricacies of Latin and Greek meant time away from the very subjects that might provide insights on the contemporary world — the sciences, mathematics, modern history, modern languages. "When one is longing to know the present world, is it wise to tie youth down to the old?" [27]

Meanwhile Lorne's mind dwelt increasingly on the vast political changes rocking the North Atlantic world of the 1860s. On the European continent German unification was charging ahead, led by Bismarck and the Prussians. Italian unification was marching in step, with only Papal Rome lying outside the new kingdom. Across the Atlantic, nationalism and nation-building were also in the ascendancy. The Northern victory in the American Civil War re-established the primacy of the United States federal government over the individual states. British North American politicians pushed towards the new confederation of Canada. Lorne felt cheated that his university studies did not touch these movements of his own day. Denied them through the classroom, he concluded that he must witness and experience them at first hand.

Such an opportunity presented itself towards the end of the 1865 fall term at Cambridge. News of an October uprising by Jamaica's black population aroused extraordinary interest among British intellectuals. Everyone was taking sides. It was either a full-scale rebellion or merely a local uprising. Governor Eyre was either a a hero who had saved Jamaica for the crown — and the lives of some 13,000 white men, women and children in the bargain — or a cruel and savage murderer as his harsh actions in putting down the trouble reveal. "For some weeks there was hardly anything (else) talked of," reported one journalist, "we might say hardly anything thought of, in England, but the story of the rebellion and the manner in which it had been suppressed and punished." [28]

Cambridge undergraduates were no exception. At a December supper party hosted by Cyril Flower, Lorne and his friends debated the Jamaica question long into the night. It was so difficlut to determine the real truth of the matter. How could anyone tell from within the cloistered walls of the university? Cambridge offered nothing but the classical world; over in Jamaica the contemporary world was unfolding. By the end of the evening two of the young men resolved to visit the West Indies for a first hand look. One was Arthur Strutt; the other was Ian Campbell, Marquis of Lorne. "In a few days we were off, and never again went back to the fogs and shades and the cloisters of Cambridge." [29]

# CHAPTER FOUR

# TRAVELLING OUT, 1866-1867

*E*arly in January 1866 Ian Campbell and Arthur Strutt sailed from Southampton on the *La Plata*. It was not unusual for a pair of young British aristocrats to set off for a few months of travel and adventure before settling down to the demands of adult society. But Lorne and Strutt forsook the usual comfort and security of the Grand Tour of Europe for the mysteries and uncertainties of the New World. Their six-month ramble took them to Haiti, struggling for credibility and recognition as an all-Black republic; to Jamaica in the wake of a Black insurrection; to the northern and southern regions of the United States in the aftermath of a civil war; and to Canada during the week of the Fenian attack at Ridgeway. Lorne began the trip as a tourist and adventurer, and ended it as an incisive student of contemporary politics and society.

Fellow passengers on the *La Plata* included British army officers bound for West Indian postings; Jamaica planters going to inspect their estates after the insurrection; Quakers and Anti-Slavery Society representatives; mysterious Spaniards on their way to colonial Cuba. The passage was quite rough at first, with two days of sea-sickness, the loss of the vessel's jib-boom, and little rest at night. Then the weather turned fine, and Lorne and Arthur spent their time promenading and sunbathing on deck. They read everything available on the Jamaica question, and found much of it contradictory.

On February 2 they stepped ashore at St. Thomas in the Virgin Islands, for their first taste of the New World, the intense tropical heat, and a predominantly black population. They strolled through the town in their white suits and Panama hats, like archetypal Britons abroad. They observed the architecture, flora and fauna, and street manners of the population. Soon the tropical sunshine overwhelmed them. "The heat was so great that we put up our umbrella, and felt as if we should like to lie down in the dust, and eat lollipops like the negroes." [1]

Lorne as a young man.

Three days later Lorne and Arthur disembarked at the tiny port of Jacmel on the southern coast of Haiti. To the horror of their fellow passengers, they proposed to ride overland to the capital city of Port-au-Prince through unknown and potentially dangerous mountain country. Being young and in love with the world, they encountered a friendly world in return. They hired local guides and pack mules for their trek through the mountains, then spent a few delightful days wandering the back streets of Port-au-Prince. As the son of a British cabinet minister, Lorne dined at the residence of the British consul and secured an interview with Haitian president Fabre-Nicolas Geffard.

Lorne was impressed with the natural environment. "Every stick and leaf was new to me, and the variety and quantity of animal life seemed wonderful." He enjoyed the spontaneity of the Haitian people. "Such energy in gesticulation, in talking, and in laughing, and how little in acting." But he was not impressed with the material progress of the country, finding "no ambition" and "too much savagery" among the population. "It is disagreeable to see a country progressing only at a jog-trot, when, with its favourable position and the fertility of its soil, it ought to drive at a gallop to prosperity." [2] Young and romantic he may have been, but Lorne was still every inch the Victorian believer in hard work and the idea of progress.

On February 14 the two travellers sailed into the harbour at Kingston, Jamaica. Everywhere they observed evidence of the recent uprising — gunboats berthed along the docks, buildings burned and gutted in the outlying towns. Here they came to learn, not to play the role of foreign tourists. The Duke of Argyll arranged for Lorne to attach himself to the party of Sir Henry Storks, the British commissioner investigating the outbreak and the brutal suppression of the Jamaica troubles. Lorne and Strutt moved freely over the island, staying with various planter families, attending hearings of the Storks enquiry, talking to survivors of ex-Governor John Eyre's repressive counter-measures.

Lorne concluded that the Jamaica "trouble" was more of a spontaneous, localized riot than an organized rebellion. He thus placed himself squarely in the camp of the Victorian liberals — men like Darwin, Huxley and Spencer — in their criticism of Govenor Eyre and their firm belief in human progress. Jamaica's future lay not in oligarchic and authoritarian rule, but in political equality between its white and black populations. It would not be easy. "It will take, I fear, several generations to put the mass of the people on a higher level than that on which they stand at present." But it had to be done, and a start could be made by attacking illiteracy among the Blacks. Lorne' solution was pure nineteenth century liberal humanitarianism. "All experience teaches us that a well-conducted system of education tends invariably to elevate mankind, white or coloured." [3]

Before sailing for Jamaica, Lorne had struck a bargain with his parents. In return for permission to leave Cambridge and travel overseas, he promised to write regular letters home, containing his observations on places visited and people met. "They contain merely superficial views of the men, manners and things that came under my notice," Lorne noted as he prepared extracts from these letters for publication. "But as the countries they refer to have recently been the scenes of important events, I hope they may not be without interest." [4] Capitalizing on British interest in the Jamaican Rebellion and the American Civil War, Hurst and Blackett published these extracts in 1867 under the delightful title, *A Trip to the Tropics and Home Through America*. Lorne was barely twenty-two years old when his first book appeared in print.

"There is nothing in *A Trip to the Tropics* to justify its publication," commented the *Spectator* in reviewing the book, "but then there is nothing for which its writer can be justly abused." The reviewer seemed to be suffering from an over-dose of travel books written by young British aristocrats. Despite this surfeit, he praised Lorne's "impartial summations" of Haitian and Jamaican affairs, delighted in the author's "dry humour" and "under-current of good sense," and support for opinions "modestly and quietly expressed." He concluded that in five years' time the more mature Lorne might look back at the book "with more amusement than annoyance." [5]

But for young Ian Campbell, short-term educational gain was more important than literary immortality. These published letters reveal an extensive knowledge of local history, geography, economics, politics, botany and zoology — more, certainly, than could have been learned in Cambridge classrooms. He returned to Britain as well versed on post-independence Haiti and post-insurrection Jamaica as anyone of his generation. In the more subtle areas of human relations he met a far wider spectrum of humanity than ever possible at school in Britain. Finally, the French milieu of Haiti and a brief interlude at Spanish-speaking Santiago de Cuba revealed Lorne's amazing facility with foreign languages, a fluency that steadily improved in real-life, not classroom, verbal interaction.

Two months in the tropics established the patterns through which Lorne recorded his thoughts and impressions as a traveller. In addition to letters home, the young man took charcoal and pencil in hand to sketch local inhabitants, natural scenery, and architecture. He also dashed off hundreds of lines of rhyming verse, much of which was doggerel, some publishable. Some of the verse is descriptive, as "Jamaica:"

> *The tropic isles in jewels glow;*
> *Their sapphire seas unfold*
> *In emerald curves and thundering snows*
> *Sea-sands of pearl and gold.* [6]

Some is political satire, as "A Planter's Lament:"

> *Our estates are in ruins, and wearied, we try*
> *To coax the dear niggers to work ere we die;*
> *But the isle that was flowing with sugar and rum*
> *Lies untilled and neglected, for scarce any come!* [7]

The stage was set. Realizing that formal schooling was not the answer for his son, the Duke of Argyll was willing to finance Lorne's travel as an alternative form of education. Connections, letters of introduction, and invitations into foreign society were easily attained through the influence of the Campbell and Sutherland names. Aristocratic birth propelled Lorne into conservative contacts abroad, while his family's own Whig views opened liberal doors. As a young man, Lorne could mix with the lower strata of foreign society his parents would have shunned. To rich and poor, high and low, the young marquis could direct insightful questions on foreign society and politics. Lorne, too, was a delightful listener — always interested in the political, economic and social views of strangers. And when the polite talk and the formal dinners were over, Lorne was always game for such outdoor adventures as riding horseback across the mountains of Haiti.

\* \* \* \* \*

After a month in Jamaica, Lorne and Strutt sailed for New York on the steamer *Caraibe*. New York City in the spring of 1866 was everything the young travellers expected — and more. "One feels as if one had leaped a century coming here from the tropics. Instead of the lazy, half-alive movements we had been accustomed to, there was a frantic haste and hurry, a general movement and hustle, that told of an eager life and dollar-scramble refreshing to witness." They spent their first few days strolling along Broadway, taking in the sights and sounds of this New World metropolis. "The town was at home, its entire population, with that active energy for which they are renowned, daily busy in the pursuit of wealth, pleasure and excitement." [8]

On to Boston, where they made the rounds of the private clubs, were welcomed at Harvard as visiting Cambridge students, and listened to debates in the Massachusetts House of Representatives. Lorne's call on Henry Wadsworth Longfellow was the highlight of this Boston visit. Rapport was easily established between veteran poet and youthful versi-fier as Lorne brought greetings from Longfellow's great English contemporary and Campbell family friend, Alfred Tennyson. Lorne bravely kept pace with Longfellow as they discussed the strengths of Tennyson and Swinburne, problems of translating Homer and Dante into English, and new work of such American poets as Dana, Holmes and Whittier. The conversation ended on a particularly happy note, with Longfellow asking Lorne to take a North American Indian peace pipe as a present for Tennyson "with his love and admiration." [9]

Secretary of State W.H. Seward was Lorne's principal contact in Washington. Here they listened to the Senate debate the admission of Colorado into the Union, inspected the new Arlington National Cemetery, dined with the British ambassador, met senators and other government leaders, and gained a short interview with President Andrew Johnson. The president was a great disappointment, not speaking one word beyond "How do?" Other American leaders were more loquacious. General Ulysses S. Grant was effusive in praising the character and abilities of his Confederate antagonists, Generals Lee and Johnston, and "very bellicose" about the presence of French troops in Mexico. Chief Justice Salmon P. Chase surprised Lorne by being "quite in favour of giving the blacks all rights, including the right to vote." [10]

Prominent American statesmen were willing to pay so much attention to a pair of young Britons because in these months following the Civil War, they were anxious to restore good relations with a Britain whose upper classes had sympathized with the South. One of the few British exceptions of prominence had been Lorne's father, whose pro-federalist and anti-slavery positions were well known on both sides of the Atlantic. At a Washington dinner hosted by the Sewards, the Secretary of State "began about my father, saying that he knew he was the best friend the North had had during the war." [11] American politicians saw Lorne as his father's son, a Britisher on their side, one who might help the cause of Anglo-American relations back in London. All doors were open.

Ironically, Lorne himself had sympathized with the Southern cause during the war years. There was something of the Highland romantic in young Ian Campbell that was attracted by the seemingly lost-cause of the ante-bellum South. In any case Lorne was his usual courteous self in arguing his views; even the United States ambassador who visited Inverary in 1863 was impressed, and not the least offended. [12]

So it was natural for Lorne to visit the South before leaving America; on 28 April 1866 he and Strutt arrived at Richmond, Virginia. The lingering effects of the war were everywhere: earthen and wooden defence works still in place, men wearing Confederate uniforms, and ladies dressed in black mourning gowns. Fredericksburg, Charlottesville and Lynchburg were the same. The visitors talked with Confederate veterans, gained entree to some of Virginia's wealthiest country homes, and secured a late evening interview with Confederate General Robert E. Lee at his home in Lexington. Lorne used his recent experience in the North to reassure Lee that "there were many who would work for reconciliation," and that "the great majority repudiated violent words." [13]

Post-war America also introduced our travellers to the Fenian phenomenon. Mostly Americans of recent Irish Catholic background, the Fenians sought every opportunity to kick Britain in the shins while espousing the general goal of Irish independence. They were particularly active during 1865-66, seeking to channel Union veterans and arms into their cause. American newspapers were full of Fenian news — reports of mass meetings and receptions, information on fund-raising drives, rumours of raids on Canada and other British territories. The New York and Boston hotels where Lorne and Strutt stayed were staffed with vocal and argumentative Fenian waiters. Lorne took their threatening boasts seriously. "I feared they would attempt something if only to justify their words." [14]   As it happened, the Fenians provided plenty of excitement as the two adventurers headed north into Canada on the last leg of their trip.

* * * * *

The young men did not expect much from this Canadian post-script to their New World odyssey. Not even Niagara Falls could excite the seasoned travellers at this stage in their journey. "I was neither disappointed nor surprised by them. They were almost exactly what I expected — minus the sunlight." Toronto proved "too dull for words," but necessitated a short stop for Strutt to visit an uncle. "Why they should have built a town on this flat wretched shore I cannot conceive." Meanwhile the weather remained "disgusting — cold, raw and wet." The train to Ottawa took them "through a dreary country with few clearings." Though it was now the last day of May, "the season is so cold that many of the trees have only just begun to come out." From the window of their Ottawa hotel Lorne mused that the city's inconvenient location might lose it the seat of government should the proposed wider federation of all the British North American colonies be consummated. [15]

Lorne and Arthur arose the next morning confident that family backgrounds and letters of introduction would smoothe their way into Ottawa's social and political world. But official Ottawa had more important matters to deal with on that first day of June in 1866. At 5:00 a.m. a telegram reached the city with news that an armed band of some 800 Fenians had crossed the Niagara River just below Fort Erie and invaded Canadian soil. The proud boasts of those Fenian waiters back in New York and Boston had been more than idle threats!

Through the efforts of an aide-de-camp, Lorne and Strutt gained a short interview with Governor General Monck. Despite the pressures of the day, Monck "was very cordial, and in good hopes that the Fenians might be caught" before attaining their supposed objective of destroying the Welland Canal. Dinner with Monck that evening at Rideau Hall was constantly interrupted by a steady stream of telegrams from the frontier. The Fenians had encamped two miles below Fort Erie and would not easily be dislodged. The Governor General excused himself; he could not waste the evening on his British guests. [16]

What an opportunity these rash Fenians now offered Lorne. In Jamaica he had witnessed only the aftermath of an insurrection, in the United States the period of reconstruction after a civil war. Now in Canada — as troops of the local militia were called up and sent to the front — he might participate in repelling this Fenian attack. Strutt "didn't fancy seeing the row" and left for Montreal. But Lorne "determined to go by the first morning train to see what was to be seen" along the Niagara River, "for it seemed unlikely that these men had come except to fight." [17]

Lorne left Ottawa early on June 2. At Prescott on the St. Lawrence he found everyone on the alert. "A large force of Fenians was on the opposite shore of the river at Ogdensburg, declaring their intention to cross." The passenger steamer out of Prescott was "full of officers going to rejoin their corps." At Brockville "sentries guarded the quays" and special editions of the day's newspapers told of a sensational battle between the Fenians and the Canadian militia at Ridgeway. At Kingston the news was all bad. "The volunteers, being unsupported, had been obliged to fall back." At Hamilton "the wounded were being hourly expected. Crowds waited at the railway station to receive them, and notices were posted requiring the services of nurses." [18]

Yet before Lorne could reach the Niagara frontier, he learned the raid had collapsed, the Fenians hastily retreating back to the United States. With train travel between Hamilton and Niagara impossible, Lorne decided to retreat himself. It was time to rejoin Strutt in Montreal and wind up this lengthy New World trip.

As he sailed home to Britain in mid-June, the twenty year-old Marquis of Lorne had plenty of time to reflect on his six-month journey of discovery through the West Indies and North America. He had seen strange sights, observed delicate political situations, conversed with all manner of people, been thrust into complex social situations that demanded tact and maturity. He had been forced to recognize the spirit of liberalism that coursed through his Leveson-Gower and Campbell blood; his attitudes towards reconstruction in both Jamaica and the United States were decidedly liberal.

The Fenian attack gave young Lorne a much deeper understanding of Canada and respect for Canadians than his brief visit had originally promised. He was impressed by the speed and efficiency with which Canadian authorities moved to seal off the border and rout the invaders. He now understood the precarious position Canada held during periods of Anglo-American trouble. And he learned to take Fenian threats seriously, even if they came from illiterate and unlearned hotel waiters! All these lessons would be remembered and acted upon when he returned to Ottawa twelve years later.

In the spring of 1866 Lorne had been privileged to dine at Rideau Hall, the official residence of the Governor General; in the autumn of 1878 he would return to Rideau Hall as Governor General in his own right.

* * * * *

The Marquis of Lorne celebrated his twenty-first birthday at Inverary on 6 August 1866. The week-long festivities included a continuous round of receptions and banquets, Highland games every day, fireworks and illuminations and dancing in the evenings. Ronald Gower, himself a younger son, showed some jealousy in describing this coming of age of the eldest son of the Duke of Argyll — "attended with much ceremony, great expense, and general rejoicings," though the honoured individual was merely "the son of his father, and the inheritor of his wealth, estates, and ailments." [19]

There was no thought of returning to Cambridge. The past few months had confirmed Lorne's belief that foreign travel was his forte, his personal means to an education, his pathway from adolescence to adult maturity. His parents could hardly disagree. Yet some compromise was necessary, for Lorne's "home folk had not altogether approved" his "cutting short the time at Cambridge" the previous winter. [20] Accordingly, Lorne enrolled at the University of Berlin in the autumn of 1866.

Berlin promised both the academic study desired by the Duke and Duchess as well as the foreign travel that had become almost an obsession with the young man. Besides, Berlin would allow Lorne to put his facility in German to the ultimate test. Lorne had already proven himself an able student of the German language. During the winter of 1863-64, for instance, Lorne carried on a running debate over the Schleswig-Holstein question with the German-speaking tutor of his younger brothers. To the amazement of the Campbell family, these intense and complicated political discussions were conducted entirely in German. When the Prussian Crown Prince and Princess visited Britain, a lady-in-waiting to the Princess remarked "she had never heard an Englishman, except the Prince of Wales, speak German as did Lorne." [21]

The Campbells of Argyll were no strangers to continental Europe. Lorne's grandfather, the Seventh Duke, spent the early months of 1803 in Paris and Geneva, until chased home by the renewal of Anglo-French hostilities. Lorne's father rounded out his education by spending two winters in Rome during the 1840s. Lorne himself had enjoyed several extended family holidays on the continent; these sojourns provided warm winter sun for Lorne's ailing mother as well as organized learning activities for the older Campbell children. In the summer of 1863, with brother Archie and Ronald Gower, Lorne spent a delightful hiking holiday in the Swiss Alps; two years later he and Ronny holidayed at Vichy, France.

Now it was the autumn of 1866, and from Lorne's perspective, Berlin was the place to be — "the young world city" he called it — the proud capital of a confident country on the march. Just that summer Prussia had thrashed its rival Austria in the Seven Weeks' War and was consolidating its hold over the smaller German-speaking states. "Berlin was indeed a happy city after her people found themselves victors over their great opponent and rival in the south," Lorne observed. "I was fortunate in visiting the city when it was full of just pride, and full of the men who in war had made themselves famous." [22]

The University of Berlin was also on the ascendancy. During the 1860s the major German universities enjoyed a high reputation in teaching and research. Berlin was especially exciting. Here the intellectual resources of the university — professors like Ranke, Gneist, Lepsius — were further enriched by the cultural resources of the capital city. "I have been wandering over galleries of art and antiquities," Lorne dutifully reported to his anxious parents. The city also offered first-rate theatre. "At the opera between the acts, one meets everybody in town." [23]

In Berlin Lorne found a good friend in Gerald Talbot, a British-born officer cadet in the Prussian army. Talbot provided Lorne with an entree into the appealing world of parades and military reviews, regimental dinners and receptions. Lorne was enthralled by the military ideals that permeated the country, musing that the Prussians were probably "right to give all possible honour to the profession of arms." Denied a military career by his parents, Lorne romanticized the close German link between militarism and nationalism. "The idea of military service being most honourable is good. The idea that every man is bound to defend his country is good." [24]

Beyond the student scene, nights at the opera, and the dazzling military world, there were further distractions to entice the young student away from his books, or, as Lorne would have argued, further opportunities to broaden his education. As in America, Lorne's family background opened doors everywhere. The Radziwill brothers, old Prince Wilhelm and Prince Boguslav, were delighted to see this grandson of their old friend the Seventh Duke of Argyll. Both Augustus Loftus, British ambassador to Berlin, and George von Bunsen, former Prussian ambassador to London, were happy to entertain the son of the Eighth Duke.

Dinner parties enabled Lorne to talk with Chancellor Bismarck himself. At their first meeting Bismarck "bent down, to tell me courteously that he was glad to meet me, as he had read about my people when he himself was a boy, in Scott's novels." On another occasion, "knowing that I intended to stand for Parliament, he remarked that surely I was too young for the House of Commons."[25]

Lorne also gained entree to the Prussian royal court. In November he joined members of the court in the annual St. Hubert's Day wild boar hunt. One afternoon he took tea with Queen Augusta, who "talked of all things with much sympathy and intelligence," and gave her friends "little souvenirs of herself — a seal, a ring or picture." In February came an invitation to dine at the royal palace. "I put on a uniform representing this country, a blue volunteer garrison Artillery, with silver belt, and a red stripe down the trousers." This produced "immediate salutes from the sentries" which "the appearance of a kilt would hardly have accomplished." [26]

Best of all were invitations from the Crown Prince and Princess, Frederick William and his spirited wife Vicky, eldest daughter of Queen Victoria. The Prince found Lorne a good listener when he talked of his recent battlefield exploits in the Seven Weeks' War. The Princess discovered in Lorne someone who shared her interest in the arts and her delight in witty conversation. Lorne enjoyed the antics of their two young sons, Wilhelm and Henry, who "used to tumble about and play marbles." He predicted Wilhelm was "likely to be the cleverest king Prussia has had since Frederick the great. He certainly has good brains." [27] In letters to her mother, the Crown Princess spoke highly of Lorne's presence in the Prussian capital. "I am so glad to hear that young Lorne is so much liked," replied Queen Victoria. "I always rejoice to see good parents have good children and then rising up to high positions who promise to be of use to their country both socially and politically." [28]

Lorne paid so little attention to his formal studies at the University of Berlin that it is tempting to write off the year as a waste of time and money. Yet it was a valuable year in training for a young man determined to stand for the House of Commons, someone who might specialize in European affairs. His linguistic facility, political curiosity, and many contacts in Berlin and elsewhere, gave the twenty-one year-old Lorne insights into Prussian affairs that rivalled those of a veteran British ambassador or a knowledgeable *Times* correspondent.

\* \* \* \* \*

October 1867 found Lorne in Vienna, embarking on a second winter of European travel, this time without the pretense of formal university studies. He was on his way to Bucharest, carrying a letter of introduction from the Crown Princess of Prussia to the new ruler of Roumania. While in Vienna he learned of a popular uprising in Rome — perhaps signalling the end of the Pope's secular power and the incorporation of the Papal States into the new Kingdom of Italy. Suddenly Italy promised greater excitement and adventure than Roumania. Lorne quickly altered his plans and caught the first train for Florence, the temporary Italian capital. Perhaps he would be in time to link up with Garibaldi's supporters in the "liberation" of Rome.

In Florence he checked in at the British embassy, interviewed *The Times* correspondent, and dined at the Prussian embassy. Rumours abounded. Garibaldi was leading an assault on Rome; no, he was in hiding. The new Italian government would support him; no, it would not. The insurrgents inside the Papal States were strong enough to mount their own revolt; no, they were too weak. Lorne realized that the only way to determine the truth was to get to Rome.

But would the frontier be open? Would a Protestant Britisher be allowed into the Papal States at this critical time? Lorne used his amazing connections to persuade the Prussian embassy to allow him to travel to Rome under the protection of their diplomatic courier, Lieutenant Stumm.

The atmosphere was extremely tense as Lorne and Stumm stepped off the train in Rome. "Gendarmes with bayonets fixed on loaded rifles, were guarding every inlet or outlet of the terminus." They were marched into an anteroom for a baggage search. "A little loose powder was unfortunately found in my valise. The suspicions of the police were aroused, and one little fellow plunged like a terrier dog among my clothes, almost burying himself in my property, in the vain hope of finding something compromising." But nothing more than a small powder-flask was uncovered.

Just as they seemed safely through the inspection, Lorne's Italian servant, Jacque Tinto, was searched for arms. Luckily the inefficient search failed to uncover the pistol Lorne had given him. "Jacque came out chuckling and triumphant, but rather inclined to be slightly hysterical about the fright he had gone through." The three adventurers then climbed into a carriage and "made the deserted streets ring with our laughter at the recollection of the pistol-hunt." [29]

From his quarters at the Hotel de l'Europe — where he had stayed with his parents on earlier visits — Lorne found little revolutionary action worth witnessing. "I was struck with the quiet aspects of the streets. During the day, except for the frequent movement of small bodies of troops and gendarmes, it would have been impossible to know that anything unusual was going on. Every shop was open and every thoroughfare crowded." Lorne even wandered the streets of the curfewed city after sunset. "Beyond occasional inconvenience from being detained by some inquisitive squad, and having to establish one's identity, I never experienced any trouble." [30]

How could he pick up the latest political and diplomatic news behind the seeming inactivity? The British diplomatic representative was "a nice old trifler, whose rheumatism prevented him from moving, and from taking in, or being able to collect the information that was afloat." Prussian and Russian officials were pleasant individuals but not much better informed, while the French charge d'affairs "kept pretty much to himself." Fortunately Monsignore Stonor, a Papal official whose sister had married Lorne's cousin Leo Ellis, proved a goldmine of information, never objecting "to tell even such a heretic as myself all the news." [31]

Early in the morning of October 29 Stonor rushed to Lorne's hotel with the news all liberals had been awaiting. Garibaldi and his volunteers had slipped across the Italian-Papal States frontier, joined the insurgents, and captured the garrison town of Monte Rotondo just twenty-five kilometres from Rome itself. Early next morning came the alarm that the Garibaldians were descending on the city in force. With Hardman of *The Times* as his companion, Lorne sped to the top of the French Academy, a building which commanded a good view of the countryside towards Monte Rotondo. "With our glasses we could make out in the distance beyond the river several bodies of men." But rather than advancing Garibaldians, they were merely Papal forces on reconnaissance patrol. [32]

Later that day Lorne witnessed the end of the abortive uprising. "About four in the afternoon I heard the blare of infantry bugles advancing from the railway station." French troops had arrived to support the Pope. "One column marched down the Via Babiuno, and I followed wishing to see the reception they got. It was mostly a silent one. The priests and some shopkeepers showed signs of joy, but the poor kept quiet." Soon 10,000 French troops took up their positions around the city and Lorne no longer felt comfortable. "As the French entry was the end and legitimate result of all we had been witness to, I thought I would get out of Rome." [33]

Back in Florence, Lorne encountered his friend Gerald Talbot "who had come down from Paris much in the same harum-scarum way as I from Vienna, to join Garibaldi." [34] His resolve strengthened by Talbot's presence, Lorne agreed to one more adventure. Together the two young Britons set off for the front, this time from the north, hoping to make contact with the Garibaldian forces still encamped around Rome.

Lorne and Talbot met Garibaldi at the Fuligno railway station the evening of November 3. Their hero was retreating by train after the defeat of his forces by French and Papal troops earlier that day at Mentana. What an opportunity for the two young adventurers! Drawing on his Sutherland and Stafford House connections, Lorne talked his way onto the train and into a short interview with the Italian hero.

"I went into the General's compartment, and told him who I was, and how glad we all were to see him safe. He was as calm-looking and thoughtful of others as usual. The only change I noticed was that he looked a good deal older than when he was in England. He had passed through much in that short time. It was impossible to ask what had happened, but we heard ample details of the last few days from officers of the staff." [35]

Up to their necks in danger, Lorne and Talbot risked further trouble by transferring to Garibaldi's train and accompanying the revolutionary leader on his northward retreat. Garibaldi's forces were irregulars, denied any official status by the Italian government at Florence. Quite likely the train would be halted at some point, Garibaldi arrested for fomenting trouble, with hangers-on detained by Italian authorities.

At first all went well. At small railway stations along the line, assembled townsfolk cheered Garibaldi and his red-shirted followers. But at Filigne, a small town about an hour outside Florence, Lorne watched in horror as a trainload of Italian regulars pulled up on an adjoining track, halted Garibaldi's train, arrested his hero for unauthorized military action against Rome, and transferred the great man to a north-bound prison train.

As passengers on the Garibaldi train, Lorne and Talbot were under automatic suspicion. Italian forces with fixed bayonets surrounded all the coaches. "It was so dark that Gerald and I were able to watch our opportunity and jump" from their coach into a coach on the official train. "The good fellows said nothing to prevent us, so we were able to leave with their train when at length it slipped away." During a ten-minute stop in Florence, "we made our escape." [36]

So, concluded Lorne, "the farce was played out." The incorporation of the Papal States into a unified Kingdom of Italy would be delayed for three years until the Franco-Prussian War caused France to withdraw its troops from Rome. In the meantime, mused Lorne, lives had been lost for nothing; the Italian government had shown weakness in not backing Garibaldi; the French continued to dominate the Italian peninsula; and Garibaldi was imprisoned.

Though he spent little time on introspection, young Lorne might have pondered his own good luck in escaping unscathed. How embarrassing back home had the Duke of Argyll's son been arrested on suspicion of aiding and abetting extra-legal military activities in the Italian peninsula! As it was, Lorne simply packed his bags in Florence and joined an autumn hunting party on the shores of the Adriatic; Gerald Talbot returned to his officer-training course in Prussia. One more sporting adventure for a pair of young British toffs!

❦ CHAPTER FIVE

# TRAVELLING IN, 1861-1870

*P*rincess Louise was thirteen when her father died at Windsor Castle in late 1861. Never a robust man, Prince Albert had caught a cold in November that stubbornly refused to go away. Unfortunately, Albert would not rest, continuing to involve himself in state affairs, even travelling to Cambridge to berate Louise's brother, Bertie, over a sexual escapade. His cold worsened. Soon Albert was down with typhoid fever. He died on December 14 at the young age of forty-two.

"Oh, why did God not take me?," Louise blurted. "I am so stupid and useless." [1] Yet Louise had never worshipped her father in the manner of her older sisters, Vicky and Alice. In later years she harboured no illusions about the unblemished character of "Dearest Papa." After Percy Colson included a rather cynical study of Albert in his 1932 book, *Victorian Portraits*, Louise asked him to tea at Kensington Palace. Colson expected a tongue-lashing. "You were very naughty," she began, "but it is all true. I have bought your book and I want you to sign it for me." [2]

Rather than the death itself, the aftermath of Albert's death made Louise's life so miserable. While the Marquis of Lorne immersed himself in the environments of Eton, St. Andrews, and Cambridge, Louise was condemned to spend her teenage years in the depths of her mother's mourning. Within a week of Albert's death, Queen Victoria gathered her four unmarried daughters — Alice and Helena, Louise and Beatrice — and left for Osborne. Here the long dreadful period of mourning began. The Queen took little interest in life, in people, in anything.

Balmoral was even worse. In Scotland, the scene of so many happy former times, the royal grief was intensified. "Here everything is more painful and grievous than anywhere else," moaned Victoria. Relations with her family changed dramatically. "The children are good and loving," she wrote, "but I do not find their company the same and it is no support. I can only have two with me at a time and I still take my meals in my own room. I feel extremely weak; I can only walk slowly and not very far." [3]

The grief was renewed at anniversary times and on special occasions. Monuments to Prince Albert were soon erected in several parts of the British Isles, and the Queen made certain her children shared in these tributes to their father. Yet occasions like the unveiling of the Aberdeen monument in the fall of 1863 served only to deepen the gloom. Victoria was dressed in solid black, Louise and the other children in suitable sombre attire. An all-day rain added to the dreariness. The ceremony went on far too long, with the Queen visibly showing her impatience. The statue was finally unveiled. The rain continued. After scanning the monument briefly, Victoria and her children retired to a small, dark upstairs room where luncheon was served by one of the royal footmen. There was little conversation. The rain continued.

The Queen continued to insist that her children share fully in the long period of mourning. Even after Albert had been dead for four years and Louise was seventeen, Victoria refused to open the Buckingham Palace ballroom for a coming-out dance. Helena accepted such a prohibition philosophically, but Louise was devastated. She sulked and she ranted, refusing to reconcile herself to the loss. The Queen was so bound up in the grief and martyrdom of widowhood, expecting all around to join in her sorrow, that she failed to appreciate the life forces stirring inside her teenage daughter.

The Queen's letters to her daughter Vicky reveal this difficulty in understanding Louise. In the fall of 1862 Louise "behaves as well as possible" and "keeps quietly, and without grumbling in her own place." On her fifteenth birthday the following March she is "poor Louise" — poor because of the Queen's misconception that she was less intelligent than her sisters. A year later Louise still had "difficulties to contend with", but was beginning so show some "great advantages." Now Louise is "so handsome and so graceful and her manners so perfect in society, so quiet and lady-like." And the Queen had to admit that Louise "has such great taste for art."[4]

Cut off from her father through death, and her mother through mourning, Louise had few confidantes within the royal family. Among the girls, Alice was closest to Louise in interests, but her 1862 marriage to Prince Louis of Hesse took her away to Darmstadt. Helena was too dull and Beatrice too young to be close companions through the difficult teenage years. Fortunately Louise and her new sister-in-law, Alexandra — Bertie's bride and Princess of Wales — developed a kind of sisterly relationship. Alix addressed Louise as "my little pet" or "my own dearest Louise," begging Louise to "think sometimes of the sister who loves you." In turn, Louise gave her sister-in-law little presents, and confided to her all the tangled complications of teenage emotions. [5]

Louise, age 13.

Beyond the immediate family, Louise enjoyed the friendship of Mary and Louise Grey, daughters of the Queen's private secretary. But her closest confidante through these teenage years was Louisa Bowater, daughter of a another member of the royal household staff. Friends from early childhood, the two Louisas were brought even closer together through the deaths of their fathers the same day — 14 December 1861. Fortunately Miss Bowater (later Lady Knightley, wife of Rainald, Baron Knightley) preserved her letters from the Princess, despite a plea to "please burn all my letters because such dreadful things can happen." [6] This correspondence provides a most intimate view of the teenage Louise.

"I always think that grief made me love you so much," the fourteen year-old Princess confided to Louisa Bowater in May 1862. "It is so curious that all of our misery came on the same day." Nearing the first anniversary of their fathers' deaths, Louise conveys the mood of the royal household. "We are approaching a sad time now. I can only feel for you very much, and you for us." And on the anniversary itself: "The loss to us all is one that nothing can efface." [7]

As the correspondence developed, the two girls came even closer together. The Princess signs her letters "your very affectionate friend" or "your most loving friend." The two Louisas pass along family news, send each other photographs and birthday presents, exchange pencil drawings and water-colour sketches, and share their intimate joys and sorrows.

These letters provide glimpses of the physical and mental state of the teenage Princess Louise. She delighted in the physical development of her adolescent body. "Everyone tells me I am grown very much, I think so myself." Yet she is bothered by the pain of severe headaches that plagued her. "I am not at all free from them," she wrote in April 1865. "There is never a day without them and they prevent me from enjoying myself as I should like. It is dreadful always having these pains, never a day without them. I try to be patient." [8]

These headaches probably resulted from a combination of physiological and psychological factors. Physically, Louise enjoyed generally good health, inheriting her mother's great strength and endurance, rather than her father's perpetual poor health. But the headaches were certainly real. Like her mother, Louise passed through much of the 1860s coping with mental and psychological stresses that produced physical pain. In Queen Victoria's case, this is usually ascribed to the tension between her desire to indulge herself in total mourning and her conscientiousness towards the on-going affairs of court and state. In Louise's case, the headaches arise out of the tension between her own wishes for a free-spirited life and the demands placed on her as a royal Princess, and by a domineering mother.

Louise could sometimes treat this gap in expectations in a light-hearted way. "I shall be so pleased to see you at Court," she wrote at the time of Louisa Bowater's first official presentation in the spring of 1866, "and will try and behave very well when you pass, because I have always an inclination to laugh when I see anyone I know." [9]

On other occasions, the temperamental princess suffered from deep depression. "I feel low and sad, and sit in my room and cry," Louise confided to Miss Bowater that July. "I cannot write and tell you why there are so many things I know ought not to be as they are, and that is what makes me so sad. I am expected to agree with them, and yet I cannot, not when I know a thing to be wrong." Five months later there was still no relief. "I am often sad," she lamented, "but I never let others see that I am."[10]

Louise had not yet found ways to let loose the devils inside her head.

\* \* \* \* \*

Princess Helena's 1866 marriage to Prince Christian of Schleswig-Holstein marked the start of a new phase in Louise's life — chief support to her mother. In her widowhood Queen Victoria demanded almost full-time moral support from at least one of her daughters. Eldest daughter Vicky had been spared this task; as Crown Princess of Prussia she had her own destiny to fulfill in Berlin. Alice had done a superb job in comforting her mother at the time of Albert's death, but she too escaped to the Continent as the wife of Prince Louis of Hesse-Darmstadt. Helena then had her turn; though she resided in Britain after her marriage, the existence of her own domestic establishment limited time with her mother.

After 1866 the natural companion-in-mourning to Queen Victoria was her senior unmarried daughter, eighteen year-old Princess Louise. Of all the daughters, Louise was the least well adapted to this role.

As her mother's principal companion, Louise was forced to endure endless days of consolation and mourning at Windsor, dreary visits with similarly morbid friends, solemn public appearances in the British countryside, plus innumerable day-long outings in the hills and glens around Balmoral. Louise was ever at her mother's side on these Highland excursions, sitting and eating with her, walking with her, sketching beside her, pretending to take an interest in the things that interested her. Of their 1867 Highland holiday the Queen remembered "these breakfasts with dear Louise, who was most amiable, attentive and cheerful." [11] Louise could endure only so much.

Occasionally she was able to release her pent-up frustrations. Duff relates the story of the royal party returning to Balmoral late in the evening of Hallowe'en 1867, after an all-day excursion. Some distance from the castle, the carriage was met by servants carrying torches. Intrigued by the idea of being a torch-bearer herself, Louise climbed down from the carriage and walked along with a flaming torch in her hand, appearing to her mother "like one of the witches in Macbeth." Nearer the castle a large crowd of servants, tenants and their families awaited the royal return. Louise and her youngest brother Leopold led the group inside, marching single file through the house, each with a torch, while bagpipes played. Later a bonfire was made of the torches, with Louise and the others dancing Highland reels around the flames. [12]

But Hallowe'en fun at Balmoral was an exception rather than the norm, as the mid-1860s were generally miserable years for Princess Louise. It was soon evident that she had neither the talent nor the desire to play the role her mother demanded. "I can't speak a *coeur ouvert* to Louise as she is not discreet and is very apt to take things in a different light to me," the Queen complained. Though continuing to praise Louise's art, and now finally admitting that "she is in some things very clever," Victoria remained generally negative about her fourth daughter. "She is very odd, dreadfully contradictory, very indiscreet and, from that, making mischief very frequently." [13]

Louise caused further outrage by refusing to tolerate her mother's hypocondria. After Albert's death, the Queen increasingly exploited imaginery ill-health to get her own way. Although physically well enough to do whatever she wanted, she was quite prepared to generate numerous afflictions as a way of deflecting unwelcome demands. The royal physician, Sir William Jenner, won the Queen's confidence by endorsing her self-diagnosis and supporting her fears that worry and overwork would drive her mad. Louise took the opposite side, supporting General Grey and Henry Ponsonby, the Queen's secretaries, in their attack on Jenner's encouragement of Victoria's fantasies. [14]

While slighting others with her indiscretions, Louise could feel terribly hurt when she herself was the victim of real or imagined hurts and oversights. She was terribly upset, for instance, at not being chosen in 1866 as a god-parent for her sister Vicky's new baby, Princess Victoria of Prussia. "She nearly cried when she heard Arthur has been asked, as she is very sensitive, [and] thinks no one likes her," wrote the Queen to her eldest daughter. "I should be very sorry if you overlooked her. She is decidedly cleverer (odd though she is) than Lenchen [Helena] and has a wonderful talent for art." [15] Victoria, as always, got her way, and Louise was asked to be a god-mother.

When she wanted, young Louise could be all sweetness and light in her relationships with others. "Louise was most tender and full of sympathy," Lady Augusta Stanley, a royal lady-in-waiting, confided in December 1866. She "spoke to me long in the corridor on Friday night." On another occasion Lady Augusta was effusive in praising a letter she had received from Louise. "There is something so natural and true in Princess Louise's letter," she told a friend, so much "the reverse of the wordiness characteristic of most of this younger generation." [16]

Given her own temperament, the usual expectations placed on a royal princess, extra demands from her mother, plus the emotional strains natural to the teenage years, Louise spent the latter half of the 1860s vainly trying to sort out her thoughts and dreams. Her sister-in-law Alexandra sensed the emotional unease and offered some sisterly advice. "My thoughts have been a great deal with you, my sweet Louise," wrote Alix in the autumn of 1866, "and I have been wondering how things have gone on and hope they have not been teasing you dear, like the last day I saw you when you looked quite worn and sad!! Pray don't let yourself be guided by so many!!! but better go straight to your Mama. She surely would give you the best advice. So pray darling, follow my advice, and listen to a sister who, God knows, means well and loves you very much."[17]

Continental visits provided some relief. In the summer of 1865 Louise travelled with her mother to Coburg to unveil a monument to Prince Albert in the place of his birth. "We enjoyed our stay in Germany very much," she wrote her friend Louisa Bowater. "We were in such a lovely place, and every spot associated with my father's youth. It is touching to hear how the people speak of him." [18]

Three years later Louise and her brother Arthur accompanied Queen Victoria on a mountain holiday to Switzerland. At a brief stop in Paris Louise had her first direct confrontation with political reality when a Fenian sympathizer "shook his stick" at her and shouted "A bas les Anglais." [19] Undaunted, the royal party continued on to Lucerne, where they rented a villa overlooking the lake. They hiked the surrounding countryside; they climbed Mount Pilatus.

Best of all the royal party travelled incognito as the Countess of Kent, Lady Louise Kent and Lord Arthur Kent. It reminded Victoria of her earlier incognito romps with Albert through the Scottish Highlands. It promised Louise a partial relief from her official role in life. But foreign travel could never do as much for Louise as for the Marquis of Lorne. Her liberation from the smothering embrace of everyday life would come through an inward voyage.

\* \* \* \* \*

That inward journey came through painting and sculpture, and it was well underway by the spring of 1868. "Today is dear Louise's 20th birthday," the Queen wrote Vicky on 21 March. "She is — and who would some years ago have thought it? — a clever, dear girl, with a fine strong character, and a very marked character — unselfish, affectionate, a good daughter with a wonderful talent for art. She is now doing a bust of me, quite by herself, which will be extremely good." This surprised Vicky. "I have seen so little of [Louise] that I can say I scarcely know her." So the Queen wrote again, underscoring her praise of Louise. "She is a distinguished girl, and very much liked and, with right, much admired — for she is very handsome. Such a beautiful figure and so quiet and graceful." [20]

"The impossible had happened," writes Daphne Bennett. "The Queen and Louise had drawn close, a warmth had sprung up between them that was to increase with the years and the effect on both of them was excellent." Bennett suggests that maturity itself had a settling effect on Louise. "Experience had taught her that as a member of the royal family it was useless to pretend that she was the same as anyone else. This had the effect of making her calmer and more resigned to her status." [21]

Louise could never effect a complete turnaround, reconciling herself to a life of mother's helper, or making trite speeches in public and opening bazaars like Helena. But she did become a better private companion for her mother. It was Louise who persuaded her mother to sing again, something she had not had the heart to do since Albert's death, and to invite musicians to perform at Buckingham Palace and Windsor Castle for the first time in years.

Far more important to Louise's new sunny disposition was the confidence gained through her formal art studies. Vicky had earlier urged the Queen to allow Louise to study art beyond the confines of private palace lessons; keeping her unoccupied and disgruntled at home was not the answer. Times were changing, Vicky argued, and institutional training need not automatically be denied an artistic princess. Above all, it would be a pity to waste Louise's artistic talents — a practical point that appealed to the Queen.

Encouragement from Louise's private art teachers, Mary Thorneycroft and Edward Corbould, was equally important. Louise had proven herself a keen observer and quick learner while Thorneycroft sculpted a series of busts of members of the royal family. She had helped Corbould design a christening cup for Prince Albert Victor of Wales, which the Queen declared "most beautiful." [22]

So Louise enrolled as a student at the The National Art Training School in South Kensington. Founded in the 1830s as the School of Design, the college had been revitalized by Prince Albert and other sponsors at the time of the Great Exhibition of 1851. Today it survives as the Royal College of Art.

Louise's program included a general painting course plus advanced sculpture lessons. The Queen at first considered sculpture a less suitable pre-occupation for a princess than sketching or water-colour painting. But she was reminded that Vicky had taken up sculpture after her marriage, and that Albert had approved, expressing the view that "as an art it is even more attractive than painting." [23] That was enough for Victoria. Soon she was writing Vicky with considerable pride that Louise was going to "try and greatly alter" a "horrid colossal statue" of Her Majesty fashioned by another sculptor. [24]

Joseph Edgar Boehm was Louise's sculpture instructor at the National Art Training School. Fourteen years older than Princess Louise, the Viennese-born Boehm had settled in London in 1862 and quickly became an established figure on the British art scene. Appointed sculptor-in-ordinary to the Queen, he executed a statuette of Victoria plus one of Louise on horseback. Such an appointment ensured him a large practice as a society sculptor and led to a constant flow of commissions for public monuments, portrait statues and busts.

The National Art Training School and the semi-bohemian milieu of Boehm's studio offered Louise a glimpse of a world far removed and far different from that of the palace. Here were other young people with similar interests. Here was artistic freedom rather than family obligation. Her teenage discontent seemed to disappear immediately. Even her mother's refusal to permit her to live in a studio of her own could be taken in stride.

And to the joy and delight of the twenty year-old artist, the Royal Academy accepted one of her pieces — a sculpted bust of her brother Arthur — for its spring 1868 exhibition. The next year Louise was back at the Academy exhibition with a bust of her mother, and again in 1874 with a bust of the late General Grey.

Most visitors to the 1869 exhibition claimed to like Louise's bust of the Queen, though diarist Emily Hall, for one, wished to hear some honest criticism on the subject. "Her Royal Highness should have sent it in the name of one of the people. Then the real truth would have been known. At present the work is judged of as the Princess's and the President of the R.A. can talk such rubbish and flunkeyism as to say 'Art has been honoured by Her Royal Highness's work'." [25]

Art historian Hilary Hunt-Lewis praised Louise's 1869 piece. She had "infused life and flesh and blood to her marble. Like Boehm she managed to thaw the chill which cold marble sheds around. The bust is full of character and has a delicate feeling for form rightly realized, the work is good in pose and line, refined in drawing and excellent in style." [26]

Hunt-Lewis was generally positive towards most of Louise's work, particularly her drawing and painting. "Her art retained much of the Victorian delicacy, the subtle charm and fragrant neatness due to her natural tendencies and her training. In much of her work she clung to that technical expression that requires laborious application and unquestioned obedience to a rather formal code of regulations." Yet in all her drawings, continues Hunt-Lewis, there is "always a freshness of treatment and delicacy of feeling." Finally, she also possessed that "rich gift of being able to transfer to paper or canvas what is termed atmosphere." [27]

Yet Louise seemed more wedded to the conventions of art history than to the innovations of mid-to late-nineteenth century Europe. She would turn her back on the French Impressionists and on the Rodin school of sculpture, and showed no curiosity to go to Paris to see their work for herself. Somehow the originality that Edward Corbould noticed when she was young never quite materialized. Her paintings and sculpture would always be technically proficient, but like her most influential teacher, Edgar Boehm, "she broke little new ground as an artist herself." [28]

Whatever critics of the future might conclude, Louise's work in 1868 and 1869 was of a quality that demanded public exposure and critical commentary. But, as Emily Hall suggested in her diary, critics and curators would hardly dare to be honest with her work. Criticizing the work of a princess was tantamount to criticizing the morals of Queen Victoria herself! Louise was totally compromised through her position as a daughter of the Queen.

With or without criticism, Louise could not put her canvasses and her sculptures on the commercial market as other promising young artists could. She did exhibit in three Royal Academy exhibitions. She did present pieces of her work to close friends, or to countrymen or hosts who had shown her special favours. She loaned or donated her work to charity exhibitions. In the autumn of 1870, for example, she placed samples of both her painting and her sculpture in a London exhibition to raise money for the relief of the sick and wounded in the Franco-Prussian War.

But in the fall of 1870 even art was relegated to a secondary position in Princess Louise's thoughts. That October she became engaged.

# CHAPTER SIX

# YOUNG ROMANTICS, 1868-1870

*H*ome for a brief visit during his foreign escapades, Lorne was the centre of attention in the Campbell household. "A certain mystery accompanied him to us younger ones," recalled his sister Frances, "his sudden departures, and unexpected returns, the romance of his expeditions." Frances listened "breathless" to tales of the wounded Lorne had seen in Rome, and the "ghastly trail" of war in the United States. "He would tell us tales, or repeat poetry, or hear our young ideas, with the amused air of a companion." Or he would scribble verse, "which sometimes rose to the level of poetry," which he and Frances shouted together in "an uncomprehending unison." Tired at last of such frivolity, Lorne would bribe the youngsters to leave him alone with his "astonishing store of copper coins." [1]

Home from his Italian adventure for Christmas 1867, Lorne seemed more serious and mature. At the ripe age of twenty-two he was ready to take the step he had discussed with Bismarck — membership in the British House of Commons. Lorne's marquisate was a courtesy title, and did not bar him from the Commons. Argyllshire offered a safe seat, controlled by the Campbell family, "his by almost feudal right." [2] A suggestion from Duke George produced the resignation of Struthers Finlay, Liberal member for the previous ten years. Lorne easily captured the Liberal nomination and won the subsequent by-election on 3 March 1868.

Two days later Lorne took his seat in the House of Commons, duly introduced to the Speaker by his great-uncle, Charles Howard, and uncle, Ronald Leveson-Gower. The Duke of Argyll watched proudly from the peers' gallery, while Lorne's mother and his sister Edith beamed their approval from the ladies' gallery. After the swearing-in, the Speaker whispered that just minutes previously, a member had quoted a passage from Lorne's *A Trip to the Tropics* during debate on a tramways bill, and

Lorne as seen by cartoonist in 1870.

that the opinion quoted had "turned the scale against the bill." Gower thought this "of good augury" for Lorne's parliamentary career." [3]

Ronald Gower took Lorne under his wing, showing him around Westminster and London. Gower was Liberal member for the Scottish riding of Sutherland, like Argyllshire a virtual family-controlled seat. "Our walks to and from the House were charming," he recalled. [4] They probably took in the Royal Academy's spring exhibition and admired the sculpture of young Princess Louise. Gower was also an avowed homosexual and no doubt introduced his colleague to London's emerging homosexual world of the late 1860s. At any rate, Lorne found the social life and the political atmosphere equally heady. "I have been dining out every day," he wrote. "Ireland is the subject of everybody's talk." [5]

The spring of 1868 proved an exciting time to enter parliament, as both parties boasted new and dynamic leaders. Benjamin Disraeli had just succeeded Lord Derby as Conservative leader and prime minister, making his first House appearance in his new role the same day as Lorne's swearing-in. Yet Disraeli was in trouble, for the Commons contained a majority of political opponents. Those opposition members were rallying around William Gladstone, who himself had recently replaced Lord John Russell as leader of the emerging Liberal party. Gladstone made the Irish Question his great cause, beginning with an attack on the rights and privileges of the established Church of Ireland. He was carrying the attack, in fact carrying motion after motion against the Conservative ministry.

The Gladstonian tide crested with a sweeping Liberal victory in the general election that autumn. Lorne easily retained Argyllshire; throughout Scotland fifty-two Liberals were returned against eight Conservatives; altogether across Britain a Liberal majority of just over 100. On December 9 the first Gladstone ministry was sworn into office, with Lorne's father as Secretary of State for India. Gladstone pledged his administration to introduce reform at home, settle outstanding disputes abroad, and solve the seemingly impossible Irish Question. "Never had new members talked so much as they talked in 1868," wrote G.M. Young in his analysis of Victorian Britain. "Never had they had so much to talk about." [6]

Gladstone came to dinner at Argyll Lodge the day before Christmas, and the talk was all of politics – support for the secret ballot, reduction of military expenses. The new prime minister shared confidences with his two Campbell colleagues — father in the cabinet and son on the back benches. At age forty-five, the Eighth Duke of Argyll was at the peak of his political influence; at age twenty-three the Marquis of Lorne seemed on the threshold of his own promising career.

Ronald Gower initially feared Lorne might "be tempted to speak too soon" in House debates, and advised him to bide his time. [7] Gower's fears were groundless. Not till 21 July 1869, did Lorne make his first contribution — a perfunctory comment on a routine Scottish bill. In his ten years representing Argyllshire, Lorne spoke just six times! Nor was he all that conscientious a constituency man; in 1878 *The Times* rapped his knuckles for not giving "an annual account of stewardship." [8]

A new member's silence might be excused for a short while; besides, having a father in the cabinet (and later a mother-in-law on the throne) precluded any strong utterances either for or against government policy. But Lorne was little more than a political eunuch during his ten years, contributing nothing of importance to the debates, obediently voting the party line with one minor exception. [9] The *Dictionary of National Biography* summed up Lorne's political career in a masterpiece of understatement: "He seldom spoke in parliament." A Canadian writer charitably spoke of Lorne's parliamentary career as being "graceful rather than active." [10]

Lorne's only steady contribution to British political life in the 1868-70 period came as private secretary to his father at the India Office. The Duke's appointment as Secretary of State for India was no surprise; he was in line for a senior portfolio, and for some time had acted as chief Liberal spokesman for India in the House of Lords. Lorne's salary as private secretary came out of his father's pocket rather than the public coffers. Nevertheless, with the presence of such Scots as Argyll, Lorne, and M.E. Grant Duff as under-secretary, livelier wits began referring to the India Office as "Nova Scotia".

At first Lorne shared in the excitement of dealing with the vast subcontinent in these years following the suppression of the Indian Mutiny. "Interesting questions about salt duties, irrigations, army armaments and promotion of officers, are coming in," he wrote in January 1869. Within a month, however, it had become rather routine. "India work of course heavy," he noted in February, as correspondence on salt duties and armaments piled up. [11] By the end of the first year the work had become positively boring. Lorne's major regret was his inability to parlay the job into a trip to India itself. Everything was done from London — the correspondence, the decisions, the private receptions and grand entertainments. It was all so tame after his travels in America and Europe.

Of course life was not all House sittings and India Office paper shuffling. The young man known to his fellow MPs as Johnny Lorne found plenty of diversions in the great metropolis of Victorian London. He joined the Marlborough Club. "I play bowls there, and sup on late nights, till three in the morning, and I find the exercise the alleys give one very pleasant." He kept up his markmanship skills by participating in the annual rifle matches between Lords and Commons. He was appointed captain and company commander of two militia regiments, the London

Scottish Volunteers and the Sutherlandshire Rifles — the closest he came to realizing his boyhood dream of a military life.

There were lunches and dinner parties. "Dined with men who were with me at the Edinburgh Academy," Lorne noted on one occasion. "A good deal of speechifying, but the dinner was otherwise pleasant." There was the theatre. There were frequent invitations to country house weekends where he usually found "a pleasant little party." [12] Most of these London activities seem to emphasize male rather than mixed company as Lorne demonstrated a definite homosexual preference, either latent or manifest.

Regardless of how pleasurable his London diversions, Johnny Lorne was restless, as always, and could hardly wait for parliamentary breaks. During the two-week Whitsuntide holiday in May 1869, Lorne sped to Berlin, to keep abreast of German developments. He talked politics with the elderly Radziwill brothers, British ambassador Augustus Loftus, and Reichstag deputy George von Bunsen. He returned via the Rhineland where he visited Gerald Talbot at a Prussian military school near Ehrenbreitstein. It was a beautiful spring on the Continent. "The country was looking lovely, the vineyards beginning to get very green, and all the meadows near the Rhine full of white flowers." [13]

Lorne also spent some time in Ireland that year, trying to gain a better understanding of the Irish Question that dominated British politics. Unfortunately, his contacts were limited to wealthy landlords who reinforced his own inherited attitudes towards property. While Lorne could support Gladstone's disestablishment of the Church of Ireland, he could not condone attacks on the landowning system then prevailing in Ireland. "Who would bring new capital in the place of that driven away?" Like his father, Lorne was beginning to distance himself from the more radical aspects of Gladstone's Irish policies. [14]

Yet Lorne's commitment to any set of policies or principles seemed to lack depth; the young member of parliament was a bit of a dilettante. He might get superficial enjoyment from the heady atmosphere of House debates, or India Office entertainments, or fact-finding tours of Ireland, but he was not prepared to apply himself rigorously to the task at hand. Both his contributions at Westminster and his constituency work in Argyllshire seem half-hearted. Somehow the golden promises of the 1866-67 years of travel do not bear fruit in the subsequent parliamentary years.

* * * * *

The Marquis of Lorne celebrated his twenty-fifth birthday on 6 August 1870. He had made little impact as a member of the House of Commons; he was bored with the routine paper work of his India Office job. Even his trips to Berlin and Ireland were an anti-climax after his continental escapades of 1866-67.

There seemed little focus to Lorne's public life. A different career might have provided greater challenges and rewards, but little else was available to a duke's eldest son. His parents had long ago ruled out a military career; he could hardly go into trade or the professions. One had to put in time in a socially acceptable way until one's inheritance came along. But with the indefatigable Duke George not yet out of his forties, Lorne was going to have to wait a long time.

Time had caught up with other members of the family. Lorne's beloved grandmother Harriet, Duchess of Sutherland, died in October 1868 after several lonely years of widowhood and ill health. His mother, Elizabeth Campbell, suffered a paralytic seizure in December 1869, following a bitterly cold trip in an open carriage at Inverary.

Lorne sped north from London as fast as he could, and found marginal improvement by the time he reached the castle. "Mother's condition is still very critical," he noted two weeks later, "but the doctors use very hopeful language, and her strength and great courage are much in her favour."[15] After a long convalescence, Elizabeth regained her mental and verbal capacities, but physical paralysis through the left side of her body ended her life at court — Queen Victoria had chosen her to succeed her mother as Mistress of the Robes — and severely restricted all public engagements.

Meanwhile, Lorne's siblings began crossing the threshold from adolescence to adulthood. In December 1868 his sister Edith married Earl Percy, later Duke of Northumberland. One month later, Lorne's brother Archie married Janey Callendar, a ward of the Duke of Argyll since the death of her own parents.

Lorne seems not to have been tempted to follow Edith and Archie to the altar. Young women, apart from his sisters, seem absent from his life. His school memoirs and travel writings introduce his male friends — Frederick Wood at Eton, Andrew Lang at St. Andrews, Cyril Flower at Cambridge, Arthur Strutt in America, Gerald Talbot in Germany, Lieutenant Stumm in Italy, and always Ronnie Gower. Young ladies do not appear.

Once upon a time Mary Gladstone had been such a young lady. Mary was the fifth child of William and Catherine Gladstone, born in November 1847, two years younger than Lorne. She and Ian were good friends as children and teenagers, since the Gladstone and Campbell families enjoyed pleasant weekends together in the British countryside and occasional winter holidays in Rome, often with children in tow.

In the autumn of 1865 Mary spent a few days at Inverary. She was almost eighteen; Lorne had just turned twenty. Mary's diary entries make those days sound like the highlight of her life.

"Up at five," reads her September 29 entry. "Coffee and off in the waggonette. Lorne riding and leading another horse for me. The hounds caught the otter trail at once. We scrambled along the river, in a deep ravine, very hard and difficult walking, jumping over burns, and missing the trail after two miles. Lorne helped us, and great fun we had. About ten we picknicked. The otter was found in a cairn. With infinite difficulty, varied by tumbles, we scrambled to the spot. The scene was most exciting and beautiful, men and hounds dotting the banks. The otter tried to swim down-stream, but suddenly changed his tactics, and dodged up the river. We were in at the death. Lorne and I jumped on our horses and rode home. In spite of my having no habit, enjoyed the ride immensely. We had a great discussion on the Scottish Established and Scottish Episcopal Churches."[16]

A pencil note in Mary's diary opposite her October 1 entry, as if added some time later, is even more revealing: "This was an interesting visit," she mused. "Lord Lorne, a Prince of Hosts, fair and very good-looking, most fascinating to a raw 17-year-old girl. We spent hours together each day, fishing, riding, driving, walking, and he always contrived we should be together. Our talks were of the deepest interest, ranging over endless subjects." [17]

Mary was as infatuated as any young girl could be, and perhaps more deeply in love than at any time in her life. Something was working on Lorne as well, for he "always contrived" they should be together. Would the relationship go beyond deep talk and wide-ranging discussions?

December 1866, a little over a year later, finds the Campbell and Gladstone families holidaying together in Rome. Mary had been there since mid-October, and Lorne came down from Berlin a few days before Christmas. Lorne was now twenty-one, Mary had just turned nineteen. It is an ideal opportunity for their relationship to blossom.

But Mary's diary entries for this period are extremely disappointing, as Lorne makes only two brief appearances. After visiting the Saint Agnese Catacombs with Lorne and two of her brothers, she notes: "Willy, Stephy, Lorne and I were lost for a few minutes, and shouted in vain. It was a horrid sensation". A year earlier Mary would have enjoyed being "lost for a few minutes" with Lorne! A few days later, after a dull party in Florence, Lorne escorts Mary in to dinner which, Mary claims, "was a decided relief." [18]

That is all; Lorne rose no higher than "relief" escort during this winter vacation in Italy. Lorne still seems the gallant young man of the previous autumn — shouting for assistance when they lose their way in the underground catacombs, escorting Mary to dinner. Yet no longer does he "always contrive" that they should be together.

Nor did Mary expect it. Had she become more discriminating among young men? Did she realize that as a commoner's daughter she had no hope of marrying the eldest son of the Duke of Argyll? Or had Mary become aware of Lorne's possible sexual ambivalence?

Whatever the case, Lorne had made his last entry in Miss Gladstone's diary. Mary, on the other hand, never once appears in Lorne's autobiographical writings. *Passages From the Past* contains no mention of Inverary in 1865. Christmas 1866 in Rome is recalled solely for a hike to the monastery at Monte Cassino with Mary's father, William Gladstone![19]

Lorne returned to Berlin in mid-January 1867, while Mary and her family made their way home to Britain. Mary retreated to her music, fell in love a year later with Arthur James Balfour — yet another disappointment, as his thoughts seemed elsewhere — and at age thirty-eight married Rev. Harry Drew, a Church of England cleric. She and Lorne remained lifelong friends, but the subsequent friendship lacked the ardour of that golden autumn of 1865.

Mary could at least console herself with the knowledge that Lorne had not forsaken her for another woman. The only women in Lorne's life through the late 1860s were his own family members — his sisters, his mother, and his mother's sister.

He was certainly an attractive young man, both in appearance and personality. "His nature was so radiant and loving," according to his sister Frances. "He had an uncommonly fair complexion, with straight regular features, and the brightest of blue eyes, the whole crowned by a wealth of yellow gold hair." Elizabeth Campbell had idolized her eldest son "from the hour he was born," and Frances herself lovingly recalled that it was next to impossible "to prevent every one from doing the same." [20]

One of Lorne's favourite dancing partners was his sister Elizabeth. They "were a fair couple to see, in the ball rooms of that date." But there was no outside young lady in the picture. In the world of formal society, concluded Frances, Lorne was "a bright peculiar star." [21]

\* \* \* \* \*

While the British public remained completely indifferent about the Marquis of Lorne's love life, it grew increasingly interested in the matrimonial prospects of Princess Louise. The Princess celebrated her twenty-second birthday in March 1870 with no husband in sight!

The problem was certainly not her appearance. Louise was by far the most beautiful of Queen Victoria's daughters. Though full-bosomed like her sisters, her height gave her an elegant rather than a dumpy figure. Everyone remarked on her clear blue eyes and her lovely blonde hair. She had an eye for style that led her instinctively to choose just the right dress or hair style to show herself to best advantage. When in good spirits, she was a witty, intelligent, delightful young woman, exhaling a kind of "psychical ozone" that could easily overwhelm all around her. [22]

Ever since Helena's marriage in 1866, the British press had been pairing Louise with virtually every eligible Protestant prince on the European continent. Prince William of Orange, a member of the Dutch royal family, was one early candidate. Willie happened to be a good friend of the Prince of Wales, sharing with Bertie a fondness for the boulevards and night life of Paris. That in itself was anathema to the Queen, never mind what Louise thought. So William of Orange was quickly ruled out.

Then on 7 May 1868 the leading Copenhagen newspaper *Dagstelegraphen* announced the engagement of Louise and Crown Prince Frederick of Denmark. Here was a more serious candidate — a brother of Alexandra, Princess of Wales, and a familiar face to Queen Victoria ever since his student days at Oxford. But Buckingham Palace denied the engagement immediately. Apart from Louise's lack of romantic interest in Frederick, Queen Victoria knew that such a match would antagonize Prussia. Prusso-Danish animosity was an important element in European diplomacy through the 1860s, and the British royal family had already made two Danish marriages — the Prince of Wales with Alexandra and Helena with Prince Christian. To avoid further Prussian hostility, the Queen had previously informed Copenhagen there would be no more Danish marriages.

Finally, there were the Prussian bachelor princes, led by Prince Adalbert (or Abbat), the thirty-two year-old nephew of King William I. Four days after the *Dagstelegraphen* announcement, Queen Victoria heard from her daughter Alice in Darmstadt. "Adalbert is here," she reported, "so much pleased with having seen you again, singing the praise of both Lenchen [Helena] and Louise. It is such a pleasure to hear others admire and appreciate my dear sisters." [23]

Adalbert was returning to Berlin after a visit to the British court. The next step in any carefully orchestrated marriage minuet would take Louise on a family visit to Prussia. Sister Vicky obliged some months later, suggesting that Louise trade the gloom and doom of Windsor for a few sunny weeks in Berlin. But Vicky was motivated by more than altruism. A Prussian marriage might restore some normalcy to Anglo-Prussian relations and strengthen Vicky's own delicate position within Prussian politics.

At first all seemed to go well on the dance floors and in the drawing rooms of Berlin and Potsdam. Vicky noticed the stir her beautiful young sister caused. With amazement she watched Louise make her entrances, "floating gracefully into a room to become the instant cynosure of all eyes in a pale-coloured dress of the lightest material." [24] The Prussian princes found Louise a fascinating creature, not the least bit shy, chatting

Louise as a young woman.

vivaciously with men and women alike. Swept off his feet by this lovely English girl, Adalbert whispered to Vicky his hopes of marriage.

But Adalbert got no further; like William of Orange and Frederick of Denmark, he was stopped by the combined efforts of Queen Victoria and Princess Louise. For her part, Louise had come to thoroughly dislike Adalbert and his Prussian stablemates; they seemed too arrogant, too chauvinistic, altogether lacking in artistic sensitivity. "Louise very properly said she could not and would not marry anyone she did not really like," the Queen informed Vicky. [25]

Such a bold declaration from a rebel daughter might have been overruled by her all-dominant royal mother, except that Queen Victoria and Princess Louise saw eye-to-eye on this particular business. While Louise had soured on Abbat personally, the Queen had come — at least temporarily — to reject the very principle of European marital entanglements. It was becoming increasingly difficult to please the various pro and anti-Prussian forces on the Continent. And it was not worth the effort! "This alliance is out of the question," the Queen wrote Vicky. "Louise and I have other views for her, and it is well that [Abbat] should know that all idea of this is at an end." [26]

The crucial decision about Louise's marriage was made in the autumn of 1869. "Louise is most decided in her wish to settle in her own country," the Queen wrote the Prince of Wales on November 24. "I am equally of the opinion, having ascertained that there are no difficulties which will not be easily overcome." Bertie was to tell no one but Alix; the Queen herself had discussed it only with Lord Granville and Dean Stanley of Westminster, both of whom, she reported "are strongly in favour." [27]

So Louise wished "to settle in her own country". This was not xenophobic nationalism at work; Louise dearly loved Europe and spent much of her later life escaping to the Continent from dreary old England. In the autumn of 1869 she was simply rebelling against the custom of the day of marrying royal princesses to whichever eligible prince offered the best dynastic and diplomatic prospects.

The new life that Louise had glimpsed through art and the London art scene would surely be snuffed out by the obligations that marriage into a European royal family entailed. Louise wanted to be mistress of her own destiny. If there was to be marriage it would be on her own terms; it would be a marriage in which her artistic interests would be allowed to flourish. It would not be found on the other side of the English Channel.

This pointed to marriage with a British subject, most likely a member of one of the senior aristocratic families. But that had not happened in over three and a half centuries. Not since Mary, youngest daughter of King Henry VII, married the Duke of Suffolk in 1515, had a princess married, with the sovereign's official sanction, outside the confines of a reigning European house. Queen Victoria, however, was Queen Victoria, and it was very difficult to stop her once she had made up her mind to do something.

But to whom marry the fair Louise? There were plenty of rumoured prospects. "A member of the peerage with a long rent-roll and a high German title was thought of," reported Henry Labouchere's anti-royalist journal *Truth*. "But he formed another matrimonial engagement". Also an earl "whose fortune and personal standing in the country rendered him a *parti sortable*, but he got entangled with an illustrious widow." [28] The *Western Morning News* reported that a young Church of England clergyman had caught Louise's attention at Windsor, and that the impossibility of such a match had led Louise to threaten to enter the Anglican sisterhood at Clever — a horrid, High Church prospect for the Broad Church Queen Victoria. [29]

Behind such public speculation, mother and daughter spent the winter of 1869-70 drawing up a list of acceptable suitors. The Queen checked out character references and political prospects. Some names were deleted; others added. By the summer of 1870 five names remained on the short list: Lord Rosebery, Lord Stafford, Lord Fitzroy, Albert Grey, and the Marquis of Lorne. One by one each was invited to spend a few days at Balmoral during September.

Rosebery wrote a description of his visit, which he found thoroughly depressing. The highlight of Saturday September 3 came after dinner when "we went off to the dreary and uninhabited drawing room." The next day he complained of "an odious drink called birch wine" served at lunch. On Monday the atmosphere was even "stiffer than usual" though Louise, on this one occasion, was allowed to remain after the Queen and to go to the billiard room "where as usual we played bowls." [30]

Poor Rosebery excited no spark with either the Queen or Princess Louise; he probably had no desire to do so. Once his allotted time was up, Rosebery was despatched without regret, and dropped from consideration. Similar fates befell Stafford, Fitzroy and Grey. The Marquis of Lorne was the last of the suitors to visit Balmoral that September, and his placing at the end seems more deliberate than accidental, as if the other four were merely there to be rejected while waiting for the chosen one.

# CHAPTER SEVEN

# THE MAIDEN ALL FOR LORNE, 1870-1871

*L*orne and Louise's engagement was not entirely spontaneous. After the other potential suitors had suffered Louise's indifference and Queen Victoria's haughtiness, mother and daughter decided — then if not earlier — that it would be the Marquis of Lorne. Lord Hatherly, a member of the household staff, was instructed "to inform the Marquis that his suit would be acceptable and had already been sanctioned by the Queen." [1]

Lorne was standing by at Inverary, ostensibly helping his parents with their annual autumn round of shooting parties and weekend entertaining. One of the house guests was Oscar Browning, an Eton master and former protégé of William Johnson (Cory). Browning was thoroughly enjoying the family's hospitality, when suddenly one morning at breakfast, with no prior warning, "Lorne took leave of us, and said that he was going to Balmoral." Afterwards Browning was told in confidence that "the object of his visit was to ask for the hand of Princess Louise." [2]

The formal proposal came on October 3. That afternoon two carriages left Balmoral on separate Highland excursions. Queen Victoria and her youngest daughter Beatrice headed for Pannanich Wells. At the same time Louise and Lorne, accompanied by Lady Ely and Lord Hatherly, headed for Glassalt Shiel.

Glassalt Shiel lay three kilometres from Balmoral Castle, at the western end of lonely Loch Muick. Here the Queen had built a secluded cottage for herself; now it would provide some intimacy for the betrothal of her daughter. Arriving at Glassalt, Lady Ely and Lord Hatherly hung back. It had been arranged in advance that the young couple would walk alone from Loch Muick over the hill to the next body of water, Dhu Loch.

*When was our loving? Oh, ask when the mountains*
*Keep but a lacing of cold Winter's snow,*
*Grass-lands are greening, and lambs by the fountains*
*Are bleating below!*

*Have you not seen, on the Loch's glassy water,*
*Dolphins leap onward in sport by the shore;*
*The Hind stand and wonder the Stag had not sought her*
*With challenging roar?*

*Were you then sleeping, when moorland and meadow*
*Woke to the call of the Plover, and song*
*Rang in the woodlands, that scarce knew a shadow,*
*For Spring was yet young?*

*If you were wakeful, then why ask the season*
*The Highlands are loveliest, − lovely alway?*
*Stay: I will tell you; − enough, in all reason! −*
*Before − we were grey!* [3]

"Love in a Cold Climate" is a title fit for the wooing of Princess Louise by the Marquis of Lorne, writes Ivor Brown in his history of Balmoral. Courtship, more often associated "with green thoughts in green shades" was pursued in the bare and lofty wilderness around Glassalt. The proposal was fitly made in a "scene so essentially Highland" as the path to Loch Dhu. [4]

Neither Lorne nor Louise left any account of their thoughts, words or actions during the hours they spent alone that afternoon. But they did take their time, and were quite late in returning to Balmoral. The Queen had arrived back at seven, and was anxiously awaiting the news. Finally, well after dark, "Louise ran into the castle, breathless, to tell her mother and sister that she was engaged." [5]

"This was an eventful day," a happy Queen Victoria wrote in her diary. "Our dear Louise engaged to Lord Lorne. Louise told me that Lorne had spoken of his devotion to her, and proposed to her, and that she had accepted, knowing that I would approve. Though I am not unprepared for this result, I felt painfully the thought of losing her. But I naturally gave my consent, and could only pray that she might be happy." [6] The Queen seemed pleased with Louise's chosen husband. "From the very high character which he possesses — his superiority in almost every sense over the young men of the present day — and the excellence of his parents — the Queen can only rejoice." [7]

As heir to the Argyll dukedom, Lorne was a natural candidate for the short-list of Louise's suitors. Queen Victoria had long admired his parents and grandparents, and had no doubts concerning his family background. Yet she wondered about Lorne himself. Was he good enough for a royal princess? What sort of young man was he? What were his religious views? What kind of moral life had he led? Where did he stand on the great social and political questions of the day? Rev. Norman Macleod, Scottish theologian and close friend of the Campbell family who had prepared Lorne for his first communion, reassured the Queen on many of these points during an interview at Balmoral in the fall of 1869.

Yet as late as the following June, Lorne still made a better impression on other members of the royal family than on Queen Victoria herself. "Lord Lorne has just been here," wrote daughter Vicky from Berlin on June 2. "I was so glad to see him; he came for the wedding of a friend of his, a Mr. Talbot — who is a Prussian officer, and who married a Miss Broadhurst, a pretty American lady." Such enthusiasm for Lorne was not entirely to the Queen's liking. "I do not fancy him," she replied. "He has such a forward manner, and such a disagreeable way of speaking but I know he is very clever and very good." [8]

Queen Victoria's opinion changed markedly during the week Lorne spent at Balmoral in the autumn of 1870. Lorne arrived Thursday September 29. By the weekend Victoria was coming around. "I think him very pleasing, amiable, clever, his voice being only a little against him. And he is in fact very good looking." By the following Thursday she convinced herself that "I always wished for him, though I did not like him so much, till I got to know him and now I do so much." [9]

Once she made up her mind, Victoria could overlook Lorne's "forward manner" and his rasping, high-pitched voice. He was handsome; he was charming; he was well versed in both domestic and international politics. He possessed an artistic temperament and artistic interests similar to Louise. In the end she judged Lorne "most superior and quite excellent." And his devotion to Louise was "quite touching." [10]

But the gossips wondered about Louise. They believed that her desire to avoid a continental marriage and settle instead on a Briton, any Briton, was much stronger than her personal feelings for Lorne Soon the ladies of the court were whispering that Louise was not really in love. "I think she will love him," remarked Henry Ponsonby, the Queen's secretary, in a manner less than convincing. "All of these Princesses have made devoted wives whatever their faults may be and if Lorne steers well all will be very well. He will make her part of his family and one of themselves."[11]

Lorne and Louise had been acquainted since childhood, and shared similar artistic tastes and talents. Yet there is tangible proof of only one meeting between them in the months immediately prior to Balmoral. This encounter took place at a breakfast party hosted by William and Catherine

Gladstone at their London home in July.

"What a great pleasure it was coming to your breakfast, and how very much I enjoyed it," Louise wrote Mrs. Gladstone. "There were many people there I had been anxious to become acquainted with — so you can judge how pleased I was when I saw them." Lorne was more explicit. "I think it was a little owing to your breakfast party," he later confided to Mrs. Gladstone, "that things have fallen out as they have." [12]

Meanwhile the young lovers descended from the heights of Glassalt Shiel and Dhu Loch to the reality of daily life. Late that evening, Lorne dined privately with Princess Louise and the Queen. He spent one more full day at Balmoral, before departing for Inverary.

With the engagement settled, Louise was anxious to leave Balmoral for the return to Windsor Castle and the London art scene. But the "Great Knee Row" interfered. In mid-October, Louise sprained her knee while riding over the Highland countryside. Queen Victoria seized this opportunity to prolong the family's stay in her beloved Scotland, insisting Louise not travel until she could walk, and sending for a Scottish doctor. Louise demanded an English physician, and loudly protested that if the journey in question had been from south to north her mother would have packed her into a carriage forthwith. "Oh what a row," exclaimed her brother Leopold, breaking into peals of laughter. [13]

Of course the Queen won the argument; the return journey was delayed until November 23. Princess Louise might be engaged, in a few more months she would be married, but the formidable Queen Victoria still ruled the roost.

\* \* \* \* \*

An old Highland story on the engagement begins with an Argyllshire woman being stopped on the street by her parish minister. "Well, Janet, this is a great day for us in the West Country — to think of marrying a princess!" Janet's reply was somewhat unexpected. "And for what should it be a great day meenister? I'm thinkin' the Queen'll be a proud woman to have a daughter married to the son o' Mac Cailean Mhor." [14]

The British public generally welcomed the engagement between the beautiful princess and the handsome lord as the love match of the generation. Louise was affectionately dubbed "The Maiden All for Lorne." A London perfume shop, the Laboratory of Flowers, offered a new fragrance named "Love-Lorne." A Glasgow photographer received 60,000 orders for a photograph of the bridegroom. *The Times* and other publications fed an avid public millions of words on the romantic young couple.

By coincidence, a new edition of Robert Blackmore's novel *Lorna Doone* appeared almost simultaneously with news of the engagement. A careless journalist mistakenly conveyed the impression that the novel bore some relation to the bridegroom's family history. So the reading public flocked to the bookstores, making *Lorna Doone* the literary sensation of the season.

On a more serious level, Benjamin Disraeli thought the engagement "as wise as it is romantic." [15] *The Times* admitted the engagement might "excite a momentary surprise," but believed Louise's happiness more important than outdated concepts of international dynastic alliances. For once, the stolid *Times* seemed quite ecstatic. "A marriage between a pair so accomplished and amiable, and drawn to one another by the force of mutual affection, promises a life of uncheckered happiness." [16]

Despite this initial euphoria, Queen Victoria knew the battle was not quite over. She may have pleased a sentimental public, she have may bested the Prussians, but she still had to convince parliament and members of her own immediate family of the match's worth.

On 9 February 1871, the Queen drove from Buckingham Palace through the streets of London to open the new session of parliament at Westminster. "Louise and Beatrice with me in the carriage," she noted in her journal. "There was a great crowd and much cheering and enthusiasm." At Westminster, "Louise and Beatrice stood on the steps of the throne, and Arthur to my right near Bertie. More cheering on the way back." [17]

This was only the third time Queen Victoria had opened parliament since Albert's death nine years earlier. On her previous appearance, five years before, the Queen had requested a dowry for her betrothed daughter Helena and an annuity for her son Alfred. Now she made similar appeals for her next two children: for Princess Louise a marriage dowry of 30,000 pounds, plus an annuity of 6000 pounds; and for Prince Arthur a similar annuity on his coming of age.

Louise's marriage could not have come at a worse time. Just as she had the misfortune to be born in the troubled year of 1848, now she was cursed to marry and dip her hand into the public purse during another upsurge in republican sentiment during the winter of 1870-71. Inspired by the Franco-Prussian War, the Paris Commune and the fall of the French monarchy, radical politicians and republican sympathizers took up the attack on the darling young couple of the previous October.

The columns of the anti-royalist *Reynolds's Newspaper* blossomed with advice on how state dowries and annuities might be replaced by the Marquis of Lorne earning an honest living. Boot-riveting was the suggestion of a Northampton correspondent, who added, "perhaps his wife could do a little on the machine." [18] On a more serious level, members of parliament were questioned at public meetings on their attitude towards

Louise's dowry; in early February an anti-dowry protest meeting was held at Holborn.

Prime Minister Gladstone anticipated spirited opposition to the dowry proposal from at least two members of the House of Commons — "one of them, though well meaning, is weak; and the other is perhaps the most fractious spirit in the House." Nevertheless he assured the Queen she would "have no cause to complain of any want of explicitness or decision" on the government's part. [19] Once the shouting was over, the dowry motion carried by a vote of 350 to one. Henry Fawcett was the lone holdout, objecting on principle rather than personality for, as Lorne noted, "he was a personal friend of the bridegroom." [20]

Louise's dowry was saved in part by her choice of a husband, or rather by whom she chose not to marry. Lorne had his detractors — Tories objecting to his family's Liberal politics, Englishmen fearful of too much Scottish influence on the throne — but the nation as a whole, at a time of anti-German feeling prompted by the Franco-Prussian War, considered him much superior to some German prince. Good for Louise for choosing a Briton!

Yet Queen Victoria had the most trouble persuading her two oldest children. Daughter Vicky, despite liking Lorne personally, had always hoped and assumed Louise would follow family tradition and choose a German prince.

"I know well that abroad such a marriage, until it is thoroughly understood, may startle people," the Queen wrote Vicky, "but it is what I have long thought it must come to. Great alliances like yours are right and well for some of the family, but small, foreign Princes are very unpopular here, R. Catholics illegal and totally repugnant to our feelings; therefore one turns towards those in one's own country, who possess large fortunes and rank certainly equal to small German princes." [21]

Unfortunately, Vicky read about the engagement in the anti-British Berlin newspapers several days before she received her mother's letter. She was naturally upset and angry. So the Queen wrote again, stressing additional advantages. "The popularity of this step and this marriage all over the empire, including Ireland, is quite marvellous! And, when the Royal Family is so large, and our children have (alas) such swarms of children, to connect some few of them with the great families of the land — is an immense strength to the monarchy and a great link between the Royal Family and the country. Besides which, a new infusion of blood is an absolute necessity — as the race will else degenerate bodily and physically." [22]

The Prince of Wales also disapproved of the match. Since the Marquis of Lorne sat in the House of Commons as a Gladstonian Liberal, would not this marriage be seen as exposing the Crown to partisan political influences? And since Lorne was not of royal blood, would there not be constant difficulties in assigning correct official rank to the new husband and wife?

Queen Victoria wrote Bertie in the same vein as she had to Vicky. "Times have changed; great foreign alliances are looked on as causes of trouble and anxiety, and are of no good." As to politics and protocol, the Queen saw no difficulty whatever. "Louise remains what she is and her husband keeps his rank only being treated in the family as a relation when we are together. It will strengthen the hold of the Royal family, besides infusing new and healthy blood into it." [23]

As the Queen championed Lorne to her children, private secretary Henry Ponsonby tackled the doubters within the royal household. "No use talking now of this or that Seidlitz Stinkinger," he told Lady Biddulph. "They are out of the question. This is the best Briton. Uphold him — and make the best of him." [24]

Lorne himself did not worry about court protocol or Prussian opposition. "The difficulties really become wonderfully small when looked at as I have had to look at them," he wrote a political colleague. "There is nothing to prevent a little give-and-take policy carrying one easily over them." [25] When the Queen had finished one of her loud laments as to the strained relations the projected wedding was causing, he said quietly: "Madam, my forefathers were kings when the Hohenzollerns were parvenus." [26]

Louise was also confident that problems could be overcome. "I shall find my position difficult at first," she wrote her old childhood confidante, Louisa Bowater, "but I shall trust to a higher power to help me behave as I should." It was the same to Catherine Gladstone. "I think we shall be very happy, and we shall have pride in overcoming the difficulties which every body places before us." [27]

* * * * *

## MARRIAGE

*Thy servants come to ask Thee'*
*To bless their wedding-day;*
*Thou gavest life, now grant them*
*Love's light upon their way.*

*The sweet and sacred union*
*By Thee in Cana blessed,*
*Make fruitful in possession*
*Of all Thou deemest best.*

*And may the troth here plighted*
*Be a celestial sign,*
*The earthly bond to honour*
*By thoughts that are Divine.*

*So shall the Bride be likened*
*To vines the Home around,*
*The Bridegroom, her protection,*
*To walls with vintage crowned.* [28]

Britons called it "Queen's weather". By nine o'clock in the morning of 21 March 1871, the sun broke through the clouds at Windsor Castle and promised a gorgeous spring day for the wedding of Princess Louise and the Marquis of Lorne. The town of Windsor was in a particularly festive mood, decked out with signs and streamers proclaiming loyalty to the crown and wishing everlasting happiness to the bridal pair. "On such a day of rejoicing Windsor is indeed spirit-stirring," wrote Lorne in later years. "The immense royal standard floats in gold, blue and crimson from the Keep. Carriages, with servants in scarlet, carry guests gay in uniform and silks, the melody of chiming bells is heard from belfries of tower and town, the houses of the citizens are bright with flags." [29]

By ten o'clock crowds lined the streets from railway station to castle gates, hoping to glimpse important guests arriving from London. Inside the gates 900 boys from nearby Eton College, the groom's former school, lined roadways to cheer the bride as she drove from her apartments to St. George's Chapel. A Highland pipe band marched across the castle green, lustily playing "The Campbells Are Coming".

The scene inside the chapel, observed Ronny Gower, was "superb, full of pomp, music, pageantry, and sunshine." [30] Bright sun streamed through the rich coloured glass of the windows, lending a warmth and gaiety to what otherwise would have been a cold and bare interior. Male guests wore full dress uniform, adorned with glittering gold lace and stars and sashes. The ladies were even more dazzling, in dresses ranging from heavy velvet to gauzy silk, from deep maroon to the palest of pinks and blues, all bedecked with jewels.

The Duke of Argyll was the first member of the wedding party to arrive. Duke George never suffered from a lack of pride; now, with his son marrying a daughter of the Queen, this was his proudest moment yet. His Grace wore full Highland dress, complete with kilt, philibeg, sporran and claymore, with green Campbell scarf and the Order of the Thistle across his shoulders. Duchess Elizabeth followed her husband in a dress of silver and white satin. The duke and duchess took their seats with eleven of their children — four brothers and seven sisters of the bridegroom.

Lorne and Louise's wedding, St. George's Chapel, Windsor Castle.

The groom himself — John George Edward Henry Douglas Sutherland Campbell, Marquis of Lorne — awaited his bride at the altar. He was dressed in the rather sombre military uniform of the Argyllshire Regiment of Voluntary Artillery. Uncle Ronny Gower and brother-in-law Earl Percy were his supporters. "He stood waiting for the bride during a very trying eight minutes," observed one guest, making "a much more successful attempt than usual to look as if he did not know that everybody was staring at him." [31]

Members of the royal family sat across the aisle from the Duke and Duchess of Argyll: Alexandra, Princess of Wales, with her young children; Louise's own sisters — Helena in cerise satin, Beatrice in pink; her brothers — Arthur in military uniform, Leopold in Highland dress. Her two older brothers — Albert Edward, Prince of Wales, in Hussar uniform, and Alfred, Duke of Edinburgh, in white tunic — waited by the door where the Queen and Louise would enter.

The chapel organ burst forth in triumphal strains as the eight white-satined bridesmaids make their appearance. Then a blare of trumpets and a roll of drums announced the grand entrance of Queen Victoria and Princess Louise. The bride was stunningly radiant in her gown of white satin and veil of Honiton lace. She "stops for a moment at the door, says something to her mother with a half-nervous smile, and then walks along with a great deal of maidenly grace and self-possession." [32]

The Bishop of London read the service in a very faint voice. The responses of the bride and groom were inaudible. Such a painful, prolonged silence was finally broken by the loud, clear voice of the Bishop of Winchester as he read a short epistle for the newly married couple. The choir then sang a chorus by Beethoven. The Queen kissed her daughter and the groom kissed Her Majesty's hand. "The Bride and Bridegroom behaved uncommonly well," noted the Duke of Cambridge. "Nothing could have gone off better, or been better arranged." [33]

The bride took her husband's arm and walked with bright and happy face into the vestry. Vestry cupboards still house the 1871 marriage register, officially recording the solemnizing of marriage between Lorne and Louise, "by special licence in the King's Free Chapel of St. George's," duly witnessed by — the signatures follow one another in the records — "Victoria, Albert Edward, Alexandra, Argyll, Elizabeth Argyll," etc.

Following the ceremony the wedding party and guests drove by carriage from St. George's Chapel to the castle itself. The Queen received the guests in the State Drawing-Room. At 2:15 the wedding breakfast was served in the Oak Room. The Queen herself proposed the toast to Princess Louise and the Marquis of Lorne. "We had a capital luncheon and champagne," noted the goggle-eyed rector of Rosneath parish church, "and everybody got very talkative and familiar." [34]

At four o'clock the newlyweds left the castle for their honeymoon spot at Claremont Lodge. Riding in an open carriage drawn by four grey horses, they were accompanied by Lord Mount Charles and Lady Churchill, with an escort of Life Guards and a shower of old shoes and satin slippers. John Brown, the Queen's favourite Highland ghillie, threw a new broom at the departing carriage, for such was the old Scottish custom.

Down Castle Hill, along High Street and Park Street in Windsor town, every balcony and window was filled with cheering spectators. Dense crowds lined the streets and the Long Walk was packed with people for nearly a mile. One observer noted the Princess in high spirits, and remarked that Lorne, "with great good taste appeared to desire that his fair young bride should be the sole object of the popular demonstration, and only raised his hat from time to time." [35]

Esher was reached at six o'clock, and there again an enthusiastic crowd cheered the newlyweds. At Bear Green a triumphal arch had been erected; here an address was read by the local vicar on behalf of the villagers, and the sheriff's young daughter presented the royal bride with a fresh bouquet of camellias and orange blossoms. On drove the bridal carriage, through the welcome arch and towards the royal lodge at Claremont.

\* \* \* \* \*

Today's visitors reach Claremont either by British Rail from Waterloo Station to Esher, or by car along the A244 highway. The residence stands about one kilometre south-east of Esher village on the road to Oxshott, opposite Milbourne Lane. The old estate was broken up in the 1920s, the eastern part developed for housing, the western half acquired by the National Trust, the house itself becoming a girls' school. Today Claremont is a co-educational school, run by the Christian Scientists, open to visitors on Saturday and Sunday afternoons of the first weekend each month.

Claremont Lodge was state property in 1871, at the disposal of Queen Victoria. The home was one of the Queen's favourites, and held many happy memories for her family and relatives. Claremont was the site of several previous royal honeymoons: Princess Caroline and Prince Leopold in 1816, and the Queen's own parents, the Duke and Duchess of Kent two years later. In turn, Claremont served as Leopold's English residence until he became King of the Belgians in 1831, and provided refuge for exiled King Louis Philippe and Queen Marie-Amelie of France after 1848. Later it would be the honeymoon site of Louise's two younger brothers, Prince Arthur and Prince Leopold.

But Claremont was also associated with many tragedies. Its original owner, Lord Clive, died of suspected drug poisoning shortly after the completion of his new residence. Princess Caroline died at Claremont in childbirth in 1817. Both Louis-Philippe and Marie-Amelie died there in unhappy exile. Shortly after receiving Claremont as a country residence, Prince Leopold would also die. Perhaps the residence laid a curse on its occupants.

In the early evening of their wedding day, Lorne and Louise's carriage drew up before the dignified, white-brick, Palladian-style Claremont Lodge. Climbing a flight of twenty steps from the driveway, the honeymoon couple entered a great oval hall, eighteen feet high, opening to a splendid suite of rooms on the ground floor and leading to the upper rooms by a grand staircase. One of these upper rooms was a special bridal suite, featuring a "lovers' carpet" into which was woven a design of orange blossoms and myrtle entwined with white ribbons.

The wedding night of Princess Louise and the Marquis of Lorne, that night of 21 March 1871 at Claremont Lodge, can only be surmised. Whether the marriage was consummated or not remains unknown. But the stay at Claremont was certainly short. Within six days, Princess Louise and her husband were back at Windsor Castle, summoned by the Queen to attend a formal reception for recently deposed Emperor Louis Napoleon of France. Next day they accompanied the Queen to London, experiencing "immense crowds" who "cheered tremendously" and showed great "friendliness to Louise." The following evening they joined the Queen at the official opening of the Albert Hall, where Louise "shone pre-eminent in dazzling white from top to toe." [36]

The newlyweds were the darlings of the British public, drawing crowds and cheers wherever they went. Even the possibility of Louise's presence was enough to stir the blood. Following one court function, a somewhat disappointed lady noted that Louise "wasn't there after all, but the rumour of her intention to be present was the cause of an immense crowd." [37]

After a week of public adulation, Lorne and Louise left for a two-month, extended honeymoon journey through the Rhine Valley to Darmstadt and across the Alps to Florence. "Louise looks well and happy," observed her sister Alice in Darmstadt. "Their visit was so pleasant." [38]

Yet Lady Walburga Paget offers a different, and somewhat disturbing picture of Louise on this continental trip. Lady Paget acted as hostess for the honeymooners in Florence, laying on dinners and receptions and frequently accompanying Louise on afternoon shopping trips. Lady Paget believed the princess was neglecting her husband. Louise seemed "so delighted with all she saw" in the shops that "she lost count of all time." Lady Paget had to remind her that "Lord Lorne must be waiting." And how to explain Louise's curious behaviour at a party her hostess arranged with a number of Florentine ladies? "Suddenly in the midst of it all, she became shy, or tired, or both, and insisted upon beating a retreat through my bedroom." [39]

This Florentine episode illustrated Louise's nerves giving way under the strain of constant public exposure — especially if some aspect of the milieu bothered her. Perhaps she was annoyed with Lorne or with Lady Paget over some trivial matter. Yet when everything went well, when nothing "got on her nerves," Louise easily kept up a frantic pace and enjoyed herself for hours on end. Consider Lorne's description of a typical day during a Dublin visit later that year:

"Louise had no time at all to herself, for directly after breakfast we had the Review till nearly two o'clock, then changing dress for lunch, which was to be at Lord Sandhurst's at 2:30, and did not really take place till 4 o'clock, then a visit to The Queen's Institute, where girls are taught painting and how to work telegraphs . . . then to a china shop where some Belleek purchases were made, then home at 7, and dinner at Lord Hartington's at 7:30. After this, home for ten minutes, and then a ball at the Exhibition Building till two or three in the morning." [40]

This Dublin visit with the Prince of Wales and Prince Arthur was designed as a "show-the-flag" exercise in the Irish capital. While Louise galivanted around, and her brothers made the appropriate public appearances, Lorne acquainted himself with the Irish political scene, and gauged the extent of support for the monarchy. "All who speak to me," he wrote Queen Victoria, "are most anxious that yearly visits be paid, if it be not possible for any of the family to live permanently in the country." [41]

Lorne was hinting at an Imperial role for himself. When this Irish visit was first announced, *The Times* suggested Lorne "will afterwards be offered the Viceroyalty." Though the paper denied the rumour four days later, speculation continued over the next few months — indeed throughout the next two decades — that this son-in-law of Queen Victoria might be appointed as Lord-Lieutenant of Ireland.

Back from Dublin, Lorne and Louise prepared for the final round of their honeymoon journeys — a September visit to the Campbell family home at Inverary. Louise got things off to a proper start when she stepped out of her carriage at Inverary's front door wearing a shawl of Clan Campbell tartan. Cheers and huzzahs roared up from the assembled estate workers and townsmen. From the steps of the castle Lorne thanked everyone for such a splendid welcome. More cheers.

Louise was set to work almost immediately, distributing prizes for local volunteer work. That evening at dinner, she was seated next to Lord Colonsay, whose witty talk "made her very merry." The Duke was especially pleased. "Louise's manner to the people has been all one could desire," he wrote his sister Emma, "and everybody was delighted with her." [42] A few days later the Duke gave his tenants a great feast in honour of the occasion, and personally asked the assembled throng to give "three cheers for the Princess, my daughter." Even the usually cynical Ronald Gower was impressed with this home-coming celebration. "The Princess seems quite at home and very cordial to all." [43]

# CHAPTER EIGHT

# MR. AND MRS. CAMPBELL, 1871-1878

*B*ack from their honeymoon and post-honeymoon trips, the Lornes — as family and friends now called them — leased a townhouse at No. 1 Grosvenor Square in the heart of London's fashionable Upper Mayfair district. The house was a classic 1730s structure, three windows wide, with three full storeys above ground and an attic for servants' quarters, commanding a fine view westward across the park-like square.*

Within easy walking distance of Hyde Park, and a short carriage ride to Piccadilly and the West End, Grosvenor Square in the early 1870s was ideally located for city living. Yet the Lornes seemed to prefer their rented rural retreat at Dornden near Tunbridge Wells. Dornden provided both geographical and psychological distance from family, court and society expectations. Here Lorne spent long hours writing, while Louise sketched and painted all day without interruption.

Ronald Gower thought Louise was especially happy at Dornden. "She bustles about all day, looking after and superintending all the domestic arrangements, carving at meals, and making herself generally useful. After dinner we stroll out in the grounds of the pretty little domain, and visit the stables and the kitchen garden; and generally finish the evening by a game of billiards or pool." [1]

---

* The building was demolished in the 1930s and a new United States embassy constructed on the site. After the Second World War, when the Americans moved to a larger embassy on the other side of the square, the Canadian government purchased No. 1 and christened it Macdonald House after Sir John A. Macdonald, Canada's first prime minister. By the mid-1980s the Canadian government had transferred most of its High Commission business from the old Canada House on Trafalgar Square to Macdonald House. This was most appropriate for the site where the Marquis of Lorne once lived, since as Governor General of Canada his administration established the post of High Commissioner in London.

Louise in 1871.

Within a very few years, however, the Lornes gave up both Grosvenor Square and Dornden. Duff suggests it was Lorne's "real Scottish caution over money matters" that led to such forced economies. [2] There may also have been pressure from Queen Victoria, who wanted to exercise closer supervision over this young couple with their quasi-Bohemian tendencies. But No. 1 Grosvenor Square, at least, was never intended to be anything but a temporary residence for the newlyweds. As a royal princess and daughter of Queen Victoria, Louise was to have something much greater and grander than a Mayfair townhouse.

State apartments at Kensington Palace became available in the autumn of 1873. "We went to London for ten days to look after the apartment which we are to have," Louise wrote her friend Lady Holland from Inverary in early December. The rooms were in the south-west corner of the palace, once inhabited by the Duke of Sussex, a younger son of King George III, and had housed his voluminous library. "They are very dirty at present," observed Louise, "not having any attention since George III's reign". Seven weeks later Louise sounded more anxious. "The repairs and cleaning have not yet begun but we hope they will be soon." [3]

Given the condition of the rooms, inevitable government delays, Queen Victoria's interfering nature, and Louise's own high standards of interior decor, another full year elapsed before the Lornes moved in. From that point, Kensington Palace served as their London residence until Lorne's death in 1914 and through Louise's widowhood for another quarter century. Living there for sixty-four years, Louise in later life quite naturally acquired the name of "The Grand Old Lady of Kensington Palace."

The building had suffered from the whims of successive monarchs and the design schemes of several architects during its long history. Cassell's *Old and New London of* 1870 described Kensington as a "plain brick building, of no particular style or period, but containing a heterogeneous mass of dull apartments, halls and galleries, presenting externally no single feature of architectural beauty; the united effect of its ill-proportioned divisions being irregular and disagreeable in the extreme."

Yet other writers ascribed a certain charm to Kensington Palace. "It can be imagined full of English comfort," wrote Leigh Hunt. "It is quiet, in a good air, and, though it is a palace, no tragical history is connected with it; all which considerations give it a sort of homely, fireside character, which seems to represent the domestic side of royalty itself." While Windsor Castle was a place to receive monarchs, Buckingham Palace to see fashions, Kensington "seems a place to drink tea in." [4]

Kensington was especially dear to Queen Victoria, who had spent her childhood there. Early in March 1875 she paid her first formal call at her daughter's new residence. "Louise took me upstairs to her sitting rooms, which are very nicely arranged," the Queen wrote in her journal. Mother was quite impressed with daughter's new home. "Louise has several rooms opening into each other & a fine Drawingroom. The Diningroom is also nice, but a great deal still has to be furnished, & the long corridor to be cleaned". Later that day Victoria wrote Louise: "I loved the old Home — tho' it was not a very gay or even happy one! And I am happy to think one of my daughters should live in a part of it." [5]

First from Grosvenor Square, then from Kensington Palace, the Lornes made their initial ventures into the world of Victorian philanthropy. During 1872 they convened an "Educational Parliament" at Grosvenor Square, where leading educators planned the Girls' Public School Day Company. The object was to provide a sound education for modest fees, giving middle-class parents an option between sending their daughters to lower-class state schools or paying exorbitant fees to install them in elite private schools.

The scheme was typically English in its perpetuation of class divisions, but proved very appealing to the Victorians. The Girls' Public School Day Company (later Trust) opened its first school in Chelsea in 1873. By the end of the century, thirty-three schools provided secondary education for more than 7,000 girls. Lorne served as a founding member of the board of management, while Louise, as the organization's patroness, appeared at innumerable school openings, prize days, and fundraising events over the next fifty years.

Early in 1873 Lorne set out to raise seven million pounds to provide financial assistance for some 4,000 rural Church of England clerics whose annual incomes were then less than 200 pounds. Since religion had never particularly excited Lorne's passion, his support for these vicars was a charitable rather than a spiritual act. "I cannot say that Lord Lorne had any clear conception or plan," Gathorne Hardy noted in his diary on June 21. "He has taken up the plan hastily and not seen its difficulties. He will end with some eleemosynary scheme." [6]

Nevertheless, Lorne meant to do a good job. He wrote all Church of England bishops in July, requesting support from clergy and laity in each diocese. He and Louise co-sponsored a public meeting where the Archbishop of Canterbury and other notables pleaded for public subscriptions. Thus was launched the Church of England Incumbents' Sustenation Fund, or Queen Victoria Fund or Religious Beneficiaries Fund. Forty years later Lorne reported its success in raising a considerable sum, "but not nearly large enough, and it still continues." [7]

In addition to her Girls' Public Day Schools, Louise also served as first patron of the Ladies' Work Society. Founded in 1875, the movement enabled poor women to earn a livelihood from needlework done at home. The products were to be artistic as well as functional, and the society enjoyed the active support of William Morris and the Arts and Crafts Movement. As with the Girls' Schools, Louise took an unusually active interest in the Ladies' Work Society, contributing "many of the designs herself" that the ladies embroidered in their homes. [8]

Girls' schools and ladies' needlework are the earliest examples of Louise's lifetime of good works aimed at improving educational, artistic, and economic opportunities for Victorian women. As early as 1869 Louise began corresponding with women's rights champion Josephine Butler. "I do take great interest in the happiness and well-being of women," she wrote, "and long to do everything I can to promote all efforts in that direction." There had been talk of founding an international women's review, though Louise advised against putting "anything about women in the title, as I think all appearance of exclusiveness should be avoided. Only with the co-operation of the cleverest of men can we hope to succeed." [9]

Lorne inherited upper class obligations and expectations from both his father's and his mother's families. The convening of the Educational Parliament at No. 1 Grosvenor Square was perhaps an attempt to replicate the activities of his maternal grandparents, the Duke and Duchess of Sutherland, at Stafford House. Yet there seems to be little focus in Lorne's philanthropic activities of the 1870s. Neither Girls' Public Day Schools nor Religious Beneficiaries particularly interested or excited him.

* * * * *

September 1875 provides an ideal opportunity to observe the Lornes while they holiday with the Duke and Duchess of Argyll at Inverary. The observers are three other visitors to Inverary that month — Richard Henry Dana, Queen Victoria, and Henry Ponsonby — who recorded contradictory impressions of Lorne and Louise, and of the relationship between the young couple and the rest of the Campbell family.

Richard Henry Dana III was an impressionable twenty-four year-old American. Grandson of Dana the poet, son of the author of *Two Years Before the Mast*, Dana III was taking a year away from his studies at Harvard law school to do the Grand Tour of Europe. With letters of introduction from the New England literary and legal elite, he was a welcome house guest at Inverary.

Dana arrived on Wednesday September 1 and spent the first evening at dinner sizing up the Lornes. Louise impressed him as "good-sized, well-developed, with a German cast of face and a slight German accent. Her r's are gutteral, instead of lingual." Lorne was even more fascinating — "handsome and strong, with delicate features, bright complexion, a small mouth, very light hair, blue eyes, and a manly and kindly bearing." [10]

Dana soon found himself the recipient of little kindnesses and courtesies from Louise. She "talked pleasantly and easily and showed me some etchings of hers drawn for embroidery patterns." Next morning she helped him select a fishing rod and showed him how to tie flies. Dana "fell a bit in love with Princess Louise." He could hardly resist. "Besides her most agreeable manners, she has many fine traits of character and is amiable with all and not in the least demanding attention, modest without being retiring or sensitive." [11]

Lorne proved every bit as congenial as Louise, lending Dana his personal salmon rod and providing him with a flask of fine Scotch whiskey for a Friday fishing expedition. On the Sunday he gave Dana a personal tour of the Duke's private yacht.

Inverary seemed a happy place, everyone getting along well, the Princess and her in-laws on particularly good terms, dining room and drawing room conversation always pleasant and cheery. Dana readily dismissed the current gossip that the marriage was not a love match. "It is clear the Marquis and the Princess are more than fond of each other." They made a point of driving out each day in a pony cart, in order to have time to themselves. "They often chat together just because they like to, and their amiable ways together are too natural and spontaneous to be merely assumed for effect." [12]

Dana delighted in catching little intimacies between Lorne and Louise. At lunch one day Louise had asked Lorne a question. "He did not hear at first, as he was talking to someone else, and she put her hand on his shoulder to draw his attention in a gentle, loving way which struck me quite pleasantly." It was evident, Dana concluded, that Louise was "a happy woman". [13]

Dana left Inverary on Monday September 6 to continue his tour of country houses and European capitals. Two weeks later, on Wednesday September 22, Queen Victoria arrived with her youngest daughter Beatrice and a large entourage of attendants. It was her first visit since 1847, "when Lorne was only two years old. And now I return, alas! without my beloved husband, to find Lorne my son-in-law." [14]

The Queen's journals make the visit sound idyllic. On the road to the castle the first day, the royal party were met by Lorne and Louise, "looking pleased and well." Victoria found Louise "so kind and attentive, so anxious that I and all my people should be comfortable, thinking of everything." She was pleased when an elderly lady tenant told her: "We are all so fond of Louise; she is a great pet." [15]

Yet Henry Ponsonby, the Queen's private secretary, saw things very differently. "There seemed to have been various troubles arising out of Inverary," he claimed, "where Princess Louise took the opportunity of pouring out her grievances, such as that her rooms were not good enough, that she could not dine alone when she wished, and the ladies Campbell did not treat her with becoming respect." Ponsonby concluded that Louise was a royal mischief-maker. "Louise plays old Harry with every household or person she touches. The once happy home of the Argylls seems to be perfect Pandemonium now and the departure of the Lornes for the rest of the winter in the south has caused but little grief to the worthy parents."

Louise was bad enough, but her husband was no better. Ponsonby was appalled that "Lorne seems to support her in all these complaints and thinks that the Duke should do more for her." He concluded "Lorne is overborne by her." [16]

So the rumours surrounding the engagement and marriage were given greater credence. Louise was a trouble maker. She did not get along with her Campbell in-laws. She ran roughshod over her husband. The marriage was not a love match. Lorne and Louise stayed together merely to keep up appearances. Do we believe Richard Dana, Queen Victoria, or Henry Ponsonby?

The Queen is the least credible observer. A selfish and self-centred individual, she saw everyone's relationships only as they affected herself and only as she wanted to see them. Thus everything was fine between Lorne and Louise because she wanted everything to be fine. Her main concern at Inverary was her own personal comfort; since Louise was solicitous on her behalf, Louise was a loving daughter and a delightful person.

In fact Queen Victoria was a major part of the problem. Her week-long stay at Inverary completely disrupted the Campbell household. She demanded a suite of rooms all to herself and her personal attendants. She insisted on taking her breakfasts, lunches and sometimes even dinners alone with Beatrice and Louise. She decided where she would drive each afternoon, and who would accompany her. Throughout her stay the Queen behaved more as if she were in her own home than as a guest of the Duke and Duchess of Argyll — at considerable inconvenience to her hosts.

Louise and Lorne were caught in the middle. The Princess wanted her mother's visit to be successful, but often found that what pleased the Queen often inconvenienced her in-laws. As the mediator between two forces, Louise found herself resenting both. Anxious to please both his wife and his mother-in-law, Lorne was of little comfort to his parents.

But can the jolly observations of Richard Henry Dana be squared with the dour report of Henry Ponsonby? Dana had the good luck to precede the Queen to Inverary, and to catch the Campbells at their best. The young American was an easy house guest who brought out the best in Lorne and Louise, in the gracious Duke and good Duchess, and in the fluttering hearts of Lorne's unmarried sisters.

Much of the happy aura surrounding Dana's visit in the first week of September evaporated by the time Queen Victoria arrived later in the month. While the Duke enjoyed entertaining his many political, literary and scientific friends, the Duchess found such merry-making an increasing strain. Elizabeth had not fully recovered from the stroke she suffered six years' earlier. Dana reported that "she talks in so low a tone and with such slight articulation that I find it hard to understand her at times." [17] The Queen was simply too much for her.

Louise, too, grew weary of the incessant stream of visitors and the pressure to be her charming, royal self all day, everyday. She had a short social fuse, and her nerves simply did not stand up to such pressures over an extended period of time. By the end of September she was less gracious with the Duke and Duchess, less friendly with her young sisters-in-law, even less attentive to Lorne's needs and interests. Her mother's week-long encampment proved more than she could bear!

The weather was another factor. During 1875 the weather grew progressively worse as the season advanced. Dana mentions rain during some of the days of his visit, but not every day, and certainly not enough to dampen people's spirits. By the time of Queen Victoria's visit, however, it rained hard every single day. How much fun could it have been sitting around Inverary Castle in a cold, driving late-September rainstorm?

So Ponsonby's inferences must be weighed against Dana's observations form earlier in the month. The Queen's private secretary saw a different Inverary and a different cast of characters than the young American. Critics of the royal family and Argylls could agree with Ponsonby and draw conclusions that were not at all flattering to the Princess and her husband. Friends of Lorne and Louise could agree with Dana, and continue their fascination with the couple.

* * * * *

Lorne had other things on his mind in September 1875 besides mediating between his in-laws and his parents. Amidst visits from Richard Henry Dana and Queen Victoria, he was proof-reading the final draft of his first book of poetry — a long, narrative poem entitled *Guido and Lita: A Tale of the Riviera,* scheduled for a November publication by Macmillan.

During the 1870s Lorne turned increasingly to poetry as an outlet for his somewhat frustrated and as-yet-unrealized talents. Inheriting a poetic aptitude from his father, Lorne had composed verse since his boyhood — everything from nonsense rhyming couplets to lengthy descriptive stanzas. He knew and admired Tennyson as an old family friend, and had conversed with Longfellow in America. His pieces had occasionally appeared in student publications and small literary magazines. He had sprinkled his 1867 book, *A Trip to the Tropics,* with descriptive poetry of the West Indies and United States.

Lorne in 1871.

Lorne spent the spring and summer of 1875 polishing *Guido and Lita,* — a 2500-line poem of adventure, fidelity and love set along the Italian Riviera during mediaeval times. Lorne spun out the tale of young Guido as he makes his way in the world. In a dramatic encounter between the forces of good and evil (Christians versus Muslims), Guido triumphs over all adversity, earns his father's respect, and claims the beautiful young Lita as his bride.

Lorne possessed initial doubts about *Guido and Lita,* attempting to pass it off as an anonymous publication, and seeking suggestions for improvement from Lord Houghton, a senior poet and literary scholar of the day. "I venture to ask a favour of you," Lorne wrote Houghton, "to be so kind as to wade through this accompanying story in rhyme, and tell me afterwards if you think that, in case of its anonymous publication, it would find any favour among the many who are fond of spending the winter in the Riviera. If you could mark what you disapprove of I should be very grateful." Houghton would do nothing until he was certain of the authorship. "The story is mine," Lorne admitted two weeks later, "and the sternest sentence will be most gratefully received." [18] Houghton's verdict is unfortunately unknown, for his replies to Lorne's pleadings have not been preserved.

But correspondence between Lorne and his publisher Alexander Macmillan does survive, and shows how quickly the work passed through the stages of editing and production. Lorne forwarded his manuscript to Macmillan on July 14, together with suggestions for illustrative material. Convinced of the book's quality and marketability, Macmillan took only six days to decide on publication, and just three more days to prepare a specimen page set in type for Lorne's examination. In early August Lorne provided a frontispiece and agreed to copyright and royalty arrangements. During September at Inverary, he read and returned the corrected proofs and decided on a dark maroon binding.

On November 8 Macmillan brought out 1500 copies of *Guido and Lita* at a price of seven shillings and sixpence, and deposited 112 pounds in Lorne's London bank account as an advance on royalties. Before year's end Macmillan ran off second and third printings of 1500 copies each, made arrangements for American and Canadian editions, and discussed possibilities for a German translation. On the second printing, Lorne received another advance sum of 112 pounds. By the third printing, with sales perhaps beginning to slacken, Lorne's contract called for him to receive half the profit realized or pay half the loss incurred should sales prove disappointing. [19]

Brief press notices of *Guido and Lita* appeared in mid-November. "On the whole I did not get nearly so much knocked about as I had expected." [20] But lengthier reviews carried in the literary magazines over the next few months were extremely negative. *Guido and Lita*, claimed the

*International Review*, was not at all innovative, but "more decidedly a continuance of past fashion in literature," the work of a man of conventional culture, imbued with a great reverence for old, accepted models in literature." The verse reflected the form of Byron's "Corsair" without "its fiery rhythm," and the slow movement of Crabbe "without his fine and delicate painting of details." Had the lines been written a century earlier, "they might have secured the author a certain amount of poetic fame." [21]

Undaunted, Lorne pushed ahead with his second poetic effort, *The Book of Psalms, Literally Rendered Into Verse*, published in 1877, again by Macmillan. This re-writing of the traditional Psalms arose out of personal rather than religious conviction. While attending church, Louise occasionally criticized the "dull way in which some of the grand old Psalms were put into verse." Agreeing with her, Lorne "ventured to attempt in some cases an improved arrangement of his own." Forty years later, Louise still kept the prayer-book in which his revised versions were first scribbled. [22]

But how to render a Psalm more comforting to church congregations than the authorized version? Consider the revered Twenty-Third Psalm:

> *The Lord's my shepherd, I'll not want.*
> *He makes me down to lie*
> *In pastures green: He leadeth me*
> *The quiet waters by . . .*

compared with Lorne's unsatisfactory "literal rending into verse":

> *My Shepherd is the Lord, and I*
> *Shall never want or fear;*
> *To streams of comfort he me leads,*
> *By quiet waters clear . . . .*

Only with the one Hundredth and Twenty-First Psalm did Lorne produce verse that endured. Here he began with an undistinguished authorized version:

> *I to the hills will lift mine eyes,*
> *From whence doth come my aid.*
> *My safety cometh form the Lord,*
> *Who heav'n and earth hath made . . . .*

and turned it into the inspirational:

*Unto the hills around do I lift up*
*My longing eyes:*
*O whence for me shall my salvation come,*
*From whence arise?*
*From God the Lord doth come my certain aid,*
*From God the Lord, who heav'n and earth hath made.*

Sung to the same tune as "Lead, Kindly Light," Lorne's "Unto the Hills" eventually found its way into most hymnals of the English-speaking world. Canadian folklore likes to believe the hymn was inspired by Lorne's first glimpse of the Rocky Mountains in September 1881. [23] But *The Book of Psalms* was published in 1877, four years before Lorne visited the Canadian West. The inspiration came either from the imagination or from the Scottish Highlands around Rosneath and Inverary.

But such limited fame lay in the future. Correspondence between author and publisher during 1876 and 1877 reveals both Lorne's feverish devotion to the task of re-writing all 150 Psalms, as well as Macmillan's doubts about the project. "I send the first 59 [Psalms] in two manuscript books, and will send the rest as I fill up other books," Lorne wrote in early February 1876. "The next will contain versions up to the 90th or thereabouts. I would be glad to have the proofs as soon as the printer has set up the versions now sent." Lorne finished the rest of the Psalms over the next twelve months, and then began second literal renderings of many of them, "which I find many people like much more than the bald and literal first versions."

Through the spring of 1877 the author took pains to assure his publisher that both the Scottish and American Presbyterian churches would be interested in the book, provided "the price of the volume should not be too high." Alexander Macmillan was obviously worried about length. "I quite agree that 570 pages make too large a book," Lorne wrote in June, "but I think the Scotch will never be satisfied with anything that does not [contain] in the same volume, the excellence of some of the authorized versions and paraphrases I like so much."

Macmillan decided to go ahead, and Lorne signed and returned his contract on June 6. Five hundred copies of a first edition had been printed, when Lorne unexpectedly requested some changes. Macmillan reluctantly agreed, stopped the print run at that point, made the changes, and ran off a second edition of 1000 copies. Author and publisher were not experiencing the happy relationship that had characterized *Guido and Lita.*

Lorne's next complaint concerned marketing. "I visited two large bookshops in Glasgow yesterday," he wrote Macmillan in early August. "At both I asked for the new Psalter, and the shop men had not heard of it. Surely Glasgow and its newspapers should see some of the advertisements." [24] It is the same today; while *Guido and Lita* regularly appears in second-hand bookshops on both sides of the Atlantic, *The Book of Psalms* is a difficult item to find.

Nor did *The Book of Psalms* — with the exception of "Unto the Hills" — make any major impact on church liturgy. At the time of Lorne's death the *Manchester Guardian* dismissed his versions as "never once sung even in his native churches, and now forgotten." Though his version of the Psalms was an improvement on that of Tate and Brady, observed *Reynolds's Newspaper*, "it was, nevertheless, a failure. Why should any writer presume to improve upon the beautiful language of the Psalms in the authorized version? Hebrew poetry consisted largely of a repetition of the same idea in different words, and it is not at all suitable for being put into rhyme. Milton failed in the attempt, so did Burns." [25] And so did Lorne!

\* \* \* \* \*

From Kensington the Lornes made their way in London society — trooping off to luncheon and dinner parties, attending the theatre and the art openings, and entertaining their own circle of friends. Theirs was a wide circle, extending from the royal family through various strata of the aristocracy to artists, musicians, and writers. Sensitive and artistic Prince Leopold was their favourite royal brother-in-law. On Lorne's side, brother Archie and sister Mary were frequent guests at Kensington, while a bevy of younger Campbell girls often accompanied Lorne and Louise on excursions. Uncle Ronny Gower, by now a confirmed homosexual, society gossip, sculptor and art critic, remained popular with both husband and wife. Friends like Mary Gladstone from Lorne's youth and Cyril Flower from his university days became Louise's friends as well.

Louise never let royal protocol — nor marriage conventions— prevent her from enjoying the company of people she chose to befriend. She announced her intent in a frank letter to her art teacher, Edward Corbould, shortly before her marriage. "You have been one of my true friends that I have looked up to all my life and from whom I have always had encouragement and sympathy, and from whom I have learnt much besides art, tho' art was the foundation of all things," she informed Corbould. "When I am Married, I shall hope often to see you and [hope] that our interest in each other's work will not diminish but increase." [26]

Her friendships spanned the arts of music, writing, painting and sculpture. "My Princess Louise is coming tomorrow," composer Arthur Sullivan confided to his mother in July 1877. "Bring a lot of roses — never mind what it costs — I don't get her every day." [27] Determined to know the talented but socially ostracized novelist George Eliot (Mary Ann Evans), Louise asked George Goschen, the banker and Liberal politician, to invite Eliot to a dinner party he was giving for the princess. "Instead of Madonna [Eliot] being presented to her she asked to be presented to Madonna," wrote an amazed George Lewes, "and at once sat down beside her and entered into a friendly chat." [28]

Louise and her brother Leopold were occasional visitors at the shabby apartment of George Francis (Frank) Miles at the top of a creaking staircase in an old house on Salisbury Street. Miles made his living as a magazine illustrator and portrait painter (including one of Lillie Langtry), and turned his apartment into a meeting place for society and Bohemia. Here congregated people like poet Violet Fane, actress Ellen Terry, painter James Whistler, and actor Johnston Forbes-Robertson. [29] Stimulating company for Louise the sculptress, but hardly appropriate for a Queen's daughter and marquis' wife in Victorian Britain!

Visits to Joseph Edgar Boehm's sculpture studio were even less appropriate. It seems that Boehm had been much more than Louise's teacher prior to her marriage. While at Balmoral, working on a statue of John Brown — probably in autumn 1869 — Boehm and Louise almost became lovers. Louise, according to the story, "used to come to him in his studio on the pretence of modelling and they become intimate, though not to the extent of actual love-making, and one day the Queen coming to see how the statue was getting on found her there and a violent scene occurred between them." [30] Immediately the Queen set about finding a husband for her!

This story comes to us in the 4 June 1909 diary entry of poet Wilfrid Scawen Blunt following a conversation he had with Catherine "Skittles" Walters, the "bedfellow of half the men in London society, not excepting the Prince of Wales." Blunt's credibility as a witness, argues historian Angela Lambert, can safely be presumed, since no credit would accrue to him through his secret diary until long after his death. Skittles's reliability, like her memory, is less certain. She was nearly seventy years old when she told Blunt the story of her life, and in poor health. Accordingly, Blunt "cross-questioned her pretty closely," so as to test the story's accuracy, and found that in all essentials it held well together." [31]

Marriage failed to cool the ardour between Louise and Boehm. Throughout the 1870s, from Grosvenor Square and Kensington Palace, the Princess continued to visit the sculptor in his Fulham Road studio. This continuing dalliance undoubtedly related to marriage-bed problems between Lorne and Louise. Either Lorne's homosexual inclinations propelled Louise toward Boehm, or her continuing fascination with the sculptor rendered her incapable of responding sexually to her husband.

No children blessed the marriage of Lorne and Louise. Behind the gala facade of friends and parties, art and poetry, the gap of childlessness was readily apparent. Within a year or two of the wedding, the absence of a pregnancy caused tongues to wag. Throughout Argyllshire, supporters of the Campbells whispered that Louise had never had a menstrual period and was unable to bear children. If this was true it ought to have been made clear to any potential husband, but it has not been substantiated. Louise herself once said she had received hundreds of letters telling her how she might have a child, but that "none of them were any good." [32]

Lorne and Louise's seventh wedding anniversary on 21 March 1878 provides an opportunity for stock-taking. Whatever the crcumstances — his homosexual inclinations, her barrenness, her attraction to Edgar Boehm — no children had arrived and no children were likely to arrive. The marriage was and would continue childless. There would be no noisy and happy domestic circle at Kensington such as both Louise and Lorne had known as children themselves.

Artistically, their careers had not progressed much beyond the gifted-amateur stage. Lorne's *Guido and Lita* and *The Book of Psalms* owed their publication as much to the author's station in life as to his literary talents. The reviews were generally negative. Louise's paintings and sculptures were occasionally seen at charity exhibitions, though she spent most of the decade working for her own private pleasure. Neither husband nor wife had earned critical respect from the artistic community.

Nor could they derive much satisfaction from their public lives. Lorne continued to make little impact as a member of parliament; his performance on the backbenches was even more silent after his marriage than before. His charitable and philanthropic work was sporadic. While Louise's charitable causes were more focussed, she was having difficulty establishing a position within the royal family independent of her mother's whims and wishes. Despite Queen Victoria's championing of their marriage, she became quite tiresome once the wedding was over. She insisted that Louise keep up the usual round of family obligations — Osborne in summer, Balmoral in autumn, Windsor Castle for Christmas. Louise and Lorne's desires counted for naught.

This smothering embrace might have been tolerable had Lorne been fully accepted within the royal family. But court protocol assigned him a much lower precedence than his wife. Queen Victoria tended to treat him more as a monarch would than a mother-in-law. Louise's three oldest brothers — Bertie, Alfred and Arthur — "look upon him as a regular outsider" and "certainly do not care much about him." Bertie had never approved of the marriage. Over the years, Lorne's "earnest views on life" and "priggishness in manner" made him distinctly unpopular "with the gay friends and companions" of the Prince of Wales. [33]

On the other side of the family, the Campbells did their best to make Lorne and Louise feel at home at Inverary. Yet Louise was not just any daughter-in-law, but a royal princess who required careful handling. Not only her wishes, but those of her mother had to be dealt with — as in September 1875. Then came the traumatic fire that partially destroyed

Inverary Castle in the early morning hours of 12 October 1877. Behaving "with the most conspicuous gallantry and coolness," Lorne personally rescued his brother Archie's two youngsters. [34] Yet his mother, who had suffered an initial stroke eight years earlier, slipped noticeably in the months following the fire.

Seven months later, on the evening of 25 May 1878, the Duke and Duchess of Argyll were dining at the London home of Elizabeth's cousins, Lord Frederick and Lady Cavendish, when the fatal stroke occurred. She died within seven hours. The Duke of Argyll undoubtedly mourned the death of his wife and helpmate of thirty-four years, the mother of his twelve children, though he would remarry within four years. The most grieved mourner at Elizabeth Campbell's funeral may well have been her eldest son, Ian, Marquis of Lorne. The bond between Ian and his mother was extremely strong, perhaps the strongest of his life.

Death had ended this emotional bond. Fire had weakened Lorne's physical bond with Inverary, for the castle required a long time rebuilding. Other bonds such as parliament, poetry, or philanthropy, were not strong enough to engage his full attention. How long could the marriage bond itself be sustained? By the summer of 1878, the Marquis of Lorne needed a new challenge in life. Louise was always looking for fresh challenges.

# CHAPTER NINE

# THE CANADIAN PROMISE, 1878

*T*he Marquis of Lorne was enjoying a yachting holiday in the Hebrides in June 1878, when one night, as his small vessel tossed off the wild northwest coast, he dreamt he was in a small room with Prime Minister Benjamin Disraeli, now Lord Beaconsfield. Disraeli was smiling at him, and talking, and asking if he would accept one of the great imperial viceroyalties. Would Lorne take up the position of a colonial Governor General?

Such was Lorne's most dramatic encounter with the psychic phenomenon known as second sight — a visual scenario unfolding in the mind with extreme clarity prior to the event's occurrence. Second sight had been a popular topic during Lorne's student days at St. Andrews; later he would incorporate the phenomenon in his novel *From Shadow to Sunlight*. But nothing matched this Hebridean dream of June 1878.

The dream became reality at 10 Downing Street on July 24. "My interview with Dizzy today was so exactly as I had expected." After some initial pleasantries, Lorne waited for the Prime Minister "to open fire, which he did at once, saying that he wished to see me about a very important matter, namely, that one of our great Viceroyalties [Canada] was vacant and he wished me to take it. Then full stop, to see if I was surprised, which I was not, having seen it all in a vision beforehand."

Lorne thanked Disraeli for this expression of confidence, then politely suggested other, more highly qualified men. But the Prime Minister "was most anxious that I should take it, and believed I had the abilities." Lorne asked time for consideration, made his bow and left the room. But there was no doubt he would be the next Governor General of Canada. [1] Disraeli's own opinion, which proved correct, was that "Lorne was personally not disinclined to entertain the suggestion," but that — and here he quoted Lorne's own words — "the wrench would be with Her Royal Highness." [2]

Queen Victoria reached the same conclusion when Disraeli discussed the appointment with her. "I was rather divided in my feelings," Victoria confided to her journal, "satisfaction at the distinction for Lorne, and the fine, independent position for poor Louise; but uncertainty as to her liking to leave her home interests and go so far away from all her family. The thought, too, of parting from her for so long was very painful. Still, I would not object or oppose the offer." [3] Perhaps in her heart Victoria regarded the Ottawa appointment as the best possible solution to the difficult and perplexing problem of her daughter's marriage.

It was settled. "You will be greatly surprised to hear that Lorne and Louise are going to Canada," the Queen wrote her daughter Vicky. "But for three not five years. It is of course painful to part from her for so long — and so far away — but she can come over each year and there will be an immense field for doing good and for him to distinguish himself. There being so many Scotch there will be an additional satisfaction. In Canada the effect will be immense and it is carrying out beloved Papa's views, for he wanted our children to be useful in the Colonies." [4] Even the Prince of Wales, never a great fan of his Campbell brother-in-law, seemed pleased. "He has a fine career open to him," thought Bertie, "and my sister living in one of our most important colonies cannot fail to have a most excellent effect." [5]

The proposal originated with Michael Hicks Beach, foreign secretary in the Disraeli cabinet. "I got Dizzy to settle with the Queen about sending the Lornes to Canada," Hicks Beach confided to his wife on July 31, "as I thought she wouldn't have agreed if I had proposed it to her. But the idea was mine, and — so far — seems a success." [6]

On the surface it appeared to be another in a long series of imperial coups for Disraeli. He had purchased for Britain a controlling interest in the Suez Canal Company; he had proclaimed Queen Victoria Empress of India; now he would send out Princess Louise as chatelaine of Government House in Ottawa. It seemed a logical extension of John A. Macdonald's idea of a Kingdom of Canada. Retiring Governor General Lord Dufferin believed the time had come when the presence of someone more than a mere official was needed in Canada to inspire and hold the loyalty of the new country. Lorne would hold the office, Louise the royal aura. Before Louise left for North America, Disraeli referred to her as "Her Canadian Majesty" and suggested, only half in jest, that she wear a crown.

Lorne welcomed the prime minister's offer. The Ottawa appointment offered a chance to do something on his own, out from the long shadow cast by his prominent father and away from the smothering embrace of his royal mother-in-law. "The Governor-Generalship opens a care to the Marquis of Lorne that may be some compensation for political activity from which his marriage cut him off at home," observed *The Times*. [7]

Perhaps Ottawa might serve as a stepping-stone to even more prestigious posts such as Lord Lieutenant of Ireland or Viceroy of India. At the very least, Canada offered Lorne new opportunities to indulge his old interest in travel. The entire continent of North America now beckoned.

Lorne's commission and instructions, handed down by the Colonial Office on October 7, outlined his responsibilities. On the ceremonial side, the Governor General represented the Queen on those state occasions like the opening of a session of Parliament, where the presence of the constitutional monarch was deemed necessary. On the diplomatic side, he represented the British government — specifically the Colonial Office — playing a quasi-ambassadorial role between fledgling Dominion and Mother Country, when neither side was certain of just how much autonomy was possible within an imperial framework.

Constitutionally he guaranteed the orderly succession of government in case of a ministerial resignation, not free to choose anyone as the next prime minister, but only one who commanded majority support in the Commons. Politically, the Governor General acted on the advice of his Canadian ministers, duly assenting to orders-in-council and parliamentary acts as passed by the House of Commons and the Senate.

Instructions given to Lorne in 1878 reduced the Governor General's sphere of independent action. No longer was he required to reserve various types of bills for London's approval, to preside at council or cabinet meetings, or to exercise a personal discretionary power. It seemed perfectly clear now that the Governor General took political action only on the advice of his ministry. Opportunities for errors in judgement were reduced.

Yet it was not an easy position. At the level of day-to-day operations, the Governor General was continually called upon to clear up all the little misunderstandings that arose between Ottawa and London. "Would your Excellency be good enough to inform" began many letters from Prime Minister Macdonald to Lord Lorne. Britain tended to blame the Governor General for disagreeable actions on Canada's part — like the imposition of a higher tariff — while Canadians blamed him for British oversights — such as the concluding of imperial arrangements binding on Canada, without consultation with the Dominion. The Governor General was often caught in the middle, walking "inevitably on a razor edge," in the words of a later incumbent. [8]

Beyond politics lay the world of Canadian society and culture. The Governor General and his wife were expected to provide leadership for Ottawa society while Parliament was in session, and for the country as a whole at all times. These expectations went far beyond lending the vice-regal names as patrons for artistic endeavours or philanthropic efforts. The Governor General and his lady were expected to set the tone, to inspire, to elevate, to lift society and the arts into major league realms.

Failure to meet these expectations could be even more drastic than any political mistakes; for in the realms of society and culture, the Governor General's wife was judged just as critically as her husband.

All this was to be accomplished on an annual salary of 10,000 pounds, British currency, paid from the consolidated revenue fund of Canada, as stipulated in Section 105 of the British North America Act. Out of this salary the Governor General was expected to pay operating and entertaining costs at Rideau Hall, salaries of his personal staff, and his own travels throughout the country. The result was inevitably a dipping into one's personal or family income as expenses each year totalled well over 10,000 pounds — a prospect not particularly welcomed by the Campbells of Argyll.

\* \* \* \* \*

The announcement that royalty would occupy Rideau Hall caused quite a stir throughout the young Dominion of Canada. Shopkeepers hurriedly ordered commemorative plates and souvenir pressed-glass creamed jugs and sugar bowls stamped with the heads of the Marquis of Lorne and Princess Louise. Politicians and their wives took time out from a federal election campaign to learn the rudiments of court etiquette. A new railway carriage was ordered for the Princess, and a special corps of guards formed to protect her. The daily press outdid itself in expressions of loyalty and predictions of Canada's future within the British Empire — "an amusing mixture of gush and canny speculation," observed the more dispassionate New York *Times*. [9]

In his hastily written *Royalty in Canada* — the instant gift-book of the 1878 Christmas season — Charles Tuttle recorded the "thrill of joy" that "burst upon the Dominion" with the announcement that a daughter of Queen Victoria was on her way across the Atlantic. "We felt we were moving nearer to the throne of our Gracious Sovereign; that we were being rewarded, as a people, for our faithful allegiance to the Crown; that we were rising to the full dignity of British citizenship." Louise's presence would "impart a new life, a new brilliance to the social circle" at Ottawa; she would be the "centre of a grand social sentiment, the rallying point for a rising aristocracy." Finally, Louise's presence during a period of ever-increasing Canadian-American economic ties, would "arrest our drifting into the Republic of the United States." [10]

Back home, *The Times* greeted Lorne's appointment "with great pleasure," informing Canadians they were no longer the "poor relations of the Imperial household." Yet the London *World* considered the new Governor General a "nonentity in the House of Commons and a nonentity without." Because of his anomalous position — accepted neither by the royal family nor by his political colleagues — perhaps a five-year exile in Canada was the best way to get rid of him. The London correspondent of the New York *Times* agreed that Lorne "was not much thought of on this side of the channel." Though a "respectable young man" with a "clean social record" and "no blemish on his name," he was an "untried man in public business," whose "greatest achievement in life is his marriage to a Princess." Perhaps Disraeli was banking his hopes on the "cleverness and feminine discretion" of the princess rather than on the talents of the Governor General himself! [11]

Canadian papers looked on the positive side. How flattered the young country was to receive a royal princess and her handsome husband! The Toronto *Globe* imagined great benefits arising out of the appointment. It would "turn all eyes in Britain towards Canada," bring "thousands of tourists to admire our natural scenery and study our material resources," and secure "an even greater share" of trans-Atlantic emigration. Nevertheless the Canadian press raised two rather embarrassing questions. How could Lorne — and especially the delicate Louise — stand the isolation and provincialism of Ottawa? "It remains to be seen," mused the *Globe*, "whether this intelligent pair can find in Canada sufficient of interest to induce them to remain during the duration of a Governor General's term." In addition, the Montreal *Gazette* thought Lorne would have to possess "no ordinary abilities" if he ever hoped to match the success of his very able and popular predecessor, Lord Dufferin. [12]

Both Queen Victoria and Prime Minister Disraeli overlooked Lorne's lack of political, diplomatic and administrative experience. He had done little to merit such a senior colonial appointment as Governor General of Canada – ten years as a silent backbencher in the House of Commons and three years as his father's private secretary at the India Office. Perhaps his only claims were having the name of Campbell of Argyll and marrying the Queen's daughter.

Lorne knew little of Canada in general, and Ottawa in particular, his home for the next five years. In 1857, when the city was proposed as a capital for the old Province of Canada, the Duke of Argyll asked his twelve year-old son to find the spot on a map of North America. "The search was wholly unavailing," lamented Lorne. [13] Later, during his brief stop in Ottawa in June 1866, following the excitements of the West Indies and the United States, Lorne was decidedly unimpressed with the new Canadian capital. "The position of the town is most inconvenient; it is never likely to gain much importance in commerce." [14]

Between 1872 and 1878, however, Ottawa had been enlivened by the presence of Governor General Lord Dufferin. Could Lorne match the reputation of his predecessor? Dufferin was at the beginning of a long career in diplomacy that led to the viceroyalty of India and ambassadorships in Rome and Paris. He was enthusiastic about the new country and equally enthusiastic about imperialism, vigorously promoting the idea of a united Canada within the Empire.

But there was more. The Dufferins enlarged Rideau Hall and made it the centre of Ottawa social life while Parliament was in session. They hosted an endless round of luncheons, teas, concerts, receptions, dinners, private theatricals, musical plays, costume balls, skating and toboganing parties and curling matches. They established a summer residence at The Citadel in Quebec City, and spent many weeks travelling the length of the country — Dufferin being the first Governor General to visit Manitoba and British Columbia. Dufferin was also an excellent orator, lauding Canada's praises in equally eloquent English or French or, if necessary, Latin or Greek. Dufferin was brilliant; he was interesting; he was energetic; and he was full of good old Irish blarney. Lady Dufferin easily matched her husband in charm and energy and public spirit.

Everyone knew Dufferin would be difficult to follow. In its issue of 30 November 1878, the Canadian magazine *Grip* featured a cartoon depicting the interior of a classroom at the Ontario School of Art. Lorne sits on a footstool, artist's pad in hand, about to begin a sketch of a plaster statue of Lord Dufferin. John A. Macdonald and Alexander Mackenzie are at their own easels off to one side, though Macdonald is keeping a close eye on Lorne's work. The instructor leans over Lorne's shoulder and whispers, "There, my dear Marquis, copy that carefully; it's a fine constitutional model."

As a close friend of the Duke and Duchess of Argyll, Dufferin greeted the appointment of young Lorne with considerable interest. "I cannot conceive any arrangement more conducive to the interests of this country, than that you and the Princess should come and preside over its expanding destinies," he confided to Lorne in early August. Over the next three weeks he wrote his successor three very long letters dealing with his Canadian experiences — one on the social and ceremonial side of the office, a second on the Canadian political scene, and a third on the financial aspects of the Governor Generalship. [15] No one could have been better briefed by his predecessor.

Dufferin went out of his way to praise his young friend and successor. "A more conscientious, high-minded, or better qualified Viceroy could not have been selected," he told a Canadian audience. There was just one problem. "Unfortunately," continued Dufferin with tongue in cheek, "an irreparable and a congenital defect attaches to this appointment. Lord Lorne is not an Irishman!" [16] Dufferin's own Irish background had not been significant in itself. But such Irish traits as a gift for the blarney and a capacity for making people laugh had endeared him to the Canadians. Lorne would be expected to measure up, while Louise must duplicate Lady Dufferin's support for her husband's enthusiasms!

Crossing the Atlantic in November 1878.

The Dufferins were not so naive as to think Lorne and Louise would have an easy time in Ottawa. Lady Dufferin thought Lorne's "administrative capabilities have still to be developed;" indeed, she found the young Marquis "very vague in his conception of the duties of his office." And how would Louise treat people in Canada — "if as royalty there will be trouble, but if in the same way as Lady Dufferin, they will be flattered."[17]

Meanwhile Lorne and Louise prepared for their departure for Canada. Lorne was created a Knight Grand Cross of the Order of St. Michael and St. George in honour of his appointment. He said goodbye to his Argyllshire constituents, resigning his seat and cavalierly handing it over to his brother Colin, who held it for the Liberals in the ensuing by-election. He and Louise hosted a grand farewell dinner at Kensington Palace. "Lorne the most genial of hosts," noted Disraeli, "and directed his conversation to your humble servant, who could not keep up the ball, for I never for a moment understood what he was talking about." [18]

So the Lornes said farewell to family and friends, and late in the evening of November 13 left London by train, accompanied by Prince Arthur and Prince Leopold. Next morning the city of Liverpool gave them a grand civic reception and dockside sendoff. Lorne put in a word for Canada as a mecca for settlers, Louise waved her brothers goodbye, the bands played, and the RMS *Sarmatian* slipped out into the cold grey waters of the North Atlantic. Canada was ten long days away.

\* \* \* \* \*

The *Sarmatian* was the pride of the Allan Line, the premier line serving the Britain-Canada run. Designed for Admiralty use in wartime, the *Sarmatian*'s speed and power might be needed that autumn of 1878, for disturbing rumours surfaced of an armed Fenian vessel laying in wait to capture the vessel and "make prisoners of Lorne and Louise." [19]

The *Sarmatian* had been specially refurbished for its important passengers. Lorne and Louise each had a suite consisting of bedroom, sitting room and private bath. The upper deck boasted a ladies' boudoir and a men's smoking room for the vice-regal party of fourteen "persons" and twenty-five "servants." But the *Sarmatian*'s most novel feature was its newly-patented self-adjusting beds, which made sea-sicknesses impossible, "the bed adjusting itself to every motion of the vessel, so that its pitch and roll cannot be felt." [20] Barring any Fenian troubles, a pleasant voyage seemed assured.

Stormy weather, not Fenian threats, soon became everyone's main concern. The *Sarmatian* encountered rough seas shortly after leaving Moville on the Irish coast, late in the evening of Friday November 15, rolling heavily and taking in large amounts of water. That set the pattern for the crossing. Every day brought high winds, heavy clouds, strong seas, driving rain and impenetrable fog. Heavy squalls on Monday turned into a raging afternoon gale, damaging sails and masts. "The ship rolled and pitched heavily, and all on board suffered in consequence," despite the self-adjusting beds. [21]

How to amuse oneself on a ten-day Atlantic crossing in rough late-November weather? Louise took to her bed, overcome by a combination of sea-sickness and neuralgia, and was attended by the Queen's personal physician, Dr. A. Clarke, who "made himself very useful." Not till the final day did Louise appear on deck. Lorne may have read background papers on Canadian politics or attempted some writing, but the only incident he recorded was catching a seagull, making a drawing of the bird, then setting it free. "I think it was a kittiwake," he mused, "but am not sure." [22]

Saturday November 23 and the *Sarmatian* lay twenty-three kilometres off Halifax in the midst of a rotten Atlantic gale. The ship's captain desperately needed a harbour pilot, but had no way of signalling his needs through the foul weather. Ashore the Duke of Edinburgh, Louise's brother and Royal Navy commander at Halifax, had no way of locating his sister's ship. "We are close to our destination," noted Lorne, "but dark has come on and the captain says he must lie to, to the disgust of the ladies, who have another night of rolling in the trough of the sea before them." [23]

Just before midnight the lights at the entrance of the harbour became visible, and the captain decided to make the run without a harbour pilot. "The rain is making the deck wretched, but the captain's anxieties seem to be over," observed Lorne. [24] The engine-room bell rang, the ship's bow sought out the passage, and a few minutes later they were safe in the relative calm waters of Halifax harbour.

The late night arrival allowed the vice-regal couple to claim Sunday as a day of rest, and to delay official welcoming ceremonies till Monday 25. Yet Sunday was busy enough on the *Sarmatian,* as a launch from the Duke of Edinburgh's ship ferried local dignitaries back and forth from shore. The British military commander and Lieutenant Governor A.G. Archibald of Nova Scotia paid their respects. *Sarmatian* owner Hugh Allan popped in, "very anxious" that Lorne and Louise attend a "great St. Andrews Society Ball" in Montreal on their way to Ottawa. [25]

Sir John A. Macdonald was the only notable absentee from the list of shipboard visitors that Sunday. Canada's Prime Minister was in no condition to meet a new Governor General and royal Princess. He had begun one of his celebrated drinking bouts on the train ride down from Ottawa, and had taken refuge in his room at the Lieutenant Governor's residence. The drinking continued, the days slipped by, the *Sarmatian* arrived. A secretary tip-toed into the bedroom and found Macdonald pale and haggard, "looking more dead than alive." [26] The Prime Minister's "lumbago" was acting up, according to the public announcement.

Monday November 25 witnessed the official welcome to Canada of a new Governor General. "The landing was the prettiest sight imaginable," wrote Lorne, "the town looking its best in bright sunshine, with its many steeples and houses covered with flags." Guns boomed from ship and shore. Thousands of Haligonians cheered themselves hoarse. Dockside pleasantries were brief — flowers for the Princess, introductions to assorted politicians. Then a carriage ride to Province House for the swearing-in ceremony. Welcome arches all along the streets. Guns still booming their salutes. People still cheering. That evening Lieutenant Governor Archibald hosted a formal dinner for some forty people, followed by a reception for "the whole adult population who could appear in evening clothes in Halifax." It was past midnight when an exhausted Lorne and Louise returned to the *Sarmatian*. Still, Lorne remained buoyant. "Nothing could have been more pleasant than the welcome given by Halifax." [27]

Tuesday was a working day for the new Governor General. Every major society clamoured for the right to present formal addresses of welcome — and to read them, word for word, in the vice-regal presence. Lorne listened patiently to hour after hour of verbiage from the Nova Scotia cabinet and the Halifax and Dartmouth municipal councils; from Church of England and Presbyterian clergy — separately, of course; from local English, Scottish and Irish ethnic societies; from the Dalhousie University faculty and the Sons of Temperance. No matter that each address covered the same ground. Lorne was expected to listen with great interest and respond with appropriate and original remarks in each case.

Enough! At eleven o'clock the next morning, the vice-regal train pulled out of the Intercolonial Railway's Halifax station and began its journey to Ottawa. Such a journey in the spring or summer months would have shown off the beauty of the small towns and countryside along the way. But it was now the last week in November. Outside the train's windows lay the death-grey colour of late autumn.

Yet everywhere the Canadian welcome was warm and generous. Intense excitement built up all day at Newcastle, New Brunswick, and late in the evening the crowds began to gather about the station, hoping for even a brief glimpse of the distinguished party as the train sped through. The crowd was spotted in the glare of the engine's headlight, and Lorne gave the signal to stop. "The Princess was weary of the riding," according to one contemporary account, "but smiled genially at the simple-hearted people, and his lordship, with much grace, listened to a sonorous, though genuinely cordial address, making a brief reply." [28] The crowd cheered and the train thundered away through the darkness.

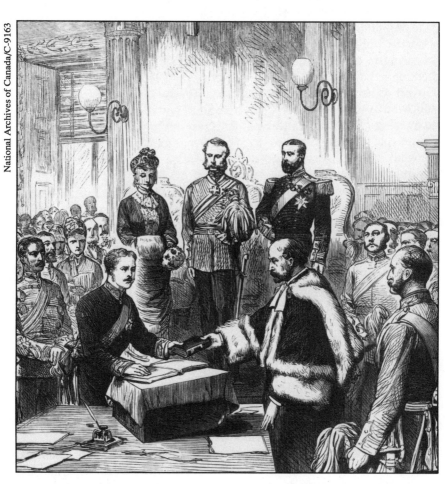

Lorne being sworn in as Governor General.

Presenting a bouquet to Louise in Halifax.

Demonstrations of loyalty throughout the Maritimes and Quebec impressed Lorne. "Nothing can exceed the desire of the people everywhere to show their loyalty and goodwill," he wrote his father. Scots-Canadians, "everywhere overflowing with enthusiasm," sang their own version of "The Campbells Are Comin'"at every stop of the train:

> *The Campbells are comin' hurrah, hurrah,*
> *The Marquis of Lorne, the Princess an' a'*
> *The Campbells are comin' hurrah, hurrah,*
> *They come to a land that has won some renown,*
> *A people most loyal to Queen and the Crown,*
> *They come to hold court at fair Ottawa,*
> *The Campbells are comin' hurrah, hurrah.*

The Scots were not alone in their goodwill. The Irish "have as yet found it very hard to work up a grievance," while French-Canadians "cheered as heartily as any of the Britishers." [29]

At Montreal the welcome lasted three full days, with fireworks and illuminations, bands parading through the streets, receptions and speeches, luncheons and dinners. At the St. Andrews Society ball, Lorne "delighted the citizens by the ease and abandon with which he danced Scotch reels." A little later Louise "came forward and disputed the laurels with her husband by likewise engaging in the national Scottish dance, acquitting herself with fascinating grace, and an old-time air at once delicate and charming." Ladies whispered about the "light that sometimes breaks over her face," the "depth and expression of her eyes," the "purity of her expression," and the "charming alternation of repose and vivacity in her features." [30]

The bubble soon burst. Led by the New York *Times*, the press grew tired of all the hoopla, particularly when a teeming rainstorm on Monday December 2 showed everything and everyone in the worst possible light. That day's train trip from Montreal to Ottawa began "in a storm of sleet" and finished "in a wretched rain-storm." At Montreal's Bonaventure Station the vice-regal suite entrained amidst "a dripping military guard, under dripping triumphal arches" with "a crowd of dripping people" looking on. Even the gas-lit mottoes "sputtered in a drizzle that found its way through a canopy of British flags." Lady Sophia MacNamara, Louise's lady-in-waiting, looked "as if she would be glad to say good-bye to Canada, and return straight to England." [31]

"Rain poured on their royal heads without abatement," during a brief stop at St. Ann's. Here, according to the New York *Times*, Lorne "spoke his speech in his usual style, in a snuffy, grating tone, with the strong English accent affected by the Bowery imitators of the Cockney." [32] The train continued west to Prescott, then north to Ottawa over the same dreary route Lorne had travelled in the spring of 1866.

Entry into Montreal.

The storm increased in intensity as the vice-regal train pulled into Ottawa shortly after four o'clock in the afternoon. Prime Minister Macdonald, in much better shape than a week earlier in Halifax, made the most of a wet situation by claiming the heavens were weeping tears of joy at the arrival of the Princess and her husband. Such miserable weather was not without its advantages as official welcoming ceremonies were drastically curtailed, and a thoroughly soaked Lorne and Louise were quickly spirited off to their new Canadian home at Rideau Hall.

* * * * *

Ottawa in the late 1870s remained part frontier lumber town, part national capital. The river itself was dotted with lumber barges and log booms, while along both shores stood the sawmills and pulpmills that still provided the bulk of the city's employment and the base of its economic and social structure. Culturally the city was a backwater compared with the glittering capitals of Europe. Its population stood at about 20,000, roughly — and European sophisticates could indeed describe Ottawa's populace as "rough" — one-third French-speaking, one-third Irish, and the remainder of English or Scottish origin. Though many Britons might have seen this English-French cultural duality as a liability, Lorne and Louise welcomed such a doubly enriching challenge.

The Parliament Buildings — "very picturesque," noted Lorne, high up on a "beautiful cliff, cedar-covered" overlooking the dramatic Ottawa River — consisted of three separate structures facing into a broad expanse of grass. The Centre Block contained the House of Commons and Senate chambers, the East and West Blocks offices for politicians and civil servants. The Governor General's office was Room 211 of the East Block. Situated at the top of a red-carpeted, private stairway, and complete with private bathroom — bath-tub and all — it was the most luxurious of all Parliament Hill offices. Yet Lorne did most of his work from Rideau Hall (Government House), the official residence a few kilometres east of Parliament Hill in suburban Rockcliffe.

Rideau Hall was originally an eleven-room, bow-fronted Regency villa built in 1838 for Thomas Mackay, chief contractor of the Rideau Canal. Acquired by the government of the old Province of Canada after Ottawa was designated the capital, Rideau Hall was enlarged in 1865 just before the arrival of its first vice-regal occupant, Lord Monck. Dufferin's additions in the 1870s transformed the residence into the entertainment centre of Ottawa. A large and handsome ballroom, with a stage at one end, now stood to the right of the main entrance. To the left was an even more ingenious addition — a full-sized indoor tennis court which could be converted in a few hours into a splendid banquet room.

Rideau Hall underwent additional improvements in preparation for Queen Victoria's daughter and son-in-law in the autumn of 1878. The tent room was given a permanent foundation and faced with brick to harmonize it with the ballroom. A telephone was installed. A log skating hut, a new laundry house, and additional staff houses were built on the grounds.

Lorne's staff included his secretary, Major Francis De Winton, who functioned like a modern executive assistant; a military secretary, Colonel Littleton; a comptroller or treasurer, Richard Moreton; and two or more junior military officers as aides-de-camp. Princess Louise's personal staff was headed by her lady-in-waiting, Lady Sophia MacNamara. Staff members informally referred to Lorne as "His Excellency" or "His Ex"; Louise was always "the Princess".

De Winton was the key figure in this operation. "Major De Winton is excellent," Lorne confided to his father on just his third day in Ottawa. "His manner is the very thing wanted for dealing with the ministers to whom he has occasionally to be sent." [33] De Winton was a graduate of the Royal Military Academy, Woolwich, served in the Crimean War, and gained colonial experience as secretary to the Lieutenant Governor of Nova Scotia. After Lorne's term ended, De Winton served as colonial administrator in Africa before ending his career as Sir Francis De Winton, comptroller to the household of the Duke and Duchess of Cornwall and York, later King George V and Queen Mary.

Both the De Winton and Moreton families lived in staff cottages on Government House grounds. Moreton's young daughter Evelyn, later Lady Byng of Vimy and herself chatelaine of Rideau Hall, fondly recalled the children of the various household families going to Rideau Hall for lessons, bundling up in huge buffalo robes for sleigh rides and tobogganing, and taking Sunday walks through the grounds and into surrounding Rockcliffe, with Lorne and Louise leading the procession. [34]

Such recreation would have to wait a few days. On the afternoon of Tuesday December 3, his first full day in Ottawa, Lorne sat in the Senate Chamber and endured a repeat performance of Halifax and Montreal as every patriotic, religious, benevolent and chartered society for miles around — from the Hamilton Board of Trade to the St. Patrick's Literary Association — insisted on formally reading its own individual welcome to the new Governor General. Fanny Meredith and her daughters braved the crunch and "saw nothing, but felt a good deal, to wit, two or three fat men who nearly crushed them to death." [35]

"We have had so much to do in the way of travelling and receiving addresses," Lorne wrote his father the next day, "that there has been no peace and quiet." The stormy Atlantic passage had been followed by the gruelling rail trip from Halifax, then the Ottawa ceremonies. "I am as hoarse as an old crow for 25 out of 40 speeches had to be delivered in the open air to large crowds. We hope there is an end to these things." Louise "has been able to undergo the long Drawing Room pretty well, though the one held at Montreal was trying, over 750 people passing." There was more to come: "Today we are to drive through the town to see the illuminations and tomorrow I hold a levee. It is to be hoped that there will soon be time for a little reading for hitherto I have had none." [36]

Yet before long the Lornes were imposing their own imprint on Rideau Hall. "Here we are settling down in this big and comfortable house, which I tell Louise is much superior to Kensington, for the walls are thick, the rooms are lathed and plastered (which they are not at Kensington) and there is an abundant supply of heat and light." The faint note of persuasion suggests Louise may not have been quite so enthusiastic as Lorne. She, however, soon had everyone busy making alterations to the inside of the house. "Louise has two carpenters at her disposal," noted Lorne, "and she has set everybody to work their arms off, all through the house." [37] Outside in the Rideau Hall grounds, she had the "Princess Vista" cut through the woods to give a better view of the Ottawa River.

At Rideau Hall that first winter Louise entertained two of her artist friends from London, sisters Clara and Henrietta Montalba. Henrietta sat for a portrait painted by Louise, a piece now owned by the National Gallery in Ottawa. Henrietta in turn worked on a bust of Lorne in fur cap and coat; it was cast in bronze and despatched to Inverary.

Ottawa writer Annie Howells Frechette was impressed by the way Lorne and Louise turned Rideau Hall into "the home of an artist and a poet." Their presence permeated every aspect of the large official residence. "An air of culture and refinement pervades it," observed Frechette, "and whichever way you turn you are delighted by some pretty conceit, or tasteful fancy successfully carried out." Old tapestry hangings and exquisite ornaments were displayed with taste rather than ostentation. Louise's "presiding genius" followed the visitor from room to room. "Here is a panel of flowers, and here a door decorated by her brush; an unfinished study hangs in one corner; and rare paintings glow upon the walls." [38]

# CHAPTER TEN

# THE CANADIAN REALITY, 1879

"*Y*ou will be glad to hear the Marquis of Lorne has made a very favourable impression, and the Princess is winning all hearts," wrote Charles Tupper, Canada's Minister of Railways, five weeks after the arrival of the new vice-regal couple. [1] The Ottawa correspondent of *The Times* concurred. "Those who come in personal contact with the Marquis of Lorne freely confess they believe him to be the stuff successful Governors General are made of." Louise was even better. "Matters of state pale in popular estimation in comparison with the movements of the Princess. The fact that she has been skating, she has been out walking daily, visiting the Chaudiere Falls and city shops, she carries a light cane when walking — these matters call forth lively comments wherever men or women congregate." [2]

Informal actions and words of the vice-regal pair quickly passed into the oral folk-lore of the capital city — Louise walking into a dry goods store unannounced; Lorne and an aide-de-camp helping a wagon driver replace a wheel; Lorne inviting a group of youngsters to join him in a skate along the frozen Ottawa River despite a constable's efforts to clear the ice for him; Louise making small talk with a watchmaker in his shop. On December 8 Janet Hall recorded in her diary that she looked out her window on Wellington Street and was astonished to see the Princess and her party briskly stepping by. A few days later the two women almost bumped into each other on Sparks Street. "I got a very good view, and she seems rather good-looking." [3]

Canadians need not have feared the imposition of a regal stiffness at Rideau Hall. As early as December 10 the Hamilton *Spectator* informed its readers how simple and informal Lorne and Louise had been at an after-noon reception for members of the St. Andrews Society. The vice-regal pair "passed gently and unostentatiously among the visitors, cordially shook hands with each; and after a little easy chat, in which they made the delegates feel perfectly at home, they bade them a kindly good-bye." And to the amazement of all clothes-conscious observers, Lorne wore a plain morning suit, while Louise graced the reception in a very simple, unadorned dress.

The anonymous *Spectator* columnist listed some of Louise's daily habits — plenty of exercise, brisk walks through Rideau Hall grounds, shopping excursions into the city. Louise walked into town nearly every day "in good, stout English walking-boots in which she tramps through the mud and slush with a bold, firm step, which puts to shame the mincing ladies who pick their way tenderly as if they were walking on eggs." What a delight she was! "Plain, simple, unostentatious, affable, and courteous, Her Royal Highness has already won the affections of all who have come within her influence."

Meanwhile Lorne delighted everyone by sounding more Canadian than British in his public addresses. Just one month in the country, in a speech to Ottawa educators, he skillfully sorted out the relationship between public and separate schools, and knew enough to pander to the vanity of the Ontario education department by praising its recent exhibit at the Paris Exhibition. While reminding Canadians of their loyalty to Queen and Empire, he closed with a strong plea to his young audience to be "true Canadians," who would "devote your energies for the welfare of this wide Dominion." [4]

The only jarring note through December was the death from typhoid fever of Louise's sister Alice, Grand Duchess of Hesse. Alice had served as role model for Louise, showing through her philanthropic and nursing activities among the underprivileged classes how to be one's own woman in the face of family and societal expectations. Alice's death at least gave Louise an excuse to retreat from the madding Ottawa crowd for a two week period of mourning over Christmas. "My poor dear Loosy," lamented Queen Victoria that holiday season, "far away in a distant land, in another quarter of the globe!" [5]

By early January Lorne and Louise were back in the public eye, hosting a belated Christmas party for Ottawa's Sunday School children. Government House was decorated in grand style and the delighted youngsters found a glittering Christmas tree and presents for all. One little boy remembered pounding the table for plain bread and butter instead of the fancy cakes he was given. Another youngster asked Louise how her mother was. "Her Majesty is very well, thank you," replied the Princess [6]

By this time the Canadian winter had set in. Louise found the dry, cold air produced a static electricity inside Rideau Hall that enabled gas jets to be lit by a finger touch. Lorne noticed even his breath froze, forming icicles on his beard. But much winter fun awaited on the Rideau Hall grounds. "We have three rinks of curlers, all playing at the same time on

Group at Rideau Hall, c1879. Louise is standing centre right, beside Francis De Winton, Lorne's Chief-of-Staff. Lorne is seated, second from the right. At the extreme right is Lorne's brother, Lord Archibald Campell.

the skating-pond," noted the Scottish-born Governor General. The giant toboggan slide provided another source of amusement. "On a fine frosty day the thing goes down at a tremendous speed, the snow rising in dust clouds behind it; and when at the end of the course there is an upset, the cedar thickets ring with laughter." [7]

The Lornes took one break from Ottawa that first winter — a hurried trip to Niagara Falls to witness the famous cataract in all its ice-coated, mid-winter splendour. The visit was a spur-of-the-moment thing, almost a lark. On January 17 Lorne's secretary, Francis De Winton, informed Prime Minister Macdonald that "His Ex is thinking of leaving for Niagara for a short visit on Monday night to return about Saturday," hoping it would not inconvenience public business. "Please keep this private," De Winton begged Macdonald, "as H.R.H. is exceedingly anxious that her movements be kept as secret as possible." Lorne and Louise would travel as Lord and Lady Sundridge. [8]

"We set foot on Yankee soil at Niagara," Lorne noted, "and as soon as we arrived near the suspension bridge a great white-headed American eagle sailed out and accompanied our carriage in the most respectful and proper manner. There was so much ice about the falls that the sound of the water was a little hushed, by the curtains of icicles and the mountains of ice piled on the rocks below the falls. But the effect of the whole in winter is marvellously grand." [9] Niagara in winter with Louise certainly made a better impression than Niagara in the rain with Arthur Strutt back in 1866!

The arrival of "Lord and Lady Sundridge" at Niagara on Tuesday January 21 fooled no one, as the press eagerly reported the antics of Lorne and Louise on the loose. Reporters questioned Lorne on Dufferin's idea of an international park along both sides of the Niagara River. Yes, he supported the proposal in principle, but refused to be drawn into any detailed discussion of costs or operations.

Louise was of infinitely greater interest than her husband. "She is of medium height, has an exceedingly petite figure and is very attractive," the Buffalo *Courier* informed its readers. Then came a detailed description of her clothes, right down to her footwear. "Her size is number three and her foot is very pretty. Her step is elastic and firm, and she knows how to use her feet to the best possible advantage." [10]

Enough! It was time to return to Ottawa and get on with the political work of being Governor General.

\* \* \* \* \*

The first session of the fourth parliament of the young Dominion of Canada opened on 13 February 1879. The weather was extremely cold, with flawless blue skies and glistening white snow — royal weather, the newspapers called it, in honour of Princess Louise. Despite the weather, Ottawa was crowded with people, and for years there had not been so much bustle in the capital. The star attractions were a new, or resurrected Prime Minister in Sir John A. Macdonald and a new Governor General in the Marquis of Lorne. The extra bonus was a possible peak at the Princess.

The vice-regal couple left Rideau Hall in the early afternoon for the short trip to the Parliament Buildings, riding in separate carriages. Louise's carriage arrived on Parliament Hill at 2:45 and was greeted with a twenty-one-gun royal salute; Lorne received only a nineteen-gun vice-regal salute when he arrived fifteen minutes later.

Members of both houses assembled in the Senate to hear the Governor General read the Speech from the Throne. Louise sat beside Lorne on the raised dais at the front of the chamber. Representatives from the far reaches of the country packed the floor; gawkers jammed the visitors' galleries. There was great anticipation all round. George Ross, Liberal member for the Ontario riding of West Middlesex, called up his "Scottish prejudices" and basked in confidence that the "prosperity of Canada is assured." But Lorne's anglicized manner caught Ross off guard. "His Excellency read his speech, strange to say, without Scottish accent. How he avoided the burr of his native hills was a mystery." [11]

The Throne Speech itself, written by Prime Minister Macdonald and read verbatim by Lord Lorne, announced a "readjustment of the tariff" and the "vigorous prosecution" of the Pacific railway to meet the "reasonable expectations" of British Columbia. Loyal Conservative papers applauded the speech, while the Liberal press predictably dismissed it as "barren" of any proposal for economic improvement. The New York *Times* commented on the "irksome necessity imposed on a British Liberal of formally recommending the protectionist policies of Canadian Tories." [12]

The opening of Parliament brought an increase in formal social activity for the Governor General and his wife, for the Ottawa "season" coincided with the parliamentary session. The State Drawing Room was the first gala event, held in the crimson and gold Senate Chamber on the night of the first Saturday following the opening.

Lorne and Louise stood on the steps of the dais, surrounded by a glittering staff of military aides and ladies-in-waiting. As the Governor General's military secretary announced each name, a long line of odds and sods of Ottawa citizenry filed by to be presented, "exactly as at home except there is no handshaking, no kissing and no feathers and few low dresses." The 1879 soiree brought the usual mix of young debutantes and elderly judges, Senators and MPs and their wives, diplomatic and consular officials, senior civil servants, whatever landed and mercantile wealth the capital could muster.

Louise, c1879.

This State Drawing Room was a singular event, not repeated till the following year. But the more routine receiving and entertaining of the "sessional" people — those political representatives and various hangers-on who inhabited Ottawa only while Parliament was in session — continued week after week. "I am very busy seeing all the senators and M.P.s, beginning at 8 o'clock with them, and going on till 1:30," Lorne wrote on February 24. Three weeks later he and Louise were "trying to dine and entertain all the M.P.s, and give three dinners of fifty-four each week, besides two theatrical parties of three hundred and fifty each next week and the week after." [13]

Even at such social festivities, the Governor General had to preserve a detached non-partisan position. "The Opposition are trying to make out that I am embroiled with my Ministry," Lorne wrote his father, "and each handshake is watched by the bloodshot eyes of angry politicos." [14] So he and Louise made certain not to overlook Alexander Mackenzie, leader of the Liberal Opposition. Learning of Mackenzie's ability on the ice, Lorne challenged him to a widely publicized and well-attended curling match. Louise captured the heart of the Scottish-born Mackenzie by telling him of her mother's love for the Highlands, trying a few words of Gaelic, and confessing that she and Lorne felt as much at home in Ottawa as in Argyllshire because "we meet so many Scotchmen." [15]

The climax of the Ottawa season came on February 19 when the Lornes hosted their first Government House state ball. Nearly all the ministers, senators, M.P.s, and senior civil servants were there, as well as the city's business and professional elite. Lorne took Agnes Macdonald as his partner in the opening set of quadrilles, while Louise danced with Sir John. The pairings for the rest of the evening were equally exciting: Lorne with Mrs. Tilley, with Mrs. Mackenzie, with Madame Laurier, etc., etc, and Louise with Louis Masson, Chief Justice William Ritchie, "and other gentlemen."

Unfortunately, a few of the guests imbibed too freely of the champagne punch, which one participant thought "insipid to the taste, but actually very potent." [16] "Several persons drunk before it was over," observed Edmund Meredith. "It is said that Senator Carroll kicked aside the Princess' train — if he did not actually push her aside by the shoulder."[17] Word quickly spread through the Ottawa rumour mill that Louise had been insulted by an inebriated Prime Minister Macdonald, and that Lady Macdonald had treated her with a lack of respect.

Sir John wrote Lorne, asking if steps could be taken to deny the rumours immediately. "Certainly it is worthwhile to contradict such reports," Lorne replied. "There is no foundation for the statements made."[18] But tongues would not stop wagging about the alleged "incident" between Macdonald and the Princess, and of cool relations between Agnes and Louise.

More than thirty years later, long after the death of Macdonald himself, veteran Liberal politician Richard Cartwright returned to the story in his published *Reminiscences*. Princess Louise, he wrote, was "unmistakably a great lady and one of the very last persons with whom any man in his senses would presume to take a liberty, and Sir John had given her very just cause of offence by his conduct on the occasion of a state function, so much so, in fact, that she was obliged to request his retirement from her presence." Directly Cartwright's *Reminiscences* appeared, the Montreal *Star* cabled the sixty-seven year-old Lord Lorne: "Cartwright's Memoirs say Sir John Macdonald on unfriendly terms with Princess Louise owing affront put on her by Macdonald." To which Lorne replied: "Rubbish."[19]

Macdonald's former secretary, Sir Joseph Pope, attempted to counter Cartwright's 1912 charges of "unpardonable rudeness towards the Princess," plus the long-standing talk of a jealous feud between Louise and Agnes Macdonald, by releasing to the Toronto *Globe* a series of friendly letters that passed between Louise and Macdonald during the winter of 1883. As far as Pope was concerned, nothing of import had taken place, and Louise honoured the Prime Minister "with her friendship and regard — a regard and friendship ever cordially and respectfully reciprocated."[20]

Here is a case where perception becomes the accepted truth. Whatever happened at the Rideau Hall ball on 19 February 1879, whatever relationship subsequently existed between Louise and Sir John, and between Louise and Lady Macdonald — many people came to believe that all was not as it should be between Ottawa's two leading couples. Canadians were accustomed by now to Sir John's behaviour, and they could empathize with Agnes Macdonald's difficulties in coping with a member of the royal family. Perhaps Louise was the aggrieved party; perhaps she had been a contributing factor. But a Princess's behaviour should always be above reproach. Now there was some small bit of suspicion.

* * * * *

Underneath his drinking, his personal quirks, and his sometimes unpredictable private behaviour, Canada's prime minister was a master politician. Lorne's arrival in the country coincided with the resurgence of Sir John A. Macdonald and his Conservative party. Forced out of office by the Pacific Railway Scandal five years' earlier, Macdonald had rallied his troops and swept back to power in the general election of September 1878.

Lorne's initial assessment was favourable. "Macdonald is certainly very agreeable in conversation," he wrote his father on December 4. "He can make pretty speeches as well as anyone. The prime minister's smooth talk led Lorne to think the government would be very "go-ahead" in military matters and that a protective trade policy would not be inaugurated. [21]

Yet the two men soon found areas of disagreement. Lorne was reluctant to approve a batch of civil service and militia dismissals, a product of the spoils system and the recent election. Lorne also tried to avert the dismissal by the federal government of Lieutenant Governor Letellier of Quebec. But in the honeymoon period of that first December, such differences seemed minor. Lorne and Macdonald compromised over the civil service and militia positions; in time they might come to an agreement on the Letellier business.

Meanwhile the tariff question moved to the centre of the political stage. The Conservative election victory suggested higher tariffs, but just how high? Macdonald had been rather cautious and moderate in his campaign statements; in October he told Dufferin his purpose was not protection; and on the train from Halifax to Ottawa with Lorne, had insisted the British press was quite mistaken in assuming Canada intended to go beyond a revenue tariff. [22]

Through December, however, pressure from Canadian manufacturers pushed the government towards protection. For a while Ottawa considered a 20 to 25 per cent British preference; Finance Minister Leonard Tilley asked Lorne to sound out London on that possibility. But the pressure for commercial nationalism kept building up. Early in February Lorne made one last effort to save the preference, but Macdonald and Tilley refused. [23] It would be a protective tariff clothed in the high-sounding words of the "National Policy".

Macdonald had earlier promised to submit his new tariff proposals to the Colonial Office for approval before introducing them into the Canadian Parliament. But Tilley's continued adjustments to very complicated rate schedules meant Lorne was unable to send the finished proposals to London till the very last moment, with the reply reaching Ottawa only forty-eight hours before the time scheduled for Tilley's budget speech on March 14.

The British were clearly disappointed in the new import duties — and some of that disappointment seemed to be directed at Lorne's inability to persuade his Canadian ministers otherwise. But London was forced to bow to the inevitable; Colonial Secretary Hicks Beach informed Lorne that however regrettable the general effect of the new tariff, the fiscal policy of Canada was a "matter for the decision of the Dominion legislature." Lorne agreed entirely. Despite his own free-trade Liberal principles and the use of his office to mediate the worst effects of the tariff, the new Governor General had quickly embraced the cause of Canadian self-determination. If self-government within the Empire meant tariff differences between Britain and the Dominion, so be it. "However much we in England may disapprove of Protectionist Doctrines," Lorne wrote, "it seems to me the Canadians have a right to try the experiment on which they are bent." [24]

Despite its charting of new directions, the tariff question provided Lord Lorne with a rather routine introduction to Canadian politics and to Colonial Office workings. At the same time a more controversial issue bubbled to the surface, embarrassing the young Governor General and providing the one major blot on his otherwise satisfactory first year in office.

On March 13, the night before Tilley's budget speech, a motion to censure Luc Letellier de St. Just, Lieutenant Governor of Quebec, passed the House of Commons. A Liberal appointee, Letellier had incurred the wrath of both provincial and federal Conservatives early in 1878 by dismissing his Conservative cabinet at Quebec City, on grounds of its neglect of his office. Victorious in both provincial and federal elections later in the year, the Conservatives were determined to have Letellier's head.

Macdonald would have preferred to leave Letellier alone, for the lieutenant governor's term expired in another two years. But his Quebec supporters pressed on, introducing the censure motion at Ottawa. In the Commons, both sides argued the question on the basis of provincial autonomy, the Liberals charging that Letellier's dismissal would be a gross violation of provincial rights, and the Conservatives pointing out that Letellier himself had violated provincial autonomy by dismissing his ministry without due cause. The motion passed by a crushing majority of one hundred and thirty-six to fifty-one. On March 29 Macdonald informed Lorne that the federal cabinet had decided to press for Letellier's dismissal. While such a decision was the cabinet's prerogative, its formal execution would be in the Governor General's name.

Lorne was not prepared immediately to act on the cabinet's advice — as he had intimated to Macdonald when they had first discussed the affair on the train ride from Halifax to Ottawa in the fall. [25] The young Governor General was appalled at the vindictive spirit of the Quebec Conservatives. They were denying the very basis of responsible government and invading provincial autonomy. No doubt Lorne realized he would have to yield ultimately, but to protect himself at this point he asked Macdonald to give his reasons in writing for requesting such a step.

"My face was so solemn and long when I told Sir John that he must put down his reasons for this dismissal," Lorne wrote his father, "and that I should place in writing my reasons why I thought the precedent was a dangerous one." Macdonald countered with an alternate suggestion. Since the Letellier case presented an unprecedented problem in Dominion-provincial relations, perhaps the Governor General should refer the whole matter to the British government for a settlement. Lorne was delighted at this way out. "I assented readily, because this gives me an opportunity of getting the Colonial Office to write a public despatch pointing out the dangers of the proposed course." [26]

Both parties saw merit in referral to the Colonial Office. Lorne did not want to get into a long, public argument with his prime minister, yet he believed that someone in authority should confront the Canadian government on the serious constitutional step it proposed to take. Nor did Macdonald relish a public argument with the Governor General.

Yet Lorne had been manoeuvred into a difficult situation. While it was evident to the general public that the Governor General found dismissal unappealing, that same public could only regard referral to Britain as shirking vice-regal responsibilities. Conservative supporters of dismissal argued that Lorne should have set aside his own scruples and followed the advice of his ministers; Liberal opponents of dismissal urged him to show some backbone and refuse that advice. Both sides seemed eager to teach the young marquis his duty as Governor General.

To make matters worse, Macdonald's April 3 announcement to the Commons of reference to Britain conveyed the impression that the idea originated with the Governor General, contrary to the collective advice of cabinet. Next day Lorne despatched a brief but firm note to the Prime Minister, asking him to correct the public misapprehension. To his credit, Macdonald did that, assuring parliament that reference had been made on the advice of cabinet. But the damage had been done. Regardless of where Canadians stood on the question of Letellier's dismissal, many concluded that their inexperienced and naive Governor General was no match for the wily Sir John A. Macdonald.

Reference to the Colonial Office was just as unpopular in Britain as in Canada. Hicks Beach made it clear he did not want to be bothered with the internal affairs of the new Dominion. "I did not expect the matter would be referred home and regret it," he informed Lorne. [27] Why had the Governor General not acted upon his original advice, privately given, to hesitate upon and then yield gracefully to the dismissal of Letellier?

Through the spring Lorne waited for London's definitive answer, never doubting he would be told to act on the advice of his ministers. Meanwhile he used the time to force his ministers into confronting the seriousness of their step and accepting full responsibility for an act which he felt was wrong. Upon receipt of Hicks Beach's final despatch on July 14, Lorne informed Macdonald he would accept the advice to dismiss Letellier if this were the considered opinion of the cabinet. But he insisted that all ministers must concur, including those absent in Britain. A week later Sir John replied that the advice, after reconsideration, was still tendered. Lorne had no alternative but to sign the order-in-council which deposed Letellier.

Lorne always stuck by his decision that reference to Britain was an appropriate course of action. Such a line of reasoning had not been accepted by the Colonial Office, as Hicks Beach bluntly informed the Governor General. Nor has it been accepted by Canadian historians. W. S. MacNutt maintains that Lorne "had his knuckles gently rapped," while John Saywell argues that "had Lorne not been the Queen's son-in-law it is likely he would have been placed on the rack." [28] Lorne waxed philosophical about his treatment in the Canadian press. "I have been abused through the length and breadth of the land," he wrote his father. "The press language here is as foul as the country is fine, and I have made a vast collection of this garbage for transmission home to Downing Street." [29]

Poor Letellier was dismissed, humiliated, and broken in both spirit and body. "When you see the Marquis of Lorne," he whispered from his death bed eighteen months later, "tell him that Letellier forgives a moment of weakness." [30]

\* \* \* \* \*

Parliament was finally prorogued on May 15, and the Lornes made their getaway from Ottawa and the Canadian politician scene as quickly as protocol and decorum allowed. For the next four months the country witnessed a peripatetic Governor General and Princess, dividing their time between official tours and private vacations. Lorne indulged his love of travel and his growing admiration for the Canadian countryside. Louise put John and Agnes Macdonald out of her mind while she painted and sketched the landscape.

Their first stop was Montreal for the May 24 celebration of Queen Victoria's birthday. They attended a military review at Fletcher's Field; Lorne conferred knighthoods on five prominent Canadians; the city hosted a grand civic banquet for its vice-regal guests; finally the young couple hurried to the official opening of the Art Association of Montreal's new building.

Lorne and Louise gave this art opening their very best effort, making a grand entrance before the admiring locals, Lorne in formal evening dress, Louise dazzling in white satin with lace draperies and diamond ornaments. The Princess delighted the city's art community by presenting her own painting, "A View of Glen Shira, Inverary," to the new museum.

Lorne's remarks drew even more press attention than Louise's looks and actions. The Governor General told the Art Association of Montreal that he looked forward to the day "when there may be a general art union in the country" and to a time when one of his successors might be called upon "to open the first exhibition of a royal Canadian academy." [31] Lorne was already involved with Ontario and Quebec artists in discussions that within a year would lead to the establishment of a Royal Canadian Academy, and eventually to the National Gallery of Canada.

From Montreal the vice-regal pair moved on to Kingston, where Lorne received an honorary degree from Queen's University and Louise distributed prizes to cadets at the Royal Military College. Then to Quebec City, where the handsomely refurbished old fortress known as The Citadel awaited the vice-regal couple as their official summer residence.

Quebec was everything that Ottawa was not. Cool breezes wafted up the broad St. Lawrence; narrow streets and crowded antique shops invited walking and browsing; beyond lay delightful day trips into the country-side of Montmorency and the Ile d'Orleans. "No man has known what pleasure life can give," recalled Lorne in later years, "until he has ridden out of Quebec with a joyous company to Lake Beauport, and has there fished for trout and dined on fish caught by himself, and thereafter has partaken of buckwheat cake with maple-sugar, and finished his dinner with wild strawberries and cream, and then seen the sunset on water and forest and hill." [32]

On June 9 Lorne officially opened Dufferin Terrace, that marvellous promenade overlooking the St. Lawrence and named after his predecessor. On the 11th Louise laid the foundation stone of the new Kent Gate, named after her maternal grandfather, Edward, Duke of Kent, whose army career had brought him to Quebec in the 1790s. That was followed by an evening of music, featuring a "Cantata of Welcome" composed by Calixa Lavallée.

"The reception everywhere has been excellent," De Winton informed Macdonald from Quebec, "the people enthusiastic and our journeys without a hitch." Lorne concurred. "We have been received with marked and remarkable kindness." It was not surprising. "To see the daughter of the Queen," observed De Winton, "is the general wish of every inhabitant of Canada." [33] Louise seemed to be enjoying the trip every bit as much as her husband.

But they dare not tarry too long in Quebec, for the Letellier business "makes it advisable that we should not be there when the Provincial Parliament meets in the middle of June." [34] Joined by Lorne's father, his brother Archie, and sisters Mary and Elizabeth (Libby), the Campbell entourage then sailed down the St. Lawrence on the government yacht *Druid*, bound for a salmon-fishing and sketching holiday at Indian House Pool on the Restigouche River in the Gaspé Peninsula.

Here was Canada in the wild — Indian guides, sleeping under canvas, troublesome black flies and mosquitos — the best and the worst of Canada's untamed wilderness. It appears to have been a success. "You never saw such fish," exclaimed Lorne's father, "40 lb. is a common weight, and such beautiful shapes." [35] Even Louise enjoyed herself in the Canadian backwoods. "She has taken a great fancy for salmon fishing,"

De Winton informed Macdonald with pride, "and has had very fair success, owing to her patience and perseverance." [36] "She seems in good health and able to rough it," observed her delighted father-in-law, "sleeping in tents and barges where the changes of temperature are very trying." Lorne, however, had put on too much weight during his first year in Canada. "He is rather too stout and will be a very heavy man unless he takes care." [37]

With the cultural stimulation of Quebec and the physical challenge of the Restigouche behind them, a refreshed and envigorated Lorne and Louise embarked on an official vice-regal tour of the Maritime Provinces. Every city and town lucky enough to be selected for a stop went through a period of emotional intoxication. Planning and preparations began weeks in advance. As the great day approached public buildings and private homes were decorated with flags and bunting; lavish welcome arches were built along the streets; final arrangements were made for parades, torchlight processions, receptions, banquets or whatever could be squeezed into the itinerary. Inevitably the great day itself was declared a local public holiday.

The small communities of New Brunswick, Nova Scotia and Prince Edward Island swept by in quick succession, as one gala evening merged into the next crowded day. British North America had seen nothing like it since Louise's brother Bertie, the Prince of Wales, had toured in 1860; there would be nothing to match it till the royal visits of the twentieth century.

Officially the communities of Atlantic Canada may have been observing the Governor General's visit, but it was undoubtedly the flesh and blood of a royal princess that sparked the extraordinary greeting. The departure of the golden couple produced a warm after-glow in people's minds. Children released their pent-up energies dismantling the decorations; elderly grandmothers put their Lorne and Louise souvenir plates safely out of harm's way; newspaper editors featured human interest items for the next few days illustrating the warmth and charm of the Princess; the names Lorne and Louise became popular for babies born over the next few months.

Ontario was next. After an August respite at The Citadel, Lorne and Louise took on Canada's most populous and prosperous province during September harvest time. Once again, both the countryside and its people responded with their best efforts. Small town agricultural fairs displayed 1879's bountiful harvests and shouted forth Ontario's prosperity. "A very fine country," Lorne observed, and the tour seems most thriving, each place pouring out its thousands to meet us." [38] Everywhere the sight of a Campbell of Argyll delighted the local Scottish population. At Berlin (Kitchener) the Governor General delighted another segment of the population by speaking German.

Lorne, c1879.

Toronto provided the climax. Here in Ontario's proud capital Lorne opened the first Toronto Industrial Exhibition, later known as the Canadian National Exhibition. He conferred with American Secretary of State William Evarts on Indian problems in the West. He and Louise met the city's leading citizens — members of those fine old Ontario families that ruled Victorian Toronto. "Toronto is just now in a paroxysm of vulgar flunkeyism, called forth by the visit of the Princess and her husband," wrote the anti-monarchist Goldwin Smith. Getting away to Boston for a breath of fresh air, Smith and his wife "left all our neighbours literally practising presentation bows and curtseys for a monkeyish imitation of a Drawing-Room which the Princess was to have." [39]

The antics of Torontonians at vice-regal presentations made even the dour Alexander Mackenzie smile. "Lady Howland went through in grand style curtseying so low that every one wondered how the whole of that 300 pound woman ever got up again," Mackenzie wrote his daughter. "Another stupendous woman a head taller than me and three times as thick went through with the preliminary movement to a curtsey. The officer immediately behind stepped back hurriedly, evidently seized with a sudden apprehension of what might become of his family if the curtsey should fail in the recovery. Someone whispered, 'is that whole woman to be presented at once?'" [40]

Luckily there were no casualties, and the Toronto visit was every bit as successful as the others that year. But Lorne and Louise were themselves wearing down. Apart from their Quebec City breaks and Gaspé fishing holiday, they had been on the road and on display for almost four months. "We have been fearfully busy," Lorne wrote his brother Archie from Toronto, "spouting at dinners, luncheons, institutions, etc., having been the order of the day, together with great entertainments given by ourselves, and it is a wonder we are alive." [41]

# ☙ CHAPTER ELEVEN
# THE MISSING PRINCESS, 1879-1880

*I*n a lengthy article reviewing Lorne's first year in Canada, *The Times* concluded that the experiment of appointing a royal son-in-law to a major overseas post had been "crowned with complete success." Lorne had shown it possible to appeal to Canadian sentiment without jeopardizing the dignity of the crown or the imperial connection. "Lord Lorne has played a difficult part with remarkable ability." [1] Apart from the Letellier business, the young marquis had fared well. His hard-to-please father certainly thought so. "I saw Lorne at work," noted the Duke of Argyll after returning from North America in the summer of 1879, "and saw plainly that he delighted in it, and seemed to be very popular with the people in all the Provinces. He seems to have a personal interest, almost a party spirit, in everything Canadian." [2]

The tour through the provinces had also endeared Louise to the people of Canada's small towns and rural communities. Despite the strain of constant travel, her energy never appeared to wane, and she seemed equal to every occasion — laying cornerstones, opening exhibitions, presenting medals and prizes, visiting schools and hospitals, hosting formal receptions. During a visit to Britain that summer, Macdonald was quick to praise Disraeli for sending Louise to Canada. "He says the Princess is a great success," Disraeli noted, "extremely gracious, speaks to everybody and is interested in everything," and "skates divinely." [3]

Then on October 18, Louise boarded the *Sarmatian* at Quebec City and sailed for England for a three-month break from Canada and her husband. Lorne accepted the separation as a matter of course. "I mean to live economically here for the next three months," he wrote his brother Archie, "and shall enjoy whatever quiet time I can have before the meeting of Parliament. There is always no end of work to do, and then there is the all important task of good skating to be learnt. I hope before

Louise dressed for the Canadian winter.

I leave Canada to be a thoroughly good skater and a Frenchman." [4] No word about missing Louise!

But the public on both sides of the Atlantic had difficulty accepting the explanation that Louise was back in England for a short holiday break, to attend the wedding of her younger sister Beatrice to Prince Henry of Battenberg. They questioned her need to leave Canada after less than a year's residence. They wondered why she did not remain with her husband. Wild suggestions and imaginative speculation began emerging in the press.

The London *World* suggested Louise returned to help launch the Lake Winnipeg Colonization Company, a scheme for the development of Manitoba farm lands. Such a company did exist, with Lorne's brother Walter Campbell as a director, but it was inconceivable that a Governor General's wife would be personally involved in such a project. "It requires some degree of credulity," concluded the Toronto *Globe*, "to believe that Her Royal Highness has gone home for the purpose of furthering it." [5]

Perhaps, then, Louise needed a respite from the rough-and-tumble Canadian political scene and its more nefarious practitioners? The dark rumour persisted, fostered by the Prime Minister's political opponents, that John A. Macdonald had "taken a liberty" with the Princess after imbibing too much punch at the state ball the previous February. Lady Macdonald was equally at fault, continued this line of thought, by continually trying to upstage Louise as Ottawa's first lady.

Officially, Louise's absence was referred to as a holiday and much-needed rest from the public pressures of Rideau Hall. "Princess Louise returns to England," noted Ottawa diarist Janet Hall, "having been ordered by her physicians." The "unexpected journey" had been "decided upon the advice of her physicians," according to *Truth*, the London weekly gossip sheet. [6] The public was asked to believe that a royal princess, a member of the nineteenth century's fragile and weaker sex, deserved some relaxation from the strain of official duties.

Considerable speculation centred on Louise's mental health. "Soon after her arrival in Canada," reported the Birmingham *Post*, the Princess "began to lose the habitual cheerfulness, not to say gaiety of mind, with which she had brightened the somewhat sombre atmosphere of the Royal domestic circle, and fell gradually into a state of depression which at one time threatened to pass into settled melancholia." The *Post* was confident that in England, "amid the scenes of her youth," Louise would "regain her youthful buoyancy of spirits." [7]

The wildest rumour had Princess Louise pregnant, with the baby's father someone other than her husband. She was returning to London for the last weeks of confinement and for the birth. This rumour began in the more sensationalist American papers, and was picked up by *Reynolds's Newspaper* of London on 1 February 1880. Readers were told of the "little

Lorne dressed for the Canadian winter.

stranger" that Louise would take back to Ottawa, "from Windsor Castle, with a grandmother's blessing." But Louise proved much too active during her holiday for any confinement or delivery. Her three months in England, from 28 October 1879 to 23 January 1880, were filled with a steady round of family visits, private parties, public engagements — including a Girls' Public Day School opening in Blackheath —and evenings at the theatre. No "little stranger" was taken back to Ottawa.

No matter how effectively the sensational rumours were dispelled, no matter how often health reasons were put before the public, whispering continued and questions kept being raised. Had something gone wrong between the Princess and her husband? Victorian society expected a wife to support her husband's public role and to stay at his side. Louise had erred.

Meanwhile, the Prince and Princess of Wales accepted the challenge of restoring Louise's spirits. They met her at St. Pancras Station on her arrival in London, escorted her home to Kensington Palace, gave her a luncheon party the next day at Marlborough House, then whirled her off to their country home at Sandringham for the Prince's birthday festivities. Bertie and Alix were full of high-spirited fun. What a contrast between the dull provincial society of Rideau Hall and the witty and artistic Edwardian set that frequented Marlborough House and Sandringham.

Louise spent the weeks before Christmas with her mother at Windsor, the obligatory Christmas at Osborne with most of the family, then early January with her sister Helena at Cumberland Lodge. One can imagine Louise's boredom in listening day after day to the detailed accounts of family births and christenings, marriages and deaths provided by Queen Victoria and Princess Helena.

Unlike Ottawa, however, London always provided a variety of escapes from claustrophobic obligations. Here Louise had her circle of friends in the arts and society; there were art exhibitions to visit and theatrical evenings to attend; there were luncheons and receptions and parties; there was witty conversation and hearty laughter wherever one went. "A miscellaneous and an aesthetical crew, to interest and amuse the Queen of Canada," noted Disraeli of a dinner gathering at Stafford House, the London home of Louise's Sutherland in-laws. [8]

At first there was speculation that Louise would not return to Canada. "The Princess will not go back again," the Birmingham *Post* informed its readers. Either she intended to live apart from her husband or, more likely, "the Marquis of Lorne would be recalled, and rejoin his Royal consort" in Britain. [9] But Lorne was not recalled, Louise's English stay was always spoken of in official circles as a rest holiday only, and in mid-January her return to Canada was announced.

Accompanied by her usual retinue of ladies-in-waiting, an equerry, and aides-de-camp — but with no "little stranger" — Louise left Liverpool on January 23. Once again the weather was "boisterous throughout the whole passage" and the *Sarmatian* delayed by "incessant gales of head winds" with the result that "the Princess suffered much." [10] On February 2 Lorne met his returning wife at Halifax. Guns boomed from Citadel Hill and crowds cheered their welcome to their still-adored but ever-more-mysterious royal princess. Husband and wife then embarked on the long four-day rail trip back to Ottawa, through extreme temperatures and deep snow of a Canadian winter. At the capital city, Janet Hall wrote in her diary, "quite a large crowd assembled at the station." [11]

The Duke of Cambridge, Queen Victoria's cousin and a perceptive observer of her children, noted in his diary that Louise left England "with a very heavy heart." *Truth* concurred. "It is no secret that Princess Louise returned to Canada with great reluctance," announced the usually authoritative weekly. "She complains of her utter isolation there, arising from the want of congenial society, there being few outside her own home with whom she has two ideas in common." [12]

* * * * *

Thursday 12 February 1880, a cheerless day of driving snow and bitter wind in Ottawa, the second session of the fourth Canadian Parliament opened. The usual formula was followed. Guns thundered from Nepean Point; militia units formed the guard of honour; Princess Louise sat on her throne in the Senate chamber; the Governor General read the short Throne Speech prepared by Prime Minister Macdonald; Lorne informed Parliament that Louise was "happy to return." Ottawa was back in business. The city's middle and upper classes looked forward to another lively season of parties and dances and gala dinners at Rideau Hall.

Saturday February 14, St. Valentine's Day. Lorne and Louise left Rideau Hall at 8:15 in the evening for the first official social event of the new season — the Drawing Room or formal reception in the Senate chamber. Accompanying them in their covered sleigh were Eva Langham and Colonel McNeill, lady-in-waiting and aide-de-camp. The night was cold; the streets were slippery with ice and snow.

Trouble began half-way down the avenue leading from the front door to Rideau Hall's main gate. One of the horses began pulling against its side straps and when checked, threw up its head in protest. The other horse grew restless. As they drew near the lodge gate the pair got completely out of control. About fifty metres from the gate the road took a half turn to the left. The charging horses took the corner too sharply. The sleigh slid sharply to the right and overturned.

Coachman and footman were thrown off into the snow, while the horses bolted through the gate and along the main road to Ottawa, pulling the overturned sleigh and its terrified passengers behind them. Louise was pitched head first against a vertical iron rod supporting the roof — her right ear severely lacerated and bleeding profusely.

The sleigh was dragged some 350 metres before the horses gradually slackened their pace. At that point Captain Jocelyn Bagot, another aide-de-camp and a distant cousin of Lorne's, jumped from a second sleigh, caught the runaway horses' heads and brought the overturned sleigh to a halt. Bagot pulled open the upper door, and assisted the passengers to safety. Louise was whisked back to Rideau Hall, escorted upstairs, and put to bed. Doctors were summoned. The Drawing Room on Parliament Hill was cancelled.

"We have had a narrow escape," Lorne wrote two days later. "L. has been much hurt, and it is a wonder that her skull was not fractured. The muscles of the neck, shoulder and back are strained, and the lobe of one ear was cut in two. As we pounded along, I expected the sides of the carriage to give way every moment, when we should probably have all been killed. L. was the only one much hurt, although Mrs. Langham was a great deal bruised. McNeill and I escaped almost untouched." [13]

Louise's recovery was slow and painful. She "is able to be downstairs now and has taken short walks," Lorne wrote his father a month after the accident. "Any fatigue, and almost everything gives her fatigue, brings on much pain in the injured side of the head, and I fear there will be nothing for it but long periods of rest and quiet in England, and that the travelling here and the taking part in ceremonial receptions, will be out of the question. At the same time she looks so well and is so vivacious in talk, that no one will believe she suffers." [14]

That was the problem. Few people were fully aware of the seriousness of the accident and the slowness of the recovery. The communication gap began when Francis De Winton, Lorne's secretary, imposed a news blackout on information about the accident. De Winton argued that Queen Victoria deserved an official report rather than wild newspaper speculation. Unfortunately the delay in accurate news coverage led both Canadians and Britons to conclude the accident was much less serious than it really was.

"Canadians laugh at the lugubrious accounts of the sufferings of P.L. since the sleigh accident," *Truth* informed its British readers. [15] "They think no more over there of being thrown out of a sleigh than hunting men of getting a fall. The general opinion was that the Pss. was delighted to have an excuse for another excursion to Europe." Certainly Ottawa's social set were disgruntled at the sudden cessation of public entertaining. The February 14 Drawing Room was not re-scheduled. There were no state balls nor formal dinner parties, no skating and tobogganing evenings at Government House that winter.

Yet private fun continued. Arthur Sullivan took time out from an American tour of *The Pirates of Penzance* to visit the Lornes just nine days

Sitting room at Rideau Hall, early 1880s.

after the accident. While staying at Rideau Hall, Sullivan set to music the words of Lorne's "Dominion Hymn," a proposed national anthem for Canada.

God bless our wide Dominion,
Our fathers' chosen land;
And bind in lasting union
Each ocean's distant strand;
From where Atlantic terrors
Our hardy seamen train,
To where the salt sea mirrors
The vast Pacific chain.

O bless our wide Dominion,
True freedom's fairest scene;
Defend our people's union;
God save our Empire's Queen.

On Saturday March 15 the hymn received its premiere performance by the band of the Governor General's Foot Guards, before a few private guests at Rideau Hall. "The stanzas are gracefully tuned, and effective in their simplicity," noted the Ottawa *Citizen's* society columnist, who somehow was privy to the entertainment. "They interpret the highest spirit of Canadian patriotism." Unfortunately, Sullivan's music was not as stirring. "It is flowing and melodious, but not equal to the words and thoughts it is intended to illustrate and enforce." [16]

Sullivan was followed to Rideau Hall by Albert Bierstadt, the American landscape painter. In common with many nineteenth century artists, Bierstadt quite openly courted the patronage of European royalty and aristocracy. He had met Queen Victoria and Lorne's brother Archie; he was a longtime friend of the Dufferins, visiting them at least twice in Ottawa. In May 1880 he was again a house guest at Rideau Hall, this time to the delight of the artistically starved Lorne and Louise. He promised to send Lorne photographs of "some very curious cliff dwellings in Northern Mexico and Central America." [17]

Ottawans read in their newspapers of these visits by Sullivan and Bierstadt. They knew of Louise's own excursions to the courts and to the House of Commons when the debates interested her. Yet there was no resumption of public appearances and official entertaining. If the Princess was up and about, why was she not taking her expected place as the leading hostess in Ottawa's public life?

Critics believed Louise was using the excuse of the accident to withdraw from her public responsibilities. The Toronto *Mail* suggested she felt "lost and lonely in a new country like ours," and regretted "the refined society and the aesthetic enjoyments left behind her." *Reynolds's Newspaper* began making comparisons with the previous vice-regal administration. "Lord Dufferin was always accessible, but Lord Lorne and his wife are precisely the contrary." [18]

The accident proved to be one of those traumatic life incidents that caused both participants and onlookers to re-evaluate their lives and situations. Half-formed thoughts and latent ideas now became manifest. Inarticulate mutterings became screams. Louise used the accident to vent her frustrations at the frigid Canadian climate, the equally hostile Canadian social and cultural environment, and her continuing discomfort within her unsatisfactory marriage. Lorne used the accident to justify sending Louise back to Britain for a prolonged stay, leaving him free to pursue his own interests in Canada. The Canadian public used it to express their frustrations towards the Princess. Never for a moment accepting the seriousness of Louise's injuries, Canadians concluded that she was using the accident as an excuse to escape her obligations. Since she did not like them, they decided they did not like her.

\* \* \* \* \*

Louise should not have missed the March 6 opening of the Canadian Academy's painting exhibition at the Clarendon Hotel. Her presence that night before the cream of Ottawa society might have made up for the cancellation of the February 14 reception on Parliament Hill. This was no ordinary painting exhibition. This show in makeshift galleries at the Clarendon was the culmination of a proposal Lorne had launched the previous May in Montreal — the idea of a national association of artists, holding annual exhibitions in the leading cities of the country.

But three weeks after the sleighing accident, Louise still suffered frequent headaches and stabbing pains along the side of her face. She did not feel physically or mentally strong enough to endure a major public engagement on a cool Ottawa evening. Lorne would have to open the show on his own, and take whatever criticism the public wished to direct at his absent wife.

Vice-regal patronage of the arts did not originate with the Marquis of Lorne. Half a century earlier, Dalhousie founded the Literary and Historical Society of Quebec. Both Elgin in the 1840s and Head in the 1850s gave their financial patronage to individual artists. Dufferin characteristically threw his energy and initiative into advocating a national association of artists. The trend continued in the twentieth century — Bessborough and the Dominion Drama Festival, Buchan and the Governor General's Awards for Literature, Massey and the Royal Commission on National Development in the Arts, Letters and Sciences.

Interview with Lorne in his Rideau Hall study, 7 February 1880.

Lorne used his enthusiasm and the prestige of his office to bring Dufferin's idea to fruition. In May 1879 he won over the Quebec artistic community with his remarks to the Art Association of Montreal. In September the Ontario Society of Artists accepted his draft proposal for a Canadian Academy. The new association would embrace painting, sculpture, architecture, engraving and industrial design. Full members would be called academicians; others would be known as associates. A National Gallery would be established in Ottawa, exhibitions held in principal cities of the country, and schools of art and design encouraged.

Controversy plagued the selection of the charter list of academicians — eighteen painters, six architects, and one sculptor. "There is a marvellous amount of bitterness and bad language," observed Lorne from Rideau Hall. "Half the artists are ready just now to choke the other half with their paint brushes." The selection process was heavily paternalistic, determined through consultation between Lorne and various local groups, particularly those in Montreal and Toronto. The Governor General's drive kept the project on the rails. Despite the infighting and petty jealousies, he remained "quite enthusiastic about the affair." [19]

Lorne spared no effort to launch the Academy in style. He talked the prime minister into providing at least the government's moral support; he secured Ottawa's Clarendon Hotel — recently purchased by the government for a geological museum — as a locale for the first exhibition; he encouraged academicians to complete their diploma or member-qualifying works for this show; he subscribed $500 of his own money to head the list of honorary members.

Regardless of Louise's accident and her slow recovery, there was no postponing the opening date for the first exhibition. All paintings, drawings and sculptures were required to be in Ottawa by February 28, when the selection committee of five academicians began their work. Lorne visited the committee members at the Clarendon every day, and entertained them at Rideau Hall. Louise was still confined to bed, though she insisted that Lorne bring nearly every picture up to her room for her personal inspection. [20]

Ottawa's political and social elites turned up at the Clarendon on the appointed evening. The Macdonalds, the Tilleys, the Tuppers, and other ministerial and official couples were there to give the Academy their stamp of approval. The Clarendon's rooms were rich with works. Lucius O'Brien's "Sunrise on the Saguenay" held the place of honour; there were fine paintings from Allan Edson, William Raphael, Charlotte Schreiber, Robert Harris, plus exhibits from sculptors and architects. It was a huge show, filling twelve rooms of the hotel, with some 388 works of art in the main exhibit itself. The Ottawa *Citizen* concluded that the high standards represented "the cornerstone of the quality of Canadian art in years to come," and would "elevate incalculably the art of Canada." [21]

With the crowd milling and surging through the building, the exhibition's climactic moment came with the arrival of the Governor General, complete with guard of honour and all his retinue in uniform. He was greeted with rounds of applause as he made his way towards the dais. Standing beneath O'Brien's grand painting, Lorne gave a lively, thoughtful speech, commenting on the incredibly short time since the project had been proposed, and ardently promoting the future of Canadian art and artists.

The Canadian Academy was launched; two years later it would become the Royal Canadian Academy; more than a century later it continued to hold an important, if not unchallenged, place in the Canadian art establishment. "The Academy has turned out a great success," Lorne wrote his father, "there being many good pictures, and the whole country joining in praise of the initiative of such an institution." He was conscious of his own role. "I think myself lucky to have been able to get it on foot, off my own bat, the first year, as it will be a lasting thing, and grow with the nation's development." [22]

The most conspicuous absentee at the Clarendon Hotel gala was Princess Louise. Whatever the public may have whispered privately about the seriousness of her injuries, Canada's artists were pleased and honoured to have her as an official patron. Absent or not, from the beginning she seemed to hold the Academy in real affection. In subsequent years she went out of her way to submit her own paintings for the annual exhibitions. She was delighted in 1930, when the Academy presented her with a silver scroll to mark the fiftieth anniversary of its founding.

Still, the Royal Canadian Academy was primarily Lorne's child. Vice-regal support for such a venture was to be expected, but Lorne far exceeded expectations in this case. Besides lending the prestige of his office, and his personal moral support, Lorne over the years donated considerable sums of money through prizes, purchases and outright donations. Instead of retiring gracefully from the scene in 1880, Lorne promoted the Academy's subsequent annual shows, — Halifax in 1881, then Montreal, then Toronto. After his return to Britain, Lorne remained a lifelong promoter of Canadian art and artists.

Although there would be many generous and important supporters of Canadian art in the future, Lorne was set apart from the rest in that he was "blessed with a large enough spirit to be able to look with equanimity on the often capricious behaviour of artists." A rare bird among art patrons, Lorne was able to "maintain his trust in the essential integrity of the artists" and "allow them a full voice in their own affairs." [23]

The Academy's most difficult objective was the establishment of the National Gallery as a physical reality. Lorne's ideas on a permanent national collection were clearly enunciated in a letter to Macdonald in

November 1879. "Members will be required to give a Diploma work, which will be presented to the country. In this way we shall at the outset get 20 or thereabouts good or fair pictures to start a National Gallery at Ottawa." The Clarendon Hotel was fine for the Academy's first exhibition. But "the future National Gallery must find a place afterwards." [24]

With the successful Clarendon exhibition behind him, Lorne made a serious approach to the federal cabinet. On May 10 he sent a formal memorandum to the Privy Council outlining the "desirability of the erection of a small gallery to contain the pictures presented by the Canadian Academy to the country." He reminded ministers that artists donating their works "will not feel their gifts are appreciated unless they are placed permanently on view in Ottawa." Besides, a permanent location "is likely to increase the presentation to the nation of pictures by others, who may wish to give or bequeath works of art to a National Gallery." [25]

Two years later, on 27 May 1882, the Royal Canadian Academy's picture collection moved into its first permanent home. This incipient National Gallery of Canada had to be content with humble quarters — an eleven-by-six metre single room shared with the Supreme Court in a small stone building at the foot of Bank Street. There was no grand formal opening, but one of the visitors that first morning was the Governor General himself, taking "great interest in pointing out to his friends the many beauties of the works of art on exhibition." [26]

After further temporary homes above the Government Fisheries exhibit on O'Connor Street, and in the Victoria Memorial Museum on McLeod Street, the National Gallery of Canada finally found a building of its own in 1960. Originally planned as an office building, and converted to an art gallery during construction, this structure again proved unsatisfactory, with its low ceilings and weather-proofing problems. But at least it was the National Gallery's own building. Most fittingly, it was called the Lorne Building.

* * * * *

In late May 1880 Louise and Lorne travelled to Quebec to greet Prince Leopold on his arrival for a North American holiday. The youngest of Queen Victoria's four sons, Leopold was the most sensitive and scholarly of all her children. He was a patron of the opera and theatre, and a close friend of actress Sarah Bernhardt, painter Gustave Doré, and singer Paolo Tosti. He amassed a great library and pursued research on ceramics. Since 1876 he had served as private secretary to his mother the Queen. Leopold was also a hæmophiliac, a bleeder, and never out of danger.

Leopold was Louise's favourite brother. There was always a strong bond of understanding between them, despite the five year difference in their ages. They shared similar artistic temperaments, similar tendencies to shut out the rest of the world and lead their own inner lives. They had been planning this holiday for months. They would ignore Leopold's hæmophilia and Louise's recent sleighing accident. They intended to cavort around North America seeing and doing whatever they wished, travelling as private citizens, as brother and sister, rather than prince and princess.

Off they sped to Niagara Falls and then to Chicago. When time constraints and physical exhaustion forced them to abandon a proposed trip to San Francisco, they made the most of Chicago. They attended the Republican national convention that nominated James Garfield for the 1880 presidential election campaign. "The royal party drove on the boulevards and through the south park," reported the Chicago *Tribune*. "Later they spent an hour and a half looking through the jewelry and silver ware of N. Matson and Co., and made several important purchases." [27]

Their arrival in New York occasioned star treatment by the popular press, and one newspaper published a long article of welcome under the heading "Vic's Chicks". Now it happened that Leopold owned a dog named Vic, and when he sent the article to the Queen she either failed to understand the journalistic jargon or thought it in bad taste. "How odd of them," she wrote Leopold, "to mention your dog." [28]

After ten days in the United States, Leopold and Louise rejoined Lorne at Quebec. "Prince and Princess returned this morning much pleased with their trip to the West," noted De Winton on June 12, "but I think a little tired with travelling. Lorne was quite relieved the jaunt was over. "The vulgarity of the Yankee papers about them surpasses belief," he confided to his father. [29]

The Governor General then offered an additional treat to his "convalescing" wife and "delicate" brother-in-law — a fishing holiday on the Cascapedia River, sixteen kilometres upstream from the small town of New Richmond on the southern side of Quebec's Gaspé Peninsula. He had reconnoitred the site the previous year when they fished on the nearby Restigouche River, and now it was his — a public gift to the Governor General and his successors from the Quebec provincial government. One of Lorne's successors, Lord Stanley, built a handsome nineteen-bedroom fishing lodge on the site; as Stanley House this later became the property of the Canada Council and was used extensively for summer cultural seminars.

That was all in the future. In June 1880 the vice-regal party made do with a pre-fabricated cabin purchased in Quebec. Still, with its four bedrooms, sitting-room, kitchen, large verandah and servants' loft, the cabin was quite comfortable. Lorne sent Louise and Leopold on ahead while he remained in Quebec for the June 24 St. Jean Baptiste Day festivities, which included the first public presentation of Calixa

Lavallée's "O Canada." Then he joined his wife, brother-in-law, and his own brother Archie for a full month in the outdoors.

Lorne considered the Cascapedia the "best salmon stream in the world," offering catches averaging twenty to thirty pounds, all in a "sylvan paradise" of luxurious flora and fauna. [30] The party rose nearly every morning at dawn, paddled upstream to one of the deep, still pools of water that marked the river's course, and fished from their canoes. They caught far more than they could eat themselves, distributing the surplus to local notables in New Richmond, and sending carefully packed boxes back to Ottawa and even to Windsor and Inverary.

"We are catching very fine salmon," Lorne informed Lord Granville. "The river is lovely almost beyond belief, and were it not that the Princess is not feeling strong, and that the flies are odious, our happiness would be perfect." [31] Odious flies were to be expected, and could be endured. Perhaps by this time even Louise's condition was predictable. Strong enough to travel furiously through the United States with her brother, she became weak on a supposedly restful fishing holiday when in the presence of her husband!

Instead of accompanying her husband on daily fishing excursions, Louise sought refuge in sketching and painting. Some of her best Canadian painting originates from this summer in the Gaspesian wilderness. "Wooden House - Cascapedia" is a delightful watercolour capturing the eerie stillness of early morning. "On the Cascapedia," an oil on canvas, demonstrates a sensitive use of colour and a fine sense of paint handling.[32] Despite the ruggedness of the surrounding terrain, the paintings reflect a serene, almost pastoral sense. This represented a typical response of the British artist to an unfamiliar landscape. Yet it also suggests an inner peace Louise found along the Cascapedia and which had escaped her in Ottawa.

At the end of July the Cascapedia party broke up and returned to The Citadel at Quebec. There on the 29th, Louise laid the coping-stone of the new Louise Embankment, named in her honour. Two days later, accompanied by Prince Leopold, she sailed for Britain. Less than a year earlier she had taken a three-month break from Canada; this time, as Janet Hall wrote in her diary, "a great many believe the Princess will not return." [33]

After a few days with her mother at Osborne, Louise left for Marienbad, the continental spa that attracted the cream of European royalty and wealth in the latter half of the nineteenth century. She travelled privately as Lady Sundridge, and meant to enjoy and indulge herself. At Marienbad she took rooms at the Villa Hapsburg. With her were Captain Collins as equerry, his sister, a Miss Collins, as lady-in-waiting, and three servants.

Her daily routine at Marienbad was not limited to a formal treatment program in the mineral waters. Lunches with vacationing friends, perhaps; carriage rides and country walks in the afternoons; plenty of time for sketching and painting. Dressing for dinner, parties and dancing late into the evening. No Ottawa and no husband; no London and no family or court obligations. Here Louise could defy convention even more.

Back from Marienbad and from a brief visit to Inverary in late October, the Princess was expected to announce plans for her return to Canada. *Truth* speculated she would return "in about three weeks." But she did not. All fall and through the winter of 1880-81, *Truth* announced postponements in Louise's sailing — because of family Christmas plans, to allow for an Easter visit to Italy, etc., etc. Finally in June 1881 *Truth* admitted there would be no early return. Louise had made any question of return "as remote and uncertain as it could be." She might never rejoin her husband in Ottawa, but would await the return of Lorne to England, "which is almost sure to take place in the autumn." [34]

The supposedly weak and convalescing princess gave the press and public much to talk about during 1881. At no time in her life did she appear to enjoy herself so much. She did another private Lady Sundridge visit to Italy at Easter. At home she entertained friends at Kensington Palace and visited their country places on weekends. She explored London's art galleries and artists' studios — including, frequently, the studio of Edgar Boehm — and spent evenings at the theatre. Her spirits remained remarkably buoyant during her long sabbatical leave from Ottawa. "Louise was amusing," noted Disraeli after one London dinner party; on another occasion she had "never looked prettier." [35]

## ❦ CHAPTER TWELVE
# SEPARATE AND HAPPY, 1880-1881

*T*he explanation for Louise's prolonged absence from Canada from July 1880 to June 1882 is complex. First there was some fear for her security — fear prompted by possible attempts on her life by the Fenian movement, the nineteenth century terrorist group that promoted Irish independence by striking at British interests at home and abroad.There was also her physical health — caution prompted by her seemingly slow recovery from the sleighing accident of February 1880 and a desire to protect her from more icy Ottawa winters. Finally, there was her mental state — an aversion to Canada in general, to Sir John and Lady Macdonald, perhaps even to her husband?

As a royal princess of Great Britain, a daughter of the reigning monarch, Louise was an obvious target for Fenian extremists. During a family holiday in 1868, she had been verbally abused by an irate Fenian sympathizer on a Paris street. Rumours of a Fenian attack on the *Sarmatian* had plagued the initial voyage of Lorne and Louise to Canada in November 1878.

Since then the Fenians had stepped up their North American propaganda and recruiting. In Canada they counted on sympathy and support in cities containing substantial Irish Catholic populations — Halifax, Saint John, Quebec, Montreal, Ottawa and Toronto. Occasionally speakers came from Ireland or the United States, whipping up support for the Home Rule cause. There were rumours of arms build-ups from time to time. Lorne never underestimated the potential mischief of the movement. He had been alarmed at the dedication expressed by Fenian waiters during his 1866 visit to the United States; his sojourn into Canada that year coincided with a Fenian attack on the Niagara Peninsula. He was inclined to take seriously the occasional rumours of threats against Louise.

On 7 January 1881 Lorne was warned by an anonymous Fenian to "get out of Canada" if Home Rule leader Charles Stuart Parnell were convicted by British courts of membership in the outlawed Irish Land League. "One hundred thousand Fenians" would invade from the United States "in 24 hours notice" to deal with the Governor General. [1] Though Lorne was not about to leave Canada, certain precautions had to be taken. Security was increased at Rideau Hall, the British garrison at Halifax kept at full strength, and the British embassy at Washington established as a clearing house for intelligence. In the coming months ambassador Henry Thornton passed along to Lorne a steady stream of reports of Fenian activities along the Canadian-American border. [2]

Yet the alleged Fenian threats on Canada and Canada's princess were perhaps more an excuse than a reason for Louise to remain on the other side of the Atlantic. Exposure to potential Fenian trouble had not cramped Louise's activities during her jaunt to Chicago and New York with Leopold, nor her sketching and painting activities on the Cascapedia. Certainly Rideau Hall offered far greater security than American hotels or the Gaspesian wilderness. Nor did the Fenian presence in Europe keep her away from Marienbad in the autumn of 1880 or Italy the following Easter. The Fenians seemed enough of a threat to keep Louise from Ottawa, but not serious enough to interfere with her other activities.

Health reasons, rather than Fenian threats, offer a more plausible explanation for Louise's prolonged absence from Canada. "She had not yet entirely thrown off the effects of the carriage accident," notes Duff in justifying her Marienbad holiday. "But two months of mild German air, coupled with excellent treatment, proved very beneficial." She returned to England in October 1880, Duff tells us, "feeling much stronger." [3] Strong enough to maintain an active life in Britain, and travel on the Continent, but not nearly strong enough to return to her husband in Canada.

Throughout 1881 Lorne was in constant communication with the royal doctors over Louise's health. He accepted Dr. W.F. Cumming's statement that she "always looks well — but still suffers a great deal from headaches and sleeplessness, and is very thin." By early May Lorne realized Louise would be unable to accompany him on his proposed summer trip to the Canadian Northwest. "I fear the N.W. journey would certainly be too fatiguing," he confided to his father. "Flies, heat, dust and long drives across the Prairie would knock her up." [4]

Lorne was not alone in asserting medical reasons. A certain Dr. Dupuis of Kingston, for example, assured readers of the Ottawa *Citizen* that he had it on the personal word of Erasmus Wilson, "one of the ablest and most eminent surgeons of England," who had been "consulted on her care as soon as she came home," that Louise was indeed "very seriously injured" in the sleighing accident. "The old gentleman then went on," continued Dupuis, "and detailed to me the nature of the injury and the consequences that had resulted from it, and convinced me that what we had ignorantly considered as a trifling bruise, not knowing the facts, was an injury of grave import." As a consequence, "it was by the advice of her medical advisers" that Louise remained so long in Britain. [5]

The sleighing accident most probably left Louise with a combination of physical and physiological symptoms best described as neuralgia. Medical dictionaries define neuralgia as an abnormal condition characterized by severe stabbing pain. Its causes stem from a variety of disorders affecting the nervous system, including pain from a damaged nerve. Certainly the severe lacerations and bruises suffered by Louise could have damaged a nerve in her right ear or along the right side of her face and head. If the damage was to the trigeminal nerve, the major nerve in the face, then Louise was suffering from very painful trigeminal neuralgia.

Trigeminal neuralgia produces excruciating pain along the side of the face. The attacks may be triggered by touching a sensitive spot or even by sitting in a draft. The pain is sharp and hard to bear, shooting along the affected nerve. Though the initial pain usually lasts only a few seconds, the attack may return again and again, every few minutes.

Today trigeminal neuralgia is treated by surgically severing certain nerve connections, or by injecting opiates or alcohol into the damaged nerve. But in Victorian times, the prescription usually went no further than rest, proper diet, oral ingestion of modest pain killers, and a general admonition to avoid stressful situations. Research by an American doctor during the 1870s suggested that severe changes in weather — particularly cool breezes and icy drafts — could trigger neuralgia outbreaks. [6] Following this line of reasoning, it seemed to make good medical sense to keep Louise away from Ottawa's cold winters. Britain and the European continent were permissible, but not Canada.

Yet attacks of trigeminal neuralgia can be induced by psychological as well as physical and climatic factors. Louise's often perplexing behaviour as a teenager and young woman had frequently been ascribed to "nerves" — her tearful outbreaks, sudden exits from formal receptions and banquets, cancellations of public appearances. If nerves had caused such problems in the past, how much more troublesome could they be now that an important facial nerve had been physically damaged. [7]

It is tempting to conclude that Louise could trigger an attack simply by thinking of the unpleasant people and dull society that awaited her in Ottawa. And that the combination of Ottawa, the Macdonalds, and her husband was both physiologically and psychologically more than she could endure. Her persona cried for release and freedom from her domestic and vice-regal obligations. As long as she remained in Britain and Europe, and led her own life, she could keep the neuralgia attacks to a minimum.

Did she really care about her husband? One story making the rounds at the time of Louise's birthday in March 1881 had Lorne telegraphing an official in the Queen's household, requesting him to convey his congratulations to his wife, "as he was not acquainted with her whereabouts." [8] Whether true or not, the story embodied a perception shared by many on both sides of the Atlantic: the marriage was in serious trouble!

\* \* \* \* \*

Facing a prolonged separation from his wife, Lorne busied himself in Ottawa with the myriad of political and ceremonial duties that defined the role of the Governor General. August 1880 featured a second tour of the Maritime provinces. Up and down the long indented coasts of New Brunswick, Prince Edward Island and Nova Scotia sailed the vice-regal party — minus the Princess. At every stop Highland settlers boosted the Governor General's ego. "They kissed my hand and behaved like their ancestors, who were proud to follow [the Campbell laird] to death." [9]

September took him through rural Ontario for that province's "annual epidemic of Fairs." [10] Later in the fall he sampled other aspects of North American popular culture — a football match between Ottawa and Harvard universities, a wild west show featuring Buffalo Bill Cody, a concert by a black spiritual ensemble, and a Sarah Bernhardt performance in Montreal, where he squirmed uncomfortably as the audience burst forth in a spontaneous rendition of the Marseillaise.

The new year brought another session of the Canadian parliament, another series of gala entertainments at Rideau Hall — "entertaining all the world at the rate of about 500 a week" — and another round of political sparring with Prime Minister Macdonald. "Sir John is by no means well," observed Lorne on the eve of the opening, "and I am afraid will not last long — but he has great recovering power." [11] He certainly did; enough staying power, in fact, to see him through another full decade of public life.

Meanwhile Lorne adjusted to subtle shifts in emphasis in Anglo-Canadian affairs. The defeat of Disraeli and the Conservatives in the British general election of April 1880, and the return to power of Gladstone and the Liberals, saw John Wodehouse, Earl of Kimberley, replace Sir Michael Hicks Beach as Colonial Secretary. Correspondence between London and Ottawa began to feature the Pacific railway scheme, a proposed trans-Pacific telegraph cable, and the imminent appointment of a Canadian High Commissioner in London.

Lorne was as anxious as Macdonald to get the Pacific railway moving. His own hopes of promoting British emigration to the Canadian West depended on cheap and direct transportation to the prairies. But hundreds of miles of track remained unbuilt. Now, however, with the country's acceptance of the new protective tariff, and a moderate upturn in the economy, it was time for bold ventures. Lorne agreed with Macdonald's plan to encourage a private company or syndicate to tackle the mammoth construction project.

He advised Macdonald on potential investors; Lord Dunmore was a notorious speculator with "a very good heart, no head, and no money."[12] He rejoiced in the agreement reached in October 1880 with a syndicate that included George Stephen, Donald Smith, and Duncan McIntyre. In December Charles Tupper presented the agreement to Parliament; both Commons and Senate approved the Pacific Railway bill early in the new year; on 15 February 1881 Lorne gave royal assent and transmitted copies of the act to Kimberley at the Colonial Office.

Meanwhile Lorne promoted the idea of a resident Canadian minister, or High Commissioner, in London. He agreed with Macdonald that such an individual was necessary in representing Canada to Britain and foreign governments. This was "the beginning of a difficult question," he had earlier written Hicks Beach, "for Canada will more and more wish to make her own treaty arrangements." Still, such an office could work to the advantage of Imperial unity, for it might "stave off, for a very long time to come any wish on the part of Canada for a separate set of representatives in foreign countries." [13]

Lorne saw his main role in allaying British fears. "Among sensible men here," he wrote from Ottawa "there is no wish to conduct negotiations separately, but only that the interests [of Canada] be pushed as the interests of an integral part of the whole." By accepting the concept, Britain had more to gain than to lose, for through it "we may hope to keep public men here content with the present system." [14]

Britain reluctantly agreed to the idea, and accepted Sir Alexander Galt as Canada's first permanent representative in London.* Lorne realized Galt would have difficulty gaining entry in the imperial capital, for Sir Alexander had committed the unpardonable Victorian sin of marrying his deceased wife's sister. "Will you be civil to Galt if he calls on you in London," Lorne urged his father, "and ask him and Lady G. to dinner and help him a little? Canadians think so much of such attention." [15] He suggested Galt concentrate first on the ceremonial side of the job, and only gradually raise questions of political and commercial interest, since the new Gladstone ministers were in no mood to have their "digestions overloaded." [16]

---

* The High Commission office was originally located in very cramped quarters in Victoria Street. The present Canada House on Trafalgar Square was purchased from the Union Club in 1924 and, after much renovation work, opened as the Canadian High Commission the following June. Today most of the work of the Commission is done from Macdonald House, on the site of Lorne and Louise's former residence at No. 1 Grosvenor Square.

In the long run the office of Canadian High Commissioner in Britain reduced the role and power of the Governor General as a political go-between in Ottawa-London affairs. It was just as well. Within a short period of time at Rideau Hall, Lorne had come to see the positive side of complete Canadian self-government (within an Imperial framework of course) and the absolute necessity of Canadian self-promotion of her own interests. Lorne in fact was increasingly identifying his office with the interests of Canada. Macdonald was quick to note that the Governor General had quickly become "a good Canadian."

Such enthusiasm was continually regenerated through travel. Late spring and early summer of 1881 produced Lorne's third annual vice-regal tour through the provinces. At Chambly, Quebec, he unveiled a monument to Colonel De Salaberry, a hero of the War of 1812. He reminded his audience of the friendship between De Salaberry and Louise's grandfather, the Duke of Kent, adding that Louise "wishes me to convey her sorrow that she is not here today." [17] Then Albert Bierstadt joined Lorne for a few days at The Citadel and a fishing break on the Cascapedia. The first of July took the Governor General to Camp Sussex, New Brunswick, for a Dominion Day military review. Three days later he opened the Canadian Academy's second annual art exhibition at Halifax.

Lorne remained at his best on these public occasions. "The Marquis of Lorne is as good a Canadian as if he had been to the manor born," concluded the Saint John *Daily Sun*. He had proven himself "a lover of our country" by "throwing himself heartily into various non-political movements calculated to benefit the country," doing "all that lay within his reach to promote Canadian interests." This was mere prelude to what lay ahead. The *Daily Sun* was as excited as any Canadian newspaper about the Governor General's next project — a visit to the West. "It is impossible to over-rate the importance of the visit which His Excellency proposes. We shall be greatly mistaken if it does not give an impetus to emigration far greater than anything the North West has yet witnessed." [18]

\* \* \* \* \*

## WESTWARD HO!

*Away to the West, Westward Ho! Westward Ho!*
*Where, over the prairies, the summer winds blow!*

*Why known to so few were its rivers and plains*
*Where rustle so tall in the ripeness their grains?*
*The bison and Red-man alone cared to roam*
*O'er realms that to millions must soon give a home.*

*Away to the West, Westward Ho! Westward Ho!*
*Why waited we fearing to plant and to sow?*

The vast expanse of the Canadian prairies meant much more than the Great Lone Land of Red Indians and Paul Kane buffalo. To Canada's Governor General it represented both the logical home for Britain's surplus population and the fulfilment of his new country's trans-continental destiny. During his first year in Canada, he wrote home enthusiastically about prairie settlement, joked that his next sister to marry "should settle under my wing in Manitoba," and "had all the politicos" jumping at his proposal to name "a new province beyond Manitoba, almost as big as France, Alberta." [19]

Now in the summer of 1881, having paid his respects to Eastern Canada, and with Louise safely out of the way in Britain, Lorne prepared to indulge his wanderlust and embark on his most adventurous travel since the Garibaldi episode of 1867. Though Dufferin had visited both Manitoba and British Columbia, no Governor General had as yet shown the flag in the intervening region of the North West Territories. Yet the CPR was about to launch its mammoth prairie construction, settlement had to be encouraged, Indian anxieties quieted and capital attracted.

The trans-prairie trek might jolt the British out of their general indifference toward Canada. Aware of residual interest in the North West, Lorne invited members of the British press to accompany him on his tour. Favourable publicity for the Canadian West would aid the Pacific railway on London's money markets and attract British emigration. "I have great hope," wrote Lorne, "that this journey may be of some use in advertising the new territories." [20] Promised an expense-free tour led by an adventuresome Governor General, offered the chance to meet with "great councils" of Indians, the British press responded to the challenge.

Preparations completed, the vice-regal party left Toronto by rail on July 19. The 180 kilometre journey to Owen Sound on Georgian Bay took eleven long hours as citizens of every community along the line insisted on presenting long-winded addresses to their Governor General. "Dust, sun and speechifying took much out of one." [21] At Owen Sound the exhausted travellers boarded the steamer *Frances Smith* for a leisurely four-day trip across Lake Huron and Lake Superior to Prince Arthur's Landing on Thunder Bay.

Beyond Thunder Bay there was little opportunity to relax. The still-unfinished Canadian railway line stopped at Lake Wabigoon. From there to Winnipeg, a succession of steamer, barge and canoe transport was interrupted by uncomfortable overland portages. One fifteen kilometre portage was rendered even more uncomfortable by a forest fire which destroyed the half-way house prepared for the party's refreshment.

Winnipeg was reached without further mishap — a bustling city of more than 10,000, anticipating its future as the gateway to the Canadian West. "Winnipeg is in a fever," Lorne wrote, as he too was swept along in the rising tide of optimism. [22] On the outskirts of the city Donald Smith, a leading Canadian Pacific Railway shareholder, entertained the visiting Governor General at his grand home, Silver Heights, where the music of bagpipes and a triumphal arch resembling the front of Inverary Castle added to the festive atmosphere of the occasion.

From Portage la Prairie, Manitoba, on August 8, the Governor General's party left the transcontinental rail line and headed northwest across the almost unbroken land. In addition to the press, the group included Francis De Winton and members of the Rideau Hall staff: Edgar Dewdney, Commissioner of Indian Affairs, and other government officials; a North West Mounted Police escort; a chaplain, a physician, and a retinue of servants to cater to everyone's wishes — including Lorne's personal chef, M. Boquet, promptly dubbed "Maître Cuisinier de la Prairie." The expedition — totalling seventy-seven men, ninety-six horses, twenty-seven vehicles and twenty-one tents — was part military in its assertion of Canadian sovereignty over unsettled lands and restless Indians; part promotional in Lorne's use of the British journalists; part pure adventure for the Governor General.

Each day the party moved off at sunrise to complete a march of fifty to sixty kilometres, travelling at an average rate of eight kilometres an hour in three stages. Between nine and ten o'clock a halt was made for breakfast; lunch followed at two. Somewhere about six, the long train of wagons, carts and riders would stop for the night. Carriages were wheeled around to form a line; baggage wagons formed another. Every move followed a well-practiced plan; each wagon was numbered and each driver knew exactly what to do. Horses were unyoked. Escorts pitched the tents in a double line, forming a street. Servants brought in the luggage, fixed the camp beds and mosquito curtains, and carried water for the nightly baths. The camp now appeared like an animated village, with fires blazing in the darkness.

Lorne was overawed by the natural beauty of the prairie. "The distance seems infinite. You gaze, and the intense clearness of the air is such that you think you have never seen so distinctly or so far over such wide horizons before. Plateaux, hollows, ridges, and plains lie beneath you, on and on, and there is nothing to keep the eye and mind from the sense of an infinite vastness. There is no special mark to arrest the gaze, and it wanders and wanders on to those pink and blue shades, where the skies, light and beautiful in tint, are joined in harmony and colour to the endless swell and roll of the uninhabited world beneath them." [23]

The vice-regal party was eagerly awaited at Battleford, the tiny capital of the Northwest Territories. "We are in a great state of excitement," wrote William Parker of the local NWMP detachment. Constable Parker and friends were not the least bit disappointed in their young Governor General. "He is a very nice man," Parker wrote his mother, "our fellows think a great deal of him, especially so before leaving he made every man a present of a pound of tobacco and the Non-commissioned officers two pounds." Even a committed non-smoker like Parker felt obliged "to try a pipe of it to do honour to the Marquis." [24]

On September 1 the party left Battleford for the two week overland journey southwest across the prairies to Fort Calgary in the shadow of the Rocky Mountains. In some ways this was the most exciting leg of the trip. Four days out of Battleford the party encountered a herd of buffalo, one of the first seen in several years, and chased and killed three of the beasts in one of the last buffalo hunts on the Canadian plains.

Yet Battleford-to-Calgary was also the toughest leg of the trip. Higher elevations and the advancing autumn season produced below-freezing nights and heavy morning frosts. Day after day of cold driving rain and long wet grass taxed man and beast alike. Horses and wagons faced the ultimate challenge in negotiating the steep banks of deep-cut valleys like that of the Red Deer River. Carts had to be abandoned with broken axles and wheels, horses died of exhaustion, mosquitoes swarmed about the riders, prairie wolves howled dismally at night.

This was no longer white man's country. The fringe of European and even half-breed settlement had been left behind. The Governor General's party relied on Indian guides like Poundmaker, great chief of the Crees, to lead them through this largely unknown and unmapped countryside. Poundmaker was a skilled guide by day and an entertaining story-teller by night. He made many professions of loyalty to the Great White Mother, as the Indians called Queen Victoria.

But could Canadian authorities continue to take Indian loyalty for granted? True, native irritants to Canadian-American relations had been largely resolved in July, when Chief Sitting Bull and the last of his Sioux warriors returned to the United States. But problems remained north of the 49th parallel of latitude. Until now the Indians had had room to retreat westward before the advance of civilization. But that advance threatened to accelerate with railway construction and white settlement. The Indians would soon have their backs against the Rocky Mountains.

\* \* \* \* \*

Since Fort Qu'Appelle in early August, the Governor General had held important meetings with native groups along the way — listening to their grievances and protestations of loyalty, presenting gifts to the chiefs and promising to take Indian complaints back to his government at Ottawa. Now Chief Crowfoot, leader of the Blackfoot, greeted the vice-regal party as they set up camp at Blackfoot Crossing on the Bow

Conference with the Blackfoot Indians at Blackfoot Crossing, September 1881.

River in the evening of September 9. Lorne agreed to his request that a great pow-wow or council take place the next day with the Blackfoot and their allies from across southern Alberta.

The Blackfoot camp was alive at sunrise the following morning. Beginning at nine o'clock, and lasting for almost a full hour, the Indians rode to the meeting place on horseback and in full battle array, shouting and waving and firing their rifles. Behind them tripped the women and children, for everyone wanted to be part of this pow-wow with the Great Brother-in-Law, as the Indians called Lorne.

Riding hard and shouting wildly, over 200 Indians rode up to the official party, sprang from their horses, and advanced to shake hands. Chiefs sat down in front of the Governor General, head men behind in a second row, the rest of the Blackfoot ranged around in a deep half-circle; on the right an allied set of cousins, with their aunts and sisters behind them; while on the left, in triple ranks, crouched on the ground, sat the warriors, "round limbed and lithe young fellows," Lorne noted, "clad with little but paint on the body." [25] When all were present the chiefs, each carrying a Union Jack, came forward to shake hands with Commissioner Dewdney and Lord Lorne.

Serious discussion did not begin until pipes were smoked and dances danced. "Strange and weird and uncouth these dances are," Lorne later told an enthralled British audience. "The magicians sit on the ground beating a tom-tom, and in a circle, following each other in single file, strut, bow, howl, and jig the braves detailed for the duty; pretending occasionally to be in pursuit or in flight, round and round they go until the music ceases, when all sit on the ground." [26] The young braves insisted on recounting their deeds in war, boasting of stealing cattle and of killing their foe.

Having sufficiently gathered their thoughts, the native spokesmen rose in succession and voiced their desires in fervid and flowery language. They spoke of losing their lands to the white man, the disappearance of the buffalo, and the increasing numbers of white men who were moving in. They spoke of the small rations and the poor flour, and they asked for more help. Crowfoot was the last to speak. He made an impassioned plea for more rations for his people and more help to make them self-sufficient. Standing in his tattered robes, Crowfoot presented himself unashamedly as a destitute spokesman for his starving people.

Responding to Crowfoot's plea, Lorne advised him to lead his people in breaking the land and turning to agriculture as a livelihood. He told him that the old days were gone and the Blackfoot could no longer wander in search of buffalo. Crowfoot replied. "Grasping my hand, and putting round my arm the bridle cord of his horse," wrote Lorne, "he asked me to accept the animal as a present, and repeatedly assured me that, although he had hitherto been first in fighting, he would now be the first in

Rocky Mountains from the Elbow River near Fort Calgary, September 1881. From a sketch by Lorne.

working." As a parting gift, Lord Lorne gave Crowfoot a shotgun, but would not take the chief's horse from the destitute tribe. [27]

Everything after Blackfoot Crossing might have been anti-climactic had Lorne not fallen in love with the southern Alberta countryside. The love affair began with the first sight of the Rocky Mountains. Heading west towards Fort Calgary, late one evening the Governor General trained his field glasses on a "row of stupendous craggy peaks, clear-cleaving that fair air," almost 200 kilometres away. "They looked like the serrated black jaws of some crocodilian reptile's spine as he lay all hidden but his back, guarding a golden treasure from which the yellow light poured out behind him." [28]

The Rockies acted as a beacon for the weary travellers: a vertical backdrop relieving the tedium of a month's travel through horizontal grasslands. The weather also turned in their favour, as the previous fortnight's rain gave way to glorious days of golden September sunshine. Here in this generally dry, lightly rolling foothills countryside of southern Alberta, Canada's infant ranching industry was beginning life. Both Lorne and De Winton were anxious to investigate investment possibilities.

On September 12 the vice-regal party rode into Fort Calgary, a tiny settlement around a mounted police post, soon to emerge as a major ranching centre. Lorne and De Winton talked land prices and agricultural conditions with settlers John Glen and Sam Livingstone. They observed a huge cattle drive, a herd of several thousand just arrived from Montana, bound for nearby Cochrane Ranch. De Winton ultimately succumbed to the lure, organizing the Alberta Ranche Company, which operated for a number of years in the Bow River and Pincher Creek areas. [29]

Meanwhile in September 1881, Fort Calgary marked the westward limit of the vice-regal tour. There was not time to push into the Rocky Mountains, still eighty kilometres away. Boats had been built in Calgary to carry the party east by river, but at the last moment Lorne decided to return via Fort Shaw, Montana, and the Union Pacific Railway. This allowed a few extra days in the delightful Alberta foothills — south through High River to Fort Macleod. The weather continued favourable, "like a time in an English June." [30]

Macleod was unlike anything seen by the party so far. If Canada had a "wild west", this was it. The fort itself — a North West Mounted Police outpost — was enclosed in a wooden stockade. The village's one dusty street was lined with squalid, one-storey buildings, hiding all manner of recreation and debauchment behind their white-washed fronts. The most colourful spot was Camoose House, a saloon run by a former Indian trader and preacher. Its smoke-filled interior was crowded with ranchers, bull whackers, mule skinners, traders and working cowhands. How they must have smiled at the delicate manners of the Governor General's party!

One last Indian council with the Bloods, members of the Blackfoot confederacy, illustrated the scramble for good land and the hope that the Governor General could solve the natives' problems. "What His Ex told them, I am not in a position to say," remarked a local white identified as 'Grumbler No. 1'. "The Bloods wanted Standoff bottom where they could raise something, and came back with the impression the G.-G. had given it to them, and commenced building in the bottom accordingly." [31]

Lorne stayed overnight at Kyleakin, home of Colonel James Macleod, former NWMP Commissioner, founder of Fort Macleod, and Southern Alberta patriarch. Continuing south toward the American border, he forded the Waterton River (then called the Kootenay River) at a spot afterwards known as the Governor General's Crossing. Atop a hill offering a grand view of prairie and mountain, Lord stopped his team and exclaimed, "It is rightly called God's Country." If "I was not Governor General of Canada," he told a Rideau Hall visitor the following year, "I would be a cattle rancher in Alberta."[32]

Winter approached, and storm clouds massed overhead as the party crossed into Montana. At Fort Shaw on the 28th "a gallant American regiment" welcomed the bone-weary travellers. "All spent a delightful time with our American friends," Lorne noted, "the men greeting our fellows as if they were old comrades." Here at a colourful parade ground ceremony, with the blue uniforms of the American army mingling with the red of the North West Mounted, Lorne bade farewell to his police escort, "as fine a troop as I ever saw." [33]

The great trans-prairie trek was over. A United States Army escort accompanied Lorne to the nearest railway point for his journey east. "Looking perhaps better than at any other period since his arrival in Canada," enthused the Globe, "denotes how thoroughly he has enjoyed and benefited by the trip." [34]

## ❦ CHAPTER THIRTEEN
# STILL APART AND STILL HAPPY, 1881-1882

*D*uring the eastward rail journey through the United States, Lorne detoured north to Winnipeg to address the Manitoba Club on October 11. He was fulfilling a commitment made two months' earlier to speak on his impressions of the Canadian North West. The extra time and travel were well worth while. Before an audience which included journalists from major Canadian, British and American newspapers, the enthusiastic Governor General gave the most inspired speech of his life.

Keeping his introductory pleasantries brief, Lorne began by denouncing those nay-sayers who sought to disparage the potential of Canada's West. Nothing, he charged, could exceed the fertility and excellence of the land along the Saskatchewan River and the parkland immediately to its north. Here would be "room for a great population whose opportunities for profitable cultivation of the soil will be most enviable." Even on the more open plains to the south, the Governor General and his party "passed over land whose excellence could not be surpassed for agricultural purposes."

The Canadian West was by no means "a great lone land." It was not "flat, dreary, unwooded, devoid of animal life, and depressing in the extreme." There could be no greater mistake than to think so. "The open prairie," he cried, "is a green sea of rich grasses, over which the summer winds pass laden with the odour of countless flowers." Clumps of trees provided firewood and shelter; swamps and lakes teemed with fish and bird life; coal was available along the upper reaches of many of the prairie rivers; American cattlemen were jealous of the stock-raising potential of southern Alberta.

All Canadians should be aware that the country's future would be determined on the western plains. "For a Canadian, personal knowledge of the North-West is indispensable. Here, he told his Winnipeg audience, "you have a country whose value it would be insanity to question," a land that "must support a vast population." With the completion of the Pacific railway and the agricultural settlement of the plains, Canada would soon "be a land of power among nations." [1]

Press reaction to Lorne's Winnipeg speech was extremely positive. The Toronto *Globe* judged it "eloquent, manly, sensible," in its praise for prairie agricultural potential and its predictions for Canada's future. The Quebec *Chronicle* termed it "brilliant, exhaustive and analytical;" the Montreal *Evening Post* believed the young Governor General had shown himself "superior to the suave and eloquent Lord Dufferin." The speech, predicted one editorial after another, would break down "the skepticism which prevails in the Old Country regarding the value and attractiveness of the Territories." [2]

The speech made great immigration propaganda. Before the year was out the Department of Agriculture in Ottawa published Lorne's address in pamphlet form, under the title *The Canadian North West*. The pamphlet was reprinted in 1882 and again in 1883; it appeared in German as *Der Nordwesten Canadas*; it quickly became part of the growing body of Canadian immigration and tourist promotional literature.

At the same time, reports of the various expedition correspondents aroused the most Canadian interest in Britain since Confederation. Rev. James MacGregor's articles in *The Scotsman* helped convince farmers they had much to gain by emigrating. Charles Austin's pieces in *The Times* raised Canada's economic profile and attracted British investment.

Sydney Hall's one hundred drawings in *The Graphic* appeared regularly between August 1881 and February 1882. Most famous was his large double-page illustration entitled "The Pow-wow at Black Feet Crossing" in the November 7 issue. Lorne also commissioned Hall to paint a large oil of the event — "Last Indian Council Held on Canadian Soil between the Governor General of Canada, and Crowfoot, Chief of the Blackfeet Indians, 1881" — now owned by the Gilcrease Institute of American History and Art in Tulsa, Oklahoma. The Public Archives of Canada has its version, a large charcoal and watercolour by Hall entitled "Conference of the Marquis of Lorne and Blackfeet Indians, September, 1881."

Lorne's own sketches appeared in the *Illustrated London News* and were later reproduced in his book *Canadian Pictures* and in George Grant's *Picturesque Canada*. Lorne used a variety of media to capture the prairies — pencil drawings, pen and ink over pencil, sepia drawing with wash over pencil, pen and ink with wash, watercolour and pen and ink over pencil, watercolour over pencil, pencil with wash. The lively, anecdotal quality of both Hall's and Lorne's sketches helped create a new, more human image for the Canadian West. The Governor General had opened everyone's eyes to the potential of the region.

The public now perceived Lorne as a key individual in the settlement of the West. On both sides of the Atlantic it became known that he was the man to see in order to get the right people on the right block of land at the right time. Take the case of Harry and Frank Sawyer, Spencer and Willie Page, and Grant Taylor. Soon after emigrating to Canada in the spring of 1882, the men met at Rideau Hall as guests of the Governor General, to whom each "had been sent by friends at home for guidance and instruction." Lorne, in turn, directed them to the Moose Mountain region of the North West Territories. [3]

Ottawa's role was crucial in facilitating prairie settlement. In an October 28 memorandum for Macdonald, Lorne detailed the responsibilities of the federal authorities: complete the Pacific railway with all possible haste; settle the Manitoba-Ontario boundary dispute without rancour; grant generous leases on federal lands for cattle ranching. [4]

Lorne's greatest fears concerned the Indians. To avoid potential conflict between native peoples and white newcomers in the prairie West, he passed on a number of specific suggestions to Macdonald: make legal grants of land to Metis families; survey all settled lands along the Saskatchewan and Bow rivers within a year; give all possible encouragement to Indians wishing to farm; establish an industrial school on each native reserve; strengthen the North West Mounted Police to improve monitoring of cross-border Indian movements. [5] Unfortunately most of the Governor General's advice, like that of many knowledgeable westerners, went unheeded. Important Metis and Indian grieveances remained unresolved, and the country drifted towards the North West Rebellion of 1885.

*****

Throughout 1881 newspapers on both sides of the Atlantic speculated on Lorne's forthcoming resignation as Governor General. It was alleged that "the Marquis does not find his relations with the Gladstone Ministry altogether harmonious." It was whispered that Queen Victoria, unwilling to let her daughter spend another winter in Ottawa, now demanded her son-in-law home at Louise's side. Spring and summer reports had Lorne resigning following his trip to the West; autumn despatches suggested he would leave after the close of the next session of Parliament, with either Lord Rosebery or Lord Elgin replacing him. [6]

The Toronto *Globe* regretted Lorne's supposed departure, fearing the public would conclude he had been a failure, "which would be an error." The Governor General "has done his duty and filled his position as well as any other person could have done." The London *Telegraph* singled out Lorne's "honesty of purpose in promoting the best interests of the Dominion" as the great secret of his success. That, plus hard work. "He has not hesitated to work night and day in order to bring Canada into as prosperous and happy a condition as could be desired by her warmest friends."[7]

Speclation continued as Lorne sailed from Quebec on November 5. Did the swearing in of Sir Patrick MacDougall as Administrator or acting Governor-General indicate vacation or resignation? Why had neither Rideau Hall nor London denied the rumours? What did the delay in naming a successor signify? The London (Ontario) *Advertiser*, a persistent opponent of the Governor General, remained convinced that Lorne would not return. "He has not been quite at ease in his office. He has found the moral temperature of the place neither pleasant nor invigorating."[8]

Politics aside, most Canadians were far more titillated by the soap opera aspects of the Lorne-and-Louise love story. The royal couple had been apart more than fifteen months since Louise sailed home in the summer of 1880. Now husband was returning to wife rather than wife to husband. Was it a voluntary trip or had Queen Victoria summoned him home for a face-to-face confrontation about her daughter's welfare? Would Louise be waiting for her husband at Liverpool?

The reunion in Liverpool harbour on November 14 was enough to inspire a Harlequin romance — at least in the eyes of the Toronto *Mail*'s British correspondent. Picture Louise on the tender *Stormcock* setting out from the docks to intercept the *Sarmatian* at the end of its Atlantic run. "Nearer and nearer came the tiny tender to the huge leviathan, and then the Marquis was picked out of the crowd on the latter, waving his handkerchief to his wife, as if his right arm was being worked by steam-power. Immediately afterwards he stepped off the *Sarmatian*'s deck, and the next moment — all the good wives of Canada will be glad to learn — he gave his better half a regular downright emphatic hug."[9]

Such a well-documented embrace helped dispel rumours of strained relations. The cheers of the Liverpool crowds as the couple drove from dockside to railway station harkened back to the old fairy-tale image of this royal pair. Their reunion destination of Eaton Hall, near Chester, home of Lorne's aunt and uncle, the Duke and Duchess of Westminster, seemed to signal all was well between Louise and her in-laws.

Eaton Hall was the first in a steady round of socializing with family and friends during Lorne's eight-week break from Ottawa. He and Louise visited the Gladstones at Hawarden Castle, stayed with the Duke of Argyll at Inverary, with the Prince and Princess of Wales, the Duke and Duchess of Edinburgh, with the Duke of Connaught and Prince Leopold, and of course with Queen Victoria. They seemed to make a good impression.

Following a luncheon at Hawarden, Mary Gladstone described Louise as "amiable and highly delighted", Lorne as "hearty and warm." [10]

Yet Louise and Lorne spent very little time alone together during this two month period. Only for a few days at Kensington Palace and at Claremont — their old honeymoon haunt — were they on their own. "Louise is still very weak," Lorne confided to his Aunt Emma, "and is good for nothing, but is slowly mending." [11]

During his weeks in Britain, Lorne's heart seemed closer to Canada than to Louise. "I have been running about seeing relatives ever since I came 'home'," — he put the word in quotation marks — "and now I shall have only a few days in London before sailing for my blessed Canada." After Canada, he found the dull, damp English winter "mysterious and unwholesome." He missed "the bright light and the dry and beautiful snow with its sapphire coloured shadows." [12]

\* \* \* \* \*

On 11 January 1882 Lorne sailed back to Canada without his wife. It was his own "particular desire" that Louise remain behind until she was "sufficiently recovered;" only by the "urgent representations" of her doctors had she agreed to stay in Britain. He hoped she would be able to join him at Ottawa in the spring. [13] Instead of his wife, the Governor General was accompanied by his sister and brother-in-law, Frances and Eustace Balfour; Frances would take Louise's place as official Rideau Hall chatelaine during the coming parliamentary season. "With Frances's red head to warm me," Lorne assured his Aunt Emma, he would "feel quite comfortable." [14]

The Atlantic in January brought grey skies and howling winds, unusually low temperatures, and thick ice inside the porthole windows of the S.S. *Parisian*. Frances and Eustace were "absolutely unable" to leave their berths. Lorne, however, seemed "quite happy, like a second David of ruddy countenance," returning to his blessed Canada. Bad weather followed the travellers on their train trip from Halifax to Ottawa. Heavy snows caused delays all along the line; temperatures plummeted to minus 30 degrees Celsius. To Frances, the cold was "truly awful." But the gallant Governor General was "intensely happy at being back again." [15]

The Balfour visit coincided with the longest parliamentary session since Confederation, stretching from February 9 to May 17. The onus of entertaining all and sundry continued to rest with the Governor General. Rideau Hall that winter and spring hosted two state balls, dinner parties every Tuesday and Thursday, toboggan parties Saturday afternoons, and special theatrical entertainments on Saturday nights. The entertainments, complained Frances, "come thick and fast." [16]

Rideau Hall in 1880s.

Meanwhile, to the Governor General's embarrassment, the 1882 session of parliament featured a series of resolutions supporting Irish Home Rule. Lorne agreed with Macdonald that the resolutions seemed "inoffensive", though he reminded the Prime Minister that Canadian politicians were too distant from the scene "to feel the patient's pulse."[17] He expressed greater annoyance in a letter to Gladstone. The Canadian Parliament was "meddling in Irish matters," the resolutions a "piece of folly" thrust on members anxious to "get the Irish vote." [18] Colonial Secretary Kimberley instructed Lorne that Britons were "not in any temper to be trifled with by anglers for Irish votes at elections for colonial Legislatures." [19] Once again, the Governor General was caught in the middle; he could not entirely please either his Canadian ministers or his British overseers.

With the Irish issue out of their system, Canada's parliamentarians ended their lengthy session on May 17 and prepared for a June 20 general election. There was little doubt about the result. Macdonald was able to link modest economic improvement with his protective tariff and stepped-up construction on the Pacific railway, and the Conservatives were swept back into office.

*  *  *  *  *

The prorogation of parliament may not have been foremost in Lorne's mind on May 17. That day also marked the wind-up of Oscar Wilde's thirty-six hour assault on the staid, provincial city of Ottawa — a day and a half of anguish for the Governor General.

Twenty-eight years old in the spring of 1882, Wilde was in the midst of a year-long North American lecture tour. Though his major writing lay in the future — his only published work to date was his 1881 *Poems* — Wilde's reputation as a flamboyant dresser and outrageous lecturer and his uninhibited lifestyle were well known on both sides of the Atlantic. While Wilde's biographers differ on whether he was yet a practising homosexual, all agree that his sexual predilections already had the gossips whispering.

Wilde looked forward to encountering Canada's handsome young Governor General. "Tomorrow night I lecture Lorne on dadoes at Ottawa," he wrote from Montreal on May 15. [20] Wilde was a close personal friend of Ronny Gower, and of Lorne's sister-in-law Janey Campbell. Clearly he expected to be honoured by the Governor General's attention.

On the evening of the 16th Wilde lectured on "The Decorative Arts" to an enthusiastic audience at Ottawa's Grand Opera House. During his stay in the city he met Prime Minister Macdonald, attended a House of Commons debate, and held court in his suite at the Russell House Hotel.

In a *Globe* interview he was brutally frank about Canadian art, wondering "what we have been doing here all the time," and expressing surprise that Princess Louise, "who was such an admirer of art, had not accomplished greater results." [21] Hope for the future lay with such young Canadian artists as Frances Richards, who "has already civilized the Marquis of Lorne." [22]

At least two Ottawa newspapers had announced that Wilde would be the overnight guest of the Governor General at Rideau Hall. Certain of Wilde's biographers assert that he did indeed stay at Government House. Wilde even gave his address as "Government House, Ottawa" when he signed Frances Richards's birthday book on the 16th. [23] After carefully studying the movements of both Wilde and Lorne on May 16 and 17, however, Wilde scholar Kevin O'Brien concludes that Wilde was not invited to Rideau Hall, nor did Lorne attend the evening lecture at the Grand Opera House. There is "no evidence for any connection between Lord Lorne and Wilde in the Ottawa visit." [24]

O'Brien views the snub as evidence that Wilde was not respected "by the upper orders" of British art and society. [25] A royal son-in-law could not act as host for the disreputable Wilde. Journalist and historian Sandra Gwyn sees the vice-regal snub as evidence of Lorne's homosexuality. "Already over his governor-generalship there hovered a whiff of heliotrope, a lingering scent of the green carnation." [26] Any contact with the seemingly gay Oscar Wilde would only have increased the whispering about Lorne's sexuality.

Certainly the male figure continued to attract Lorne's eye. Cadets at Royal Military College were "as strong as horses." Southwestern Ontario produced "bronzed and manly farmers." Competitors at a Dominion Rifle Association annual match were "fine soldierly fellows," the members of the Manitoba team "particularly good looking strapping fellows." [27] Lorne's writings are peppered with comments about attractive males; one searches in vain for similar remarks on the women he encountered in Canada.

Whether discretion or the avoidance of temptation, or both, it was best not to have anything to do with Oscar Wilde that spring in Ottawa. Instead of meeting the illustrious and notorious visitor, Lorne spent most of those two days playing golf with Francis De Winton.

\* \* \* \* \*

Cultural interests provided welcome relief from both Oscar Wilde and politics during the long drawn-out spring of 1882. The third annual exhibition of the Canadian Academy opened in Montreal on April 11. "All the beauty of Montreal there and many of the City Fathers. Some of the pictures excellent."

With the Academy now well launched, Lorne looked forward to the inaugural meeting on May 25 of the Society for the Encouragement of Science and Literature, soon rechristened the Royal Society of Canada, comprising the leading men in science and literature. The Royal Canadian Academy and the Royal Society, Lorne boasted, "are my 2 Canadian children." [28]

A year earlier, before leaving for the West, Lorne had proposed the establishment of a national academic organization combining the scientific thrust of the British Association and the literary bent of the French Academy. It would do for scholarship what the Canadian Academy had done for visual arts.

French Canada responded enthusiastically, but opposition arose from English-speaking Canada. Alpheus Todd fretted over different standards of excellence in English and French-Canadian writing. Goldwin Smith doubted whether Canada "had the material for even a respectable Academy," and believed the democratic North American environment would be hostile to such an elitist group. [29] The Toronto *Globe* dismissed the proposed organization as a "mutual admiration society of nincompoops," refusing to hold Lorne responsible for a "project so absurd." [30]

But the Governor General was responsible, and his 1881 western trip only strengthened his resolve. While travelling through southern Alberta Lorne had been disturbed to learn of an archaeological expedition from the Smithsonian Institute, collecting Indian relics on Canadian soil and carting them off to Washington. "These things are sure to happen until we have some such Association of our own," he wrote from Fort Macleod. "As soon as I get back to Ottawa, I am going to set about the founding of a Canadian Scientific and Literary Institute." [31]

In late October, he requested a government grant of $5000 to publish the proceedings of the first meeting of his proposed Society for the Encouragement of Science and Literature. In December a small organizing committee began work under Principal J.W. Dawson of McGill University. The Society would consist of four sections of twenty members each: French literature and history; English literature and history; mathematical, physical and chemical sciences; geological and biological sciences. Membership would be restricted to Canadian or Newfoundland residents who had published original works or memoirs "of merit".

Lorne asked Dawson to propose charter members on the science side, and Daniel Wilson of the University of Toronto the literary side. Wilson considered his task the more difficult. "I know not who to name," he wrote Dawson. "It is like making bricks not only without straw, but without clay. However I shall try and make out a list of the illustrious nobodies; the more insignificant they may be, the higher will be their delights when Honours are thrust upon them." [32]

Lorne was convinced "the best men in the country" accepted membership. Yet even more public controversy surrounded the naming of these initial Royal Society fellows than the selection for the Royal Canadian Academy. Critics argued that some of the more prominent writers and scholars had been omitted, and that some charter members in the English literature section were totally unworthy. "Some had published no original work," wrote one such critic, "while many were almost innocent of authorship of any character."[33] Nicholas Flood Davin launched the most savage attack in a pamphlet entitled *The Secretary of the Royal Society - A Literary Fraud*, a tract supposedly criticizing the literary pretensions of J.G. Bourinot, but pointedly dedicated to the Governor General!

Lorne outlined his long-range hopes at the Society's inaugural meeting in the Senate chamber on May 25. Even the Prime Minister had delayed his usual fast escape from Ottawa after the close of a parliamentary session to attend the event. Lorne spoke eloquently of parallels between the Society and the Royal Academy — repositories for permanent treasures as well as annual exhibitions of talent. While the Academy might some day give birth to a national painting gallery, the Royal Society could promote national collections in geology, archives, and "objects illustrating ethnology and all branches of natural history." [34] He was planting the seeds of the future National Museums of Canada, National Library of Canada, and Public Archives of Canada.

Within a year the federal government began an annual grant of $5000 for publication of the Society's transactions. These published papers provided Canada with a new and powerful medium for the distribution and exchange of scientific ideas. Year by year the Society's annual meetings attracted more and more attention. In later years other academic bodies representing single disciplines, like the Canadian Historical Association, began meeting at the same time and place as the Royal Society. Collectively these groups became known as the Learned Societies, and their annual meetings became a high point each spring in the academic year.

Lorne was proud of this second Canadian child. "The success of the institution," he wrote in 1893, "has certainly been greater than I anticipated, although I was hopeful enough." The following year he boasted of the Society's success in becoming a "record of Canadian intellectual activity and vision." He believed the Society and the Academy were part of a Canadian renaissance. "Just as in some war periods, so in the time when great enterprises like the C.P.R. were undertaken, adornment and elevation of thought is coincident with sterner effort." [35]

# CHAPTER FOURTEEN

# HALFWAY TO HEAVEN, 1882-1883

*T*he usual family occasions demanded Louise's presence during the early months of 1882 — lunches and dinners with the Queen; the christening of her niece Princess Margaret of Connaught in March; the wedding of her favourite brother Leopold to Princess Helen of Waldeck-Pyrmont in April. But Louise was seldom seen at formal court events; her strength, it was announced, would still not allow her to stand through long receptions and Drawing Rooms. Still she had enough energy to tour art exhibitions in the afternoons, dine with friends, and attend evening concerts and theatricals.

Louise was also actively seen promoting various schemes dear to her husband's heart. She became a patron of the Women's Emigration Society, where her name raised Canada's profile among intending emigrants. She met with William Spottiswoode to further Lorne's plans of having the British Association for the Advancement of Science meet in Canada in the near future to stimulate his own Royal Society. Some critics believed this was mere window dressing to mask underlying tensions between the couple; more likely, Louise was genuinely interested in her husband's activities.

Consider Lorne and Louise's joint contribution to *Good Words*. The 1882 edition of this annual fiction, travel and inspirational publication featured six of Louise's sketches under the title "Quebec: Pictures From My Portfolio". The drawings portrayed views of the St. Lawrence River from the heights of The Citadel; Lorne added the descriptive text and a lengthy poem "O Fortress City". [1]

And if Louise really did wish to distance herself from Lorne, she would not have spent so much time with her Campbell in-laws that spring. She presented her new mother-in-law, Amelia Anson, to the Queen, for the Duke of Argyll had recently remarried. She trooped off to Harrow for a school fair in the company of three of Lorne's sisters and his old admirer, Mary Gladstone. "Brilliant day and the arrival was delightful and exhilarating," noted Mary. [2]

Would Louise really return to Canada and her husband? The voyage had been delayed and postponed so many times that skeptics thought it would never take place. But in late May Louise finally sailed from Liverpool on board her old nemesis, the *Sarmatian*. This time the voyage was quite pleasant. Demonstrating her commitment to the new Women's Emigration Society, the Princess "conversed freely with the passengers", and "manifested considerable interest in the condition of the steerage passengers," visiting their quarters the first day out. [3]

All Quebec seemed on the streets to welcome her back on June 4. Forget her long absence; rejoice in her return. The mayor greeted her in a brief dockside ceremony; Louise replied in French. Despite a light rain shower, she and Lorne delighted the crowd by driving to The Citadel in an open carriage. Quebec would remain home for the Governor General and his wife for the remainder of the summer.

It was not unusual for the country's leaders to desert Ottawa during the heat of summer — the prime minister and most of his cabinet got away whenever possible. In addition, the well-protected Citadel offered Louise a safer place than Rideau Hall in a period of renewed Fenian threats. Newspaper despatches from Quebec reported that "Louise is closely guarded, there being a rumour that American Fenians intend to kidnap her." [4] Certainly the Queen, the Governor General and the British and Canadian governments took these threats seriously.

At the end of June Lorne informed Macdonald that he had received "a nasty Fenian warning" of an attempt against Louise, and "must take precautions as the devils are mad enough to try anything." The plotters supposedly left New York on June 12, masquerading as a fishing party, intent on kidnapping Louise on Canadian soil and holding her as hostage for the release of Fenian suspects under detention in Ireland. [5] Macdonald was as alarmed as Lorne. "These demons will stop at no atrocity and I don't think any risk should be run," he confided. "Both her Royal Highness and Your Excellency are exposed to the dangers of capture, and the consequences are so grave that no fear of being charged with over-caution or timidit, should prevent the most extensive precautions from being undertaken. '[6]

Still, while the Fenian scare may have provided an excuse to avoid Ottawa, it did not prevent Lorne and Louise from enjoying the delightful shops of Old Quebec, day trips into the surrounding countryside, or a fishing holiday on the Cascapedia. Nor did it interfere with their much more dangerous plan to travel by train across the United States at the end of the summer, bound for San Francisco and a vice-regal tour of British Columbia.

This Pacific coast trip attracted as much interest as Lorne's prairie trek the previous year. Because of the ever-present Fenian scare, Lorne reluctantly agreed to the presence of American security officials aboard the train. "I think these precautions necessary," De Winton informed Macdonald. "It will show that the matter of safety has not been neglected."[7]

Lorne and Louise left Quebec on August 30 and spent the first weekend of September at the Prospect House in Niagara Falls with painter friend Albert Bierstadt. Louise ordered her large painting case brought from the railway station and set up for sketching on the hotel balcony overlooking the waterfall. Lorne and the more vigorous members of the party "amused themselves by strolling about the grounds, clambering up the rugged foot-paths and discovering new vantage points of observation."[8]

The Niagara weekend set the tone for the entire trip, as Lorne and Louise meant to enjoy themselves. They moved on to Chicago, where the party took on generous supplies of Budweiser beer and Worcestershire sauce. They paid a surprise call on a Nebraska farmer while their rail coach laid by for an evening of sketching and strolling on the American prairie.

Louise almost experienced a repeat of her Ottawa sleighing accident as the train neared San Francisco on September 13. At Port Costa they were rammed by a yard engine and delayed fifty minutes. The occupants of the vice-regal car were "shaken up, crockery broken and parcels strewn about." Fortunately no one was injured. At the time of the collision Louise "was making her toilet, and was thrown down, but received no injury beyond the most trifling bruise."[9]

Still, the rail accident provided sufficient excuse for Louise to absent herself from formal receptions and presentations, and to enjoy San Francisco on her own terms. She and Lorne sampled Chinatown's exotic food and theatre; they took a boat trip around the bay; Lorne journeyed out to Menlo Park at the invitation of Leland Stanford. Everywhere they were treated as celebrities. They were "serenaded at the Palace Hotel by a very large crowd." Their eventual balcony appearance produced "loud and long continued cheers of welcome."[10]

The outside world refused to leave them alone. On September 18, shortly before they boarded HMS *Comus* for the sea voyage north to British Columbia, the ship's captain received an anonymous note threatening "the sloop would be blown up by a torpedo as soon as the vice-regal party stepped aboard."[11] A squad of American marines searched the vessel and found nothing, but for safety's sake an American revenue cutter accompanied *Comus* out of the harbour. Lorne found such incidents a constant worry, but by this time was accustomed to handling all manner of rumours and scares.

"The Fall of Niagara," watercolour by Princess Louise, September 1882.

The trip on the *Comus* proved quite pleasant, as "the Princess suffered very little from seasickness." Crew members remembered her "always making sketches;" one drawing of boatswain's mate Tom Mitten, in naval uniform with wide-brimmed straw hat, was later rendered in oils, and became a favourite of Louise's nephew, the future King George V. [12] After two pleasant days at sea, and without further incident, HMS *Comus* delivered Lorne and Louise to Victoria, British Columbia, on 20 September 1882.

\* \* \* \* \*

The British Columbia visit had both political and personal dimensions. Lorne had long observed the deteriorating relationship between Ottawa and Victoria over the slow progress on the Pacific railway, and believed a personal visit might soften British Columbia's criticism. At the same time an extended trip to the west coast would legitimately excuse Louise from Ottawa. "He will take her over to B.C. about October and stay there till Xmas so as to break the winter," De Winton had informed Macdonald in March. "This is very much private and I have only obtained it piecemeal for sometimes His Ex is most reticent about his plans." [13]

Victoria had previously welcomed a Governor General, when Dufferin paid his respects in 1876 — but never a Princess. Anticipation had been at fever pitch for several days prior to the arrival. "The town is full of strangers and more are arriving by every conveyance," reported the *Daily British Colonist* on September 19. "Every hotel is overrun with applications for quarters, and steamers at the wharves are berthing a large number. Victoria is en fete and has never before presented an appearance so lively."

The morning of the 20th dawned hazy with a threat of rain, but soon "the mist rolled away and before ten o'clock the sun shone in splendor from a bright autumnal sky" — Queen's weather for the Queen's daughter! At eleven o'clock Lorne and Louise steeped ashore at the Esquimalt navy dock, entered their horse-drawn carriage, and crossed Point Ellis Bridge for their triumphal entry into Victoria. The city was mad with bunting and banners and flags, with welcome arches and other "hideous monstrosities" to honour the vice-regal pair. Lorne informed the mayor that the reception was "the best he had ever been recorded." Everything pointed to a happy and successful visit. [14]

Cary Castle, residence of the provincial lieutenant governor, served as home for the Lornes and their large retinue of aides and servants. Lieutenant Governor C.F. Cornwall proved a perfect host. Son of a Gloucestershire rector, graduate of Trinity College Cambridge, successful barrister, Cornwall had succumbed to gold rush fever twenty years earlier and made a new life for himself in British Columbia. Louise and

Welcome Arch at Government House (Cary Castle), Victoria, BC, 1882.

Lorne delighted in his combination of old world urbanity and new world informality.

On their first full day ashore, Thursday September 21, Lorne inspected the Esquimalt dry dock while Louise "began to employ her pencil in depicting the scenery from Government House." Next afternoon the carefree couple were seen "strolling along Government Street, where they visited several stores." The following days brought a heady round of parties and receptions, luncheons and dinners, visits and speeches. After a Government House garden party on the 26th, the *Daily British Colonist* remarked that the couple were "winning all hearts by their affability and kindness and the interest they manifest in all that concerns the people." [15]

But there was more to British Columbia than the city of Victoria, and Lorne was determined to see as much of the province as possible. On Friday the 29th he and Louise sailed to New Westminster, former capital of the once-separate mainland colony. Here they encountered more of the west coast's famous arches — this time with inscriptions in English, German, Chinese, and the local Chinook jargon — and met the usual aglomoration of local digniteries and Indian chiefs. Once again, "their kindness and affability ensnared all hearts." [16]

Sending his wife back to the comforts of Victoria, Lorne then embarked on a three-week, 1600-kilometre expedition through British Columbia. It was part fun and adventure for the lifelong traveller, but it was also serious vice-regal work. Like his prairie trek the previous year, Lorne's trip into the interior was designed to generate favourable publicity for the province and for the Canadian Pacific Railway.

The journey took the vice-regal party up the Fraser and Thompson rivers to Lake Shuswap and Lake Okanagan — just 300 kilometres west of the spot Lorne reached on the east side of the Rocky Mountains the previous year. At Yale he inspected railway construction progress with CPR engineer Andrew Onderdonk. At Drynoch near Spence's Bridge, he partook of a humble chicken dinner in the crude cottage of the resident construction boss. At Kamloops the party drove to a hilltop behind the town where "His Excellency took a sketch in water colours," expressing himself as "highly delighted with the scenery." [17] At O'Keefe's Ranch on Lake Okanagan, he drew out local settlers on the area's development possibilities.

Hearing that the Governor General was at O'Keefe's, Donald Graham and a friend saddled their horses and rode eleven kilometres to meet him. "He was outside when we arrived and sat on the end of a log talking to us. He shook hands cordially and was very frank and free in his conversation, which made it easy for us to talk to him. He questioned us as to what acreage of land we possessed, number of livestock, also how we liked the country and what we thought of its prospects." [18]

This episode was typical of the trip. "His Excellency cross-questioned anyone and everyone who could furnish him with information concerning the capabilities, prosperity and general state of the country," De Winton informed Macdonald. [19] These conversations were recorded and despatched to eastern newspapers. As always, Lorne saw the value of publicity in attracting settlement. For the immediate future, Lorne recommended a speedy completion of the railway, improved stage coach and telegraph routes through the mountains, and assistance to help the Indians cope with increased white settlement.

While in the interior he received a telegram from CPR Vice-President William Van Horne, with the exciting news that the long-sought pass through the Selkirk Range had at last been found. But all this did was remind Lorne of the split between Vancouver Island and the mainland. Van Horne's news might please the mainlanders, Premier Robert Beaven informed the Governor General, but there would be no permanent peace until Ottawa committed itself to an island line between Esquimalt and Nanaimo as an integral part of the Pacific railway scheme.

Stopping at the tiny settlement of Granville — the future Vancouver — on his return trip, Lorne was shown around the thriving lumbering operations and witnessed a huge tree cut down in his honour. It was also planned to fell a giant fir for Louise, but at Lorne's request it was allowed to stand; this was the famous "Princess Louise tree" which stood in magnificent isolation along the Vancouver waterfront until 1887. Just before leaving the townsite, Lorne encountered a colorful local character, William "Protestant Bill" Macdonald. "Your family and mine have been at odds since Glencoe," Macdonald told the Campbell heir, "but come have a drink with me and we will call it square." They adjourned to the nearest bar where Lorne set up drinks for the assembled crowd. [20]

In the meantime Louise had spent three weeks delighting Victorians with "the graceful, unaffected mien of her movements, and her smile and warmth." She took a picnic lunch to a cricket match in Beacon Hill Park. She talked with all and sundry on her daily shopping rounds. She dropped in unannounced at various public functions. The only dissenting note in the chorus of good will seems to have been that of a small boy who, when asked by his mother if he had seen the Princess Louise, replied, "Yes, but she's only a woman; I thought she was a steamboat!" [21]

Back from his interior tour on October 21, Lorne joined Louise for another six weeks of pleasure in the capital. Apart from a civic banquet, a St. Andrews Society dinner, and a grand ball at the Philharmonic Hall, most of their remaining time was unstructured. So they enjoyed themselves and their adopted city. No one asked when they planned to leave; perhaps they might stay forever. Lorne's popularity was enhanced by his "remarkable affability and painstaking efforts to obtain every possible information with regard to the wants and resources of the country." Louise

Princess Louise's tree, Vancouver waterfront.

too. "By her unostentatious manner, her kindly, courteous and amiable disposition," she "won for herself the lasting esteem of the community."[22]

The British Columbia sojourn saw Louise at her absolute public best, as the warm, moist air, the pleasant surroundings, and the informal nature of public life prevented any outbreaks of nervous disorder. Describing Cary Castle as "halfway between heaven and Balmoral," [23] Louise settled in for her happiest three months in Canada. Here she produced work that rivalled her Cascapedia River scenes. Both "Victoria, B.C.," an oil on canvas of the view across the Strait of Juan de Fuca from Cary Castle, and a watercolour entitled "Lawn Tennis Ground in the Garden, Government House, Victoria," show an openness of vista and an enthusiastic relationship with her new surroundings. [24]

Louise loved the climate — "softer and more constant than that of the south of England," claimed Lorne, which ensured "at all times of the year a full enjoyment of the wonderful loveliness of nature around you." De Winton agreed. "The Princess seems to enjoy the climate," he informed Macdonald. So why not take advantage of the situation? "I think of staying here a month longer as I find the climate and surroundings of this place suit the Princess very well," Lorne wrote Macdonald on October 24. "Nothing can be pleasanter for those who prefer soft weather to the dry air of the East." [25]

Between formal dinners and garden parties and receptions at Government House, Louise visited everything from the usual schools and hospitals to an unlikely local brewery. Victorians grew accustomed to her black shawl and bonnet over her black-figured silk dress — black was her favourite colour that autumn — on her daily shopping excursions along Government Street. Storekeepers proudly announced her patronage. Premier Beaven half-seriously proposed she become Queen of Vancouver Island! [26]

Lorne enjoyed the scenery as much as the climate. He had never seen a more magnificent country than British Columbia — "more majestic than Switzerland, more fertile than Italy, more picturesque an island scenery than the Hebrides, more glorious in its forests than any of the Old-World countries." Back in Victoria, the view of Mount Olympus across the Strait of Juan de Fuca was as spectacular as anything in the interior. "I used to say it was a mixture of Scotland and heaven," he wrote in later years, and "I have seen nothing since 1883 to qualify that description." [27]

For once in Lorne and Louise's Canadian experience, everything exceeded expectations. The vice-regal couple arranged their itinerary to allow each other considerable freedom. Lorne indulged his travel interests with his trek into the interior; Louise stayed behind at Cary Castle and painted away the days. As a result, both husband and wife remained in good spirits, and fell in love with the Pacific province. British Columbians reciprocated with a mad infatuation for their Governor General and their Princess. The planned three week official visit stretched into a pleasant sojourn of almost three months. Not till December 7 did the party leave Victoria on HMS *Comus*.

"The visit of His. Ex. & Princess to B.C. was well worth the money," De Winton informed Macdonald, "for you won't have any trouble either there or from the home govt. for the next three years." [28] Lorne had persuaded Victoria of Ottawa's sincerity regarding the railway question and had "dampened down separatism." [29] Macdonald hardly needed to be reminded. "I have been watching with keen interest the accounts of your progress," he wrote Lorne. "The press here are loud in their expressions of gratitude for what you are doing for Canada." [30]

* * * * *

Planning for the trip back from British Columbia had been left deliberately vague. "No plans have yet been decided for our return," De Winton informed Macdonald in August. "My private idea is that they will have had enough of travel by that time and will be longing for the comforts of home, and so we shall find ourselves at Ottawa." But not immediately and not directly. In October De Winton wrote again. "As far as I can see His Ex's intention is to return via the Southern Pacific [Railroad] and visit New Orleans and some of the larger cities of the United States with the Princess." Such extended travel alarmed De Winton, who was most "anxious about Irish movements." [31]

When the vice-regal party finally sailed from Victoria on December 7, De Winton's worst fears were realized. There would be no speedy return to Ottawa. The couple would take a private holiday in California, before embarking on a leisurely rail trip across the United States. At Charleston, South Carolina they planned to separate. Lorne would visit Washington on his way to Ottawa in January — altogether, a seven month absence from the capital. Louise, meanwhile, would cause further annoyance and gossip by travelling on to Bermuda for three more months of holidays. When she finally set foot in Ottawa in April 1883, it was after an absence of nearly three years.

The California holiday of December 1882 continued to bring out the best in Lorne and Louise. A San Francisco journalist observed that Louise "seemed in better health than when she arrived here early in the autumn."[32] She and her husband explored the city's shops by day and spent their evenings listening to Christine Nilsson at the Grand Opera House. From San Francisco they took the train to Monterey, spurned any official greeting, and walked the four blocks from the station to the Hotel del Monte.

The first night in Monterey was party night. "The Princess was the most affable of the party," ran a gossipy press account. "Her laugh resounded through the corridors, and it was evident that she led in the conversation and joking." Louise and a lady-in-waiting sat down at a piano, failed to whip up enthusiasm for a dance, then settled on some vocal duets, "with indifferent success." In the meantime, "the Marquis had retired to his rooms," so Louise and aide-de-camp Jocelyn Bagot "inspected the billiard tables, and evidently passed a pleasant quarter of an hour rolling the ivory balls around." [33]

They moved on to Santa Barbara, where Christmas day festivities featured an exhibition of skill by Mexican horsemen in front of their hotel. Southern California gave Lorne and Louise all the pleasures of British Columbia with none of the obligations. Both the climate and the Spanish culture were reminiscent of the Mediterranean. Long sandy beaches and quiet dusty towns provided ample time and pleasant vistas for sketching and strolling. "Santa Barbara, California," and "Garden of the Hotel at Monterey, California" are two particularly delightful watercolours rendered by Louise during their stay. [34]

Reluctantly they boarded the Southern Pacific Railroad on January 6 for the return trip east. A detachment of United States army troops offered protection against Fenian threats and the possibility of being "robbed by desperadoes." Still, they were in no hurry, taking time to visit orange groves in Arizona, inspect the pueblo culture of the New Mexican Indians, and chat with a "pleasant governor of Missouri." On through St. Louis and Cincinnati to Lorne's "dear old Virginia" of 1866 memories. They reached Charleston on January 19, "a little battered after their long journey." [35] Here they rested for a few days, confirmed their separate winter plans, and said their goodbyes.

Lorne headed north for "an interesting three days" in Washington. Seventeen years after his youthful visit of 1866, he returned as Governor General of Canada. Congress treated him to a reception, General Sherman gave a private dinner party, and President Chester Arthur a state dinner at the White House. The highlight was a grand ball at the British Embassy, hosted by Ambassador Lionel Sackville-West and his daughter Lady Victoria Sackville — the capital's exciting twenty-one year-old hostess.

Dancing began at 10 o'clock for the lucky 400 guests, broke for supper at midnight, and continued long into the morning hours. Lorne, who reportedly "enjoyed this keenly," [36] lead off the first quadrille with the wife of the Swedish ambassador, waltzed with the beautiful Lady Victoria, and threw himself into the less formal Virginia reels that ended the evening. But why was his wife not with him? Official Washington was polite enough not to mention the missing Louise. But the whispers and rumours continued. The Associated Press quoted an unnamed embassy attaché who confirmed that a "disagreement" between Lorne and Louise "was the true cause of their separation." [37]

Meanwhile, on the morning of January 25 Louise and her party of two ladies-in-waiting, two maids, and Captain Jocelyn Bagot as aide-de-camp, sailed from Charleston on HMS *Dido* for Bermuda. The colony was in a "state of delightful uncertainty." For security reasons, neither the arrival date nor the visit itself had been officially announced, but there were few secrets on the tiny island. The town of Hamilton prepared for its royal visitor by trimming trees, erecting flag poles and paving its streets. "Nearly every resident," reported a local correspondent, "is whitewashing his house and putting a fresh coat of green paint on his jalousie blinds."[38]

Louise sailed into Hamilton harbour on January 29, where she was lustily greeted by a crowd of 3,000 flag-waving Bermudians, and subjected to the usual boring addresses of welcome. "Arrived Monday," Louise cabled Lorne five days later. "Good passage. Very kind reception. Trust you got home all right." Then she added, no doubt for political reasons: "Remember me to Sir John, Lady Macdonald and all at Ottawa."[39] Her duties to her husband and to Ottawa and Bermuda officials fulfilled, Louise settled in for three months of self-indulgence.

Home was the hillside estate of Inglewood, rented from J.H. Trimingham, a member of the Bermuda Legislative Council. Ingelwood was a short distance outside Hamilton, on a high piece of land giving views of both the harbour and the south coast of the island. Here Louise executed one of her most spacious and opening-out watercolours, "Hamilton Harbour, Bermuda, from Inglewood House." [40]

After its initial welcoming euphoria, the Bermuda public left its royal visitor alone, taking notice only when a minor fire caused some smoke and water damage at Ingelwood, and when Louise's visit to the old capital of St. George's was spoiled by the stench of rotting fish on a welcoming arch. Otherwise, she was free to hike, to sketch, and to paint with hardly an official care in the world. She could drive out in her carriage, shop the stores of Hamilton town, walk to nearby St. Paul's Church — all without fuss and bother.

Louise's decision to winter in Bermuda "caused great disappointment here," reported the New York *Times* from the Canadian capital. Ottawa residents "do not conceal their chagrin at the turn affairs have taken." The real reason for Louise's absence, speculated the *Times*, was "the repugnance" Louise entertained towards Agnes Macdonald, who "threatened" the Princess by seeking "to rule in society as her husband does in politics."[41] Lady Macdonald was so upset at the rumour that Sir John wrote De Winton to express her concern. Soon he had a reply from the Princess herself — not completely denying the reported rift, but merely expressing annoyance "that such stories should have been circulated." [42]

Official pronouncements stressed Louise's health, and the need to avoid "the icy north" in January and February. "Ottawa does not suit her in winter," Lorne told the British admiral responsible for her passage to Bermuda. [43] Louise "desired to return to Canada," but "on the advice of a London physician, and by the express command of Her Majesty," went to Bermuda instead. [44] At the end of the stay, Lorne informed Governor Galloway of Bermuda that Louise derived "much benefit from the rest and quiet secured to her." [45]

The continuing Fenian threat may also have been a factor. Though Lorne "had to send two good detectives" to Bermuda, he still felt "quite free of anxiety about L. there, as no one can move on the Islands without being watched." [46] Canada was a different matter, as Fenian rumours abounded through the spring of 1883 — suspicious looking characters around Government House, plots to dynamite the Welland Canal in the Niagara Peninsula and public buildings in Halifax.

Fenian threats proved serious enough to throw a heavy blanket of security over Louise's return from Bermuda on HMS *Tenedos* in April. "The Princess will land at Newport [Rhode Island] but this is not to be known," Lorne informed Macdonald. "I shall designate Portland as the probable place." [47] In the end, Lorne staked himself out in Boston, while Louise docked at Newport virtually unnoticed on April 15.

Louise looked "hearty and well" and "as brown as a berry," with a face "as bright and happy as a schoolgirl." [48] The reunited couple spent twenty-four hours in Boston — not alone, but with Albert Bierstadt there to humour them and guide them on a tour of local artists' studios. On the evening of the 16th they left by overnight train for Ottawa. Security at the capital was heavier than ever, but no unusual incidents were reported. Princess Louise was safely back in the city she detested.

# ❧ CHAPTER FIFTEEN
# AN ENTHUSIASTIC CANADIAN, 1883-1884

*L* ouise would not have to spend too much time in her least favourite city, as she and her husband soon would be going home permanently. "My term is up in November," Lorne informed Prime Minister Macdonald on April 10, "and although I should like to stay here all my days it will not be possible for me to stay longer. It is all for the interests of this country to have a change in five years." [1]

Lorne's resignation surprised the Earl of Derby, the new Colonial Secretary in the Gladstone administration. "Our usual term is six, not five years," Derby cabled Ottawa. But Lorne was adamant: both the good of the country and the future of his marriage demanded that he and Louise return to Britain as soon as politically and diplomatically appropriate. Derby acquiesced. "After this clear expression of your wishes and feelings, I should not think myself justified in pressing upon you a longer stay." [2]

Lorne coasted through his last few months in office. The political scene was stable with Macdonald's convincing triumph in the previous year's election; the economy was on the upswing and the Pacific railway nearing completion; Ottawa finally pacified British Columbia by agreeing to build the Vancouver Island rail line. Details of daily administration needed some attention, and relations between Ottawa and London claimed some time. But there would be no new policy initiatives, no more grand schemes to elevate Canada's cultural life.

With Louise's return to Ottawa in mid-April — well after the end of the parliamentary session — husband and wife avoided the irritating problems of politics and enjoyed visits from various friends. Spring and summer 1883 saw a constant flow of guests through Rideau Hall. The Sackville-Wests, father and daughter, came up from Washington. They were followed by George and Marie von Bunsen, son and granddaughter of the Prussian diplomat once such a good friend of Lorne's parents. Painter Albert Bierstadt paid two visits. Finally Prince George of Wales, then a young naval officer and later King George V, spent time ashore with his Aunt Louise and Uncle Lorne in both Ottawa and Quebec City.

Marie von Bunsen provides a good picture of the couple that spring. Lorne struck her as "a fair, cheery man, not a personality, but keen, and with many interests." Louise seemed "even shier than most of the Queen's daughters, although most likeable." Marie enjoyed the informal atmosphere of Rideau Hall, "where etiquette was whittled down to a minimum," but wondered whether Louise suffered from playing "second fiddle on every occasion" to her Governor General husband. [3]

Albert Bierstadt thought everything in good order at Ottawa. Louise was "not only a clever artist but a charming woman in every way." Lorne was "a right good fellow and takes care of Canada." During a March visit with just Lorne, Bierstadt had enjoyed the large formal dinners and the skating parties. Now, in May, he loved the picnics and sketching expeditions with both of them. "Everything is very free and easy," he noted. [4]

The final months provided one last exercise of the routines Lorne had built into his Canadian life — summer residence at Quebec, fishing on the Cascapedia, a shooting holiday at Long Point on Lake Erie — "there was never such a paradise for ducks" — and a final round of visits and speeches through the Canadian autumn countryside. In Toronto he opened the annual Exhibition and proclaimed himself "so enthusiastic a Canadian." In Montreal he suggested official residences for Supreme Court justices and cabinet ministers, comparable to Paris and Berlin, "in a manner suited to the dignity of this nation." [5] In Ottawa he called for a civic beautification program of public parks and broad, tree-lined avenues — an early plea for a kind of National Capital Commission. "The parting from the Ottawa people was a great trial for me," he confided to Macdonald. [6]

Lorne summed up his Canadian sojourn in a farewell address to members of the Senate and House of Commons, at a time when "the happiest five years I have ever known are nearly spent." It had been his good fortune to serve as Governor General during a period in which "all domestic discord has been avoided, our friendship with the great neighbouring republic has been sustained, an uninterrupted prosperity has marked the advance of the Dominion," and Canada and Britain stood "side by side, working for the commercial advancement of each other." He concluded by asserting that it would be "my pride and duty to aid you in the future to the utmost of my power." [7]

Macdonald was sorry to see Lorne leave. The young marquis had brought good luck — an expanding economy, a revitalized Pacific railway company, the High Commissioner's Office in London, good times for the country and its government. Everything had gone well for the prime minister and his Conservative party. And now Lorne and his wife were departing. "We are all unaffectedly sorry to part with you," Macdonald wrote as the vice-regal party left Ottawa for Quebec. "Even the apathetic Ottawa people were stirred to the depths." [8]

It ended in Quebec City on October 27. At 10.00 a.m. the Governor General and Princess Louise left The Citadel by carriage. They were accompanied by Major De Winton and Major Collins, equerry to Louise, and escorted by twenty officers and men of the Queen's Own Canadian Hussars. The carriage headed down into Lower Town, towards the Allan steamship wharf where the *Sardinian* awaited. Despite drizzling rain, large crowds lined the streets; hundreds more crammed Dufferin Terrace and other vantage points overlooking the river. They cheered as their fair-haired Scot and his storybook princess drove by.

Alighting from their carriage at dockside, Lorne and Louise shook hands with the clutch of civic, provincial and federal officials gathered for the final leave-taking. His Ex and the Princess strode up the gangway. The *Sardinian* loosed her moorings, and amid the booming of the royal salute from The Citadel guns and the cheers of thousands who crowded the wharves and terraces, steamed down the river.

On their way from The Citadel to the docks, the vice-regal couple had passed under banners proclaiming "Revenez Encore" and "Come Back Again". But it was an unwritten rule that former Governors General never returned, lest they cause their successors embarrassment. Lorne would never see his beloved Canada again.

\* \* \* \* \*

How successful a Governor General had he been, this young Marquis of Lorne, still in his thirties when he ended his term? Despite minor irritations, Canada was not a burden on the Colonial Office, and Lorne — despite the fuss over the Letellier affair and the Irish Home Rule resolutions — had done his part to further that tradition. "If the rest of the Empire gave as little trouble as Canada, C.O. would have an easy time," Lord Derby noted. "Your departure is much regretted by all who take an interest in the colony." [9]

After just six months in Canada, Lorne was already quite realistic about the extent of his actual power. At Kingston's Queen's University in the spring of 1879, he referred to his position as that of a "political doctor," since "whatever prescriptions I give must be such that they can hardly be visible to or appreciated by the public. They must be written in invisible ink." Drawing gales of laughter from his appreciative audience, Lorne summed it up as "a peculiar position, and one which is totally incomprehensible to foreign doctors." [10]

The Governor General might charm the crowds from the Atlantic to the Pacific. He might speak in English or French, even Gaelic or German. He might promote national cultural movements. But "the topics on which a Governor general may speak without offence are limited," he told the Toronto Club in the fall of 1879. [11]

One of Lorne's major problems was measuring up to his predecessor. Without doubt, Dufferin was the most capable and most popular Governor General in late nineteenth century Canada. Dufferin was older and more experienced in politics and diplomacy than Lorne. By sheer force of personality, Dufferin was able to overshadow his dour and inexperienced prime minister of the 1870s, Alexander Mackenzie. Lorne, however, had to deal with the more ebullient, craftier, and above all more experienced John A. Macdonald.

Journalist J.E. Collins believed the "pernicious regard for Lord Dufferin" lay at the root of Lorne's popularity problem. Unlike Dufferin, Lorne was not naturally given to a lot of blarney and huge doses of personal flattery in public. He treated people "according to his inclination, and in deference to what he believed to be his duty." [12] But the public, it seemed, preferred flattery to straight-shooting!

The public was also disappointed that Princess Louise was not another Lady Dufferin, content to play a strong supporting role to her husband's star billing. Louise was simply out of her element in a cold and somewhat egalitarian capital like Ottawa. A princess raised in the rigid etiquette of a strict European court, and accustomed to the automatic adulation of the British public, noted *Truth*, was "as much out of place in a distant colony as a reindeer would be in central Africa or a camel in St. Petersburg." [13] Louise's problems began when she showed her irritation at the pretensions of Ottawa's social leaders. Senators and their wives — a snobbish, self-important, but totally inconsequential colonial political aristocracy — failed to impress her.

Writers familiar with the Ottawa scene believe Louise "took a deep interest in the welfare of our people," and that "in doing her duty in art and education she always seemed to be happy." After that, the line was firmly drawn. "The gnarled old pines that towered through the wintry weather about the Rideau Hall grounds were very much dearer to her than the most pompous Senator in his seal coat." She preferred mosquitoes on the Cascapedia to buffoons in Ottawa! [14]

Lorne's administration did not live up to expectations in promoting a closer link between Canada and the British crown. The Queen's own daughter seemed to let the side down. Princess Louise turned her back on Ottawa, and spent very little time there after the first year. Even if Louise had been an accommodating, full-time chatelaine at Rideau hall, there is no guarantee that Canadians would have fully embraced the idea of a vice-regal court. After their initial euphoria, most Canadians soon fell back on more egalitarian North American ways, declaring theirs was a country in which social and aristocratic distinction did not count.

What, then, had the country accomplished during Lorne's administration? "The most important development," he confided to his successor, Lord Lansdowne, "has been the appointment of a High Commissioner to England." The step signified Canada's growing status within the Empire and demonstrated the continuing vitality of that Empire. "As long as we back Canada's representatives," Lorne cautioned, "the small independence party will never have much vitality." [15]

The high commissionership was certainly important, but the main concern on Lorne's mind as he left the country in October 1883 was the Canadian Pacific Railway. In his final letter as Governor General, written aboard the *Sardinian* as it prepared to weigh anchor at Quebec, he implored Macdonald: "That railway must be backed. Any failure to do so would be disastrous to all Canada." [16]

Like Dufferin before him, Lorne had taken every opportunity to use his office to promote Canada at home and abroad. He visited every province and the North West Territories, carrying the message of national unity wherever he went. His speeches and writings, his sketches and paintings, proclaimed the natural beauty and the tremendous economic potential of the country. "None could have been more enthusiastic Canadians," concludes one vice-regal observer, than Lorne and his predecessor. "It is doubtful whether the first wave of national feeling that swept the country in the seventies and eighties could have gained momentum without their influence behind it." [17]

Through his two "Canadian children" — the Royal Canadian Academy and the Royal Society — Lorne did more than any nineteenth century Governor General to stimulate national movements in the arts and learning. He hoped Lansdowne would continue vice-regal support for both bodies. "Besides the actual good accomplished by these institutions," he told his successor, "in a country like Canada where people are scattered, they form a national centre and rallying point for men interested in Art, Science and Literature." This was extremely important. "What is wanted in this land is moral glue, to get men to stick together. The climate has the effect of loosening and drying up all things glued together, and these societies counteract to a certain extent the same tendency in other than physical things." [18]

Lorne and Louise also left behind their names to grace the Canadian landscape. In the West the Princess gave the first of her Christian names to that most beautiful of lakes in the Canadian Rockies, Lake Louise, and her third name to the province of Alberta. Though Macdonald balked at "Louiseland", Lorne's initial suggestion for one of the new districts carved in 1882 out of the North West Territories, the prime minister happily accepted "Alberta". Lorne considered this most appropriate, since the Princess, "in inheriting her father's name, has desired to fulfil his wishes in being of use to this portion of the Empire." [19]

## ON THE NEW PROVINCE "ALBERTA"

*In token of the love which thou hast shown*
*For this wide land of freedom, I have named*
*A province vast, and for its beauty famed.*
*By thy dear name to be hereafter known.*
*Alberta shall it be! Her fountains thrown*
*From alps unto three oceans, to all men*
*Shall vaunt her loveliness e'en now; and when*
*Each little hamlet to a city grown,*
*And numberless as blades of prairie grass,*

*Or thick leaves in distant forest bower,*
*Great peoples hear the giant currents pass,*
*Shall still the waters, bringing wealth and power,*
*Speak the loved name, the land of silver-springs,*
*Worthy the daughter of our English kings.* [20]

In the East the city of London, Ontario, like many Canadian communities, christened one of its streets Lorne Avenue and sent successive generations of children to Lorne Avenue Public School. The Lake Ontario shoreline west of Toronto boasted a summer cottage and recreation community called Lorne Park; for two decades its central feature was the Hotel Louise. And for several generations throughout English-speaking Canada, mothers chose "Lorne" and "Louise" as favourite names for their new babies. No other country has produced so many men bearing the Christian name Lorne.

\* \* \* \* \*

"London looks very bleak and dismal," Lorne wrote Macdonald from his study at Kensington Palace on November 7, two days after arriving home. He missed Canada. "I wish I were still able to back you in your spirited policy." [21] Lorne need not have worried; for the rest of his life he was frequently called on to back Canadian interests. Charles Tupper, Canada's High Commissioner in London after Galt left, sought his advice on both policy and tactical matters; cabinet ministers requested his support in raising money for the National Gallery; lesser political lights begged letters of introduction as they embarked on trips to the Old Country.

Sculptured bust of Lorne by Henrietta Montalba.

The former Governor General kept up a sporadic correspondence with Macdonald on the Pacific Railway, Canadian-American relations, and Ottawa political life. When Macdonald visited Britain in the fall of 1884, Lorne arranged a reception at Windsor Castle and presided at an Empire Club dinner in the Canadian prime minister's honour. "No one, except a foreign potentate," Lorne whispered to Tupper, "had ever had such a reception." [22] Lorne himself deserved most of the credit. "What a good and true Canadian he is," exclaimed George Stephen, president of the Canadian Pacific Railway. [23]

But Lorne was not content merely to grease the wheels for Tupper and Macdonald. Within days of his return to Britain in 1883 he arranged a series of public addresses "to talk the advantages of Canada into the hearts of the city people" in hopes of sending "over a few newcomers in the spring." [24]

In his first Canada speech at Birmingham on December 4, Lorne took his audience on an imaginary trip across the vast country, complete with graphic descriptions of the natural scenery, "praising the salubrity of the climate," and "lauding Canada as a field for emigrants." [25] On December 18 and 19 he gave the same talk in Glasgow and in London. Finally he presented the Royal Colonial Institute with a more formal address on "Our Relations With Canada and Other Great Colonies."

"We have had very satisfactory outings at Glasgow, Birmingham and London," Lorne wrote Macdonald just before Christmas. Personally, he "found it a great refreshment in the middle of London gloom to talk of Canada." The response was encouraging. Even the ultra Liberal newspapers, despite their "No Emigration" policy, spoke of Canada "in a very kind spirit." Of course Canada had to pull its weight. "People seem to connect the recent progress of the country with the opening up by rail of the West," he informed Macdonald, "and I do hope the government will stand firmly at the back of the CPR." [26]

Lorne's speeches were "capitally reported" in the Canadian press, wrote Lansdowne from Rideau Hall. Tupper was "wildly enthusiastic." Hector Langevin, Minister for Public Works, was certain the talks would have a "beneficial effect" in diverting immigrants towards Canada. All agreed it was fine to have Governors General saying nice things while in office, but quite a "new thing to find one making speeches for us after his term has expired." [27]

These addresses were merely the first round in Lorne's public relations campaign for Canada — and his desire to keep his name and his political views before the British public. Round two consisted of a spate of articles in leading magazines, averaging about one a year over the next two decades. The initial article, "Canadian Home Rule," appeared in the November 1883 issue of *Contemporary Review*, coincident with Lorne's return home; it argued that Canada's federal system provided a model for a system of provincial rather than national Home Rule in Ireland.

Subsequent articles continued this perspective on Imperial affairs informed by Canadian experience. "The Unity of the Empire" in *Nineteenth Century*, March 1885, argued that Imperial Federation schemes must satisfy colonial as well as British interests, which were not always identical. "The Saskatchewan Scare" in *Fortnightly Review*, June 1885, assured prospective emigrants that Ottawa had successfully quelled the Riel Rebellion. "The Canadian Fisheries Dispute" in the March 1887 *Fortnightly Review* argued that good Anglo-American relations had to be balanced against Canada's own economic interests. "Obstacles to Annexation" in the February 1889 *Forum* countered Goldwin Smith's view that Canadian absorption into the United States would benefit Britain.

While his December 1883 speeches had but momentary impact, and his journal articles reached a limited academic audience, Lorne's popular writings of the mid-1880s had a more lasting effect on a much wider audience. Relieved of day-to-day administrative and ceremonial responsibilities for the first time in five years, Lorne was able to re-engage the literary and creative side of his mind. Four books, an important tourist pamphlet, and contributions to at least two other books poured from his pen over the next three years.

*Memories of Canada and Scotland: Speeches and Verses* was published in 1884 by Dawson Brothers of Montreal. Next year produced *Imperial Federation* from Swan Sonnenschein of London, and *Canadian Pictures Drawn With Pen and Pencil* from the Religious Tract Society. In 1886 came an abbreviated version of *Canadian Pictures* entitled *Canadian Life and Scenery, With Hints to Intending Emigrants and Settlers*; the first of the Canadian Pacific Railway's hundreds of promotional pamphlets, *Our Railway to the Pacific*; and an introductory chapter in M.G. Bixby's *Industries of Canada*. In 1887 Lorne re-worked *Our Railway to the Pacific* into a chapter for W.C. Proctor's *Round the Globe Through Greater Britain*.

These writings celebrate the Canadian landscape and its peoples in verse, descriptive prose and pictorial illustration. *Memories of Canada and Scotland* contains verses that take the reader across the country from Quebec in the east:

> O fortress city, bathed by streams
> Majestic as thy memories great . . . .

to the Northwest Territories:

> Away to the west! Westward ho! Westward ho!
> Where over the prairies the summer winds blow . . . .

*Canadian Pictures, Our Railway to the Pacific*, and *Industries of Canada* repeat this coast-to-coast journey. Each successive location outdoes the previous one for spectacular scenery. Once the view of the Rocky Mountains from Fort Calgary is the "most beautiful on the journey;" elsewhere "there is no fairer land in the world" than the countryside around Victoria.

Literary critic Elizabeth Waterston ranks Lorne's *Canadian Pictures* with Lady Dufferin's memoirs and Rudyard Kipling's sketches as the three most widely read travel books on Canada in the years between Confederation and the First World War. Such books "helped fix the picture of Canada for the next generation" on both sides of the Atlantic. In particular, Lorne's "romantic sketches of the wilderness beauty of the West" set a "visual image" never given such previous exposure. *Canadian Pictures* went through several printings in the mid-1880s, making it the "most important [travel] book of the decade." [28]

Lorne's own illustrations strengthened the impact of *Canadian Pictures*. These were engravings made from his sketches and paintings of the natural landscape — Cascapedia River, Niagara Falls, and the majestic "Rocky Mountains From Our Camp on the Elbow River" — and winter scenes of snow-shoeing, skating and tobogganning. *Our Railway to the Pacific* was enhanced by engravings of three of Louise's paintings. "Junction of the Gatineau and Ottawa" seems a rather pedestrian piece, but the pamphlet was brought to life by two haunting works Louise executed during her Victoria stay — "View From Governor's House, Vancouver Island," and "View From Vancouver Island, Mount Baker in Distance."

*Canadian Pictures, Canadian Life and Scenery*, and *Our Railway to the Pacific* were aimed at the potential British emigrant. In his descriptive sections, Lorne balanced scenic description with detailed attention to physical and climatic factors that made the Canadian prairies prime agricultural land. Lorne down-played unrest among western Indians and emphasized the advantages of familiar British institutions. Still, prairie life was not for everyone. Only "people of good physical ability" should head for the Northwest; "fine ladies and gentlemen will find themselves altogether out of the race." [29]

These writings also offered a defence of Lorne's actions as Governor General and his thoughts on the Imperial future. He applauded the Canadian tariff and the appointment of a High Commissioner as steps "which promoted unity." Rather than wanting to weaken imperial ties, Canadians were "thoroughly devoted to the connection which exists between them and the mother country." A strong, confident Canada could lead the way to Imperial Federation. Again, the federal nature of Canada, with powers divided between central and provincial governments, might provide a model for Ireland. [30]

More than a decade would pass before the tide of British emigration swung north towards Canada, a swing due more to global economic forces than to Lorne's writings. And neither Imperial Unity nor Irish Home Rule would unfold as Lorne proposed. Nevertheless, he was doing more than anyone else — with the possible exception of the High Commissioner — to promote his beloved Canada. And Lorne was proud of his publications. Sending a copy of *Canadian Pictures* to George Stewart, editor of the *Quebec Telegraph*, he declaimed with false modesty that "there is little in it, but it has found favour with the British press."[31]

Lorne's outspokenness on British Empire issues did not make him a leader in the rising imperialist movement. He played no more than minor roles in the Royal Colonial Institute, the Imperial Federation League, and other late-nineteenth pan-imperial organizations. His growing estrangement from the mainstream of Gladstonian liberalism proved a liability as did his connection with the royal family. At the same time his propensity to speak out on each and every imperial issue compromised his credibility.

Lorne's persistent championing of the Canadian cause seems to have been the main obstacle. Most supporters of Imperial Federation saw closer unity as benefitting Britain. They might pay lip service to increased Canadian autonomy, but expected Canada and the other colonies to fall in line whenever Britain called. Yet Lorne's experience as Governor General gave him a different perspective. On the trade question, Canada was "practically an independent state, and does what she thinks best." On defence, Canadians would "wish to judge of the necessity of war before entering on its troubles."[32] All this might be true, but it was not what rabid imperialists and leading British politicians wished to hear. Lorne was too enthusiastic a Canadian!

# CHAPTER SIXTEEN

# BRITISH REALITIES, 1884-1886

*L*orne's five years in Canada led to speculation that he might be in line for one of the two great imperial positions that opened up in the mid 1880s — either Lord Lieutenant of Ireland or Viceroy of India.

Lorne's interest in the Irish post had first been roused during his 1871 honeymoon visit to Dublin. In 1880 the Prince of Wales suggested him for the lord lieutenancy, though perhaps more for Louise's sake than Lorne's.[1] But the Duke of Argyll's subsequent resignation from the Gladstone cabinet over the Irish Land Reform Bill made it difficult to consider a Campbell for the position at that time.

Lorne's Canadian experience proved a mixed blessing for his future Irish hopes. He touted the Canadian federal system as a possible resolution for internal Irish problems, stopping short of complete Home Rule at the national level. Gladstone seemed "very anxious to have more in detail" of such views "in connection with your Canadian experience." [2] But this had to be balanced against the embarrassment to Britain caused by the sympathetic resolutions on Home Rule passed by the Canadian House of Commons in 1882. Though Lorne denounced such resolutions in his private correspondence with British leaders, their passage marred his record.

Lorne came close on Ireland when the lord lieutenancy was again discussed by the Gladstone cabinet in early 1886. This time the possibility of sending Lorne and Louise was initially hurt by Lorne's comment that "he would be glad to do so later on if the Government went on well and a place could be found for him." Other candidates were proposed, but no one seemed to have clear support. The office was pressed on Lorne, and Gladstone telegraphed Queen Victoria for approval. But the Queen replied negatively, "really on political grounds." [3]

In the end, too many factors stood between Lorne and the Dublin post: he and his father's disagreements with Gladstone's Irish policies; the danger of exposing Louise to Fenian threats; Louise's preference for London. Doubts still lingered over Lorne's own political and administrative abilities; *Truth*, for example, continued to characterize him as no more than "la mari de sa femme." [4]

The Indian viceroyalty was even more tantalizing than the Irish post. Serving as his father's private secretary at the India Office from 1868-70 had whetted Lorne's appetite for a taste of the sub-continent. He certainly thought he would be considered as he prepared to leave Ottawa. "If Dufferin does not get India," he wrote his father in March 1883, "it is possible, I think, that I may get it." [5]

Gladstone and his foreign secretary, Lord Granville, did not encourage Lorne's candidacy. "Albany for Canada, Lorne for India, are coming on, I fear," noted Granville in April; a month later the Queen sent Granville "an application from Lorne for India." Gladstone had been expecting it. "Lorne's claim was mentioned to me some time ago by the Prince of Wales," he replied, adding caustically that Ripon, the incumbent viceroy, "ought certainly to have for a successor the best man the field will yield." In mid-May Granville met with Queen Victoria on the India position. "I told her that it was the most important appointment she had to make, hardly less important than that of prime minister. She rather assented. I did not tell her that Lorne's own reasons seemed scarcely sufficient — that it would probably suit Princess Louise's health and enable him to buy a country home at the end of the term." [6]

Neither position came Lorne's way — Lord Carnarvon got Ireland and Dufferin got India. Queen Victoria proved reluctant to send Louise abroad again or, more embarrassingly, to have Lorne abroad and Louise remain behind. While Disraeli had gambled on the royal connection paying off in Lorne's 1878 appointment to Ottawa, Gladstone was less idealistic and less romantic. Lorne's name was subsequently mooted for such posts as Governor of New South Wales, Governor of Cape Colony, and ambassador to Berlin; but no action was forthcoming. [7]

Gladstone offered Lorne no more than the largely ceremonial position of Lord High Commissioner to the General Assembly of the Church of Scotland when Lord Aberdeen stepped down in 1884. Lorne declined. "He would not like to exercise less hospitality than Aberdeen," noted the prime minister's secretary "and he cannot face the incurrence of any great personal outlay." [8] Lorne was also anxious to avoid Scottish church politics; his own support of disestablishment would be compromised by such an office. [9]

The Queen had her own proposal for rewarding Lorne's imperial service, and recognizing his special relationship with the royal family.

She would award him a newly created dukedom, separate from his titular Argyll inheritance. Lorne's father was adamantly opposed. "I should not naturally wish for the heir to the Argyll title to wish for any other one," wrote the Duke. "It is one of the most historical of all titles." Apart from Lorne's "personal connection" with the royal family, the young man had not yet "rendered such services as would ordinarily be rewarded by a dukedom." The Queen accepted Argyll's advice; Lorne would have to wait for his legitimate ducal inheritance. [10]

* * * * *

An independent ducal title would have given Lorne a seat in the House of Lords. His father, however, had long been aware of the almost total shift of power from Lords to Commons. "Lorne's good abilities" would be wasted in the Lords; a return to the Commons should be encouraged. Neither Lorne's previous record nor his marriage to a royal princess need prevent him from taking an "active part" in the House. [11]

British politics had changed considerably during Lorne's Canadian interlude. Disraeli's 1881 death deprived Lorne of a benefactor within the Conservative party, while Argyll's departure from the Gladstone cabinet over Ireland lowered his influence among the Liberals. Though in power, the Liberals were in disarray over Gladstone's Irish policies; Argyllshire itself was being hotly contested by candidates partial to the Highland Land Reform League. Still, a seat in the Commons offered Lorne his best chance now of continuing in public life.

"I intend to stand for some place at the next election," Lorne casually wrote Charles Dilke, a Radical Liberal member, in January 1885. [12] But now an English, rather than a Scottish seat, given the criticism he had received as an "absentee" member for Argyllshire. An easy London seat, an "inexpensive constituency", would be best.

Gladstone's private secretary was less than delighted with Lorne's intention to return to the Commons. "I doubt the expediency of his standing for any constituency," E.W. Hamilton noted in his diary. "As a son-in-law of the sovereign, he ought to keep clear of political contests." There were additional defects. "He will never be anything but a crotchetty member and an untrustworthy supporter." Hamilton was disappointed that the plan to pension Lorne off with a seat in the Lords had been blocked by the Duke of Argyll. [13]

Lorne's first choice was his own London riding of South Kensington. "If South Kensington would not at once reject me, this constituency would suit me well," he wrote Dilke on the morning of 23 January 1885. Did he really believe a palace occupant would be acceptable to the local Liberal organization and to the borough electorate? A few hours of frank conversation dissauded Lorne. Later that evening he wrote a second letter to Dilke. "I have been making enquiries today which have led me to believe I had best look elsewhere for a constituency." [14]

Elsewhere turned out to be the new riding of Hampstead in northwest London. It would not be easy. While the Conservatives seemed united behind Sir H.T. Holland, the Hampstead Liberals were split between the official riding association and a breakaway Radical group.

Lorne had re-entered British politics during a period of growing division within the Liberal party. The more conservative Whig faction championed the old Liberal standbys of free trade, freedom of contract, and freedom of land-ownership from historical and legal encumbrances. The Radicals were more interventionist, proposing to use the legislative machinery of the state to solve the evils and anomalies of agricultural and industrial Britain. The Radical threat from the left struck Lorne as more worrisome than the Conservative opposition on the right. "An irreconcilable ultra Radicalism, detesting all property and superiority," he wrote Gladstone, "seems to have a much larger place among the Liberals than when I was last in England, and in some places will produce division, in spite of all your magic." [15]

Lorne attempted to appeal to both factions during his Hampstead campaign in the 1885 general election. He took a reformist position on housing for the poor, on shorter working hours for labour, on free education, and on disestablishing the Church of Scotland. Yet in other areas his reform was tempered by a Whiggish conservatism. He opposed universal suffrage and payment of members of parliament, and while advocating an extension of local self-government, he stood firm against Irish Home Rule. [16]

It was a losing battle for Lorne and the divided Liberals in solidly Conservative Hampstead as Holland out-polled Lorne 2785 votes to 1910. The Liberal victory at the national level, however, led to the formation early in the new year of Gladstone's third administration. Queen Victoria at once urged the prime minister to appoint Lorne Under-Secretary for the Colonies. The scheme was quashed by the Prince of Wales, never a fan of the Marquis of Lorne, but above all a realist. "I hardly think the Queen's son-in-law should form part of the Government, no matter what party is in power," counselled Bertie. And how could Lorne possibly be part of a Home Rule government? "He would be in an utterly false position, and I can hardly imagine that my sister would wish it." [17]

Meanwhile Lorne and his father were moving toward their dramatic break with Gladstone. Following his victory at the polls in November 1885, and aware that continued support in the Commons depended on pacifying the large and noisy block of Irish Nationalist members, Gladstone became a convert to complete Irish Home Rule. Early in 1886 a

Home Rule Bill was drafted, and presented to Parliament on April 8. The legislation spelled out a form of complete internal autonomy for an Irish parliament at Dublin, with Britain retaining control over external trade, foreign affairs, and defence. But Gladstone could not carry all of his own party on this question. Ninety-three Liberals bolted ranks in the House of Commons to vote against the bill, more than enough to defeat it.

Outside the House these anti-Home Rulers were joined by Argyll, Lorne and thousands of other disaffected Liberals. The Whig-Radical ideological split within the party could no longer be contained. Radicals might support Gladstone on Ireland for the present, but the more conservative Whigs wanted out. They began calling themselves Liberal Unionists, emphasizing their position on the Irish Question. Following the defeat of the Home Rule Bill, Gladstone called a summer election; Conservatives and Liberal Unionists captured the Commons with a 117-seat majority, and Lord Salisbury formed a Conservative government with Liberal Unionist support.

Lorne hoped the division among the Liberals was only temporary. "With continued discussion, the two sides should be able to reconcile their differences," he told the Birmingham Reform Club in October 1886. [18] But the reconciliation did not come, the Liberal Unionists drifted further away from the majority Gladstonian Liberals, and gradually found they had more in common with the Conservatives.

The opposition of Lorne and his father to full Irish Home Rule stemmed in part from their commitment to the abstract political concept of union or federation. This started with traditional family support of the 1707 parliamentary union of England and Scotland, which father and son sincerely believed helped Scotland leap from mediaeval to modern times. From this federalist background Argyll supported the Union cause during the American Civil War, while both father and son applauded Italian and German unification and Canadian Confederation. Lorne saw in these larger, united geo-political entities greater hope for the achievement of liberal principles, protection of minority rights, and growth of trade and commerce.

So with Ireland. Lorne simply believed the Irish owed what little progress they had made to British rule. "Without England, Ireland would be poorer than she was in her worst days of ancient rapine, savagery, and starvation." Any separation from Britain would be disastrous. "If England did not stand at Ireland's back in finance, the smaller country would have little commercial credit, Erin would get poorer and poorer." Political repercussions would be even more chaotic, for an independent Ireland would be "self-misgovernment," a "harking back to barbarism," something like a dog "returning to his own vomit." [19]

Lorne's Irish views were uncharitable, anti-Catholic, chauvinistic, even racist. Indeed his 1907 memoirs, *Passages From the Past*, contain four pages of what he called "smoking-room stories" but were really anti-Irish racist put-downs. [20] Most important, Lorne's views on Ireland were a product of his aristocratic background as a member of the landowning class. By 1884, as he found on returning from Canada, landowners were under severe attack in Scotland as well as Ireland.

* * * * *

Denied both a seat in the Commons and a further imperial appointment, a man of Lorne's background and connections might have been content with his ducal inheritance, over-seeing his family's estates, sitting in the House of Lords, and enjoying a modest reputation as a writer. Yet in the mid-1880s Lorne's father, a vigorous man in his early sixties, still held the title, the land and the seat in the Lords, and would do so until his death in 1900. Duke George even threatened to overshadow his son's writing career. During 1883-84, while Lorne churned out his several books and articles on Canada, his father published pamphlets and journal articles in fields ranging from geology through Scottish history to Irish politics.

Nor was the eighth Duke of Argyll content to play the role of the grieving widower. In August 1881, three years after his first wife's death, George married Amelia Claughton, widow of Colonel Augustus Anson. Lorne disliked his new step-mother, dismissing her as a "tiresome woman" and vowing never to go near Inverary if she was "to roost." To make matters worse, the press gave prominent coverage to George's telegraphed proposal to Amelia while he travelled through North America. Lorne was disgusted by his father's "electronic lovemaking." "It all makes me very sick," he wrote his brother Archie. [21]

Lorne was equally appalled at his brother Colin's 1881 marriage to Gertrude Blood, "a pennyless and groatless grenadier of a girl" with nothing more to offer than "much flesh and stature." [22] The marriage turned out even worse than Lorne feared — first a legal separation, then a scandalous divorce suit that titillated London's social scene from 1883 to 1886. It was a blessing that Lorne's mother had not lived to witness the spectacle, nor to read the tens of thousands of words on the Campbell divorce suit in *The Times*. Colin himself resigned his Argyllshire seat in the Commons, withdrew from British life, and went off to practise law in India.

While Lorne's kin made such front page news, more fundamental problems were unfolding on the Campbell's own Argyllshire estates — problems that kept father and son working together despite their differences over Duchess Amelia. "I am going off to one of my father's estates in the Hebrides," Lorne wrote Macdonald in April 1884, "where agitators are endeavouring, and probably successfully, to get the crofters to seize on the neighbouring cattle farmer's land." If "you hear that I am kept a hostage," he joked, "I shall expect a company of Canadian militia to come and rescue me." [23]

But Highland land agitation was no joking matter. "We are in a nest of troubles," Lorne wrote J.G. Bourinot, "and property seems to me far less secure than in the United States or indeed many parts of the new world, for men's ideas are all 'on the wobble' and political perspective is all awray. When men here are more educated the wobbling will cease — but queer things may happen in the meantime." [24]

For decades tenant farmers in the Western Highlands had sunk lower and lower into poverty, beset by changing agricultural economics, poor soil and rotten weather, and inadequate opportunies for retraining. "It is not the man that is in fault for this," wrote Lorne. "It is the chain of circumstances that has tied him down." As remedies, Lorne suggested government loans for tenants wishing to purchase land, stimulation of the West Coast fisheries as an alternative form of employment, and continued support of emigration to Canada and elsewhere. [25]

Disaffected crofters of Argyllshire and the Western Isles provided personal impetus for Lorne's emigration campaign. Though the tenant-farming population on the Argyll estates had fallen from 14,000 to 4750 between 1781 and 1881, too many people were still trying to wring a livelihood out of the agriculturally-poor countryside. The home estates around Inverary supported 946, those at Morvern 828, at Iona 243, with another 2733 on the Isle of Tiree. [26] Lorne hoped to continue the incentive program begun by his father and grandfather. "I shall try to get some of our crofting friends to accept 100 pounds and emigrate to Manitoba," he informed Macdonald. [27]

But radical crofters in the mid-1880s were more likely to be swayed by extremists than by the likes of the Marquis of Lorne. It was not enough that Lorne's father and grandfather had been near-model landlords over the years, that they gave generously of their time and money to assist their crofters, or that Lorne's mother was known as the "Good Duchess" among them. The situation had become desperate. The Eighth Duke of Argyll's 68,000 hectares made him one of the largest landowners in the western Highlands; he was now fair game for the "agitators" of the Highland Land League. [28]

Moreover, since his resignation from the Gladstone cabinet over the Irish Land Bill in 1881 — a seemingly modest measure conceding fair rents and security of tenure — Argyll had become the self-appointed spokesman of the landed classes and leading defender of private owner-ship of land. Through his speeches and writings, Argyll opposed every attempt at land reform in Britain and Ireland. Land was sacred, it was the key to economic development, relations between landlord and tenant should be determined by market forces, and governments should keep out.

The Duke might argue theories of political economy and point to his own record as a model landlord. But the Irish Land Act of 1881 inspired crofter organization in the Western Highlands and especially on the Western Isles. The Highland Land League was formed in 1882; three years later it elected five members to the House of Commons, just narrowly failing in Argyllshire itself. Militant agitators called for rent strikes, public protest meetings, and intimidation towards those crofters still co-operating with their landlords.

Successive governments in London attempted to preserve law and order by strengthening local police forces and deploying troops in areas of particular trouble. To the landlords, such augmented forces were never strong enough. In October 1884 Lorne urged Home Secretary William Harcourt to send a force "which they can't resist" so "this growing spirit of defiance of all law will be effectively checked." [29]

Harcourt took a somewhat different view. The root of the problem, he instructed Lorne, was not a few outside agitators stirring the local pot. Highland discontent was "bred by want exasperated by a sense of injustice." [30] So a succession of Liberal and Conservative governments turned to the more fundamental areas of economic and legal reform as a long-term approach to crofter agitation. An 1883 royal commission under the chairmanship of Lord Napier largely upheld crofter complaints; the Crofters Act of 1886 guaranteed security of tenure and compensation for improvements to crofters, and set up a land court which fixed fair rents. The worst of the crisis was over.

Crofter agitation affected several members of the Campbell family. Brother Colin escaped the worst impact when his divorce case forced his resignation from the Commons prior to the 1885 election. Lorne's sister Victoria was particularly saddened; the unrest seemed a personal slap in her face after years of philanthropic and missionary work among the Western Isles. "The crofter agitation is our great trial," she confided to her diary at the end of 1884. [31] As patriarch and estate owner, Duke George took the brunt of the attack. With the passing of the 1886 Crofters Act, the Land League attained its major objectives, landlord-tenant relations were brought under government control, and the Duke's theories on the sanctity of private land consigned to history.

In the short run, the Marquis of Lorne emerged unscathed. Apart from his visit to disaffected Tiree crofters in the spring of 1884 and his correspondence with Harcourt that fall, Lorne kept his distance from the problem. The Queen's son-in-law had to be politically circumspect. Yet there were long-term implications for the heir to the Argyll estates. By the time of Lorne's succession to the ducal title in 1900, the old order in the

Western Highlands and on the Western Isles was long gone. Agriculturally, the entire region had declined through the nineteenth century to one of marginal production and profit. Legally, the balance of power in landlord-tenant relationships had tipped markedly in the latter's favour. As the ninth Duke of Argyll during Edwardian times, Lorne would face more hardship than joy as estate owner.

Meanwhile at Inverary itself, strands of young trees would always remind Lorne of his Canadian days. In 1880 he shipped home some maple seed for his father to plant. Nothing came up for over a year, and "the gardener thought they must be dead." Finally the shoots poked through, and Duke George promised to "plant out a lot of them so as to show as much as possible from the castle." [32] So Lorne sent other varieties of seed home for planting. Twenty years later they were all flourishing — black walnut and oak, cedar and Douglas fir — though "the maple leaves do not repeat their Canadian glories." [33]

\* \* \* \* \*

Prince Leopold's death in the spring of 1884 produced an additional burden for Lorne and Louise in the months following their return from Canada. The haemophilic Leopold died of internal bleeding caused by a slight fall while on holiday in the south of France. Louise had absolutely "doted" on Leopold and was "terribly crushed" by the tragedy. "I have lost the truest and dearest friend — besides the best of brothers — I ever had, the joy and object of a lifetime." [34]

Even more than Louise's favourite brother and Lorne's favourite royal brother-in-law, Leopold was indispensable in keeping the couple together. With his wit, his irreverence, and his aesthetic interests, young Leopold brought out the best in Lorne and Louise. His very presence helped supply a missing link in their relationship. Deprived of his company, the Lornes now had no family confidante with whom they could both share their intimate thoughts. Thrown back on their own resources, how would they fare as a married couple?

They were not faring very well. The supposed reunion year of 1884 saw Lorne and Louise spend as much time apart as together. Following Leopold's funeral, Louise took a long Easter holiday with the Prince and Princess of Wales at Sandringham, while Lorne left for three weeks in Scotland, to help his father deal with crofter unrest on the family estates. Early August found Lorne back at Inverary, while Louise sojourned at Osborne and cancelled a scheduled appearance at a church bazaar in Rosneath, owing to "the state of her health." [35]

Louise had become as skilled as her mother in using health problems to excuse herself from unwanted obligations. In the summer of 1884 she wanted nothing to do with crofter unrest, with dreary old Inverary castle, with the Duke of Argyll and his rather plain second wife, even with her own husband. Neuralgic headaches — still bothersome four years after the Ottawa sleighing accident — were readily invoked as reason for dallying at Sandringham or Osborne instead of joining Lorne in Scotland.

More extended relief from domestic and social obligations awaited Louise in the mineral waters and hot springs of continental Europe. Since her return from Canada the previous autumn, she had been scheming to get away to Gastein or Marienbad — without Lorne, of course. Finally in mid-August, accompanied by her half-cousin, Count Gleichen, and his daughter Feodore, Louise left for Gastein and "a course of twenty-one baths." [36]

Gleichen and his daughter were Louise's kind of people. The son of Queen Victoria's half-sister Feodore (from her mother's previous marriage), Gleichen had taken up sculpture following his retirement from the British navy. The loss of his personal fortune forced him to regard sculpture as a serious profession, and by the time of his death in 1891 he had executed a number of well-received public monuments and portrait busts. This talent he shared with his eldest daughter Feodore, who later became the first female member of the Royal Society of British Sculptors.

Nothing proved more delightful than three sculptors holidaying together at Gastein. Princess Louise found her half-cousin and his charming twenty-three year-old daughter the most enjoyable of companions. So much to talk about; so many things in common. They bathed in the soothing mineral waters; they hiked the surrounding countryside; they sketched and painted; they joined the cream of European society for evening dinners and dancing. It was all so much better than Lorne and dull old Inverary.

Queen Victoria attributed Louise's growing aversion to her husband as an aftermath of the 1880 sleighing accident. Had Lorne not dragged her off to dreadful Ottawa, the tragedy would never have occurred. Twentieth century observers might place more emphasis on basic differences in temperament and sexual preference. Temperamentally, Louise remained much more vivacious and spirited than Lorne; for her a good time meant partying and dancing, while he increasingly favoured quiet evenings in the library.

Profiles in the popular press of the day illustrate these differences in personality and temperament. Lorne was portrayed as a "gentleman of pleasant, picturesque appearance, thoroughly courteous and kindly, of reflective habits, studious tastes." He appeared "resolved to live his own life, reading much, writing a little." [37] Louise, however, was usually depicted as enjoying a good time in public. She "keenly relishes fun, wit or humour," was "strongly impulsive" and "acts very much according to her personal inclination." [38] Lorne seemed willing to ease gracefully from his thirties into his forties, while Louise was determined to remain young.

Louise's self-portrait in sculpture.

Sex remained the major problem between them. Speculation suggests that even if the marriage had been physically consummated back in 1871, by 1884 it had become a purely Platonic relationship. Lorne's latent homosexual preference led him increasingly to shun the marriage bed. While Louise might have tolerated such aberrant behaviour early in the marriage — after all she and Lorne shared similar artistic tastes and inclinations, and Lorne had saved her from a Prussian partnership — the maturing princess soon became the victim of sexual frustration.

Like her mother and like many of her Hanover and Coburg forebears and relatives, Princess Louise had a high sexual drive. Certainly she got on well with her male relatives and in-laws and artistic acquaintances. She "liked Louis Battenberg," recalled Leopold's daughter Alice, she "got on well with the Kaiser — indeed, with any man — she ran after anything in trousers." [39] Any normal marriage would have provided a safe outlet for such desires of the flesh. But hers was not a normal marriage.

Whether the aftermath of the sleighing accident, differences in temperaments, different sexual drives — or more likely, some combination of all three — the marriage of Princess Louise and the Marquis of Lorne reached its lowest ebb in the summer of 1884.

Queen Victoria did what she could to keep them together. For propriety's sake, they must try to live on friendly terms under the same roof, but Louise could not be "forced" to do so. "That is all we can do," the Queen wrote her daughter Vicky in September. Short of allowing a formal separation, Queen Victoria in fact did everything in her power to ease the pressure on Louise while "feeling very much" for poor Lorne. She allowed Louise to traipse off to Gastein. Yet she also tried to have both Lorne and Louise invited to holiday with Vicky in the Tyrol later in the fall, believing that the relaxed mountain environment and Vicky's sisterly charms might patch everything up. [40]

There was no Tyrolese reconciliation. Louise went there by herself, while Lorne continued to busy himself with crofter unrest and estate administration in Argyllshire and the Hebrides Islands. The Queen tried again in late October, summoning Lorne from Inverary to Balmoral, where Louise had roosted since her return from Europe. Still no luck. In November — with Lorne still at Inverary and Louise living by herself at Kensington Palace —she summoned the Duke of Argyll "for a conference respecting the affairs" of her daughter and son-in-law. [41]

Queen Victoria may have failed to get Lorne and Louise in bed together, but she finally succeeded in getting them to stay under the same roof — though just barely. They would remain legally married, fulfil family and state obligations as a couple, and be legally domiciled at Kensington Palace. But their time together would be as brief as possible; separate holidays and separate family visits would be pushed as far as a suspicious and inquisitive press would tolerate.

Christmas 1884 set the pattern for the next few years. Lorne holidayed at Inverary while Louise divided her time between her mother at Osborne and her brother and sister-in-law, the Duke and Duchess of Edinburgh, at Eastwell. Early spring of 1885 found them together at Kensington, busy with a full round of philanthropic and charitable activities. Later in the spring Louise took country holidays with Lord and Lady Southesk at Longwood, and with Lady De Winton at Blyth Wood. In July they were together for Princess Beatrice's marriage to Prince Henry of Battenberg. In August Lorne escorted his wife to the spa at Aix-les-Bains; as soon as she settled into the Hotel de l'Europe he rushed back to Britain.

While Lorne tarried at Inverary, Louise spent the autumn at nearby Balmoral. Most of the royal family passed through Balmoral that fall, making it particularly nice for Louise. Fritz and Vicky came from Berlin; Bertie and Alix stayed longer than usual; Liko (Prince Henry) and Beatrice Battenberg alit there after their honeymoon. "Princess Louise makes our evening parties particularly pleasant," observed Henry Ponsonby, the Queen's secretary. "Whatever people say of her I must say she is charming and I don't know what I should do at these long dreary evening parties if it were not for her." Still, beneath her "sweet smile and soft language, "she says such bitter things." [42]

**❦ CHAPTER SEVENTEEN**

# RESTLESS PRINCESS, 1887-1896

*G*olden Jubilee celebrations of 1887 — the fiftieth anniversary of Queen Victoria's accession to the throne — illustrate both the continuing court demands on Louise's time and the precarious position Lorne held within the royal family. The year began on a positive note as the Borough of Kensington commissioned Louise to do a sculpture of her mother — later known as the Broad Walk statue — as its Jubilee gift to the nation. Meanwhile, Lorne led a campaign for public support of a proposed Imperial Institute as a permanent exhibition spot for colonial products, and attended the Colonial Conference held in conjunction with the Jubilee.

Yet once spring arrived, the Lornes had little time to themselves or for their own individual interests. Jubilee festivities brought a steady round of public appearances and family entertainments for visiting European royalty. The celebrations climaxed on June 21 when the Queen drove in triumphal procession from Buckingham Palace to Westminster Abbey for a national service of thanksgiving.

The Princess of Wales and the Crown Princess of Germany rode with the Queen in the principal carriage. Louise, Helena and Beatrice followed in a second carriage. Lorne joined his royal brothers-in-law and other European royalty in a mounted escort. Cheers reverberated in the streets as the crowds waited for the procession to begin.

But the stars were not with the Marquis of Lorne that day. While waiting in the palace quadrangle, Lorne's horse began to act up, and before he could mount, a handkerchief had to be thrown over the animal's eyes. As the procession left the palace gates the roar of the cheering crowd further upset the animal. Three hundred metres along Constitution Hill the horse suddenly reared, bucked violently, and threw the Queen's son-in-law to the ground.

Rank-conscious European princes thought it fitting that Lorne had been removed from the procession, "for he was after all a mere commoner." [1] Fortunately, Lorne was not injured. He returned to the palace, borrowed a second horse, and rode to Westminster Abbey via the Birdcage Walk shortcut. But his pride was certainly wounded! Less than four years before, Lorne returned from Canada as a respected pro-consul of Empire; now he was the laughing stock of Jubilee Week.

This fiasco on horseback and its accompanying titters illustrate one of the main external problems facing the Lornes while they tried to work out their own personal difficulties. As long as they lived in Britain, and as long as Queen Victoria reigned, Louise would be but her mother's daughter and Lorne but his wife's husband and the royal family's outsider of a brother-in-law.

Queen Victoria's dictates still prevailed. Christmas had to be spent within the royal embrace, either at Windsor or Osborne. Should Lorne wish to spend the holiday season with his own family at Inverary, he went without Louise. The pattern continued through the year — summers at Osborne, autumns at Balmoral, weekends at Sandringham with the Prince and Princess of Wales. When the Queen demanded her presence, Louise responded.

The necessary compromises put a strain on the marriage at a most inappropriate time. Louise had to put her mother's wishes ahead of her husband's and her own desires. Tension, headaches and neuralgia attacks were much more frequent at home than when abroad on a European holiday. Matters were not helped by the condescending way in which Lorne continued to be treated within the royal family. He accepted such rebuffs with his usual grace, which struck others as hesitating and ineffectual. Frequently this set off yet another series of neuralgia attacks in Louise!

Louise certainly proved difficult for members of family and the court. She stirred up trouble amongst her sisters, and was often at odds with the Queen. "Auntie Lou is not right at all," remarked Princess Victoria of Prussia (Vicky's daughter) during a visit to Windsor. "She complains of every sort of thing, but is charming as usual to look at." [2] Lady-in-waiting Marie Mallet agreed. "She is so fascinating, but oh, so ill-natured I positively dread talking to her, not a soul escapes." In one letter to her husband, Mallet concluded she had "never come across a more dangerous woman" than Louise, "to gain her end she would stop at nothing." [3]

Louise's frustrations at court were matched by Lorne's failure to resurrect a political life. He did not receive another imperial appointment; his attempt to regain a seat in the Commons had failed; the long wait to inherit the Argyll dukedom promised additional frustrations. Even his writing reached a low ebb in 1886-87; Lorne's creative burst of "Canada" books was finished, with nothing new to replace it.

Lorne might have muddled his way through his forties — he would celebrate his forty-second birthday in August 1887 — patiently awaiting the literary muse or the political opportunity. Not Louise; she was a woman of action. If their lives were to be put back together — both as individuals and as a couple — she would have to take the initiative.

Her immediate and continuing need was breathing space, periodic escapes from her role as wife and princess. Selfish as she was, Louise was also astute enough to realize that Lorne needed similar space. She sensed solutions might be found in incognito travel and long holidays away from London — both separately and together.

* * * * *

The holidays and extended periods apart were now put to positive use. Rather than mere relief from accumulated past tensions, they were used for regenerative purposes, allowing Louise to stoke up on good spirits so she could better endure future frustrations. While Lorne spent September 1886 with his family in Scotland, Louise, travelling incognito as Lady Cowan, sped off to Aix-les-Bains. Here she spent her mornings taking "a regular course of baths, under the care of Dr. Bracket," and each afternoon making "an excursion to some pretty place in the neighbourhood." [4]

After a month at the spa Louise felt ready for a ten-day joint vacation with Lorne at Torquay in Devonshire. Again it was incognito as they registered at the Great Western Hotel as Colonel and Mrs. Campbell. *Truth* thought the disguise "highly absurd and foolish" since "everybody knows perfectly well who they are." [5] Still, the pretense allowed Louise greater freedom than she could possibly enjoy travelling through Britain or the Continent as a royal princess. Lorne readily co-operated, since it made his wife so much easier to live with.

Best of all were two extended, leisurely vacations on the island of Malta in the winters of 1887 and 1888. A favourite wintering-place for wealthy Europeans seeking something more exotic than the Riviera or Florence or Naples, Malta proved particularly popular for royalty watchers when Prince Alfred, Duke of Edinburgh, was posted there in 1886 as commander-in-chief of British naval forces in the Mediterranean.

Louise had lately developed a fondness for her brother Alfred, his Russian wife Marie, and their three engaging daughters. Lorne quickly fell in step with Louise's plans. On their first Malta sojourn in 1887, the Lornes stayed with the Edinburghs at St. Antonia Palace; next winter they rented quarters at the Imperial Hotel in Sliema.

In the warm sunshine of these Malta winters, free of London's court and social obligations, their marital tensions somewhat reduced, Lorne and Louise were able to relax as they could nowhere else. Lorne got back to his writing, working on poetry, journal articles and historical pieces. The local environment inspired a short story published in the December 1887 issue of *Blackwood's Magazine* under the title, "Who Were They? A Maltese Apparition." Though of minor literary note, the story illustrated Lorne's continuing interest in the supernatural, and marked his debut as a fiction writer.

Louise, meanwhile, sketched and painted, and went for long mind-clearing walks along the coast and over the hills. In the evenings the two of them joined other wintering royals and European aristocrats, military and naval officers, local Maltese and British dignitaries, in a gay round of opera performances, dinner parties and fancy dress balls, climaxed each season by pre-Lenten festivities of the Malta Carnival.

"Such a galaxy of Royalty has never been in our midst since Bonaparte slept in the Post Office," observed the Malta *Times*. The presence of so many royals produced an endless round of

> *Morning tete-a-tete calls*
> *Magnificent balls*
> *Luncheons, dinners, and teas*
> *Dancing parties and sprees*
> *Tennis, polo, and tip-sticks*
> *Racing, riding and pic-nics*
> *Tail coats and top hats*
> *Dress Boots, white cravats . . .* [6]

A military and naval review in honour of Louise's birthday in March 1887 almost collapsed in disarray when a confused British general called for three cheers for Princess Beatrice instead of Louise. "This little matter was soon put right," *Truth* assured its British readers, "and all the royalties expressed themselves highly pleased with the show." [7]

Both winters, the Lornes took their time travelling to and from Malta. The journey across France and up and down the long Italian peninsula offered many delights and kept them away from London a little longer. And their decision to go their separate ways on various stages of these trips provided the necessary breathing space for the marriage.

Returning from Malta in the spring of 1888, the Lornes were together long enough in Rome for a private audience with Pope Leo XIII. "He placed my wife and me right and left of him, on two wheelchairs," Lorne recalled, "and I spoke of Canada, Ireland and Italy." [8] Rome reminded him of the Garibaldi excitement of his youth. His musings on twenty years of change in the Italian peninsula appeared in print as *Rome Under Pius, And Italy Under Rome 1867-1887,* a long narrative poem published in 1888 by Thomas Ogilvie Smith. Not at all memorable literature, the poem is more a political justification of Italian unification.

A short visit with the Crown Prince and Princess of Germany on the way to Malta in early 1888 provided Lorne with another reminder of former adventures. Fritz and Vicky had been Lorne's initial entree into royal circles during his year at the University of Berlin. Now they were wintering at San Remo on the Italian Riviera, and did their best to welcome Lorne and Louise. But it was obvious that the Crown Prince's throat cancer was worsening. In fact he barely lived long enough to succeed his father as Emperor; on June 15 Lorne represented Queen Victoria at Fritz's funeral.

Next year the Lornes forsook Malta for a winter holiday at the spa at Arcachon, near Bordeaux. But once-a-year trips to the Continent were not enough for Louise. Later in 1889 she holidayed alone at her beloved Marienbad, striking up a deep friendship with Henry Campbell-Bannerman, future British prime minister, and his wife Charlotte.

Continental holidays with Queen Victoria were least enjoyable. Spring 1890 found the Lornes and Princess Beatrice attending the Queen at Aix-les-Bains. Ronny Gower stopped at Aix for a few days and found the scene excruciatingly dull. Dinner featured over-cooked English food, no wine, and hardly any conversation. After the meal Victoria disappeared with her daughters to a private sitting room, while the men adjourned for coffee and cigars and nothing much to talk about. After-noons provided mild relief as Lorne and Gower visited local museums and churches, shooting galleries and sulphur baths — anything for a break in the deadly routine. [9]

This Aix-les-Bains holiday proved that Continental travel was not an automatic release for the tensions swirling around Louise and Lorne. Clearly they must cultivate mutual friends with whom they could relax in Britain. Lord and Lady Southesk had given them a quiet weekend at their Longwood country home near Winchester following the fiasco of 1887's Jubilee Week. But among all their friends, the Lornes as a couple most enjoyed time together with Cyril and Connie Flower through these troubled years.

Lorne and Cyril ("Flos") Flower had first met in the Amateur Dramatic Club at Cambridge during their student days. While Lorne married a princess, Cyril in 1877 married Constance de Rothschild of the European financial family. Lorne and Cyril talked politics whenever they got together — Flower was an advanced Gladstonian Liberal, member of the Commons during the 1880s, and Lord Battersea after 1892. Louise found herself stimulated by Cyril's interest in the arts and Connie's international sophistication.

Cyril and Connie put on splendid dinner parties for Louise. "They have the pleasantest people in London," Walburga Paget noted after one memorable dinner at the Flowers' city home in 1889, when Louise was guest of honour. "I sat between de Stael (Russian ambassador) and

Millais, the painter, and enjoyed myself." Besides "lots of smart people, there were Gilbert, the sculptor; Mr. Henry James; Mrs. Chandler, an American actress." [10] Altogether a grand gathering of the culturati from both sides of the Atlantic to delight the Lornes and the Flowers.

That same year Louise was a house guest at The Pleasaunce, the Flowers' country place at Overstrand in Norfolk, when "the house was little more than a cottage, and no garden, but a few feet of indifferent lawn between ourselves and the general public." Louise took her paint-box and sketch-books and meant to enjoy herself in the country. She "took tea on the wee lawn," bought "her own stamps at the shop," and strolled "unattended on the sands." [11]

Next year Lorne and Louise stayed together at Overstrand on their way to the Norwich Music festival. In subsequent years as the Flowers improved their cottage and property, Louise enjoyed "giving her advice concerning the laying out of gardens, or suggesting some architectural or picturesque addition to the house." Return visits at Kensington were equally pleasant. "After dining quietly with my hosts," Connie would read aloud from *The Times* while Louise knitted and Lorne mused quietly. "This little intimate picture clings to my memory," noted Connie thirty years later, "in default of many a grander one." [12]

\* \* \* \* \*

Mutual interests in art and education also helped Lorne and Louise's relationship survive the difficult years of the late 1880s. Joint public appearances could be built around the opening of an art exhibition or a new Girls' Public Day School. In October 1889 they travelled to Edinburgh, where Lorne served as honorary president of the second congress of the National Association for the Advancement of Art and Its Application to Industry. Lorne delivered his official address, while Louise quietly enjoyed the attempt of William Morris and other radicals to capture the congress for socialism.

But Louise preferred to escape alone into the world of the visual arts, without her husband. She remained an avid gallery-hopper, attending Bond Street exhibitions of both established artists and promising newcomers. She enjoyed visiting the studios of painters and sculptors whose work and personality she valued — Feodore Gleichen, Noel Paton, Augustus John, Maud Earl, Alfred Gilbert, Seymour Lucas and Lawrence Alma-Tadema.

Edgar Boehm remained the most dominant artistic figure in Princess Louise's life, maintaining the influence that began during student days at the Royal College of Art and blossomed at Balmoral just prior to Louise's engagement. Through the 1880s, Boehm continued to dominate the field of British monumental sculpture, drawing lucrative commissions from

Joseph Edgar Boehm, Louise's teacher and mentor.

public bodies and wealthy private families. The patronage of Queen Victoria seemed more important than the negative voices of the art critics. In 1880 he was elected a full member of the Royal Academy, and nine years later created a baronet as Sir Joseph Edgar Boehm.

Boehm was a robust fifty-five year old at the time of his knighthood, Louise an attractive and engaging forty-one. They saw much of each other, both at public functions and in private sessions. Louise paid regular visits to Boehm's studio at 25 Wetherby Gardens. Gossips wondered how far their relationship had progressed. Certainly Louise was the only person present at the time of Boehm's sudden death in his studio on 12 December 1890.

"He was showing her some of his newest busts," wrote a shocked Queen Victoria to one of her granddaughters, "when he gave a shriek and fell forward and never spoke again — and she only heard a gurgling in his throat. She undid his collar, moved his arms, felt his pulse — but all in vain. She ran for help to his neighbour and pupil [Alfred] Gilbert, and he sent for a doctor and asked her to leave. Only the next morning did she know he was dead from heart and the bursting of a blood vessel. It has been a terrible shock to her, and she was dreafully upset." [13]

That was Queen Victoria's version of Boehm's death. Catherine "Skittles" Walters, a well-placed gossip and courtesan of the day, told a more compromising account of the death drama. In this version Boehm dies of a haemorrhage in Louise's arms, "leaving the courageous Princess to snatch the studio key from his pocket, call a cab and, covered with blood as she was, dash for a doctor on her own." She and the doctor afterwards "concocted a story" that Boehm died moving a heavy statue. [14]

Whatever the real story, the Queen had Boehm buried in Westminster Abbey. Skittles Walters and her confidante Wilfrid Scawen Blunt were much amused. Blunt came to believe that the "scandalous paragraphs in papers" about Queen Victoria and her favoured Scottish attendant, John Brown, were Boehm's work. "With no real evidence," Boehm spread the stories about Victoria "in order to cover up any revelations about his own relations" with Louise. "It all fits in," concluded Blunt, "and there is a great deal of truth mixed up with the invention." [15]

Following Boehm's death, Louise returned to her statue of Queen Victoria that had been commissioned by the Borough of Kensington back in 1887. She took her own good time completing it — six long years in her cottage studio at Kensington Palace. Even then, the announced day of unveiling had to be postponed while she added those all-important finishing touches. Finally, all was ready on 23 June 1893.

Late that afternoon, Queen Victoria — "all smiles," according to Ronny Gower — Princess Louise, and most of the royal family arrived for the unveiling of this Broad Walk statue just outside Kensington Palace grounds. The only notable absentee was the Marquis of Lorne, as funeral services for a business acquaintance, Sir William Mackinnon, somehow took precedence over his wife's artistic triumph!

Despite a steady rain, the bleacher seats along the Broad Walk were packed; a Kensington children's chorus stood in the front row, dressed in their best white summer frocks. A string was pulled, a giant Union Jack fell away, and the statue stood revealed. The Queen remarked how pleased she was "to be here on this occasion in my old home," and "to witness the unveiling of the fine statue so admirably designed and executed by my daughter." [16]

Then the Kensington children sang and danced. Eight year-old Estella Canziani, who lived nearby at 3 Palace Green, presented Queen Victoria with a bouquet of flowers. "I was so frightened, I only just managed not to cry until I had done my part," recalled Estella, "for I thought I should have to go and live with the old Queen." [17] Estella and her young contemporaries soon began calling the Broad Walk statue "the penny Queen," thinking of Victoria's portrait on the one-penny stamp.

Ronny Gower, himself a sculptor, thought the Broad Walk statue "looked well and full of dignity." A later critic agreed. "The Queen is shown with extraordinary dignity," noted Hunt-Lewis, "the artist as unmistakably belonging to the British order of mind." Indeed the work showed very little innovation in concept or execution. "The old simplicity of form remained, the same exquisite smoothness of finish, the same refined taste and noble sense of beauty." [18]

Boehm's influence seems present in the Broad Walk statue. Raleigh Trevelyan even concluded that the work was "in reality done by Sir Edgar Boehm, who ghosted it." [19] If correct, the "ghosting" takes on additional meaning, for Boehm died two-and-one-half years prior to the unveiling! But perhaps the bulk of the work — Louise's and/or Boehm's — took place between 1887 and 1890. Certainly Louise remained under the lasting influence of Boehm's tradionalist approach to sculpture.

In 1893 the Broad Walk piece was London's first public statue attributed to a female sculptor. The monument stands today to the east of Kensington Palace, looking east across the Round Pond over Kensington Gardens and Hyde Park. Carved from one piece of white Corrara marble, the statue depicts the young Queen, somewhat larger than lifesize, seated on her throne, clad in robes of state, her right hand holding upraised sceptre and her left hand resting on the arm of the throne. During the 1950s, unfortunately, vandals broke off the original stone sceptre; in 1966 they made off with its metal replacement and broke Victoria's right hand; in the mid-1980s part of the nose was chipped off.

\* \* \* \* \*

Broad Walk Statue.

Ronny Gower was another of Louise's close friends from the art world. Lord Ronald Leveson-Gower (he dropped the "Leveson" part of his hyphenated surname) was Lorne's "uncle" and close childhood companion. After Eton and Cambridge, Gower sat in the Commons for seven years as Liberal member for Sutherland, then pursued an artistic and literary life as sculptor, art critic and historian, and biographer.

Gower spent considerable time with his nephew and niece in the early 1890s. He and Lorne enjoyed weekends at Hammerfield, Gower's country place near Tunbridge Wells; they sailed together off the west coast of Scotland; they travelled through Europe on short holiday jaunts. Just as often it was Ronny and Louise spending time together — visiting London art galleries; carriage rides to Aldershot and Farnham; holidaying at Oban with Archie and Janey Campbell, Lorne's brother and sister-in-law; overnight stays at the same Paris hotel. [20]

Their travels through Europe in the spring of 1893 began as a threesome, with Ronny, Lorne and Louise tripping through Paris, Lucerne and Milan, before joining Queen Victoria for an April holiday in Florence. After a few days, the Queen departed for a granddaughter's wedding in Coburg, and Lorne was called back to London on business affairs.

Ronny and Louise had two weeks to themselves in Florence. At the end of the month they left for Venice, accompanied by a Miss Bulteel (niece of Lady Ponsonby), and her young cousin, Maurice Baring. Unfortunately for Ronny, "all the time we were in Venice Princess Louise was laid up with a cold." [21] Leaving young Baring with Lady Ponsonby, Ronny and Louise continued on to Milan and Lucerne. They were good travelling companions, delighting in each other's company, indulging their mutual interests in sculpture, sharing gossip about the art world.

There was no affair between Ronny and Louise. Gower was a confirmed and uninhibited homosexual, notes one chronicler of the late nineteenth century gay scene, "a thorough-paced queer who liked the rough trade and found time, in spite of a public career, to enjoy it prodigally." [22] During the 1890s, Frank Greene was Gower's steady male companion. He also travelled with such well-known homosexuals as Frank Miles and Oscar Wilde, serving as inspiration for Lord Henry Wooton in Wilde's 1890 novel, *The Picture of Dorian Gray*.

Gower turned out to be the ideal travelling companion for Louise, as Lorne was well aware. Ronny's presence discouraged heterosexual males from hovering around the Princess's entourage. And all the gossip the two of them shared en route could be repeated when Lorne finally re-joined them in Lucerne after their four-week jaunt in 1893. One can almost hear the peals of laughter that reverberated through hotel corridors and along Lucerne's narrow streets.

Louise's innocence is less certain in her relationship with another of her in-laws — Prince Henry of Battenberg, husband of her sister Beatrice. Since their marriage in 1885, the couple had lived in England, spending considerable time with Queen Victoria at Windsor Castle and Osborne, where "Liko" — as Prince Henry was popularly known — revived the royal family's interest in staging amateur theatrical productions.

Louise shared Liko and Beatrice's enthusiasms, particularly when she got the starring roles. Queen Victoria judged Louise "beautiful and sad beyond measure" as Mary Queen of Scots in the 1890 production of "Fotheringay." According to Frederick ("Fritz") Ponsonby, son of Victoria's private secretary, both Louise and Beatrice were "quite good in their parts, but very sketchy with the words." [23]

The Queen took great interest in these theatrical activities, sitting in on rehearsals and setting herself up as official censor. This produced a hilarious scene one day in 1893 during a practice for "She Stoops to Conquer". At one point in the action, Fritz Ponsonby was to mistake Louise for a barmaid, and tickle her under the chin. That was too much for the Queen. Ponsonby received a curt note that he "had better not indulge in any chucking under the chin." So at the next rehersal he kept his distance. Then came a second message from the Queen: Ponsonby was "overdoing it the other way." Fritz then consulted Louise, "who roared with laughter at my dilemma, and we finally hit off a happy medium." [24]

Perhaps Queen Victoria should have been keeping an eye on Liko Battenberg rather than Fritz Ponsonby, given Louise's behaviour at the time of Battenberg's sudden death. Prince Henry died of fever in early 1896 while serving with the Ashanti Expeditionary Force during a minor African colonial skirmish. Louise treated the tragedy as particularly her own, "calmly announcing that she was Liko's confidante and Beatrice nothing to him." Such talked poisoned the already gloomy atmosphere at Osborne. "Charming behaviour," commented the appalled Duchess of Teck. "The whole place is ringing with it." [25]

The Duchess was not alone in wondering how much had transpired between Liko and Louise. Saddened by the death of a jovial brother-in-law, and jealous of the attention devoted to poor Beatrice, was Louise simply appropriating some of her sister's grief? Or had Liko signed up for the African expedition to distance himself from Louise's advances? "He was so determined to go," mourned Louise in a letter to Catherine Gladstone. "How soon his efforts to prove himself useful were ended." [26] That remained the official explanation for Liko's adventure — the need for this unchallenged and uncelebrated prince to prove himself to the nation.

Louise's version of the Henry Battenberg affair was somewhat different. After Liko's death, Louise confessed in one of her "long talks" with her new court confidante, Sir James Reid, personal physician to the

Queen. It all began, Reid noted, with "Prince Henry's attempted relations with her [Louise] which she had declined," followed by Henry's subsequent attempts to gain revenge by exposing and exaggerating what Louise considered an innocent relationship between herself and Arthur Bigge, an assistant secretary on the palace staff. [27] Dr. Reid proved a valuable friend to Louise, using his influence over Queen Victoria to defuse both the Bigge and Battenberg incidents. Given her interest in and attraction to other men, Louise desperately needed such friends at court!

Whatever Louise's involvement with Battenberg, both she and Lorne used their art to express their grief at the time of his death. Lorne's "poetic infusion" appeared in the local Isle of Wight *Country Press*:

> *He died because on danger's field*
> *A soldier's duty lies,*
> *Tho' fame a slender wreath may yield*
> *Where plague's fell banner flies.*
>
> *So proud of him, we say, farewell*
> *With all on Maine and Rhine,*
> *In love remembering he fell*
> *Within our Army's line.*

Henry Labouchere considered this dreadful poetry. Though it was "hard to out-bathos the Laureate's poem" on Prince Henry's death, "Lorne had succeeded." [28]

Louise's sculpted tribute to her dear brother-in-law was far superior to Lorne's poetry. Her memorial piece stands today in Whippingham Church, near Cowes on the Isle of Wight, where Prince Henry was buried. The sculpture takes the form of a crucifixion, with the Angel of the Resurrection supporting the head of Jesus. Lorne thought the effect "more mediaeval German than anything else," while Ronny Gower considered it "an ambitious work, and a very original idea." [29]

## ❦ CHAPTER EIGHTEEN
# ACCEPTING MIDDLE AGE, 1891-1899

*L*orne's strange absence from the June 1893 unveiling of Louise's Broad Walk statue was due to the funeral that afternoon of Sir William Mackinnon, founder and chairman of the Imperial British East Africa Company. Established in 1887 and given a royal charter the following year, IBEA had produced grandiose economic plans for developing the region that today comprises much of Kenya and Uganda. Lorne was one of the original investors.

Lorne's stake in the company was one of his few major financial investments outside his family's Scottish estates. Perhaps he felt obliged to support Mackinnon, a fellow Scot from Campbelltown in Argyllshire. Perhaps he was swept away by the romance of this imperial adventure. IBEA's push up-country into Uganda was reminiscent of his own 1881 trek across the Canadian prairies, while the proposed rail line from Mombassa to Lake Victoria seemed like a replica of the Canadian Pacific Railway.

Lorne's political and court connections made him a potentially valuable London lobbyist for the company. Yet he was unsuccessful in securing a British government guarantee when IBEA tried to raise additional funds on the London money market, or in securing government financing for a survey of the proposed railway line. [1] When it became evident the company could not continue, Lorne urged government purchase of IBEA's assets and assumption of its territorial mandate in East Africa. By March 1892, with the company virtually bankrupt, Lorne advised "handing over to the Crown our position and rights" without compensation. [2]

In July, however, the somewhat sympathetic Conservative government was defeated in a general election by Gladstone and the Liberals. Never an imperialist, the new prime minister was more likely to be impressed by IBEA's philanthropic work. So in private discussions, journal articles and letters to the press, Lorne emphasized the company's role in suppressing the slave trade. [3] Finally the pressure persuaded Gladstone. Britain took over IBEA's few remaining assets and territorial rights, establishing a protectorate in Kenya in 1894 and in Uganda the following year.

Lorne and his fellow investors never recovered their initial capital, let alone earning any profit. "Poorly conceived, badly managed, and grossly undercapitalized," according to the historical record, "the company was destined from the start to a short existence." [4] By June 1893 the strain proved too much for Mackinnon; Lorne felt a moral obligation to attend the funeral.

Yet Lorne refused to write off the enterprise as a complete failure. At their very first meeting, IBEA shareholders were told their dividends "must be taken out in philanthropy," through the suppression of slavery and inter-tribal warfare. And the region had been secured for Christianity and British capitalism. Lorne remained convinced Britain should always go "where our duty or trade interests call us." [5]

Meanwhile, Lorne continued to hear rumours of possible political appointments for himself. Warden of the Cinque Ports and Viceroy of India were both whispered in April 1891. India "may surely be dismissed as incredible," pronounced Henry Labouchere. "Such an appointment would be a job of the most flagrant kind, and would excite universal disapproval." [6] Radical member of the Commons for Northampton, editor of the weekly gossip sheet *Truth*, and irreverent critic of royalty, Labouchere delighted in cutting Lorne down to size.

Lorne was even rumoured for Poet Laureate at the time of Tennyson's death in 1892. Relegating the laureate's function to "ceremonial writer of official verse," William Morris considered Lorne the "person pointed out for the office, should the office be thought one worth keeping up under modern conditions." [7] Labouchere was even less charitable, dismissing Lorne's verses on the centenary of Robbie Burns's death as "excruciating products of his muse." Since Lorne's "ghastly experiments" with the Psalms, continued Labouchere, "one might have supposed he would have spared the world any more of his adventures in verse." [8]

Queen Victoria's appointment of Lorne as Governor and Constable of Windsor Castle was too much for Labouchere. The governorship was a largely honorary position, providing an annual stipend of 12,000 pounds and a modicum of status. A "monstrous job" and an "absolute sinecure," snorted *Truth*, "given for doing nothing whatever." Even worse was Lorne's decision to hold this "permanent place of value" while contesting the 1892 general election as Liberal Unionist candidate for Bradford Central. "The sooner he withdraws his candidature the better." [9]

Marquis of Lorne, in formal uniform.

But Lorne had no intention of stepping down, though Windsor Castle and other court duties, plus a severe bout of the flu, rendered him at best a half-time candidate in Bradford Central. The issues in Bradford, as across the nation, were Ireland and imperialism. He attacked Gladstone's "policy of surrender to the Irish Nationalists." And with his Imperial British East Africa Company experience providing a backdrop, Lorne campaigned against Gladstone and the "Small Englanders" within the Liberal mainstream. They were "fearful of responsibility and anxious to limit all national effort to what they could themselves smell and touch without leaving their armchair." [10]

Lorne's strong positions on East Africa and Ireland were skilfully exploited by his Gladstonian Liberal opponent in Bradford Central. G.J. Shaw-Lefevre proved "uncomprising in his hostility" to a government bailout of IBEA, while at the same time catering to the constituency's Irish vote. Lorne went down to a 4710-4245 defeat in the July election, believing that "1100 Irish votes decided the contest against me." [11]

Lorne's stance in Bradford Central was consistent with the image portrayed through his political writing in the late 1880s and early 1890s. His occasional journal articles on Canada remained entertaining and enlightening, whether promoting emigration to the prairie west, arguing against commercial union with the United States, or explaining Canada's autonomy to American readers. [12] But his Irish articles seemed stale, merely repeating his unacceptable proposal for Irish regional rather than national governing bodies. [13]

Even Louise eventually tired of Lorne's views on Ireland. "She favours Home Rule all round," an astonished Henry Campbell-Bannerman wrote his wife from Balmoral in 1894, and "condemns the action of the Lords" against Irish nationalism. "Really it is quite marvellous," continued the minister, "and I think her influence will have the best effect." Completely enthralled by Louise's charm, as were many Balmoral visitors, Campbell-Bannerman concluded that "it is the Princess who is the divine influence here." [14]

Lorne finally returned to the Commons as Liberal Unionist member for Manchester South in the general election of July 1895, edging out the sitting Gladstonian Liberal, Sir Henry Roscoe, by a close 4457-4379 margin. Lorne's victory was part of a national trend, as Lord Salisbury's Conservatives, with Liberal Unionist support, rolled to a 152-seat majority over their Gladstonian Liberal and Irish Nationalist opposition.

"We have had a stiff fight for Union, but I think the result will lay the Irish separatists low for a long time," Lorne wrote a Canadian correspondent three days after the election. As for himself, "there will be another member for Canada in the House of Commons." [15] But Lorne proved no more talkative in his five years as member for Manchester South than in his previous stint representing Argyllshire. His one and only contribution to debates was a plea for electric lights in House of Commons committee rooms, "as any fog may stop the proceedings of Committees at present."[16] Beyond that, "he seemed content to remain an inconspicuous and habitually silent figure in the life of Parliament." [17]

\* \* \* \* \*

Writing rather than politics remained foremost in Lorne's mind through the 1890s, as he proved himself a most prolific and diverse writer. The "Canada" books of the previous decade were behind him. His political articles in the monthly magazines kept his name and his views before the country's leaders, should administrative or imperial appointments be in the air. But now his major literary energies were devoted to two new ambitious areas of writing — substantial non-fiction works in biography and history, plus entertaining fictional writing that appeared as short stories and novels.

His 1892 biography, *Viscount Palmerston, K.G.*, was published in the Sampson Low, Marston series on Queen Victoria's prime ministers. Palmerston was more than a figure out of history; he had led the nation during much of Lorne's boyhood and included the Duke of Argyll in his cabinet. Through his father's connections Lorne gained access to much previously unpublished Palmerston correspondence. The book enjoyed modest commercial success — as did the series itself — lasting through a third edition by J.M. Dent in 1906.

Critically, however, *Viscount Palmerston* proved disappointing. Lorne borrowed too heavily on other recently published Palmerston biographies; neither his new material nor the way he used it offered sufficient new insights. Too much space is given to lengthy quotes from letters and speeches, while analysis and evaluation are lacking. "The whole book forms a less vivid picture," lamented one critic, "than Lord Lorne, with his considerable ability, might have made it had he shortened it and sharpened it up." [18] As had happened before, Lorne did not push himself to the limit of his talents.

More satisfactory to both author and reader is *The Governor's Guide to Windsor Castle*, published by Cassell in 1895. Here was a subject for which Lorne had some passion. He had danced at Windsor at Queen Victoria's children's parties; there in 1871 in St. George's Chapel he had married his princess; family visits since the wedding had acquainted him with virtually every nook and cranny of the castle.

*The Governor's Guide* is written in a conversational tone, as if the writer were in intimate conversation with a single reader, showing him or her around the castle. The 190-page work is enhanced by Lorne's own sketches and illustrations. The book succeeds intellectually because of Lorne's thorough understanding of the castle's history and architecture; it succeeds emotionally because of the author's passionate commitment to his material. Like *Canadian Pictures*, it is Lorne writing at his best.

From political biography and castle guidebook, Lorne's non-fiction writing moved next to the myths and stories of his native Argyllshire. *Adventures in Legend; Being the Last Historic Legends of the Western Highlands* was published by Constable in 1898. Here the author records local legends before they vanish from the collective Highland memory, already endangered by the processes of urbanization, industrialization and Anglicization. Lorne takes a chronological approach, with lengthy introductions to each historical period and legends simply written as recited. The result is a popular history of Argyllshire and its people. But *Adventures in Legend* proved rather dull for outsiders, one reviewer dismissing it as "neither good legend nor good history." [19]

Fiction writing added yet another dimension to Lorne's public persona during this period. Short stories in *Blackwood's Magazine* and *Harper's Weekly* create highly realistic settings, as the author drew on his knowledge of local customs and geography. "Who Were They? A Maltese Apparition", inspired by Mediterranean holidays, and "The Double-Bedded Room", set in the Swiss Alps, also reveal Lorne's continuing interest in para-psychology and the supernatural. Both stories engulf the reader in a world of mystery and suspense, where the difference between reality and illusion is unclear. [20] "Hunting Life in the Rockies" is less satisfactory; while setting remains well handled, the overall effect is marred by a sense of the patronizing Briton explaining the Canadian West to American readers. [21]

The Canadian West also provides the setting for Lorne's 8500-word novella "Love and Peril", which appeared in an 1890 collection, *Three Notable Stories*, published by Spencer Blackett. "Love and Peril" chronicles the experiences of a young Toronto man, John Uptas, in the North West Territories. Uptas encounters one dramatic adventure after another — harsh natural environment, hostile Indian braves, pliable Indian princesses. It is pure adventure, appealing to the British fascination with the North American West.

Lorne's strangest piece of fiction is surely *The Adventures of John Pas-Plus*, where an eighteenth century North American boy encounters a fresh life-threatening adventure on every page. This 30,000-word potboiler was published in 1892 by the Railway and General Automatic Library — the first of a series of books designed to place cheap reading material in the hands of the third-class traveller. "Fresh batches will be added at frequent intervals," trumpeted the book's promotional blurb. It featured endpaper advertisements for Burgess Lion Pills, contained no words longer than two syllables, and sold for one shilling from automatic boxes at railway stations. *The Adventures of John Pas-Plus* confirmed the author's eccentric behaviour among the British aristocracy.

*From Shadow to Sunlight*, published by Appleton of New York in 1891, is Lorne's most complex and ambitious fictional work. The central characters of this novel present an interesting contrast — the naive, impetuous American girl in Britain and the sophisticated, reserved British traveller in America. The setting moves from the west coast of Scotland to San Francisco, to a final resolution in Victoria, British Columbia. Here, on the novel's final page, misunderstandings are cleared up, obstacles to marriage removed, and the young lovers agree to live happily ever after. Along the way Lorne indulges himself in overdoses of Celtic legends, discourses on Highland language and history, and excursions into his favourite worlds of superstition and second sight.

Critics who had ignored Lorne's previous fiction as not worthy of mention paid some attention to *From Shadow to Sunlight. Catholic World* characterized it as "a very silly little tale, badly constructed, and for the most part written in a worse style than should be pardoned even to a semi-royal author." *Athanaeum* thought it "a terribly namby-pamby story, full of guide-book style information about Scotland and America, padded out with dull conversations and feeble characters." [22]

Like all his fictional writing, *From Shadow to Sunlight* presents light, escapist reading, depending on circumstance and coincidence to advance the narrative and resolve the story. There is plenty of romance, adventure and intrigue to keep the reader engrossed. It is sentimental fiction at its best — or worst — with much melodrama through coincidental encounters, artificial dialogue, and happy, moralistic endings.

Lorne's fictional pieces, like his political articles and his travel books, illustrate his continuing interest in Canada, especially his hopes for the development of the West. "Love and Peril" pleads for "more troops regularly enrolled" in the North West Territories to prevent further Indian and Metis uprisings. *From Shadow to Sunlight* compares two transcontinental railway routes to Canada's advantage; while the American journey offered "horrid alkali plains" and the "dullness of the desert," the Canadian Pacific Railway delivered "wonderful scenery" in "perfect comfort and security." [23]

But the critics were right; as literature, Lorne's fiction was no better than his poetry. There would be no more published short stories, novellas or full-length novels after the mid-1890s. Instead, the ever-surprising Lorne now turned his creative attention to writing for the stage. In October 1897 London's Covent Garden Theatre presented the opera "Diarmid", with music by Hamish MacCunn and words by the Marquis of Lorne. Set in second century Scotland, the story came from two ancient Celtic ballads concerning the love of Diarmid and Grania.

With Princess Louise and the Princess of Wales beside him, Lorne basked in the opening night applause at Covent Garden. He was pleased with the Moody Manners Company's production, especially with the "excellent voice of Miss Kirby Lynn" as the soprano lead. He was delighted when Boosey & Company published the work under the title *Diarmid: Grand Opera in Four Acts Founded on Heroic celtic Legends*. Encouraged by this initial success, Lorne and MacCunn considered purchasing the Carl Rosa Company and presenting additional Scottish operas. [24]

But "Diarmid" proved so problematic that future plans had to be scrapped. To begin with, Moody Manners was the only company to brave an opera in English, against the prevailing preference for Italian and German, and then only dared stage "Diarmid" during the off-season. After its brief run at Covent Garden, a provincial tour of Manchester, Liverpool and Glasgow, and a special performance for Queen Victoria at Balmoral, "Diarmid" was never performed again.

In addition to its unpopular English lyrics, "Diarmid" contained too much ancient Scottish history and not enough drama for the average opera patron. As the Marquis of Salisbury bluntly remarked, its story was "over the heads of most of the people who went to see it." [25] By the end of the decade, it seemed unlikely that any of Lorne's diverse literary outpourings — poetry, fiction, or drama — would ever enjoy critical acclaim or realize commercial success.

\* \* \* \* \*

Meanwhile signals remained mixed on the personal relationship between Lorne and Louise. Separate holidays remained popular through these years. On 31 March 1896, for instance, they spent their twenty-fifth wedding anniversary apart, Louise travelling on the Continent while Lorne was a house guest at Sandringham. Though Louise had once been her favourite sister in-law, the Princess of Wales was now inclined "to take the side of the husband against the wife." [26] Perhaps Lorne and Alix found common ground as left-behinds, while their more fun-loving spouses cavorted around Europe!

As they grew older, Louise and Bertie came to appreciate each other more than ever. She alone of all his sisters was invited to weekend at Sandringham, either by herself or with Lorne. At Bertie's request she cut short a European holiday to help her brother survive the formalities of the 1896 Norwich Music Festival, "although she was not very well at the time, and said she did not feel up to the fatigue of it." [27]

But Bertie still stood in the wings as Prince of Wales. Queen Victoria continued to rule the royal roost and Louise remained at her beck and call. During 1897 for instance — the Diamond Jubilee of Victoria's reign —

Louise spent the late winter and early spring months with her mother at Cannes on the Riviera, June in the midst of Jubilee celebrations in London, and October again as her mother's principal companion at Balmoral.

Louise and her sisters seemed to become ever more protective of their mother as the old Queen moved through her last few years. With Louise at one side, Beatrice at the other, and Helena adding her support — a veritable "petticoat curtain" of protection — Victoria found it easier to get through the tiresome dinner parties and formal receptions of court life. One visitor to court found such daughterly protection intimidating and "rather alarming" when he was first introduced to the Queen. [28]

But Louise could also act as kindly mediator between the Queen and her subjects. Consider William Gladstone, prime minister for so many years of Victoria's reign, yet a man she had never liked. In the spring of 1897 the Gladstones holidayed at Cannes at the same time as Louise and her mother. Gladstone said he had no wish to meet the Queen, unless she wished to see him, which she did not. Louise solved the problem by inviting the Gladstones to tea at her hotel, then suggested they retire upstairs to continue chatting in the royal presence. The resulting meeting was reasonably friendly; amidst the polite and aimless conversation, Gladstone received the one and only royal handshake of his life. [29] That was about the only recognition the veteran politician received in that Diamond Jubilee year.

Lorne seems to have endured the dreary times spent with Queen Victoria with his usual grace and politeness. Christmases at Osborne must have been particularly bleak, as gentlemen guests were accommodated in cold, draughty cottages away from the main house. According to the Queen, Lorne "always makes himself so pleasant" during the long weeks at Osborne, especially when accompanying his mother-in-law on carriage rides. Yet Lorne seemed to need the relief provided by after-dinner billiards "to aid his digestion." [30]

Together, Lorne and Louise smiled their way through life at court. "Both very nice and gracious" noted Lord Esher in his diary during Diamond Jubilee celebrations. At Osborne, the husband of one of Queen Victoria's ladies-in-waiting enjoyed being coralled by Lorne for golf in the afternoons and by Louise for conversation every evening. "Much talk with Princess Louise about Watts' statue, architecture and statues in London, Somerset House, very lively and amusing," observed Bernard Mallet. [31]

Fortunately, with the purchase of Rosneath from the Duke of Argyll in 1895, the Lornes now had their own private escape into the countryside. It was twenty years since financial pressures had forced them to abandon their country place at Dornden. Then in 1892 they treated themselves by renting Hill House, Frensham, near Guildford, for the summer months.

They were enjoying time alone together more than they had just a few years earlier. Rosneath seemed ideal.

Lorne and his ageing father had always preferred Rosneath to Inverary. It was a smaller and more comfortable home, in an area of milder weather and lusher vegetation, and with much easier access to London. Yet for many years Lorne's father had been forced to lease Rosneath to ease the strain on family finances. When this lease expired in 1895, the seventy-three year-old Duke found himself with enough to care for at Inverary. It made sense to sell the property to his son and daughter-in-law.

By the 1890s the shores of the peninsula on which Rosneath stood were ringed by many handsome villas, summer residences and boat houses. Regular steamer service connected Rosneath Ferry with Helensburgh across the Gare Loch, while excursion steamers came across the Clyde from Glasgow in summer months. A small village had developed at Rosneath ferry, with the one hundred year-old Ferry Inn as its major landmark. The drive from the ferry landing to Rosneath Castle passed through a fine avenue of trees, well over 200 years old.

Rosneath Castle was of two-storey stone construction, boasting handsome north and south fronts adorned with fine Ionic columns and a high circular central tower offering a fine panorama of the surrounding countryside. To the south the view was open to the Clyde, and on a sunny day the afternoon and evening sun washed over the lawns and gardens. To both father and son, Rosneath was the most beautiful spot in Britain.

Unfortunately, Lorne found upkeep on Rosneath as much of a strain as his father, so that for most summers during the late 1890s he rented out the castle to generate some income. Still, ownership of Rosneath gave Lorne and Louise an annual excuse to escape London and holiday at the Ferry Inn at Rosneath Ferry. They became its most famous guests, contributing funds for its expansion, and assisting with its decorating and landscaping. At century's end the Ferry Inn may have been the world's only hostelry with an exterior sign designed and painted by a royal princess! [32]

Lorne and Louise were beginning to find some peace in their lives. "Lord Lorne is much improved in appearance by age," noted one observer in the mid-1890s, "a good Rubens, as his uncle, Ronald Gower, is a bad Bronzino." [33] While Lorne enjoyed his writing and his library, Louise needed physical activity to work out her tensions. Visitors to Rosneath observed with some amusement Louise's "handling, not only a pruning knife, but an axe or saw, as she tramps through the woods." She enjoyed berating cottagers for ill-tended fruit trees, "then and there remedying the mischief with her own hands. [34]

\* \* \* \* \*

Princess Louise, by Notman of Montreal.

Spring and summer of 1899 promised a sprightly end to the old century and a bright welcome to the new. The British populace enthusiastically joined the royal family in wishing old Queen Victoria a happy eightieth birthday on May 24. In July Louise gave one of her grand garden parties, with more than 1000 invited guests crowding the grounds of Kensington Palace. Louise and Lorne tripped off to the Derby at Epsom with the Prince of Wales. Court life as a whole seemed much more cheerful, as Bertie prepared to succeed his ageing mother on the throne.

But the nineteenth century had one last parting gift for the British nation — the South African War. Early signs indicated this war was no delightful imperial romp among "lesser breeds without the law." "We are all preparing for a rather melancholy Xmas," Lorne wrote a Canadian friend in December 1899, "as so many friends have been killed or wounded in South Africa." [35] Christmas at Osborne would have been bad enough, but the sombre mood of the country plus her own failing health persuaded Queen Victoria to remain quietly at Windsor over the holidays. Lorne and Louise joined her there for a dismal fortnight.

Yet in the long run the South African War forced Lousie and Lorne out of the complacency that had characterized their public lives during the 1890s, pushing both of them into a much more active public service role. In 1898 they rejoiced when their old friends Lord and Lady Minto got the Canadian governor generalship. [36] But the decade had slipped by with no imperial appointment for Lorne himself — Curzon got the Indian viceroyalty over Lorne in 1897; then Queen Victoria derailed a possible run at the governor generalship of the new Commonwealth of Australia by proclaiming it "quite impossible" due to Louise's health. [37]

Now the South African War provided an ideal platform for Lorne to air his views on questions of imperial importance. He willingly lent his name to various war relief efforts, and threw his moral support behind the Canadian decision to send troops to South Africa. Britain was obviously right in pursuing military action against the Boers — "practical civilization against the will of the closet," he informed readers of the *North American Review*. As the war dragged on, and the possibility of a clear-cut British triumph lessened, Lorne urged a cessation of hostilities and a building up of South Africa "in such a way as would make a repetition of the war absolutely impossible." [38]

Kensington Palace became the tea-party-and-reception centre for British Empire women on their way to and from teaching stints in Boer re-settlement (or "concentration") camps. At these receptions, according to Frances Balfour, Colonial Secretary Joseph Chamberlain gave "the speech of the conqueror" while Lorne's remarks were "characteristically conciliatory." The teachers loved his every word. "We take the gold out of the soil," Lorne said of South Africa, "and we pour the gold of our womanhood into it." And he was as inquisitive as ever; Canadian teacher

Florence Randal was astonished at the number of questions Lorne asked her about South Africa. [39]

Lorne's Ottawa experience suggested a co-operative approach to peace in South Africa. A "modus vivendi" must be worked out with the Dutch colonists "as English and French have found in Canada." Dutch and English settlers might even "in time form one race." Assisted emigration from Britain would strengthen the English-speaking component of that racial partnership, giving the country "the benefits of the best characteristics of the European races." Like most Europeans of his age, Lorne gave no thought to including South Africa's black population in the future government of the country. Indeed, Dutch and English would be driven together by "the common necessity each has to strengthen the other against any possible predominance of the blacks." [40]

Lorne's chosen vehicle for promoting British emigration to South Africa was the London-based Barnardo Society. Founded by Thomas Barnardo in 1870, the organization promoted child-saving and child-welfare, with assisted emigration of pauper children to the colonies as one of its main thrusts. During the 1890s the Barnardo group placed some 12,000 children in Canada, and now stood ready to re-direct its activities towards South Africa. Lorne served as the society's honorary president at this time, and enthusiastically supported the South African thrust.

Barnardo children would be "placed out [in South Africa] as in Canada with farmers, with miners, with mechanics, and with any who want them," Lorne explained, "if the employers can only show that a good home is provided." What a "happy change" this would be from the "crowded thoroughfares" of London's East End! Once settled in South Africa, the children would "permeate the districts where they grow up to manhood and womanhood with the British idea and practice of common obedience to law and justice as the best security for freedom." [41]

Dramatic results might have been expected, given Barnardo's success in Canada, Lorne's presidency of the organization, plus his offer to put land he owned in the Transvaal at the society's disposal. But South Africa differed from Canada — the black population provided cheap labour, while the Dutch resisted massive English-speaking immigration. The ageing and financially strapped Barnardo ultimately decided to stick with Canada. By the time of his death in 1905, the Barnardo Society had sent more than 50,000 children to Canada but only a handful to South Africa.[42] Lorne had no quarrel with the organization's Canadian focus; but he was disappointed that nothing more could be done in Africa.

The war in South Africa also illustrated Louise's increasing tendency to take on important public responsibilities. She had, of course, always patronized a long list of women's educational, health-care, and artistic philanthropies. Then in 1897 she accepted the vice-presidency of the National Trust for the Preservation of Places of Historic Interest and

Natural Beauty. Now, through the winter of 1899-1900 she mobilized her tremendous energy and organizational skills to fight the South African war on the home front.

She accepted the active presidency of the County of London Soldiers' and Sailors' Families Association, a group providing financial assistance to wives and families of men serving in the war. She made regular visits to the war wounded at Chelsea Hospital. She organized two sets of rooms for convalescing officers — at the Savoy Hotel in London and the Ferry Inn in Rosneath — paying for structural renovations and nursing costs.

Louise's major war contribution was a sculpted piece completed in 1904 and installed in St. Paul's Cathedral, honoring Imperial troops who served with British forces in South Africa. Coming after her Broad Walk statue and her Battenberg piece, the South African memorial illustrated Louise's commitment to sculpture rather than sketching or painting during this period in her life.

Louise's South African work is not the best known piece among the hundreds of statues, plaques and other memorials in St. Paul's; most staff members and volunteer workers are unable to locate it! The piece sits high up on the outside wall of the south transept, covered with an accumulation of twentieth century dust and partially obscured by the Royal Standard of Australia. It is a black marble, winged victory, projecting out from the wall. The inscription on the plaque underneath reads: "To the glory of God and to the undying honour of those 4300 sons of Britain beyond the seas who gave their lives for the love of the Motherland in the South African War 1899-1902," followed by the simple signature "Louise."

The South African memorial is an emotional piece of work, beautifully executed in exquisite detail. It is somewhat reminiscent of her Battenberg sculpture, featuring an angel with outstretched wings, hovering above a cross, clasping the hands of a figure which is about to soar heavenwards. Yet it goes beyond her previous work. It contains a suggestion of lightness — "the lightness not merely of sorrow past but of sorrow forgotten" — while over-all a tender reverence seems to brood. This piece in St. Paul's, concluded one critic, moved Louise's sculpture "to a modern plane of thought." [43]

# ❦ CHAPTER NINETEEN
# THE KING'S FAVOURITE SISTER, 1900-1909

---

*T*he winter of 1899-1900 brought disturbing news from Inverary as well as from South Africa. Lorne's father suffered a bad attack of gout which did not respond to treatment. The seventy-six year-old Duke had enjoyed reasonably good health during his advancing years, but this gout attack signalled the end. Ronald Gower "heard a bad account" of the Duke's health in early March; later in the month Gower lunched with Lorne and Louise, and "their account was no better." [1] Death came on April 24. "The last weeks of my father's illness were full of suffering," noted Lorne; "it is a relief to know he is at rest from pain." [2]

Lorne and his father had not been especially close during the last twenty years of the old man's life. The sensitive and caring Duchess Elizabeth had in earlier years served as a buffer between her high-spirited children and their more austere and formal father. But Elizabeth's death in 1878 and Duke George's later marriages upset the old order. Lorne barely concealed his loathing for George's second wife, Amelia (Claughton) Anson, following their 1881 marriage.

After Amelia's death in 1894, George went to the altar a third time with Ina McNeill, an Argyllshire-born member of Queen Victoria's household staff. One gossip suggested the Duke "could not do without a wife, and it had been the same after his first wife's death." Princess Beatrice whispered that "it was very hard for the family." [3] Ina proved marginally more tolerable than Amelia, but Lorne begrudged her position as Duke George's literary executor. [4]

Funeral services for the Eighth Duke of Argyll were held in the parish church at Inverary, with internment at Kilmun, the ancient family burial site on the Holy Loch. No gathering or service was planned at Kilmun, and only Lorne's step-mother and one sister, Lady Victoria Campbell, followed the funeral coach as it made its way slowly over the sixty-five kilometre journey. It was eight o'clock in the evening by the time the small cortege reached Kilmun churchyard. There, showing dimly in the flickering light of the torches, a solitary female figure awaited them — Princess Louise. [5]

Perhaps Louise was atoning for thirty years of putting her husband's family so far behind her own. Perhaps she was quietly preparing herself for a new life as the Duchess of Argyll. Whatever the case, her appearance at Kilmun was brief. Louise was soon on her way back to London while Lorne stayed on at Inverary with Ronny Gower and Frank Greene, sorting through the estate papers and contemplating his inheritance.

At the age of fifty-four, John George Edward Henry Douglas Sutherland Campbell, Marquis of Lorne, had succeeded his father as His Grace, the Ninth Duke of Argyll. He would now be called Argyll, not Lorne, though a name used for most of a lifetime was not easily shed. He could also call himself Earl Campbell and Cowal; Viscount of Lochow and Glenisla; Baron Inverary, Mull, Morvern and Tivy; Baron Campbell; Earl of Argyll; Baron of Londorne; Baron Kintyre; Baron Sundridge; Baron Hamilton; or Baron Lochow. What a marvellous fistful of names for travelling incognito!

The new Duke of Argyll took his hereditary seat in the House of Lords. His father's death also made him Hereditary Master of the Royal Household, Scotland; Hereditary High Sheriff of the County of Argyll; Admiral of the Western Coasts and Isles; Keeper of the Great Seal of Scotland and of the Castles of Dunstaffnage, Dunoon and Carrich; and Lord-Lieutenant of Argyllshire. He continued as Governor and Constable of Windsor Castle, and as honorary colonel-in-chief of five military regiments — 3rd Argyll and Sutherland Highlanders, London Scottish, Argyll and Bute Volunteers, Glasgow Highlanders, and Argyll Light Infantry (Canada).

The new Duke became titular head of the Clan Campbell and senior member of the immediate family. Among his brothers, Archie and his wife Janey now had two grown children — Niall (later Tenth Duke of Argyll) and Elspeth; Walter died in 1889; George lived a quiet life with his wife Sibyl; Colin removed himself to India after his messy divorce case, where he died in 1895.

Lorne's sisters had scattered far and wide. Edith lived an aristocratic life as wife of Earl Percy, later Duke of Northumberland. Elizabeth lived a colonial life, wife of an officer in the Indian Army, until her death in 1896. Victoria, despite her physical infirmities, continued as an active church worker in the Hebridean Islands until her death in 1910. Frances married architect Eustace Balfour, Arthur Balfour's younger brother, and supported the suffragette movement. Mary married Rev. Edward Glyn, vicar of Kensington, later Bishop of Peterborough, and settled into parish life.

The new Duke of Argyll inherited the ducal seat of Inverary Castle. It is an early example of eighteenth century Gothic revival architecture, constructed of talc-like stone from quarries at St. Catherine's and Creggan, dark green in colour, almost soapy to the touch, and extremely weather-resistant. The castle is quadrangular in shape, with four round corner towers dominated by a square central tower rising above the main building. It stands on the right bank of the Aray River, as it flows into Loch Fyne at the village of Inverary. Behind the castle rises the hill of Duniquoich, with richly wooded sides and an ancient watch tower perched on its bald crown. Around the castle, nearly fifty kilometers in circumference, stretches a wooded park with three picturesque avenues — one of lime trees, two of beechwood.

Certain defects in the castle were corrected in re-building after the 1877 fire. Interior walls were re-arranged to make better use of internal space. Now there were splendid rooms for family members and guests, all with windows commanding unrivalled views of mountain and glen. Magnificent state rooms featured Flemish and French tapestries; the library boasted fine specimens of early Gaelic painting; an armoury housed ancient weapons carried in battle by earlier generations of Campbells.

This armoury was the most impressive room in the castle, occupying the central tower, extending upwards to the full height of the building and flooded with light from Gothic windows at the top. From either side of the armoury a wide staircase led to the second floor, and on one of its many landings hung a full-length portrait of Princess Louise. Beside the painting stood the harp which figured in that sweet lilting Victorian song, "Touch the Harp Gently My Pretty Louise." [6]

Like the smaller place at Rosneath, Inverary Castle imposed a strain on the new Duke of Argyll. Theoretically, the financial situation looked promising: Scottish agriculture was once again prospering, and by investing some 554,000 pounds in property improvements between 1847-1897, Lorne's father had doubled the market value of the family estates. Yet by the turn of the century, annual rental income of 51,000 pounds from those family lands — 168,000 acres in Argyllshire, another 7,000 in Dumbartonshire — barely met estate and household expenses. [7] Times had caught up with the Campbells and other landowning families; it was now increasingly difficult to support an aristocratic lifestyle on rental income from marginal agricultural lands.

While government commissions recommended small-lot farmers for marginal regions like Argyllshire, Lorne clung to his inherited belief that the long-range answer lay in efficient management of large estates. Whatever the future held, the new Duke of Argyll had little hope of increasing his rental income; in fact during the early years of the century the Argyll estates actually showed "a serious shrinkage in the rent roll." [8]

Death duties posed the most immediate problem. "Everything is most strictly tied up," *Truth* correctly reported on 14 June 1900. By the time his father's will had gone through the courts and various government departments, Argyll owed a total of 46,000 pounds in death duties. "It will take me all my life to pay the tax demanded, which is seven times what it was before the Finance Act," he wrote Lewis Harcourt. "I have become for the estates a mere tax collector for the government, bound and gagged to the Treasury Executioners. [9]

By throwing all his private money "into the Death Tax vortex," the new Duke met approximately one-third of the government levy in 1902. The Argyll estates were mortgaged to raise the remainder. "I am told I must not 'cheep' on this to anyone," he confided to Harcourt, "or else the mortgage holders will raise the percentage and call in the loans." [10] Meanwhile, economy became the order of the day. The Duke and Duchess of Argyll would stick close to Kensington Palace, reduce their charitable givings, and live off Louise's state income — dating back to the 30,000 pound dowry and 6,000 pound annuity approved by parliament in 1871.[11]

Both family pride and market conditions weighed against selling Inverary or Rosneath. Inverary had been the Campbell seat for centuries while Rosneath appealed to both Lorne and Louise; neither could be parted with easily. And given ever-increasing land taxes, buyers for such castles were not that plentiful. In the end, Argyll Lodge in London was the only major property disposed of after Duke George's death. Inverary Castle was put on the rental market for 3000 pounds a year, while Rosneath was made available on a seasonal basis. On business or pleasure trips north, the Argylls stayed at Dalkenna Lodge near Inverary or the Ferry Inn at Rosneath.

Estate staff was reduced in size. "The estates are apparently to be managed on extreme utilitarian principles," reported *Truth* on 26 July 1900, "so that the tenants of all classes anticipate a 'dour' time under the new regime." Lorne reported on Inverary in autumn 1902: "four men have to be dismissed, no improvements can be made, no planting of trees carried out, and everything at a standstill." Rosneath was no better. "I have had to send away the head keeper and all dogs, and there are no horses or ponies in the stalls. The garden is well stocked with vegetables, but I have had to send away all but four men from the gardens." The future promised no improvement — "more dismissals must take place, more poor wives tears must flow!" [12]

While the new Duke and Duchess of Argyll pinched their pennies, many of Edwardian Britain's ducal families continued to live in great splendour, lavishly entertaining at both their country estates and town houses. The decline in Campbell fortunes seemed especially dramatic. Lorne remembered the gala entertainments hosted by his maternal grandparents, the Duke and Duchess of Sutherland, at Stafford House; he recalled the political energy surging through Argyll Lodge breakfasts hosted by his own parents. Now the Ninth Duke found himself with neither financial, social nor political strength.

\* \* \* \* \*

The death of the Eighth Duke of Argyll was but the first of many turn-of-the-century family bereavements. Louise's brother Alfred — host of those glorious Malta holidays — died in July 1900. Her sister Vicky, Dowager Empress of Germany, passed away the following year. But the most important death for both family and country was that of Queen Victoria. The Queen reached her eighty-first birthday in 1900, and she was beginning to slip. That autumn she paid her last visit to Balmoral, but the weather was bad and no one seemed able to cheer up the old Queen. On December 18 she travelled from Windsor to Osborne by train, for a final family Christmas.

The new Duke of Argyll informed his sister Frances in early January that the Queen "was failing." [13] On the sixteenth, Louise sped to Osborne to join Helena and Beatrice at their mother's bedside. With some slight improvement in the Queen's condition Louise slipped back to London on Friday January 18, only to be "summoned at forty minutes' notice" to return to Osborne with the Prince of Wales on Sunday.

That evening the bulletins seemed "more hopeful" to Frances Balfour, as she dined with her brother at Kensington. Yet on Monday morning she returned and found a depressed Argyll at breakfast. "The telegrams were more anxious," she recalled, "and I saw he thought the end was near. Everybody spent the day in painful suspense, absolutely no other thought seemed to occupy the public mind." On Tuesday Argyll was summoned to Osborne, "greatly dreading all that he would find." [14]

At Osborne he found wave upon wave of royal children, grand-children and great-grandchildren, political and state officials, members of the court and the household staff — all present to witness this great public death. At 2:30 that afternoon, the princesses summoned the rest of the family to the Queen's room. Through it all the old lady clung tenaciously to life. "The last moments were like a great three-decker ship sinking," remarked Lorne. "She kept on rallying and then sinking." [15]

At 6:30 p.m., Tuesday January 22, 1901, the Queen finally died. "I am glad she was spared what she always dreaded — a mental decline and a Regency," Argyll wrote Lewis Harcourt, "but was able to work in fair vigour to almost the last week. Her judgement was wonderful, and to her family the loss of her centering authority and counsel is very sorrowful." [16]

In the days leading up to her mother's death, Louise had not been at her best. "Louise is as usual much down on her sisters," wrote the Queen's physician, Dr. James Reid, from Osborne. "Hope she won't stay long, or she will do mischief." Then in the aftermath, while other members of the family succumbed to real or imagined grief, Louise went to work. She joined secretary Frederick Ponsonby in tackling the hundreds of telegrams of sympathy that arrived from around the world. Many had to be answered personally. Louise "found no difficulty in expressing herself," remarked Ponsonby, "and dictated some really first-rate answers." [17]

After lying in state for ten days at Osborne, the Queen's body began its final journey to Windsor on February 1. There on the fourth the coffin was taken to the mausoleum at Frogmore, and Victoria rejoined her beloved Albert. Argyll captured the scene in verse:

> We brought Her to where Windsor shows
> Her church, her walls, her tower;
> A dream in stone, whose river flows
> Beneath fair wooded slopes, and knows
> The secret of Her power. [18]

A favourite family anecdote concerned a dove which entered the mausoleum at Frogmore, as the royals knelt in prayer on an anniversary of Queen Victoria's death during the 1920s. "Dear Mama's spirit," they murmured. "No, I am sure it is not," said Louise. "It must be dear Mama's spirit," they repeated. "No," Louise persisted, "Mama's spirit would never have ruined Beatrice's hat." [19]

Despite her prickliness and stubborn push for independence, Louise had long ago made peace with her mother. Indeed, they had been on good terms for the past ten to fifteen years. Now she had to cope with the loss. For a while Louise found it difficult to "realize that she is gone . . . The desire to write to her, and feeling she expects news, is still with me. She was always wanting to hear and to know." Later Louise confessed that "the sorrow never wears off, at least for me it won't." [20] Lorne shared Louise's sense of loss. He confided to Ronny Gower that he "felt very deeply the death of the Queen, who was quite like a mother to him." For thirty years, Argyll had received "nothing but kindness from the Queen, and not one word of anything but affection." [21]

But Argyll's grief did not impede his writing. Before January was out he agreed to prepare a biography of his mother-in-law. *V.R.I. Queen Victoria: Her Life and Empire* was first published by Spottiswoode in weekly serial form through the spring and summer of 1901, as it rolled off Lorne's pen. Harmsworth Brothers published it in book form that November. *V.R.I. Queen Victoria* proved very popular, given its subject matter, its author's unique perspective, and the timeliness of publication. Harper and Brothers of New York brought out an American edition; both the British and American editions went through a number of printings; and in 1909 the book was republished by George Bell and Sons of London under the new title *The Life of Queen Victoria.*

*V.R.I. Queen Victoria* was a combination political and personal biography for the general reader. The text was largely a chronological narrative, covering the late Queen's long life from birth to death, with liberal use of quotations from her journal and from sympathetic admirers. Argyll included no critical opinions and little analysis. Instead, he gave the British reading public what it wanted in 1901 — a glowing account of Victoria's life, with just enough details on her court and her family to arouse interest but not slip into gossip. One reviewer found the book "in perfect taste, but necessarily rather colourless." Had Argyll possessed "greater freedom and less responsibility," a much better book might have been produced. [22]

While Lorne wrote, Louise became embroiled in a controversy over a public monument to her late mother. The memorial committee, led by Viscount Esher, political advisor to new King Edward VII, quickly settled on a site directly in front of Buckingham Palace. Louise, however, feared a memorial at that location might replace Nelson's Column in Trafalgar Square as a rallying point for demonstrators, producing "mobs in front of the Palace." Esher considered this was pure pique, believing Louise "furious because she was neither consulted nor employed" on the project.[23] Whatever her motives, Louise was unable to prevail over her brother, as Edward went along with Esher's scheme. London got a new rallying point, where "mobs" regularly began to demonstrate in support of the monarchy!

Louise also lost out to her brother on the disposition of Osborne House. Though Louise loved Osborne ahead of all royal residences, the new King considered it superfluous, and determined to hand it over to the nation. Early in August 1901 Bertie invited Louise, Helena and Beatrice to meet with him at Osborne to make the final decision about the fate of the estate. They withdrew into a secluded part of the grounds, and conversed in German for greater secrecy. [24] The King dictated the terms: Louise could keep Kent House, a smaller Tudor-style villa just outside the main grounds that her mother had willed her directly; Beatrice received a matching out-building, Osborne Cottage; while Helena already had Cumberland Lodge in Windsor Park. But Osborne's main building and grounds were donated to the nation as a convalescent home for officers invalided home from South Africa, and as a junior naval college.

As a youngster, Louise had stood in awe of her eldest brother. After Bertie married Princess Alexandra of Denmark, Louise and Alix became close confdantes, and Louise came to know the Prince of Wales through her sister-in-law. As she matured, Louise grew increasingly fond of her brother, and more confident of her ability to match wits with him. By the 1890s she was a frequent visitor at Marlborough House and Sandringham, and occasionally the two of them spent time abroad together. Not even the Osborne affair could harm their affection.

Part of the growing rapport between Louise and Bertie stemmed from their agreement in the family rift over foreign policy. On one side stood the "Osborne Set" or "German Set", composed of the mass of Queen Victoria's offspring, all linked to Germany through marriage, with William II of Germany — Victoria's eldest grandchild — as acknowledged leader. Bertie stood on the opposite side as leader of the "Sandringham Set" which, through Princess Alix, was more partial to Denmark, France and Russia on foreign policy questions. Louise gradually found German policies as repugnant as she had once found German suitors, and gravitated to Bertie's side of the family. [25]

An even stronger bond between Louise and Bertie was their mutual love of a good time. The rest of the surviving siblings — Helena, Arthur and Beatrice — were much too like their Coburg father, Prince Albert, in their devotion to respectability and sobriety. A larger share of Hanoverian blood coursed through the veins of Louise and Bertie, giving them a greater capacity for having fun. They danced with greater gusto, smoked cigarettes and cigars without feelings of guilt, joked and laughed uproariously, and, above all, loved a good party.

Louise was the new king's favourite sister, and she felt very much at home in the new reign. She still bristled at court invitations that dictated what she must wear, where she must sit at table — almost what she must say. "See!" she would cry, blue sparks flying from her eyes, "I am nothing but a dummy." [26] Yet the court itself was much more casual than under Queen Victoria, and palace dinners merrier with Edward and Alix.

Louise's general health and her energy quotient both reached optimum levels during the Edwardian era. The headaches, the neuralgia attacks, the sudden exits from dining tables and reception rooms, the cancelled public appearances — all occurred far less frequently. The first decade of the twentieth century may well have been Louise's happiest years.

* * * * *

The most intimate picture of Louise in late midle-age comes from a Madame Klepac, her personal attendant on the Kensington Palace staff. Klepac was of Austrian birth, from an old but impoverished family, with twelve years' service at the Vienna court. In the spring of 1908, just as Louise turned sixty, Klepac came to Kensington and stayed four years. Twenty years later — presumably still in need of money — Klepac told her inside-the-palace story to the American magazine *Saturday Evening Post*. [27]

King Edward VII.

Klepac took personal responsibility for Louise's physical care, including exercise, massage, rest and diet. Apart from cigarette smoking — which continued unabated — Louise was determined to maintain a healthy body. "Physical fitness was her fetish," recalled Klepac, and she maintained it by a "regime of exercise and diet as exacting as any athlete in training ever followed under the whip of a coach." The King loved to tease his sister about the setting-up exercises Klepac gave her every morning. "Never mind," Louise replied, "I'll outlive you all, and I won't be a broken-down, sick old woman either." And as a gentle rebuke to her corpulent brother: "I'm never going to be as fat as my mother was!" [28]

Louise followed a very strict daily routine at Kensington, and even on holidays when circumstances permitted. Each morning at 7:30, Klepac brought her a glass of hot water and some Bulgarian yogurt. Then came exercises and bath. Breakfast consisted of one hard-boiled egg, two thin wafers, and a cup of clear Chinese tea. Luncheon was either chicken or lamb, one vegetable, and stewed fruit with little sugar — no potatoes, no puddings or sweets. Dinner was much the same, plus a cup of clear soup. Rarely did she eat any beef or pork. Every afternoon included a rest, every evening bed before midnight.

The results left Louise with a flattering physique well into old age. Klepac remembered her as "tall and beautifully proportioned, with a lovely, fresh English complexion, soft, sandy colored hair with hardly a trace of gray." Still, her eyes remained her most striking feature — "blue as sapphires, piercingly bright, and looked you through and through." [29]

Her energy and youthful vigour impressed everyone. "Princess Louise looks remarkably young, and retains her brightness of manner unimpaired," noted Almeric Fitzroy in 1908, after sharing a compartment on the Windsor-London train with Louise and Lorne. To Klepac, she "seemed like a woman of forty" rather than sixty. "She never walked up stairs, but she ran." She was just as energetic away from the palace — tramping for hours in the rain, hunting with her husband or brother, always returning "as fresh as when she started." [30]

Louise still had her emotional outbursts, but by this time in her life, the flare-ups tended to be momentary, and then she was gentle as a lamb. Apparently she did not take her temper tantrums seriously, and became mildly annoyed when others did. "I like to make people mad," she said. "It shows what is really in them." Even so, it was good to have her husband nearby, for no one equalled Lorne's ability to handle Louise when her violent temper ran away from her. "Now, now Louise; what's the matter?" he would ask in his quiet, gentle way, treating her "just like a child." [31]

Klepac provides a convincing picture of Lorne and Louise's affection for each other. "No pair could have been more congenial." They shared a total interest in each other's work. "She would sit for hours in his library listening to passages as he read aloud to her," while he "loved to watch her

262

as, in great sculptor's apron, she chisled and hammered in her studio." And whenever Lorne passed his wife in a corridor, he would stop and kiss the top of her head in a tender way. "Oh Lorne, don't!" she would exclaim, and smile up at him. [32]

Louise would often dress especially to please Lorne. For several years during the Edwardian period his favourite gown was a pale blue dress of fine quality silk damask. "The colour intensified the blue in her eyes, the gold in her hair, and the creamy softness of her skin." So Louise wore the dress night after night when they dined alone at Kensington — for six long years, according to Klepac — though it was long out of fashion. [33]

Louise's wonderful upright figure showed off her clothes to perfection; she was equally appealing in old or new dresses, expensive or modest items. Lorne, however, was just the opposite. No matter what he wore, he looked frumpy. By Edwardian times he was paying so little attention to his clothes that his tailor described him as "the worst dressed man in London." At home, too, he seemed a little odd — using the servants' entrance, helping with the cooking, eating his big bowls of baked potatoes. To at least one member of the Kensington Palace staff, Lorne was much too simple, and "a bit too homely" for a duke! [34]

The Kensington staff remained relatively small during these years, due both to Lorne's love of simplicity and his continuing need to watch expenses. But Louise was still a royal princess, sister to the king, and certain standards had to be maintained. In addition to Madame Klepac, Louise employed two personal maids, known as dressers, young women who were invariably German. Constant practice with her attendants enabled Louise to keep her oral German in good shape, though still with the deep, gutteral Prussian accent inherited from her father. But her written German had grown rusty over the years, necessitating a German secretary to help her with correspondence.

Social life at Kensington Palace remained simple. With a minimum of house guests and formal ceremonies to disrupt their regular routines, the Duke of Argyll had plenty of time to write and Louise endless hours to paint and sculpt in her cottage studio in the palace garden. Lunches were intimate, with an occasional friend or two having a chance for close conversation with one or both of the Lornes. Infrequent dinner parties were much less formal and much more animated than in royal circles generally, with literary and artistic guests predominating. After dinner men and women retired together to a small cozy room for smoking and more conversation.

Louise engaged two principal ladies-in-waiting during the Edwardian period. Lady Victoria Russell usually accompanied her at court functions, while Lady Lucas went with her — often as an incognito pair — on afternoon walks, shopping trips and occasionally longer excursions.

Beyond the weekday world of London, Louise's travel diary included country weekends with her many English friends, spring and autumn visits to either Rosneath or Inverary, plus the continuing escapes to the spas and sunny climes of continental Europe.

Lorne joined Louise for a three-month trip to Egypt in 1906, with a leisurely homeward progress through Naples, Rome and Florence. The trip had its share of amusing sidelights. It happened that they accidently boarded the same Mediterranean steamer as their nephew, William II of Germany. "There's Willy," Louise called to her equery. "Hide me quick." Louise could laugh off such incidents, but Lorne found the trip a burden. "He does not like the [Egyptian] desert, and compares it unfavourably to the prairies," reported his sister Frances. "His heart is always in Canada."[35] At age sixty, Lorne seemed to find more pleasure in re-living earlier travels; the Egyptian holiday of 1906 was his last major overseas venture.

* * * * *

As a member of the royal family enjoying the benefits of a state income, Louise, Duchess of Argyll, was expected to earn her keep. Despite advancing years, despite her earlier anathema of artificial situations, even despite her constant need for privacy, Louise blossomed into one of the royal family's busiest public figures during the first decade of the new century. Perhaps she had finally conquered her neuralgia, discovered a balance between her public and private selves, or simply felt more comfortable in the Edwardian rather than the Victorian era. She was certainly much more visible than ever before.

Her public engagements for 1908 — the year she turned sixty — would have tired many younger women. Following her customary spring escape to the Continent, she returned to London to preside at a meeting of the Regimental Homes and Benefits Agency and raise funds for a Plaistow maternity hospital. After a May sojourn in Scotland, she and the London season hit full stride.

Louise presided at bazaars in aid of Charing Cross Hospital and the London Homoeopathic Hospital, opened a new children's ward at Essex County Hospital, presented prizes to members of the St. John Ambulance Association and at the Princess Louise Home for Girls, opened the Heritage Craft School for Girls at Chailey and a recreation ground at Barking, accepted the presidency of the Ladies' Guild of Charing Cross Hospital, and opened exhibitions for the Royal Drawing Society and the International Drawing Congress.

September provided a break at Inverary, followed by a further round of bazaar openings in London and vicinity. Besides all these public appearances, Louise served as an exceptionally active president of the

National Trust, and wrote letters to *The Times* soliciting funds for such varied projects as Marble Arch improvements, the Quebec Tercentenary celebrations, and the National Society for the Protection of Young Girls.

Louise disliked fashionable charities. Those she really loved, and for which she "worked like a slave," were the less fashionable ones centring around deprived and unfortunate young people, especially girls. Thus the Princess Louise Home for Girls, the Heritage Craft Schools, and the National Society for the Protection of Young Girls. Her pet project during the Edwardian period was a hospital for illegitimate children in the heart of London's slums. Few of her friends knew of its existence, and those who did know did not tell. [36]

The Edinburgh College of Domestic Science was another institution that demonstrated Louise's interest in seeing young women off to a good start in life. It also showed her capacity to stick with a project that seemed to produce the desired results. She became its official patron at its founding in 1875, and was still actively involved forty years later. This was not merely a nominal interest. "She has always taken a keen practical interest in the work and progress," reported one college official as late as the 1930s. [37] Louise was often in Edinburgh inspecting classes, congratulating graduates, and opening new additions.

From social welfare and education, it was an easy step into the field of health care. In Edinburgh she also supported the Princess Louise Nurses for Children, personally designing the badges they wore on their uniforms. In London she backed the Stepney and Mile End Dispensary and the London Homoeopathic Hospital, both in memory of her brother Leopold.

Louise's occasional public visits to more remote parts of the British Isles always evoked great demonstrations of loyalty and affection. Her July 1909 tour through the Rhondda Valley of South Wales seemed like a triumphal progress. Everything came together to make it successful — Louise was in good health, Lorne was particularly witty in his replies to formal addresses, the sun shone, and the local population turned out in the thousands.

At Ynshire on July 24 the streets were decorated with coloured flags and banners draped from Venetian masts, while cottagers hung out their own modest banners and bunting. "Your Presence Gladdens Our Hearts" read a triumphal arch near the entrance to the Standard Colliery. As the royal automobile came into sight the Ynshire Brass Band struck up the National Anthem, while a chorus of nearly one thousand miners, decked out in their working clothes, gave a stirring rendition of "Hen Wlad fy Nhadau." Next came the village of Mardy, where the Ferndale Brass Band welcomed the royals with a fanfare of music, and Louise presented a trophy to a local prize-winning first-aid team. [38]

How ridiculous it all seems, this poverty-stricken part of the country going wild over a sixty-one year-old woman who by accident of birth was a member of the royal family! No matter. A generation later, in the fateful summer of 1936, Louise's great-nephew, King Edward VIII, would make a similar triumphal tour through the mining towns of South Wales. The Welsh townsfolk were not particularly interested in royal gossip; they wanted to see the royals in the flesh, and to respond enthusiastically.

# CHAPTER TWENTY

# A MAN OF THE TWENTIETH CENTURY, 1907-1913

---

*T*he Duchess of Argyll may have been the King's favourite sister, but her husband was certainly not his favourite brother-in-law. Bertie had opposed Louise's marriage to a British aristocrat, and had never accepted Lorne as an equal in royal circles. Edward might retain Argyll as Governor and Constable of Windsor Castle, and as Hereditary Master of the King's Household in Scotland. He might throw some additional sops his way, such as the chancellorship of the Order of St. Michael and St. George. But he was not about to accept the Ninth Duke of Argyll as an equal.

Differences in temperament were as important as differences in rank. Lorne was always the idealist, Edward the pragmatist. "Every subject they discussed, whether politics or wine," recalled Madame Klepac, "invariably ended in an argument." [1] Sexual orientation contributed to their differences. Bertie led a decidedly heterosexual life, constantly boasting of his virility, and taking one mistress after another till close to the end of his life. He had little time or patience for a more gentle, sensitive, effeminate man like Lorne. He could neither understand nor sympathize with Lorne's homosexual drives.

The Edwardian public was no more tolerant of homosexuual behaviour than it had been during Victorian times. Writers like John Addington Symonds, Havelock Ellis and Edward Carpenter might explore the phenomenon of "sexual inversion" through their literary and psychological writings of the 1880s and 1890s. But the public was more horrified than sympathetic over such homosexual exposes as the Dublin Castle affair of 1884, the Cleveland Street scandal of 1889, and the Oscar Wilde trials of 1895.

Wilde was a prominent victim of the Criminal Law Amendment Act of 1885 — the so-called Labouchere amendment, after its sponsor and Lorne's perennial critic, Henry Labouchere. After 1885, any male homosexual act, even when committed by two consenting adults in private, was deemed a crime punishable by up to one year's imprisonment at hard labour. Within hours after Wilde's 1895 conviction on homosexual charges, the British gay community entered a state of panic. Some went quietly underground, some protected themselves through hastily contracted marriages, others — like Ronny Gower — left for extended holidays on the Continent.

Lorne had not been implicated in any of the scandals of the 1880s or in the Oscar Wilde trials. But he numbered many known homosexuals among his close friends, including his uncle Ronald Gower and Liberal Party stalwart Lewis ("Lulu") Harcourt. Lorne frequently stayed at Hammerfield, Gower's country house in Kent, where weekend festivities were said to revolve around "masculine entertainments".

Then came the Irish Crown Jewels scandal. The Irish Crown Jewels, also known as the Crown Jewels of the Order of St. Patrick, were kept at Dublin Castle and worn by the monarch and members of the royal family when visiting Ireland. They were valued at prices ranging up to 100,000 pounds. In the summer of 1907 they disappeared from a library safe in the castle.

The officer responsible for their safekeeping was Sir Arthur Vicars, who shared a house with his assistant Francis Shackleton, both known homosexuals. One evening Shackleton and an accomplice, Captain Richard Gorges (earlier sacked from his regiment over homosexual activities during the South African War), plied Vicars with whisky till he was insensitive, took the keys to the safe from his pocket, and made wax impressions before carefully replacing them. A few nights later they got into the safe with the counterfeit keys and removed the jewels; Shackleton allegedly sold them in Amsterdam for 20,000 pounds.

The theft was discovered on July 6. Dublin police were soon on the track of the thieves, who made no attempt to flee from justice. In fact they dared the authorities to arrest them, boasting that if charged they would reveal so many scandals that "they would shake the government." [2] Though Shackleton resigned his position, and Vicars was summarily dismissed, no arrests were ever made and no jewels ever recovered. Eventually Vicars was mysteriously gunned down by Irish terrorists, while Shackleton died destitute, destroyed by gambling and blackmailers.

Meanwhile a Royal Commission appointed to enquire into the disappearance of the jewels sat for a week and examined a number of witnesses. Suddenly, it was indefinitely adjourned and never met again. Such action was due, whispered the gossips, to the direct intervention of King Edward

Ronald Gower, Lorne's uncle and lifelong friend.

VII, who was alarmed at possible public disclosures affecting highly placed individuals, including his own brother-in-law, the Duke of Argyll.

Scholars of the case agree that "there may well be some truth in this."[3] Police inquiries revealed that Shackleton acted as a link between Vicars and a homosexual clique of which Ronald Gower was the moving spirit. Both Shackleton and Argyll spent the weekend with Gower at Hammerfield immediately before the theft was discovered. The King was naturally anxious to prevent the public from learning that his brother-in-law had been associating with the likes of Shackleton in the country house of such an obvious homosexual as Gower.

While the country buzzed with rumours, the gay weekends continued at Hammerfield. "Lovely weather, great success," observed a female guest at a September 1907 garden party. "On the spot we find the Duke of Argyll." [4]

\* \* \* \* \*

Hammerfield with Ronny Gower and company might be enjoyable, but Lorne drew deeper spiritual comfort from his extended vacations with Louise at Rosneath. Most years took husband and wife north for a week or ten days in the spring, and another two or three weeks in the autumn. With the castle rented out, they settled into the Ferry Inn. Here, life was simple, with few guests and no court functions. Louise's only regular companion was Lady Sophia MacNamara, a veteran of the Canadian years, a real Irish wit, and "a match for the Duke in any argument." Even the servants loved Rosneath, for "the Duke believed in plenty of cheer and saw to it that the keg of Scotch brew never ran dry." [5]

Louise indulged her loves of gardening and art. Every morning at eight she was up and out, in her rough tweed suit, saw or hatchet in hand. "Much clipping and mangling of unhappy plants by Aunt Louise," Argyll wrote his nephew, Ralph Glyn. "Dogs looking on, sympathizing with the plants." Another time "Aunt L. was out sketching in the sun under an umbrella all day — and part of the night.!"[6]

Argyll, too, recaptured much of his youthful vigour on these returns to his boyhood haunts. From the moment he boarded the steamer at Craigendoran, en route for Rosneath, he seemed "to take up the thread of his Highland life." He shook hands with the ship's captain and asked "how affairs had been progressing in his absence." While strolling the roads and pathways around Rosneath, he "had a kindly word for every person he met." Every village entertainment drew his attention, and "he always looked in during the evening." [7]

In the spring of 1911, Rosneath Castle was heavily damaged by a fire that originated in the heating system and broke out on the top storey of the north wing. Combined efforts of the estate staff, the Helensburgh town fire brigade, and cadets of a naval training ship fortunately cruising in the Gare Loch, managed to contain the blaze and limit fire damage to the third floor. Still, Louise's painting and sculpture studio was destroyed, and there was severe damage to the library and two other main rooms, a staircase, and a range of servants' rooms. Although the Duke was insured for the 5000-pound loss, he lost all rental income till repairs were made.

When estate business demanded his presence at Inverary, Lorne stayed — either alone or with Louise — at Dalkenna Lodge (or Dalchenna House), a recently built structure along the shores of Loch Fyne, three kilometres from the castle. Here as at Rosneath, he lived the rather plain life of a country gentleman of modest means, with few servants and no gala entertaining. He walked the village streets "wearing a tweed cap and apparelled in a brown crotal suit made by his Inverness tailor." He regaled his few guests with ghost stories of "Johnnie Campbell" and "The Bogle".[8]

Yet he was, after all, the Duke of Argyll, and ducal obligations demanded his time and support — Sunday services at the parish church, patronage of the annual Inverary Highland Games, subscriptions to various local and county causes. On one occasion he made land available at nominal rent for an extension to the town hospital; later he purchased the near-defunct Inverary Gas Light Company to keep it afloat and keep the community supplied with gas. And despite the economic pinch, he remained "a kind and sympathetic landlord," ever ready to meet "any just and reasonable request from the Argyll tenantry." [9]

Near the end of his life, Argyll sought financial relief by appealing against the assessment for super-tax on Louise's 1871 annuity. He claimed the annuity had been granted free from all taxes and assessments, though admitting he had previously allowed income tax to be deducted from the amount as a matter of grace. Britain's Attorney General, in what became a highly visible and publicized case, agreed that while the 1871 act had declared the annuity free from all taxes, an earlier act stated that future legislation granting tax-free annuities should not confer freedom from income tax. In the end the courts ruled in Lorne's favour, thus modestly easing the financial strain that dogged him during these last few years.

* * * * *

Immediately after his father's death in 1900, the new Duke of Argyll resigned his seat in the House of Commons and took his inherited place in the House of Lords. After the "invigorating and youthful" Commons, Argyll found the Lords "depressing and aged." He joked that one heard "more fun in the Commons' smoking-room in an evening than you do in the Peer's Library in a lifetime." Yet he believed the upper house played a valuable role in the political process — "second thoughts, thought out in quiet, the voice of age and experience," all "less swayed by the excitement of the day" than the Commons. Thus he regarded the growing attack on the power of the Lords as "destruction, not reform." A constitution arising from the natural growth of centuries now seemed "at the mercy of fleeting fashion or passion." [10]

British politics was changing. Following ten years of Conservative-Unionist government under Lord Salisbury and then Arthur Balfour (brother-in-law to Lorne's sister Frances), the Liberals under Henry Campbell-Bannerman took office in December 1905. "I hope you will accept my congratulations as a clansman and personal friend," Argyll wrote the new prime minister, "not politically but patriarchally!! [11]

The Duke found himself completely opposed to Campbell-Bannerman's national agenda. Irish Home Rule shared the spotlight with new issues like women's suffrage, trade union agitation, and social reform legislation. Argyll and his fellow landed aristocrats were becoming increasingly irrelevant to the urban-industrial concerns of the new century.

Argyll watched with increasing dismay as Herbert Asquith succeeded Campbell-Bannerman as Liberal prime minister in 1908, and David Lloyd George became chancellor of the exchequer. To finance old-age pensions and naval armaments, Lloyd George's "People's Budget" of the following year proposed steep levies on the rich, especially the landed rich. Taxes were raised on all unearned income, and on earned income exceeding 3000 pounds per year, with a super-tax on incomes of more than 5000 pounds. Death taxes were raised. Most provocative was a new revenue tax on land — a direct attack on major landlords.

Though he held his tongue in the Lords, Argyll attacked the Lloyd George budget away from the confines of Westminster. Speaking at a Unionist meeting in Dundee in November 1909, he demanded the bill be "thrown out, with a strong protest made against its provisions." The land-owning class was unfairly attacked, and need not be "ashamed of their record." Tariff reform, he suggested, offered a better hope for economic stability than the Liberal budget. [12]

Convinced that confiscatory socialism was about to grip the land, the Conservative-dominated House of Lords that same November voted 350-75 against the budget, thus violating the principle that the upper house not tamper with a finance bill. "The Lords do not resist the Commons of the nation," Argyll argued in Glasgow, but simply "ask that a temporary majority does not outstep the limit of its commission from the people." [13]

In a January 1910 general election, fought on the budget, the power of the Lords, and Irish Home Rule, the Liberals were returned to office. Though his majority was considerably reduced, Asquith was determined to push through the budget and trim the power of the House of Lords. In May the Commons passed a Parliament Bill which removed the veto power of the Lords over money matters, and severely weakened it in other areas. Asquith threatened to create enough new peers to carry the bill through the upper house.

Argyll staunchly defended the status quo through the spring of 1910. "If we did not have an hereditary peerage," he told a Liberal Unionist meeting in Inverary, "we should not have an hereditary monarchy." He admitted the need for new blood, perhaps by appointing a few colonial peers or even through a partially elected Lords. But he opposed the wholesale naming of new peers just to force through the Parliament Bill. "If some hundreds are created, the next Government must make 500 or 1000 more," he wrote *The Times*, "and there will be peers of succession and peers for the scrapheap, for all these members cannot be allowed in the congested House of Lords." [14]

*The Guardian* reported that Argyll intended to vote against the bill when it came before the Lords in August 1911. But the "expected speech was not delivered, nor the hostile vote recorded," for Argyll was one of many peers who took no part in the debate nor in the particular division. [15]

As always, Argyll's scope for independent action within parliament was compromised by his relationship to the royal family. He had been a passive member of the Commons for Argyllshire in the 1870s and South Manchester in the 1890s; as a member of the Lords from 1900 to 1914, he uttered nary a word at Westminster. Any parliamentary interjection during the House of Lords crisis of 1910-1911 would have been dangerous, especially since the new monarch, King George V, had agreed to appoint new peers if necessary.

King Edward VII died in the midst of the parliamentary crisis in the spring of 1910. In late April he had returned from a Continental holiday feeling tired; the first weekend in May he caught a chill while walking the grounds at Sandringham; on Friday May 6 he succumbed after a series of heart attacks. Louise had lost her favourite brother and Lorne a not-so-favourite brother-in-law.

Instead of bolstering Argyll's relationship to the throne and national life, Edward's death and George V's succession revealed how politically redundant the ageing Duke had become. In little more than a decade, Argyll moved from son-in-law to brother-in-law to uncle of the monarch, as Queen Victoria gave way to Edward VII, and Edward in turn to his son, George. A once-close relationship to the throne became very marginal. Any contributions to national life would have to come in areas other than the court and politics.

\* \* \* \* \*

273

The Duke of Argyll was as busy as ever with his writing following the 1901 biography of his mother-in-law, *Victoria V. R. I.* Another title that same year, *A Gift Book for the Home*, featured 142 pages of verse for all occasions. He contributed a short preface to *Portfolio of the National Gallery of Scotland*, a glossy art book designed to raise funds for the strapped Edinburgh institution. He wrote short "appreciations" in biographies of deceased friends, Dr. Barnardo of child-saving fame, and Quinton Hogg, a supporter of technical schools whose recent death was whispered to be a suicide produced by the threat of exposure as a homosexual. His one piece of fiction, "The Half Breed's Story," made good emigration propaganda for the Canadian West. [16]

Argyll's major literary project during the Edwardian years was *Passages From the Past,* his two-volume autobiography published by Hutchinson of London in 1907. Unfortunately, *Passages* proved disappointing. While providing a treasure-trove of information on Lorne's boyhood years and youthful travels, it is deficient on his later life. *Passges* tells much about Inverary and Rosneath, about Trentham, Dunrobin and Argyll Lodge; it provides wonderful glimpses into Lorne's adventures in Jamaica and Berlin and Italy; it shows his enthusiasm for Canada. But of marriage with Louise, life at Kensington Palace, political and public life in Britain, the autobiography reveals next to nothing. Too much of the material is tangential — stories related by friends about other people whose lives had little bearing on Argyll himself — and much of it poorly organized.

*The Times Literary Supplement* made *Passages* its feature review for 7 November 1907. The anonymous *TLS* reviewer wondered why "the book is not better than it is," since the author had "known everyone and been everywhere" — a criticism of the author's name-dropping tendency. Meanwhile, *Punch* abhorred the "more than ducal indifference to sequence," finding the absence of orderly arrangement "sometimes bewildering." Thomas Lloyd's review for *Bookman* was the most critical — an "indigestible hotch-potch of ill-assorted atoms" and a "pitiable waste of good material." Reading the early extracts, then turning to the later chapters, was "like passing from a Velazquez to a bad process-block." If the Duke could not write, concluded Lloyd, "we and posterity might pardon him." But the pity was, "he can write." [17]

And write he did, continuing to publish in an amazingly wide variety of fields. From his 1907 autobiography, Argyll moved to family history with *Intimate Society Letters of the Eighteenth Century.* Published by Stanley Paul in 1910, *Intimate Society Letters* is a two-volume edited account of Campbell family correspondence during the period of the Act of Union, the Hanoverian succession, and the Jacobite rebellions. "Rather promiscuous papers," charged the *Times Literary Supplement* reviewer, "many of them insignificant, many flat about uninteresting subjects, most of them needing more connecting thread than is given." [18] Once again, Argyll seems to have rushed a manuscript into print with insufficient editing and pruning.

Interest in Scottish history also led to "Fiona and Tera", a succesor opera to "Diarmid", with words by the Duke of Argyll and music by Learmont Drysdale and David Stephen. In late 1911 Argyll discussed production possibilities with Oscar Hammerstein, whose first London season Lorne was backing financially. [19] "Chances are it will be staged," the Glasgow *Herald* optimistically reported. Two years passed. The *Herald* remained supportive, speculating that "Fiona and Tera" might be "made the occasion of the founding of a Scottish Opera Company." [20] But nothing came of it. Given the short production run of "Diarmid" in 1897, and continuing prejudice against operas in English, it is not surprising that "Fiona and Tera" died still-born.

While ruminating on his Scottish roots and Scottish connections, Argyll never forgot Canada. "Since his retirement thirty years earlier, his interest has never waned," wrote Canadian politician George Ross in his 1913 memoirs. "On every occasion on which I have met him, his first enquiry has been 'Well, how is dear young Canada getting along?'." [21] Though custom prevented any re-visit, he continued to write of the country. A foreword in J.S. Redmayne's *Fruit Farming on the "Dry Belt" of British Columbia* stirred memories of his and Louise's happy stay in the Pacific province.

Then in 1910 his final book appeared — *Yesterday & Today in Canada*. It was the initial volume in a League of Empire series aimed at the general British reader. [22] *Yesterday & Today* is organized in Argyll's usual manner — a broad geographical framework within which he presents historical background and contemporary commentary. He discusses his well-known views on imperial federation and defence, transcontinental railways and British emigration to the Canadian West. Despite moderately favourable reviews, [23] the book is another disappointment — too many geographical errors, too many out-of-date views on changing issues, too much a warmed-over version of his 1885 success, *Canadian Pictures*.

\* \* \* \* \*

Embarrassed over the Irish Crown Jewels scandal, frustrated as a member of the House of Lords, and dismissed by the critics as a writer past his prime, Argyll ultimately left his mark on Edwardian Britain by serving as honorary president of the Franco-British Exhibition and the Royal Aero Club. In both cases he played far more than an "honorary" role. Argyll's active leadership helped mobilize public support for these decidedly twentieth century projects and pumped new vigour into his ageing body.

The Franco-British Exhibition, scheduled for London in the summer of 1908, was proposed as a showplace for the arts and industries of the two countries. "When Anglo-Saxon energy blends with French savoir faire, when British empiricism is ordered by French method, when British solidarity is adorned by French grace," read Exhibition propaganda that sounded as if written by Argyll himself, "a combination is reached which embraces the highest achievements of the human race." [24]

The Exhibition would also serve as a nice appendage to Edward VII's Entente Cordiale. It would "strengthen the bonds of friendship between the two countries," Argyll predicted, "draw them closer together, and "develop their commercial and industrial relations." Indeed, the Exhibition was an obvious manifestation that the Entente Cordiale "would grow stronger and stronger as the years went on." [25] Argyll no doubt hoped that his enthusiastic involvement might raise his stock with his brother-in-law, the King!

Together with the Earl of Derby as active president and Imre Kiralfy as commissioner-general, the Duke set about the task of enlisting exhibits from British industry. "This was not an easy job," noted Lord Mersey, one of Argyll's young recruits on the executive committee. "Some were afraid of foreigners learning their secrets, while others were skeptical of the value of an exhibition." As late as October 1907, with the opening just seven months away, Argyll still had exhibit space available, despite "gratifying support" from manufacturers. [26]

But it all turned out well. The 140-acre site at Shepherd's Bush, with its pleasant gardens and restaurants and its midway, proved a popular spot during the summer of 1908. Some twenty exhibit halls featured the best in scientific research, industrial products, applied and decorative arts, and social and educational advances from the two countries and their colonies. Everyone agreed the Exhibition generated much favourable publicity on the theme of Franco-British co-operation. Lord Blyth, for one, believed this was due primarily to Argyll's "own earnest co-operation in every step from first to last." [27]

While urging closer Anglo-French and even Anglo-German cooperation, Argyll continued to promote imperial solidarity and military preparedness. Imperial solidarity included assisted emigration of pauper children to the colonies so the Empire would remain composed of "the British element," a system of colonial preference within a moderately protective British tariff policy, and Canada and the other "sister nations across the seas" meeting "us here in the manufacture of guns and building of ships."[28]

Concern for home defence led Argyll to support a stronger Territorial Reserve Army, a Forth-to-Clyde canal so warships could move quickly between the North and Irish seas, as well as universal military training in schools. "We should find ourselves in parlous state," he told a Birmingham audience as he watched the military build-up on the Continent, "unless our young men are trained in the use of arms." [29] Military preparedness also persuaded the Duke of Argyll to accept the honorary presidency of the Aero Club in 1908, a most unusual office for a sixty-three year-old non-aviator.

The Aero Club — it gained the prefix "Royal" in 1910 — was extremely active up to the start of the First World War in training many of Britain's early aviators and organizing various flying competitions. Argyll used the Aero Club to voice his growing concern that Britain was falling behind America and Europe in the application of aerial developments for military and naval purposes. "No country could be considered by those able to use the aeroplane or dirigible balloons as having any frontier at all," he told the December 1908 annual dinner. "Every part of the country could be visited and inspected by transient visitors, who might have hostile intent." [30]

For the last six years of his life, Argyll used the club's platform to lobby for a greater military presence in the air. He frequently contrasted British spending with that of France and Germany. He regarded "command of the air as being of vital importance to the commerce and defence" of the Empire. Britain must follow the lead of other countries in "recognizing that aeronautics was a matter of importance to the state," and that large funds should be devoted to the encouragement of inventors of aerial machines." Arguing that naval aviation was as important as army flying, Lorne called for an "ample margin of air supremacy in airships, aeroplanes and aircraft generally as against the next strongest naval power." [31]

Government and military authorities gradually rose to the challenge. Argyll's strongly worded December 1908 address was followed just five months later with the appointment by the Asquith government of the Committee on Aerial Navigation, and by the ever-increasing interest of the army and the Royal Navy. An enthusiastic public, feasting on the triumphs of one aviator after another, kept up the pressure. Transportation magazines applauded Argyll's efforts. [32] Though he never personally ascended in a balloon or flew in an aeroplane, the elderly Duke of Argyll became one of aviation's spirited pioneers at the end of his life.

\* \* \* \* \*

Argyll's leadership in the Franco-British Exhibition and the Royal Aero Club contradict the impression of an ageing Scottish duke who spent his last years ruminating on the past, decrying the passing of the landed aristocracy, a man out of touch with the twentieth century. Instead, they reveal a man at the forefront of Edwardian thinking in industrial co-operation and foreign policy, transportation and military preparedness. Not every Briton was eager to accept French manufactured products and embrace the French as allies. Few military, naval and government leaders had yet grasped the strategic importance of air travel and aerial warfare. But the Duke of Argyll recognized the importance of France as an ally and advocated reforms in the army and the Royal Navy. Finally, he and his brother-in-law the King found common cause!

Argyll's Franco-British Exhibition and Royal Aero Club activities are reminiscent of his forward thinking as a young man. Inheriting a generous measure of liberalism from his Sutherland forebears, the young Marquis of Lorne threw his support behind Italian unification before the majority of his fellow Britons. As Governor General of Canada he sensed a vision of a future trans-continental nation long before most Canadians, and vigorously promoted the Canadian Pacific Railway, the Royal Canadian Academy and the Royal Society of Canada. Invigorated by his Canadian years, Lorne supported an imperial federation governed by equality among nations rather than colonial dependency — more like the twentieth century British Commonwealth than the nineteenth century British Empire so dear to the hearts of his countrymen.

Lorne's forward thinking was matched by his accomplishments during the first decades of his life. Indeed, he seemed to be running on fast time. He authored his first book, *A Trip to the Tropics*, at age twenty. By twenty-one he had conversed with the leading statesmen of Europe and the United States. At twenty-two he took a seat in the House of Commons. He was still a youthful thirty-three when appointed Governor General of Canada and just forty when his most widely acclaimed book, *Canadian Pictures Drawn With Pen and Pencil*, appeared in 1885.

Unfortunately for Lorne, the next twenty years — the usually mature, productive years of one's forties and fifties — were disappointing. Political and administrative offices failed to match his Canadian gover-nor-generalship. Though his writing proliferated and diversified over a wide range of forms and styles, his subsequent books failed to measure up to the promise of his early years. Trapped in marriage despite his homosexual orientation, a marriage made all that more difficult because his wife was a daughter of Queen Victoria, Lorne experienced years of personal unhappiness.

The skies brightened, however, as the new century opened and as he entered his sixties. His father's death made him master of the ducal house of Argyll. His mother-in-law's death and his wife's improved spirits made him more comfortable within his own household. Finally, his return to public life through the Franco-British Exhibition and the Royal Aero Club earned him a place on the Edwardian stage.

In the final analysis, however, Lorne's greatest contributions were to Canada rather than Britain. As Governor General he gave Canadians a new vision of their country with his much-publicized travels through the West, his support of a trans-continental railway, and his founding of national organizations in the arts and sciences. At the same time, his travels, his writings and his support for a Canadian High Commission Office in London forced Britons to take a new look at this young country rising across the sea in the northern half of North America.

# CHAPTER TWENTY-ONE

# LOUISE WITHOUT LORNE, 1914-1939

*L*orne had never followed Louise into the world of physical fitness. No Madame Klepac for him; no daily round of exercises and wise dieting. After his return from Canada, Lorne shunned all forms of physical recreation except an occasional round of golf. Neither hunting nor fishing, nor hiking across the Scottish Highlands, held the appeal of his youth. The result was a "relaxed and amiably lethargic" physique, carrying too much weight on a slim frame — as his father had first noticed as long ago as 1879.

His health deteriorated with advancing age. By the early 1900s the Duke became increasingly "short-breathed and subject to attacks of weakness, doubtless cardiac." [1] A severe cold in March 1911 was serious enough to warrant two mentions in the Buckingham Palace Court Circular. Later that year an influenza attack — worth seven mentions in the Court Circular — kept him from travelling to Rosneath.

The end came in the spring of 1914 at age sixty-eight. Argyll arrived at Kent House, Isle of Wight, for a short vacation in April, seemingly in fair health for a man of his age. Louise remained at Kensington, recovering from an influenza bout of her own. Towards the end of the month the Duke caught a chill, which developed into pneumonia. On Tuesday April 28 Louise was summoned from London.

Next day's official announcement mentioned double pneumonia, and listed his condition as serious. On Wednesday the disease seemed to have eased in one lung and worsened in the other; his condition remained "most critical." Louise, *The Sunday Times* assured its readers, was "assiduous in the nursing of her husband," spending practically night and day at his bedside, taking little rest herself. [2] It was of no avail.

At 10.45 in the evening of Saturday May 2, the Ninth Duke of Argyll died in his sick bed at Kent House.

Funeral wreath "from the people of British Columbia" for the 9th Duke of Argyll, May 1914.

Lorne's death plunged the court into official mourning for a month, cancelling all those formal court balls where gentlemen wore knee-breeches. "The fear that you will see me in trousers and not in breeches saddens and chastens and mortifies my corrupt affections," young Duff Cooper wrote his fiance, Diana Manners. "It is sad that the corpse of a dead Duke should come between my well shaped calves and the anxious eyes of an expectant world. A live calf (especially if well shaped) is better than a dead Duke, I say." [3]

Some Britons were more serious. On Friday May 8 memorial services for the late Duke were held at Westminster Abbey, St. Giles Cathedral in Edinburgh, and St. Mary Abbots parish church in Kensington. One week later, on Friday May 15, funeral services were held at Inverary, with burial following in the family grounds at Kilmun. On that May morning, "hot with the breath of summer, while all the trees were bursting into leaf, and the hills which girded the waterways were blue with hyacinths," the Duke of Argyll "was laid amid his race and name, who rest beside the Holy Loch." [4]

"A Staunch Imperialist," proclaimed *The Observer* in its obituary; "Great Scottish Peer" and "A Distinguished Scotsman" announced *The Daily Telegraph* and *The Scotsman*. The Glasgow *Daily Record*, however, argued that the death of the head of the Clan Campbell was no longer an "event of much importance," and judged the deceased on ability alone. Argyll, concluded the *Daily Record*, "had not talents to raise him to a position of pre-eminence" in national affairs, while under his tenure, the family estates had shrunk "to a mere fraction of their once-vast extent." [5]

Other papers offered more complete sketches. The Duke of Argyll was "in many ways a complex character," read a sketch in *The Sunday Times* by "an old friend." As Governor General of Canada he displayed "gifts of statesmanship of no mean order." Yet he "always seemed to lack that tenacity of purpose and concentration of thought" required of a public administrator. An anonymous writer in *The Guardian* spoke of Lorne's life-long "frustration, unfulfilment, and unrealized expectations." [6]

Lorne's death occurred just fourteen years after his father's, and obituary writers were tempted to compare father and son. All agreed that the Ninth Duke was the "most simple, unaffected and amiable of men," the first Argyll in whom a "proverbial family arrogance was wholly wanting." Yet this self-effacing humility was as much a weakness as a strength. Lorne never possessed the fervour of his father. In contrast to his hustling, assertive and eloquent father, Lorne seemed in later years a somewhat "inconspicuous Argyll." His failing was his father's in excess — a kind of "dilettantism, lacking any specially outstanding gift." [7]

Niel Munro's sketch in the local Oban *Times* got closer to the inner man than any of the metropolitan obituaries. Munro summed Lorne up as a "Bohemian of the refined and elegant order." As an artist he loved to look at the world with those "deep, pensive, quizzing, humorous eyes" that in latter years his friends "grieved to see becoming a little weary." There was always "something of the eternal boy; a man more guileless never walked on leather." Munro suggested that life's disappointments had been hard on the Duke, leaving him with little more than the "artist's solace — he could re-create and dream." [8]

Frances Campbell Balfour knew her brother well. He was "extraordinarily absent-minded," she recalled "always in a poetic dream." Family members often quoted a Highland estate official, talking of some poetry Lorne had published, that "but for that fatal weakness, he would be a great man." In later years Lorne struck many as a figure more to be pitied than respected, as the promises of a golden youth remained unrealized. Frances saw a certain wistful purity in this. She fondly remembered "Ian, the well beloved, always marching with his face to the sunrise, strewing his path with deeds of kindness and courteous remembrance." [9]

Frances joined Louise at Lorne's death-bed in May 1914. The only other family member present was the Duke's forty-two year-old nephew and heir, Niall Diarmid Campbell, son of brother Archie, who had died the previous year.

Niall Campbell, Tenth Duke of Argyll, had been educated at St. George's, Ascot, and Christ Church, Oxford, receiving his degree in 1896. He remained a bachelor, a scholar of Scottish history, who spent most of his time, as Duke, closeted in the library at Inverary Castle. His opposition to Scottish separatism in 1932 produced one of his rare public statements, and maintained the Anglo-Scottish tradition of the Campbells of Argyll.

After Niall's death in 1949, several rooms of the castle could hardly be entered as every bit of floor space was filled with furniture and bric-a-brac, boxes of documents, letters and manuscripts. Such delightful eccentricity was accompanied by years of inattention to financial affairs. Various death duties, unpaid timber duties, plus outstanding business and personal loans, left the estate with heavy liabilities in 1949. The grounds had been neglected for years. The castle itself lay in partial ruin, the roof gone over one turret, armour uncleaned and unpolished for years, family portraits caked in dust.

Niall was succeeded as duke by his cousin and Lorne's grand-nephew, Ian Douglas Campbell. This Eleventh Duke of Argyll restored Inverary Castle and opened it to the public as a money-making device to pay off the accumulation of heavy debts. Unfortunately, the Eleventh Duke was not destined to enjoy a tranquil private life. His three marriages all ended in divorces, the last in 1963 establishing a record as the longest and costliest divorce case in Scottish legal history. He died ten years later, succeeded by his son, another Ian Campbell, as the Twelfth Duke of Argyll.

* * * * *

Given Lorne's homosexuality and Louise's attraction to other men, and continuing doubts about the strength of the marriage, Lorne's death should have made little emotional impact on Louise. After the funeral and a proper period of mourning, she should have got on happily with her life, relieved now of the burden of an unloved and unloving husband. On the contrary, Louise was shattered by her husband's death, and remained in a state of mental depression for several months afterwards.

Suddenly Louise found herself alone, without her helpmate and companion of the past forty-three years. "My loneliness can hardly be described," she wrote Lewis Harcourt in December 1914, adding that she and Lorne "shared all our interests." Writing the following year to Boyd Carpenter, Bishop of Ripon and a recently widowed friend, Louise spoke of knowing "this awful desolation so well." Four years after Lorne's death, Louise still felt the pains of loneliness. "It is so hard to see, hear, and read things always alone now," she complained to Mary Gladstone.[10]

The loss seemed hardest to bear in Scotland, scene of so many happy memories. From Rosneath in September 1915, she wrote Lorne's nephew Ralph Glyn that "your table in the Library [is] always ready and dear Uncle Lorne's chair is empty. It's dreadful here without him and I feel lost coming here." The following spring Louise still bemoaned her fate to young Glyn. "I miss you not coming and cheering me up. I am so lonely."[11]

Lorne and Louise had shared a long life of artistic, intellectual and domestic companionship, caring deeply for each other and sharing their thoughts on a daily basis. From a low point in the 1880s, the marriage grew progressively stronger over the next thirty years. Long before Lorne's death, he and Louise became — and remained — very happy together. They may have gone their separate ways for substantial portions of each year, but their periods of deepest contentment came when together.

Lorne had been a constant source of help to Louise as she struggled to fulfil her official duties. Now she found herself "so frightfully busy, letters, letters, functions, meetings, laryngitis, late to bed, no sleep, constant worries." Kensington Palace now felt isolated from the outside world. "I really want someone I can ask advice of and who goes about more than I do," she wrote Ralph Glyn, "to let me know things and keep me up to the mark." [12]

The settling of Lorne's will presented Louise with yet another burden. Though nephew Niall Campbell succeeded to the entailed estates associated with the Argyll dukedom, Louise received life rent from landed estates over which Lorne had personal control, plus Rosneath as her dower house. "There is so much to look after on my husband's property which has been left in my charge," she wrote Bishop Carpenter. The outbreak of the First World War made it all the more difficult at Rosneath.

284

"Troops stationed there and I don't know what all." It was almost too much for Louise to bear. "I have so much on my hands," she wrote, "and have been so unwell — over-tired." [13]

Ultimately the demands of the war drew Louise out of her widow's depression, and mobilized her talents and energies. She could at least be thankful that Lorne was "spared these terrible anxious times." He had always cherished fond memories of student days in Berlin. He supported the Anglo-German Friendship Society "to bring about better feeling between the two countries and worked for it to the last." [14] Now Britain and Germany were at war.

Two of Louise's nephews confronted each other as monarchs of the warring nations — King George V of Britain and Kaiser Wilhelm II of Germany. Other nephews and grand-nephews participated directly in the armed struggle on both sides. German relatives were stripped of their English titles. When her niece and nephew, Princess Victoria of Hesse and Prince Louis of Battenberg faced public humiliation in the winter of 1914-15 — Louis's German background brought his dismissal as head of the Royal Navy — Louise presented them with Kent House as a retreat.

There was never any doubt about Louise's loyalty. She had spurned offers of a German marriage when young; she had long supported the anti-German faction within the British royal family. Now in the early months of 1915, the war effort demanded her return to public life, and prevented her repeating her mother's morbid widowhood.

In January she visited wounded Indian soldiers at Brighton. Next month she joined the general committee of the Officers' Families Fund. Soon she was regularly attending memorial services for the war dead, visiting hospitals, inspecting armament factories, reviewing troops, and launching fund-raising drives. Imperial troops became her special cause. "I have 40 Australians and one or two New Zealanders at my Dalham Hospital," she wrote Ralph Glyn, "such nice fellows and we make a great fuss with them." [15] Canadian military units demanded her presence, and she used those occasions to preach Lorne's message of imperial defence solidarity. "This was always a dream of my husband's," she told Canadian troops stationed in Britain in July 1916, "though he did not foresee this terrible struggle as a means of accomplishing it." [16]

The pattern was set for the next few years. War effort activities were added to Louise's list of longstanding charities and causes, and she became visible once more to the British public. There were no European holidays during the war years; simple spring and autumn excursions to Rosneath marked the extent of her travels. The strain of almost uninterrupted work — without Lorne's help and re-assurance — soon began to tell. June 1915 brought a severe attack of sciatica; 1916 through 1918 saw periodic outbreaks of laryngitis and bronchitis. The old lady soldiered on. In June 1918 the seventy year-old princess was named a Dame Grand

Cross of the British Empire in recognition of her war work.

\* \* \* \* \*

As the last months of war blended into the first uneasy months of peace, Louise thought increasingly of her beloved Continent. Six years had passed since she last sampled the German spas, the Italian art galleries and the sunshine of the French Riviera. Any visit to German-speaking Europe would have been politically unwise in the spring of 1919. Besides, the ageing princess now craved the warmth that only the South of France could offer. On March 14 — four days before her seventy-first birthday — Louise left London for a two month holiday at Menton on the Riviera. This set the pattern for the next decade — annual late winter or early spring holidays of one or two months duration at Cap Ferrat.

At home through the 1920s, Louise found herself an increasingly marginal member of the royal family. One by one the older family members died — Princess Helena in 1923, Dowager Queen Alexandra in 1925 — leaving only Louise, her brother Prince Arthur, and her sister Princess Beatrice to watch over a new world unfolding around them. Against Beatrice's wishes, Louise and Arthur supported Frederick Ponsonby's 1927 publication of correspondence between their sister Vicky, Empress of Germany, and their mother, Queen Victoria. [17]

But public attention now focussed on younger generations of royals — Louise's nephew and his wife, King George V and Queen Mary, and especially on her grand-nephew Edward, Prince of Wales. Louise periodically took tea at Buckingham Palace and occasionally helped entertain at formal court receptions. She enjoyed visits from the fun-loving Prince of Wales and his younger brother, Prince George. Yet ever since Edward VII's death in 1910, Louise had receded more and more into the background. Where once she had been the old King's flamboyant sister, she was now the new King's ageing aunt and a very old great-aunt to the heir to the throne.

Meanwhile Louise kept active in the public causes that had long interested her — the National Trust, Girls' Public Day Schools, Heritage Craft Schools, Soldiers' and Sailors' Families Association, Ladies' Work Society, Princess Louise Home for Girls, Edinburgh School of Cookery — plus assorted other educational, medical and artistic causes that caught her fancy.

In 1928, the year of her eightieth birthday, the Borough of Kensington made her an honorary freeman in recognition of lifelong services to local causes — Princess Louise's Kensington Hospital for Children, Kensington War Memorial Recreation Grounds, 13th London Regiment, Kensington Division of the British Red Cross Society, Kensington District Nursing Association. Undaunted by advancing age, Louise took the platform to praise the borough council for supporting improvements in health and social welfare.

By this stage in her life Louise was as familiar to Kensington shop-keepers as to its charity matrons. Afternoon expeditions took her regularly to the shops along Kensington High Street and beyond. Often she pretended to stroll incognito, with her companion and unofficial lady-in-waiting, Mrs. Edward Lascelles, daughter of Frances Balfour and sister-in-law to Lord Harewood, who had married Princess Mary, the Princess Royal. The old princess chatted up the shop assistants, gave free advice to nannies wheeling infants about in prams, helped remove a fleck of dust from a policeman's eye, secured a street-side spot for a fruit vendor. [18] After half a century in the borough, Louise had indeed become the Grand Old Lady of Kensington Palace.

In her last few years Louise posed a constant problem for her Kensington Palace staff, who felt they had to try to restrain her increasingly unconventional behaviour, and make her act with the decorum expected of a royal princess. Her equerries and ladies-in-waiting, for example, had to dissuade her from attending amusements and entertainments considered lower class. It was not easy to outwit Louise, but one tactic likely to deter her was to whisper that journalists would be there.

* * * * *

Except for regular bouts of flu and bronchitis, Louise remained in reasonably good physical health through her eighties. The winters of 1930 and 1931 took her again on the long journey to Cap Ferrat in the South of France, where she enjoyed a month of restorative sunshine. In 1932 she tried Sidmouth on the Devon coast of England — a much easier trip but not nearly as pleasant as the Riviera. So next year she returned to Cap Ferrat for a short spring holiday — her final Continental jaunt.

Though eighty-five in 1933, Louise still occasionally opened charity bazaars, laid foundation stones for hospital additions, presented prizes at Girls' Public School ceremonies, and appealed for funds for her Kensington Hospital for Children. She last appeared in public in December 1937 to open the Home Arts and Industries Exhibition.

Through the 1930s Louise spent less and less time on her sculpture and painting. The studio cottage in Kensington Palace grounds was vacated, and an inside room converted for the artistic passion of her old age — jewellery making. Conversation remained another passion — talking and reminiscing with her sister Beatrice and niece Victoria of Hesse, both now living nearby in Kensington Palace apartments of their own. The present Queen, when young Princess Elizabeth, remembers Kensington as the "Auntie Palace", and her great-great aunts, Princess Louise and Princess Beatrice, as "great talkers." [19]

With the death of her nephew King George V in January 1936, Louise faced yet another generation of royals. She had been fond of the new king, Edward VIII, during his earlier years as the debonair Prince of Wales, but could not support his marriage with Wallis Simpson. She had little in common with Edward's successor and his wife; King George VI, was too much the boy scout, while Queen Elizabeth proved too puritanical for the old rebel Louise.

Her favourite among this next generation was the youngest surviving brother, Prince George, Duke of Kent. He and his bride, Princess Marina, were frequent visitors to Kensington Palace through the last years of Louise's life. The three of them shared similar tastes in art and humour. Kent substituted for Louise when old age and failing health prevented her from attending a fund-raising dinner for her Kensington Hospital for Children in May 1938.

Louise was now ninety years old. That summer David Duff began working on an official biography. He forwarded completed chapters to the ageing Princess for her approval. After reading a considerable portion of the manuscript, Louise was kind enough to tell the young writer that she was "deeply interested." [20]

She was confined now to her apartments. Except for the new inside studio, the rooms at Kensington had changed little during the sixty years of her residency. Bedrooms, dressing rooms, dining room and drawing room — the last not redecorated since 1891 — retained a distinctive nineteenth century look. Lorne's bedroom remained undisturbed since his death a quarter century earlier, for Louise inherited some of her mother's reverence for a deceased spouse.

Outside, much had changed. By November 1939, as war descended once again on Princess Louise's Europe, the palace was packed round with sandbags, the skylights painted black. In Kensington Gardens and Hyde Park the grass was criss-crossed with slit trenches. Nearby were air-raid shelters and anti-aircraft guns, searchlight and balloon barrage stations.

European wars had circumscribed Louise's life. She had been born during the revolutionary upheavals of 1848, married at the time of the Franco-Prussian War, widowed on the eve of the First World War. She died at Kensington Palace at 6:50 a.m. on Sunday 3 December 1939, three months after the beginning of the Second World War. She was ninety-one years old, and was survived by her brother Arthur and her sister Beatrice, the last of Queen Victoria's children.

Tributes and messages of sympathy trickled in from her charities and her arts associations. Canadian newspapers featured short historical items on her years at Rideau Hall sixty years earlier. A memorial service was held at Rosneath parish church. King George VI declared a two-week period of official court mourning. The mourning order had less effect than usual, as war had already ended social functions at court. That was the story of Louise's death: the nation had more important things to worry about than the death of an old lady who had outlived her generation.

A private funeral service was held at St. George's Chapel, Windsor Castle, on December 12. Pipers of the Argyll and Sutherland Highlanders played the lament, "The Flowers of the Forest." Her coffin was buried, not with her husband at Kilmun, but with her own family in the Royal Cemetery at Frogmore. The coffin contained only ashes, for Louise's body had been cremated at Golder's Green crematorium prior to the funeral. Cremation was a most unusual event in royal circles, but as *The Times* reminded its readers, Louise was "the least bound by convention and etiquette of any of the Royal Family." [21]

* * * * *

Even more than her husband, Louise was compromised by her position within the royal family. Had she not been a royal princess, she would likely have pursued a career as a professional sculptress. She would have worked in the field of public, monumental sculpture, like her mentor Edgar Boehm and her half-cousin Count Gleichen. Her work would have been judged on professional standards, and not fawned over because it came from the hand of Queen Victoria's daughter.

Despite her royal handicap, and despite working in the traditional British style rather than the more imaginative French style of the late nineteenth century, Louise produced sculpture that endured. Her best Canadian piece is the statue of her mother standing on the McGill University campus in Montreal, a statue unveiled by Louise's friend, Lady Minto, at the opening of McGill's Royal Victoria College on 1 November 1890. Louise's best British work includes her war memorial for the Heritage Craft Schools at Chailey, Queen Victoria's statue in Manchester Cathedral, Prince Henry's memorial in Whippingham Church, the colonial soldiers' memorial in St. Paul's, and — grandest of all — the Broad Walk Statue of Queen Victoria in Kensington Gardens.

Like her public sculpture, Louise's public charities and philanthropies proved long-lasting. She channelled her vast reserves of energy and organizational skills into a variety of causes spanning the areas of women's work and health care, art and education. Those she considered helpful, she continued to support throughout her long life. Many of her causes outlived her; the National Trust and the Girls' Public Day Schools continue to thrive today.

The most unusual Canadian reminder of Louise is the regimental mascot of the 8th Hussars, a New Brunswick armoured regiment of which the Princess had once been colonel-in-chief. In the autumn of 1944, as the Hussars fought their way up the Italian peninsula, they encountered a young female colt, orphaned by the fighting, wounded in the leg and stomach, half starved and bleeding. She was given a shot of rum, bandaged up, named Princess Louise, and adopted as official regimental mascot.

In a stable at Sussex, New Brunswick, the equine Louise lived through the post-war period and accepted the homage of her regiment. But as the years passed, she became the pivot of a nagging and perplexing problem of royal succession — she had no heir. "Year after year the Regiment brought to her one suitor after another," writes Douglas How, the 8th Hussars' historian, "and still waited in vain for the pregnancy that would carry on the royal tradition." At last they brought her a mate who shared her own Mediterranean heritage — an Arabian stallion. "Whether the magic lay in geographical or in more mystical terms," continues How, "the combination worked." [22] Princess Louise foaled in the summer of 1954; the colt was promptly proclaimed Princess Louise II.

Princess Louise and the Marquis of Lorne are best known to contemporary Londoners as pubs. The Princess Louise at 208 High Holborn (Holborn tube stop) is centrally located near the British Museum and very up-market. Operated by the Vaux Freehouse group, this 1891 pub retains most of its original decor and features, from ornate ceilings to magnificent bar, right down to the superb plumbing fixtures in the gents' lavatory. The *Evening Standard* named it "pub of the year" in 1986.

The Princess Louise is a busy pub, serving young businessmen at lunch time, a more casual young set in the early evening, and jazz buffs on weekends. Pub snacks include melt-in-your-mouth roast beef sandwiches; upstairs the hot and cold buffets are among the best in town. Customers gaze at a painted wall panel of the Princess in front of Kensington Palace. Many put down ten pounds for bright red sweat shirts emblazoned with the name "Princess Louise".

The Marquis of Lorne pub presents a direct contrast. It is difficult to find — at Combermere and Dalyell roads in a no-man's land of council flats and working-class housing mid-way between Stockwell and Brixton tube stops south of the Thames. It serves an ageing local clientele. The outside retains its original charm; the interior has been recently refurbished along "Victorian" lines. There is no fine pub food available. But the Marquis of Lorne, a Charrington Pub, does possess two saving graces: a genial manager named Larry Brady, and a Canadian lager on tap — Carling's Black Label!

Princess Louise travelled a long way from Buckingham Palace to High Holborn; the Marquis of Lorne travelled even further from Stafford House to Brixton.

Marquis of Lorne & Princess Louise public houses, London, 1988.

# ENDNOTES

## NOTES TO CHAPTER ONE

1    Frances Balfour, *Ne Obliviscaris: Dinna Forget* (London: Hodder and Stoughton, 1930), I, 97.
2    Argyll, George Douglas Campbell, Eighth Duke of, *Autobiography and Memoirs* (London: John Murray, 1906), I, 264-65.
3    Balfour, *Ne Obliviscaris*, I, 33.
4    Argyll, John Douglas Sutherland Campbell, Ninth Duke of, *Passages From the Past* (London: Hutchinson, 1907), I, 2.
5    Balfour, *Ne Obliviscaris*, I, 87, 24.
6    *Ibid.*, I, 22-23.
7    Argyll, *Passages*, I, 229.
8    *Ibid.*, I, 199.
9    Balfour, *Ne Obliviscaris*, I, 33.
10   Argyll, *Passages*, I, 202.
11   Balfour, *Ne Obliviscaris*, I, 98-99.
12   Argyll, *Passages*, I, 199-200.
13   *Ibid.*, I, 200-01.
14   Frances Balfour, *Lady Victoria Campbell: A Memoir* (London: Hodder and Stoughton, n.d.), 5-6.
15   Argyll, *Passages*, I, 201.
16   *Ibid.*, II, 385.
17   *Ibid.*, II, 386-87.
18   *Ibid.*, I, 228.
19   Balfour, *Ne Obliviscaris*, I, 89.
20   Argyll, *Passages*, I, 17.
21   Balfour, *Ne Obliviscaris*, I, 96.
22   *Ibid.*, I, 99; Argyll, *Passages*, I, 227.
23   Argyll, *Passages*, I, 36, 40.
24   William Charles Maugham, *Rosneath Past and Present* (Paisley and London: Alexander Gardner, 1893), p. 46.
25   Argyll, *Passages*, I, 185-86.
26   Balfour, *Ne Obliviscaris*, I, 21.
27   Argyll, *Passages*, I, 7.
28   David Duff, editor, *Queen Victoria's Highland Journals* (Exeter: Webb & Bower, 1980), p. 53.
29   *Ibid.*; *Illustrated London News*, 28 August 1847.
30   Duff, *Highland Journals*, p. 53.
31   Argyll, *Passages*, I, 3.
32   Duff, *Highland Journals*, p. 53.

## NOTES TO CHAPTER TWO

1    Hector Bolitho, *Albert, Prince Consort* (London: Max Parrish, 1964), p. 98.
2    David Duff, *The Life Story of H.R.H. Princess Louise, Duchess of Argyll* (London: Stanley Paul, 1940), p. 19.

3       Argyll, *Autobiography*, I, 304.
4       Duff, *Princess Louise*, pp. 23-24.
5       C. Kinloch Cooke, *A Memoir of Her Royal Highness, Princess Mary Adelaide, Duchess of Teck* (London: John Murray, 1900), I, 86.
6       Sarah Lyttelton, *Correspondence of Sarah Spencer, Lady Lyttelton, 1787-1870*, edited by Mrs. Hugh Wyndham (London: John Murray, 1912), p. 381.
7       Duff, *Princess Louise*, p. 28.
8       Roger Fulford, *The Prince Consort* (London: Macmillan, 1949), p. 251.
9       Augusta Stanley, *Letters of Lady Augusta Stanley: A Young Lady at Court 1849-1863*, edited by the Dean of Windsor and Hector Bolitho (New York: George H. Doran, 1927), p. 229.
10      Duff, *Princess Louise*, p. 58.
11      Nina Epton, *Victoria and Her Daughters* (London: Weidenfeld and Nicolson, 1971), pp. 227, 45.
12      George Rowell, *Queen Victoria Goes to the Theatre* (London: Paul Elek, 1978), pp. 83-84; Duff, *Princess Louise*, p. 51.
13      Marina Warner, *Queen Victoria's Sketchbook* (London: Macmillan, 1979), p. 8.
14      Hilary Hunt-Lewis, "The Art of Princess Louise," in Duff, *Princess Louise*, p. 337.
15      Balfour, *Ne Obliviscaris*, I, 32.
16      *Ibid.*, I, 98.
17      Ronald Gower, *My Reminiscences* (London: Kegan Paul, Trench, Trubner, 1895), pp. 89-90.
18      Argyll, *Passages*, I, 3.
19      Balfour, *Ne Obliviscaris*, I, 99.
20      Gower, *My Reminiscences*, p. 88.
21      Duff, *Princess Louise*, p. 56.
22      Daphne Bennett, *Queen Victoria's Children* (London: Victor Gollancz, 1980), p. 100.
23      *Ibid.*
24      Gower, *My Reminiscences*, p. 90.

## NOTES TO CHAPTER THREE

1       *Dictionary of National Biography*, XXII, 386.
2       Balfour, *Ne Obliviscaris*, I, 88.
3       Gower, *Reminiscences*, p. 96.
4       Argyll, *Autobiography*, II, 129.
5       Public Archives of Canada, Marquis of Lorne Papers [hereafter PAC, Lorne Papers], Elizabeth Campbell to Ian Campbell, undated letters, c. 1858-59.
6       *Ibid.*
7       Argyll, *Passages*, I, 68.
8       Gower, *Reminiscences*, p. 97.
9       Patrick Strong to Robert M. Stamp, 5 March 1985.
10      Argyll, *Passages*, I, 96-98; John Campbell, Marquis of Lorne, *The Governor's Guide to Windsor Castle* (London: Cassell, 1895), p. 179; John Campbell, Marquis of Lorne, *Canadian Pictures Drawn With Pen and Pencil* (London: Religious Tract Society, 1885), pp. 21-22.
11      Balfour, *Ne Obliviscaris*, I, 82.
12      Argyll, *Passages*, I, 68.
13      Duff, *Princess Louise*, p. 78.

14    A.L. Rowse, *Homosexuals in History: A Study of Ambivalence in Society, Literature and the Arts* (N.P: Dorset Press, 1983), p. 148. See also Vern and Bonnie Bullough, "Homosexuality in Nineteenth Century English Public Schools," in Joseph Harry and Man Singh Das, editors, *Homosexuals in International Perspectives* (Delhi: Vikas Publishing House, 1980), pp. 123-31.

15    Bernard Holland, "An Eton Master," *The National Review*, February 1898, pp. 867-77; James Brinsley Richards, *Seven Years At Eton 1857-1864* (London: Richard Bentley and Son, 1883), pp. 180, 183. See also Rupert Croft-Cooke, *Feasting With Panthers* (London: W.H. Allen, 1967), pp. 103-10; Timothy d'Arch Smith, *Love In Earnest* (London: Routledge and Kegan Paul, 1970), pp. 4-11.

16    Faith Compton Mackenzie, *William Cory: A Biography* (London: Constable, 1950), p. 28.

17    *Ibid.*, pp. 183-84.

18    Richard Viscount Esher, *Ionicus* (London: John Murray, 1923), p. 252; Smith, *Love In Earnest*, p. 41.

19    Ronald Gordon Cant, *The University of St. Andrews: A Short History* (Edinburgh: Scottish Academic Press, 1970), p. 146.

20    Argyll, *Passages*, I, 72-73.

21    *Ibid.*, I, 84-86.

22    *Ibid.*, I, 78.

23    Balfour, *Ne Obliviscaris*, I, 82.

24    *Ibid.*, I, 84.

25    Argyll, *Passages*, I, 99.

26    *Ibid.*, I, 98, 103.

27    *Ibid.*, I, 96-97.

28    Samuel Bernard, *Jamaican Blood and the Victorian Conscience: The Governor Eyre Controversy* (Boston: Houghton, Mifflin, 1963), p. 13.

29    Argyll, *Passages*, I. 98.

## NOTES TO CHAPTER FOUR

1    John Campbell, Marquis of Lorne, *A Trip to the Tropics and Home Through America* (London: Hurst and Blackett, 1867), p. 18.

2    *Ibid.*, pp. 28, 58.

3    *Ibid.*, pp. 145-46.

4    *Ibid.*, p. v.

5    "Two Aristocratic Travellers," *Spectator*, XL (1867), 389.

6    Argyll, *Passages*, I, 149.

7    Lorne, *Trip to the Tropics*, p. 128.

8    *Ibid.*, pp. 171, 175-76.

9    Argyll, *Passages*, I, 223.

10    Lorne, *Trip to the Tropics*, pp. 168, 181.

11    *Ibid.*, p. 170.

12    Balfour, *Ne Obliviscaris*, I, 85.

13    Argyll, *Passages*, I, 166-67.

14    Lorne, *Trip to the Tropics*, pp. 201, 177.

15    PAC, Lorne Papers, Typescript draft of "A Trip to the Tropics and Home Through America," unpaginated.

16    *Ibid.*

17    *Ibid.*

18    Lorne, *Trip to the Tropics*, pp. 349-53.

19      Gower, *Reminiscences*, p. 167.
20      Argyll, *Passages*, I, 236.
21      Balfour, *Ne Obliviscaris*, I, 84.
22      Argyll, *Passages*, I, 237, 240.
23      *Ibid.*, I, 264.
24      *Ibid.*, I, 245.
25      *Ibid.*, I, 250.
26      *Ibid.* I, 248, 260.
27      *Ibid.*, I, 246, 263.
28      Roger Fulford, ed., *Your Dear Letter: Private Correspondence of Queen Victoria and the Crown Princess of Prussia, 1865-1971* (New York: Charles Scribner's Sons, 1971), p. 125, letter of 13 March 1867.
29      Argyll, *Passages*, I, 305-06.
30      *Ibid.*, I, 311-12.
31      *Ibid.*, I, 309-10.
32      *Ibid.*, I, 318.
33      *Ibid.*, I, 320-21.
34      *Ibid.*, I, 322.
35      *Ibid.*, I, 324-25.
36      *Ibid.*, I, 330.

## NOTES TO CHAPTER FIVE

1      Epton, *Victoria and Her Daughters*, p. 97.
2      Percy Colson, *Lord Goschen and His Friends* (London: Hutchinson, n.d.), p. 56.
3      Duff, *Princess Louise*, p. 86.
4      Roger Fulford, ed., *Dearest Mama: Letters Between Queen Victoria and the Crown Princess of Prussia, 1861-1864* (London: Evans Brothers, 1968), pp. 127, 182, 311.
5      Georgina Battiscombe, *Queen Alexandra* (London: Constable, 1969), p. 82.
6      British Library, Baron Rainald Knightley Papers [hereafter BL, Knightley Papers], Princess Louise to Louisa Bowater, n.d. (c1860s).
7      *Ibid.*, 22 May 1862, 30 November 1862, and 14 December 1862.
8      *Ibid.*, 14 May 1862 and 3 April 1865.
9      *Ibid.*, 21 March 1866.
10      *Ibid.*, 20 July 1866 and 22 December 1866.
11      Duff, *Princess Louise*, p. 96.
12      *Ibid.*, p. 98; Duff, *Queen Victoria's Highland Journals*, pp. 125-26.
13      Fulford, *Your Dear Letter*, pp. 82, 114.
14      Giles St. Aubyn, *Edward VII, Prince and King* (London: Collins, 1979), p. 79; Tyler Whittle, *Victoria and Albert at Home* (London: Routledge & Kegan Paul, 1980), p. 154.
15      Fulford, *Your Dear Letter*, pp. 70-71.
16      Augusta Stanley, *Later Letters of Lady Augusta Stanley, 1864-1876*, edited by the Dean of Windsor and Hector Bolitho (London: Jonathan Cape, 1929), pp. 66, 74.
17      Battiscombe, *Queen Alexandra*, pp. 101-02.
18      BL, Knightley Papers, Princess Louise to Louisa Bowater, 16 September 1865.
19      William Monypenny and George Buckle, *The Life of Benjamin Disraeli, Earl of Beaconsfield* (New York: Russell & Russell, 1969), III, 390.
20      Fulford, *Your Dear Letter*, pp. 184-86.
21      Bennett, *Queen Victoria's Children*, p. 106.

22 Marc Girouard, *The Return to Camelot: Chivalry and the English Gentleman* (New Haven: Yale University Press, 1981), p. 126.

23 David Duff, *The Shy Princess: The Life and Times of Her Royal Highness Princess Beatrice* (London: Evans Brothers, 1958), p. 62.

24 Fulford, *Your Dear Letters*, p. 164.

25 A.R. Mills, ed., *Two Victorian Ladies: More Pages From the Journals of Emily and Ellen Hall* (London: Frederick Muller, 1969), p. 200.

26 Hunt-Lewis, "The Art of Princess Louise," in Duff, *Princess Louise*, p. 338.

27 *Ibid.*, p. 339.

28 Bennett, *Queen Victoria's Children*, p. 105.

## NOTES TO CHAPTER SIX

1 Balfour, *Ne Obliviscaris*, I, 61, 81-82.

2 *The Times*, 26 September 1878.

3 Gower, *Reminiscences*, p. 199.

4 *Ibid.*

5 Argyll, *Passages From the Past*, II, 366.

6 G.M. Young, *Victorian England: Portrait of an Age* (London: Oxford University Press, 1961), p. 106.

7 Gower, *Reminiscences*, p. 199.

8 *The Times*, 26 September 1878.

9 British Library, William Ewart Gladstone papers [hereafter BL, Gladstone Papers], Lorne to Gladstone, 2 April 1870.

10 *Dictionary of National Biography, 1912-1921*, p. 88; Charles Tuttle, *Royalty in Canada* (Montreal: Tuttle & Simpson, 1878), p. 76.

11 Argyll, *Passages From the Past*, II, 344-45.

12 *Ibid.*, II, 348-56.

13 *Ibid.*, II, 366.

14 *Ibid.*, II, 377.

15 Bodleian Library, Oxford, William Harcourt Papers [hereafter Bodleian, Harcourt Papers], Lorne to Harcourt, 20 December 1869.

16 Lucy Masterman, ed., *Mary Gladstone (Mrs. Drew): Her Diaries and Letters* (New York: E.P. Dutton, 1930), p. 22.

17 *Ibid.*

18 *Ibid.*, pp. 38, 40.

19 Argyll, *Passages From the Past*, I, 337.

20 Balfour, *Ne Obliviscaris*, I, 82.

21 *Ibid.*, I, 123.

22 E.F. Benson, *Daughters of Queen Victoria* (London: Cassell, 1939), p. 156.

23 Carl Sell, *Alice, Grand Duchess of Hesse* (London: John Murray, 1884), p. 199.

24 Bennett, *Queen Victoria's Children*, p. 103.

25 Fulford, *Your Dear Letter*, p. 303.

26 *Ibid.*, p. 252.

27 Duff, *Princess Louise*, p. 104.

28 *Truth*, 9 November 1882.

29 Duff, *Princess Louise*, p. 117.

30 Robert Rhodes James, *Rosebery: A Biography of Archibald Philip, Fifth Earl of Rosebery* (London: Weidenfeld and Nicolson, 1963), pp. 66-67.

## NOTES TO CHAPTER SEVEN

1   A.M.W. Stirling, *The Merry Wives of Battersea and Gossip of Three Centuries* (London: Robert Hale, 1956), p. 109.

2   Oscar Browning, *Memories of Sixty Years at Eton, Cambridge, and Elsewhere* (London: John Lane, 1910), p. 166.

3   Marquis of Lorne, "Highland Courting," *Blackwood's Magazine*, May 1895, p. 789.

4   Ivor Brown, *Balmoral: The History of a Home* (London: Collins, 1955), p. 100.

5   Duff, *Princess Beatrice*, p. 69.

6   Duff, *Princess Louise*, p. 107.

7   Philip Guedalla, *The Queen and Mr. Gladstone* (London: Hodder & Stoughton, 1933), I, 281.

8   Fulford, *Your Dear Letter*, p. 281.

9   *Ibid.*, p. 301.

10  *Ibid.*, pp. 303-03.

11  Epton, *Victoria and Her Daughters*, p. 133.

12  BL, Gladstone Papers, Princess Louise to Catherine Gladstone, 15 July 1870, and Lorne to Catherine Gladstone, 22 October 1870.

13  Elizabeth Longford, *Victoria R.I.* (London: Weidenfeld and Nicolson, 1964), p. 332.

14  *Munsey's Magazine*, March 1902, p. 898.

15  Argyll, *Passages From the Past*, II, 391.

16  *The Times*, 14 October 1870.

17  George Earle Buckle, ed., *The Letters of Queen Victoria . . . Between the Years 1862 and 1878. Second Series* (London: John Murray, 1928), II, 120.

18  Tom Cullen, *The Empress Brown: The True Story of a Victorian Scandal* (Boston: Houghton, Mifflin, 1969), p. 124.

19  Guedalla, *The Queen and Mr. Gladstone*, I, 272-73.

20  Duff, *Princess Louise*, p. 128.

21  Fulford, *Your Dear Letter*, p. 302.

22  *Ibid.*, pp. 305-06; see also p. 309.

23  Benson, *Daughters of Queen Victoria, pp. 151-52; Buckle, Letters of Queen Victoria. Second Series*, I, 632-33.

24  Longford, *Victoria R.I.*, p. 368.

25  Bodleian, Harcourt Papers, Lorne to William Harcourt, 23 October 1870.

26  Duff, *Princess Louise*, p. 121.

27  BL, Knightley Papers, Princess Louise to Louisa Bowater, 24 October 1870; BL, Gladstone Papers, Princess Louise to Catherine Gladstone, 18 October 1870.

28  John Campbell, Duke of Argyll, *A Gift Book for the Home* (London: Hodder & Stoughton, 1901), p. 51.

29  Lorne, *Governor's Guide to Windsor Castle*, p. 260.

30  Gower, *Reminiscences*, p. 260.

31  *Memoir of Robert Herbert Story*, by His Daughters (Glasgow: James Maclehose and Sone, 1909), p. 108.

32  *Ibid.*

33  George, Duke of Cambridge, *A Memoir of His Private Life*, edited by Edgar Sheppard (London: Longmans, Green, 1907), I, 294.

34  *Memoir of Robert Herbert Story*, p. 109.

35  Duff, *Princess Louise*, pp. 137-38.

36  Buckle, *The Letters of Queen Victoria. Second Series*, II, 125; Masterman, *Mary Gladstone*, p. 60.

37  Mary Reed Bobbitt, *With Dearest Love to All: The Life and Letters of Lady Jebb* (Chicago: Henry Regnery, 1960), p. 74.

38      Sell, *Alice, Grand Duchess of Hesse*, p. 267.
39      Walburga Paget, *Embassies of Other Days, and Further Recollections* (New York: Doran, 1923), I, 260.
40      Buckle, *The Letters of Queen Victoria. Second Series*, II, 155, Lorne to Queen Victoria, 5 August 1871.
41      *Ibid.*, II, 156.
42      Balfour, *Ne Obliviscaris*, I, 104.
43      *Truth*, 1 January 1880; Gower, *Reminiscences*, p. 265.

## NOTES TO CHAPTER EIGHT

1       Duff, *Princess Louise*, p. 288.
2       *Ibid.*
3       British Library, Holland House Papers, Correspondence of 4th Lady Holland [hereafter BL, Holland Papers], Princess Louise to Lady Holland, 4 December 1873 and 22 January 1874.
4       Kensington Palace Archives, Miscellaneous notes on Kensington Palace.
5       Derek Hudson, *Kensington Palace* (London: Peter Davies, 1968), pp. 102-03.
6       Gathorne Hardy, *The Diary of Gathorne Hardy, Later Lord Cranbrook, 1866-1892: Political Selections*, edited by Nancy E. Johnson (Oxford: Clarendon Press, 1981), p. 183.
7       Argyll, *Passages From the Past*, II, 401.
8       Anthea Callen, *Women Artists of the Arts and Crafts Movement 1870-1914* (New York: Pantheon Books, 1979), pp.5,
9       Epton, *Victoria and Her Daughters*, P. 126.
10      Richard Henry Dana III, *Hospitable England in the Seventies: The Diary of a Young American* ( Boston: Houghton, Mifflin, 1921), pp. 105-06.
11      *Ibid.*, pp.106, 108.
12      *Ibid.*, p. 107.
13      *Ibid.*, p. 119.
14      Duff, *Highland Journals*, p. 187.
15      *Ibid.*, pp. 186, 191.
16      Arthur Ponsonby, *Henry Ponsonby, Queen Victoria's Private Secretary* (London: Macmillan, 1942), p. 123; Epton, *Victoria and Her Daughters*, PP. 149-50.
17      Dana, *Hospitable England*, p.112
18      Trinity College Library, Cambridge, Lord Houghton Papers [hereafter TCL, Houghton Papers], Lorne to Houghton, 1 June and 15 June 1875.
19      British Library, Macmillan archive [hereafter BL, Macmillan Archive], Lorne to Alexander Macmillan, 14 July 1875 to 7 December 1875.
20      *Ibid.*, Lorne to Alexander Macmillan, 26 November 1875.
21      "Three Old and Three New Poets," *International Review*, May 1876, pp. 412-13.
22      *The Times*, 7 February 1917.
23      See, for example, John Cowan, *Canada's Governors-General, 1867-1952* (Toronto: York Publishing Company, 1952).
24      BL, Macmillan Archive, Lorne to Alexander Macmillan, 3 February 1876 to 7 August 1877.
25      Manchester Guardian, 5 May 1914; *Reynolds's Newspaper*, 10 May 1914.
26      Epton, *Victoria and Her Daughter*, p. 135.
27      Arthur Jacobs, *Arthur Sullivan: A Victorian Musician* (Oxford: Oxford University Press, 1984), p. 106.

28      Gordon S. Haight, *George Eliot: A Biography* (New York: Oxford University Press, 1968), p. 501.

29      James Brough, *The Prince and the Lily* (London: Hodder & Stoughton, 1975,) pp. 85-86.

30      Angela Lambert, *Unquiet Souls: The Indian Summer of the British Aristocracy 1880-1918* (London: Macmillan, 1984), p. 42.

31      *Ibid.*, p. 41.

32      Duff, *Princess Louise*, p. 305.

33      New York *Times*, 11 August, 9 September, and 21 September, 1878.

34      Balfour, *Ne Obliviscaris*, I, 144.

## NOTES TO CHAPTER NINE

1      Argyll, *Passages From the Past*, I, 394-96.

2      Buckle, *The Letters of Queen Victoria. Second Series*, II, 633.

3      *Ibid.*, II, 630-31.

4      Roger Fulford, ed., *Beloved Mama: Private Correspondence of Queen Victoria and the German Crown Princess 1878-1885* (London: Evans Brothers, 1981), p. 24.

5      Sir Sydney Lee, *King Edward VII: A Biography* (London: Macmillan, 1925), I, 591.

6      Lady Victoria Hicks Beach, *Life of Sir Michael Hicks Beach, Earl St. Aldwyn* (London: Macmillan, 1932), I, 64.

7      Tuttle, *Royalty in Canada*, p. 123.

8      David M.L. Farr, *The Colonial Office and Canada 1867-1887* (Toronto: University of Toronto Press, 1955), p. 53, quoting John Buchan, Lord Tweedsmuir.

9      New York *Times*, 31 July 1878.

10     Tuttle, *Royalty in Canada*, pp. 17, 24.

11     *Ibid.*, pp. 121-22; London *World*, 9 October 1878; New York *Times*, 11 August, 9 September, and 11 September 1878.

12     Tuttle, *Royalty in Canada*, pp. 114, 115.

13     John Campbell, Duke of Argyll, *Yesterday and Today in Canada* (London: George Allen, 1910), p. 24.

14     Lorne, *A Trip to the Tropics*, p. 347.

15     PAC, Lorne Papers, Dufferin to Lorne, 6 August, 12 August, 22 August, and 19 August 1878.

16     Tuttle, *Royalty in Canada*, p. 118.

17     Epton, *Victoria and Her Daughters*, p. 157.

18     Monypenny and Buckle, *Benjamin Disraeli*, IV, 1262.

19     New York *Times*, 24 November 1878.

20     *Ibid.*, 14 November 1878.

21     *Ibid.*, 24 November 1878.

22     Argyll, *Passages From the Past*, II, 408.

23     *Ibid.*, II, 407.

24     *Ibid.*, II, 408.

25     *Ibid.*, II, 410.

26     Donald Creighton, *Sir John A. Macdonald. Volume II: The Old Chieftain* (Toronto: Macmillan, 1955), 249.

27     Argyll, *Passages From the Past*, II, 411.

28     J.E. Collins, *Canada Under the Administration of Lord Lorne* (Toronto: Rose, 1884), p. 39.

29     PAC, Lorne Papers, Lorne to Eighth Duke of Argyll, 4 December 1878.

30  Collins, *Canada Under the Administration of Lord Lorne*, p. 45.
31  New York *Times*, 3 December 1878.
32  *Ibid.*
33  PAC, Lorne Papers, Lorne to Eighth Duke of Argyll, 4 December 1878.
34  Lady Byng of Vimy, *Up the Stream of Time* (Toronto: Clarke, Irwin, 1945), pp. 11-12.
35  Sandra Gwyn, *The Private Capital: Ambition and Love in the Age of Macdonald and Laurier* (Toronto: McClelland and Stewart, 1984), p. 186.
36  PAC, Lorne Papers, Lorne to Eighth Duke of Argyll, 4 December 1878.
37  *Ibid.*
38  Annie Howells Frechette, "Life at Rideau Hall," *Harper's New Monthly Magazine*, July 1881, pp. 213-23.

## NOTES TO CHAPTER TEN

1   Alfred Lyall, *The Life of the Marquis of Dufferin and Ava* (London: John Murray, 1925), I, 284.
2   *The Times*, 24 December 1878.
3   Gwyn, *The Private Capital*, p. 186.
4   Collins, *Canada Under the Administration of Lord Lorne*, p. 416.
5   Barry St. John Nevill, ed., *Life at the Court of Queen Victoria 1861-1901* (London: Methuen, 1984), p. 98.
6   R. H. Hubbard, *Rideau Hall: An Illustrated History of Government House, Ottawa, in Victorian and Edwardian Times* (Ottawa: Queen's Printer, 1967), p. 52.
7   Argyll, *Passages From the Past*, II, 422, 419.
8   Public Archives of Canada, Sir John A. Macdonald Papers [hereafter PAC, Macdonald Papers], De Winton to Macdonald, 17 January 1879.
9   PAC, Lorne Papers, Lorne to Dr. W.F. Cumming, 30 January 1879.
10  Buffalo *Courier*, 23 January 1879.
11  Sir George W. Ross, *Getting Into Parliament and After* (Toronto: William Briggs, 1913), pp. 110-11.
12  New York *Times*, 15 February 1879.
13  Argyll, *Passages From the Past*, II, 421, 422.
14  *Ibid.*, II, 426.
15  Dale Thomson, *Alexander Mackenzie: Clear Grit* (Toronto: Macmillan, 1960), p. 349.
16  Vancouver *Daily Province*, 8 December 1939, from an interview with Mrs. W.J. Thicke, nee Clara Higman.
17  Gwyn, *The Private Capital*, p. 190.
18  Duff, *Princess Louise*, p. 172.
19  Sir Richard Cartwright, *Reminiscences* (Toronto: William Briggs, 1912), p. 211; Duff, *Princess Louise*, p. 176.
20  Toronto *Globe*, 2 December 1912; *The Times*, 3 December 1912.
21  PAC, Lorne Papers, Lorne to Eighth Duke of Argyll, 4 December 1878.
22  *Ibid.*, Lorne to Sir Michael Hicks Beach, 3 December 1878.
23  *Ibid.*, 1 January and 8 February 1879.
24  *Ibid.*, Hicks Beach to Lorne, 12 March 1879; Lorne to Hicks Beach, 24 March 1879.
25  *Ibid.*, Lorne to Hicks Beach, 27 March 1879.
26  *Ibid.*, Lorne to Eighth Duke of Argyll, 9 April 1879.

27 Public Record Office, Colonial Office Records, File CO42 [hereafter PRO, CO42], Hicks Beach to Lorne, 8 April 1879.
28 W.S. MacNutt, *Days of Lorne: Impressions of a Governor-General* (Fredericton: Brunswick Press, 1955), p. 36; John T. Saywell, "Review of W.S. MacNutt, Impressions of a Governor-General," *Canadian Historical Review*, June 1955, p. 157.
29 PAC, Lorne Papers, Lorne to Eighth Duke of Argyll, 9 April 1879.
30 MacNutt, *Days of Lorne*, p. 35.
31 Montreal *Gazette*, 27 May 1879.
32 Argyll, *Yesterday and Today in Canada*, pp. 1,2.
33 PAC, Macdonald Papers, De Winton to Macdonald, 13 June 1879.
34 PAC, Lorne Papers, Lorne to Eighth Duke of Argyll, 24 April 1879.
35 Balfour, *Ne Obliviscaris*, I, 300.
36 PAC, Macdonald Papers, De Winton to Macdonald, 28 June 1879.
37 MacNutt, *Days of Lorne*, p. 248.
38 PAC, Lorne Papers, Lorne to Archibald Campbell, 22 September 1879.
39 Arnold Haultain, ed., *A Selection From Goldwin Smith's Correspondence* (Toronto: McClelland & Goodchild, n.d.), p. 93.
40 Peter Waite, *Canada 1874-1896: Arduous Destiny* (Toronto: McClelland and Stewart, 1971), p. 93.
41 PAC, Lorne Papers, Lorne to Archibald Campbell, 22 September 1879.

## NOTES TO CHAPTER ELEVEN

1 *The Times*, 27 January 1880.
2 Balfour, *Ne Obliviscaris*, I, 297.
3 Monypenny and Buckle, *Benjamin Disraeli*, IV, 1349.
4 PAC, Lorne Papers, Lorne to Archibald Campbell, 22 September 1879.
5 Toronto *Globe*, 20 November 1879.
6 Gwyn, *The Private Capital*, p. 188; *Truth*, 15 November 1879.
7 Birmingham *Post*, 31 October 1879.
8 Monypenny and Buckle, *Benjamin Disraeli*, VI, 506.
9 Birmingham *Post*, 31 October 1879.
10 New York *Times*, 3 February 1880.
11 Gwyn, *The Private Capital*, p. 205.
12 George, Duke of Cambridge, *A Memoir of His Private Life*, edited by Edgar Sheppard (London: Longmans, Green, 1907), II, 80; *Truth*, 29 January 1880.
13 Argyll, *Passages From the Past*, II, 444.
14 PAC, Lorne Papers, Lorne to Eighth Duke of Argyll, 18 March 1880.
15 *Truth*, 26 August 1880.
16 Ottawa *Citizen*, 17 March 1880. Neither words nor music of "Dominion Hymn" were taken up by the public; three months later at Quebec, Lorne heard the first public performance of the country's eventual national anthem — Calixa Lavallée's "O Canada."
17 Argyll, *Passages From the Past*, II, 445.
18 Toronto *Mail*, 25 February 1880; *Reynolds's Newspaper*, 14 March 1880.
19 Rebecca Sisler, *Passionate Spirits: A History of the Royal Canadian Academy of Arts, 1880-1980* (Toronto: Clarke, Irwin, 1980), p. 28.
20 Charles C. Hill, "To Found a National Gallery," *Journal of the National Gallery*, 6 March 1980, p. 4.

| 21 | Sisler, *Passionate Spirits*, p. 32. |
| 22 | *Ibid.*, p. 34; Argyll, *Passages From the Past*, II, 444. |
| 23 | Sisler, *Passionate Spirits*, pp. 38-39. |
| 24 | PAC, Macdonald Papers, Lorne to Macdonald, 16 November 1879. |
| 25 | PAC, Lorne Papers, "Memorandum for the Privy Council, 10 May 1880." |
| 26 | Ottawa *Free Press*, 27 May 1882. |
| 27 | Chicago *Tribune*, 9 June 1880. |
| 28 | Princess Alice, Countess of Athlone, *For My Grandchildren* (London: Evans Brothers, 1966), p. 15. |
| 29 | PAC, Macdonald Papers, De Winton to Macdonald, 12 June 1880; PAC, Lorne Papers, Lorne to Eighth Duke of Argyll, 10 June 1880. |
| 30 | Lorne, *Canadian Pictures*, pp. 52-54. |
| 31 | PAC, Lorne Papers, Lorne to Lord Granville, n.d., June or July 1880. |
| 32 | National Gallery of Canada, European Painting Department, Accession Nos. 14640, 14644. |
| 33 | Gwyn, *The Private Capital*, p. 206. |
| 34 | *Truth*, 28 October 1880 and 2 June 1881. |
| 35 | Monypenny and Buckle, *Benjamin Disraeli*, VI, 599, 601. |

## NOTES TO CHAPTER TWELVE

| 1 | PAC, Macdonald Papers, J.J. McBride to Lorne, 7 January 1881. |
| 2 | William D'Arcy, *The Fenian Movement in the United States: 1858-1886* (New York: Russell & Russell, 1971), pp. 400-03. |
| 3 | Duff, *Princess Louise*, p. 184. |
| 4 | PAC, Lorne Papers, Lorne to Dr. F. F. Cumming, 16 January 1881; Lorne to Eighth Duke of Argyll, 13 May 1881; Lorne to Archibald Campbell, 3 May 1881. |
| 5 | Ottawa *Citizen*, 4 November 1881. |
| 6 | S. Weir Mitchell, "The Relation of Pain to Weather, Being a Study of the Natural History of a Case of Traumatic Neuralgia," *The American Journal of the Medical Sciences*, April 1877, pp. 305ff. |
| 7 | Louise was not the only member of the British royal family to serve from neuralgia and to use it as a reason to absent herself from public duties. Queen Victoria, for one, set a fine example for her daughter to emulate! A parallel case can also be found in Princess Maud of Wales, Louise's neice, a daughter of Bertie and Alexandra, who later became Queen Maud of Norway. See Kenneth Rose, *King George V* (London: Weidenfeld and Nicolson, 1983), p. 69. |
| 8 | *Truth*, 13 October 1881. |
| 9 | Argyll, *Passages From the Past*, II, 455. |
| 10 | Hubbard, *Rideau Hall*, p. 58. |
| 11 | Argyll, *Passages From the Past*, II, 459. |
| 12 | PAC, Macdonald Papers, Lorne to Macdonald, 24 June 1880. |
| 13 | PAC, Lorne Papers, Lorne to Hicks Beach, 25 July 1879. |
| 14 | *Ibid.*, Lorne to Lord Salisbury, 29 September 1879, and 28 November 1879. |
| 15 | PAC, Lorne Papers, Lorne to Eighth Duke of Argyll, 12 April 1880. |
| 16 | Public Archives of Canada, Sir Alexander Galt Papers [hereafter PAC, Galt Papers], Lorne to Galt, 1 May 1880. |
| 17 | New York *Times*, 11 June 1881. |
| 18 | Saint John *Daily Sun*, 2 July 1881. |
| 19 | PAC, Lorne Papers, Lorne to Eighth Duke of Argyll, 14 April and 30 April 1879. |

20    Argyll, *Passages From the Past*, II, 474.
21    *Ibid.*, II, 463.
22    PAC, Lorne Papers, Lorne to Kimberley, 3 August 1881.
23    Lorne, *Canadian Pictures*, p. 179.
24    Glenbow-Alberta Institute, William Parker Papers, Parker to Annie Parker, 18 August 1881, and Parker to Anne Parker, 7 September 1881.
25    Lorne, *Canadian Pictures*, p. 162.
26    *Ibid.*, p. 163.
27    *Ibid.*, p. 164; Hugh A. Dempsey, *Crowfoot: Chief of the Blackfeet* (Edmonton: Hurtig, 1972), pp. 136-37.
28    Lorne, *Canadian Pictures*, p. 191.
29    W. Henry Barneby, *Life and Labour in the Far, Far West* (London: Cassell, 1884), pp. 277-80; Edward Brado, *Cattle Kingdom: Early Ranching in Alberta* (Vancouver: Douglas & McIntyre, 1984), p. 139.
30    Argyll, *Passages From the Past*, II, 473.
31    Fort Macleod *Gazette*, 8 July 1882.
32    Glenbow-Alberta Institute, George Coutts Papers, F.W. Godsal to William Pearce, 25 March 1926.
33    Argyll, *Passages From the Past*, II, 516.
34    Toronto *Globe*, 14 October 1881.

## NOTES TO CHAPTER THIRTEEN

1    Marquis of Lorne, *The Canadian North West* (Ottawa: Department of Agriculture, 1881).
2    Toronto *Globe*, 13 October 1881; Quebec *Chronicle*, 14 October 1881; Montreal *Evening Post*, 14 October 1881.
3    Public Archives of Canada, Herbert Vero Shaw Page Papers, "Cannington Manor: A Tale of Early Settlement Life," typescript by Jessie H. Beckton.
4    PAC, Lorne Papers, "Memorandum to the Privy Council on Subjects Brought to His Excellency's Notice During His Tour of the North-West," 28 October 1881.
5    *Ibid.*
6    New York *Times*, 13 May 1881; Toronto *Globe*, 13 July 1881; *The Times*, 30 September 1881.
7    Toronto *Globe*, 13 July 1881; London *Telegraph*, 25 August 1881.
8    London (Ontario) *Advertiser*, 7 November 1881.
9    Toronto *Mail*, 6 December 1881.
10   Masterman, *Mary Gladstone*, p. 236.
11   PAC, Lorne Papers, Lorne to Emma MacNeill, 29 December 1881.
12   *Ibid.*
13   *The Times*, 12 January 1882.
14   PAC, Lorne Papers, Lorne to Emma MacNeill, 29 December 1881.
15   Balfour, *Ne Obliviscaris*, I, 327-28.
16   *Ibid*, I, 328.
17   PAC, Macdonald Papers, Lorne to Macdonald, 2 May 1882.
18   BL, Gladstone Papers, Lorne to Gladstone, 14 November 1882.
19   PAC, Lorne Papers, Kimberley to Lorne, 11 May 1882.
20   Rupert Hart-Davis, editor, *The Letters of Oscar Wilde* (London: Rupert Hart-Davis, 1962), p. 117.
21   Kevin O'Brien, *Oscar Wilde in Canada: An Apostle for the Arts* (Toronto: Personal Library, 1982), pp. 78-79.

22    H. Montgomery Hyde, *Oscar Wilde* (New York: Farrar, Straus and Giroux, 1975), p. 73.

23    Hart-Davis, *The Letters of Oscar Wilde*, p. 119.

24    O'Brien, *Oscar Wilde in Canada*, p. 185.

25    *Ibid.*, p. 73.

26    Gwyn, *The Private Capital*, p. 182.

27    PAC, Lorne Papers, Lorne to Archibald Campbell, 22 September 1879; Lorne, *Canadian Pictures*, p. 94; MacNutt, *Days of Lorne*, p. 180.

28    PAC, Lorne Papers, Lorne to Archibald Campbell, 12 April 1882.

29    PAC, Lorne Papers, Todd to Lorne, 16 May 1881; Smith to Lorne, 18 May 1881.

30    MacNutt, *Days of Lorne*, p. 139.

31    Argyll, *Passages From the Past*, II, 473.

32    Carl Berger, *Science, God and Nature in Victorian Canada* (Toronto: University of Toronto Press, 1983), p. 19.

33    Henry Morgan, editor, *The Dominion Annual Register and Review for 1882* (Toronto: Hunter, Rose, 1883), p. 278.

34    Royal Society of Canada, *Fifty Years Retrospect: Anniversary Volume 1882-1932* (N.P: n.d.), p. 2.

35    Public Archives of Canada, J.G. Bourinot Papers [hereafter PAC, Bourinot papers], Lorne to Bourinot, 8 June 1893, 8 June 1894, and 12 January 1894.

## NOTES TO CHAPTER FOURTEEN

1    Donald Macleod, editor, *Good Words For 1882* (London: Isbister and Company, 1882), pp. 217-25.

2    Masterman, *Mary Gladstone*, p. 244.

3    New York *Times*, 5 June 1882.

4    *The Times*, 31 July 1882.

5    PAC, Macdonald Papers, Lorne to Macdonald, 22 June 1882.

6    PAC, Lorne Papers, Macdonald to Lorne, 24 June 1882.

7    PAC, Macdonald Papers, De Winton to Macdonald, 24 August 1882.

8    New York *Times*, 5 September 1882.

9    *Daily British Colonist* (Victoria), 15 September 1882.

10    *Ibid.*, 17 September 1882.

11    New York *Times*, 19 September 1882.

12    *Daily British Colonist*, 20 September 1882; Vancouver *Daily Province*, 20 January 1940.

13    PAC, Macdonald Papers, De Winton to Macdonald, 20 March 1882.

14    *Daily British Colonist*, 21 September 1882; Margaret Ormsby, *British Columbia: A History* (Toronto: Macmillan, 1958); Cheun-yan David Lai, *Arches in British Columbia* (Victoria: Sono Nis, 1982), pp. 61-70.

15    *Daily British Colonist*, 22 September, 23 September, and 27 September 1882.

16    *Mainland Guardian* (New Westminster), 30 September 1882.

17    Vancouver City Archives, Reminiscences of Grace Melville Green; *Daily British Colonist*, 7 October 1882.

18    Vancouver *Daily Province*, 16 March 1940.

19    PAC, Macdonald Papers, De Winton to Macdonald, 22 October 1882.

20    Vancouver *Daily Province*, 18 March 1939 and 26 September 1936.

21    Derek Pethick, *Summer of Promise: Victoria 1864-1914* (Victoria: Sono Nis, 1980), p. 102.

22    *Daily British Colonist*, 24 October and 1 December 1882.

23    Victoria *Daily Times*, 20 July 1952.

24    National Gallery of Canada, European Painting Division, Accession No. 14650, and Prints and Drawing Division, Princess Louise's Watercolours, Album No. 1.

25    Collins, *Canada Under the Administration of Lord Lorne*, pp. 474-75; PAC, Macdonald Papers, De Winton to Macdonald, 22 October 1882, and Lorne to Macdonald, 24 October 1882.

26    Harry Gregson, *A History of Victoria 1842-1970* (Victoria: Victoria Observer, 1970), p. 140.

27    Argyll, *Yesterday and Today in Canada*, p. 56.

28    PAC, Macdonald Papers, De Winton to Macdonald, 27 December 1882.

29    S.W. Jackman, *The Men at Cary Castle* (Victoria: Morriss Printing Company, 1972), p. 41.

30    PAC, Lorne Papers, Macdonald to Lorne, 7 January 1883.

31    PAC, Macdonald Papers, De Winton to Macdonald, 31 August and 22 October 1882.

32    Ottawa *Citizen*, 26 December 1882.

33    San Francisco *Call*, 17 December 1882.

34    National Gallery of Canada, Prints and Drawing Division, Princess Louise's Watercolours, Album No. 1.

35    Argyll, *Passages From the Past*, II, 488-506; PAC, Macdonald Papers, De Winton to Macdonald, 20 January 1883.

36    Susan Mary Alsop, *Lady Sackville* (New York: Doubleday, 1978), p. 56.

37    Toronto *Globe*, 27 January 1883.

38    New York *Times*, 28 January 1883.

39    PAC, Macdonald Papers, Louise to Lorne, 4 February 1883.

40    National Gallery of Canada, Prints and Drawing Division, Princess Louise's Watercolours, Album No. 1.

41    New York *Times*, 4 January 1883.

42    Louise Reynolds, *Agnes: The Biography of Lady Macdonald* (Toronto: Samuel Stevens, 1979), pp. 96-97.

43    PAC, Lorne Papers, Lorne to Admiral Sir Edmond Commerell, 3 December 1882.

44    New York *Times*, 6 February 1883.

45    PAC, Lorne Papers, Lorne to Galloway, 23 April 1883.

46    *Ibid.*, Lorne to Eighth Duke of Argyll, 2 March 1883.

47    PAC, Macdonald Papers, Lorne to Macdonald, 10 April 1883.

48    New York *Times*, 15 April 1883.

## NOTES TO CHAPTER FIFTEEN

1    PAC, Macdonald Papers, Lorne to Macdonald, 10 April 1883.

2    PAC, Lorne Papers, Derby to Lorne, 12 April and 2 May 1883.

3    Marie von Bunsen, *The World I Used to Know* (London: Macmillan, 1921), p. 132.

4    Gordon Hendricks, *Albert Bierstadt; Painter of the American West* (New York: Harry N. Abrams, 1973), pp. 276-77.

5    Argyll, *Passages From the Past*, II, 497; Lorne, *Memories of Canada and Scotland*, p. 349; Collins, *Canada Under the Administration of Lord Lorne*, p. 495.

6    PAC, Macdonald Papers, Lorne to Macdonald, 17 October 1883.

7    Collins, *Canada Under the Administration of Lord Lorne*, pp. 497-98.

8    PAC, Lorne Papers, Macdonald to Lorne, 16 October 1883.

9   *Ibid.*, Derby to Lorne, 29 June 1883.
10  Collins, *Canada Under the Administration of Lord Lorne*, p. 417.
11  *Ibid.*, p. 431.
12  J.E. Collins, "Social Life in Ottawa," *The Week*, 6 November 1884, p. 775.
13  *Truth*, 25 October 1883.
14  Collins, "Social Life in Ottawa," p. 775.
15  PAC, Lorne Papers, Lorne to Lansdowne, 9 June 1883.
16  PAC, Macdonald Papers, Lorne to Macdonald, 27 October 1883.
17  R. H. Hubbard, "Viceregal Influences on Canadian Society," in W.L. Morton, editor, *The Shield of Achilles: Aspects of Canada in the Victorian Age* (Toronto: McClelland and Stewart, 1968), p. 257.
18  PAC, Lorne Papers, Lorne to Lansdowne, 19 June 1883.
19  *Ibid.*, Lorne to Eighth Duke of Argyll, 24 April 1879; PAC, Macdonald Papers, Lorne to Macdonald, 26 December 1881 and 3 February 1882.
20  Lorne, *Memories of Canada and Scotland*, p. 63.
21  PAC, Macdonald Papers, Lorne to Macdonald, 7 November 1883.
22  *Ibid.*, Tupper to Macdonald, 11 December 1884.
23  Creighton, *John A. Macdonald*, II, 392.
24  PAC, Macdonald Papers, Lorne to Macdonald, 7 November 1883.
25  New York *Times*, 6 December 1883.
26  PAC, Macdonald Papers, Lorne to Macdonald, 20 December 1883.
27  PAC, Lorne Papers, Lansdowne to Lorne, 21 December and 23 December 1883; Langevin to Lorne, 4 January 1884.
28  Elizabeth Waterston, "Travel Books 1880-1920," in Carl Klinck, *et al*, editors, *Literary History of Canada: Canadian Literature in English* (Toronto: University of Toronto Press, 1976), II, 363-64.
29  Lorne, *Canadian Pictures*, p. 36.
30  *Ibid.*, pp. 26, 28, 213, 217-22.
31  Metropolitan Toronto Library, George Stewart Papers, Lorne to Stewart, n.d. (c1885).
32  *The Times*, 6 October and 21 June 1887.

## NOTES TO CHAPTER SIXTEEN

1   Lee, *King Edward VII*, I, 233.
2   BL, Gladstone Papers, Lorne to Gladstone, 14 November 1882, 1 May 1883, and 20 July 1883; Gladstone to Lorne, 17 September 1885; Lorne to Gladstone, 20 September 1885; see also Marquis of Lorne, "Provincial Home Rule in Ireland," *Contemporary Review*, April 1884, pp. 483-93, and "Transatlantic Lessons on Home Rule," *Ibid.*, July 1886, pp. 128-36.
3   A.B. Cooke and John Vincent, *The Governing Passion: Cabinet Government and Party Politics in Britain 1885-86* (Brighton: Harvester Press, 1974), pp. 363-65.
4   *Truth*, 17 January 1884.
5   PAC, Lorne Papers, Lorne to Eighth Duke of Argyll, 2 March 1883.
6   Agatha Ramm, editor, *The Political Correspondence of Mr. Gladstone and Lord Granville, 1876-1886* (Oxford: Clarendon Press, 1962), II, 46-52.
7   *Ibid.*, II, 244, 432; Dudley Bahlmann, editor, *The Diary of Sir Edward Walter Hamilton* (Oxford: Clarendon Press, 1972), II, 745, 755, 768.
8   Bahlmann, *Diary of Edward Walter Hamilton*, II, 577.
9   Marquis of Lorne, "Disestablishment," *Scottish Review*, July 1885, pp. 1-10.

10    PAC, Lorne Papers, Eighth Duke of Argyll to Queen Victoria, 11 October 1883.
11    *Ibid.*
12    British Library, Sir Charles Dilke Papers [hereafter BL, Dilke Papers], Lorne to Dilke, 23 January 1885.
13    Bahlmann, *Diary of Edward Walter Hamilton*, II, 656, 660.
14    BL, Dilke Papers, Lorne to Dilke, 23 January 1885.
15    BL, Gladstone Papers, Lorne to Gladstone, 20 September 1885.
16    *The Times*, 25 March, 28 March, 30 April, and 26 October 1885.
17    Lee, *King Edward VII*, I, 527-28.
18    *The Times*, 7 October 1885.
19    Argyll, *Passages From the Past*, II, 377-78.
20    *Ibid.*, II, 380-84.
21    PAC, Lorne Papers, Lorne to Archibald Campbell, 22 September 1879.
22    *Ibid.*, Lorne to Dr. W.F. Cumming, 16 January 1881.
23    PAC, Macdonald Papers, Lorne to Macdonald, 10 April 1884.
24    PAC, Bourinot Papers, Lorne to Bourinot, 26 January 1886.
25    Marquis of Lorne, "The Highland Land Agitation," *Contemporary Review*, December 1884, pp. 827-37; see also BL, Dilke Papers, Lorne to Dilke, 24 March 1885.
26    Ninth Duke of Argyll, editor, *Intimate Society Letters of the Eighteenth Century* (London: Stanley Paul, 1910), I, 95.
27    PAC, Macdonald Papers, Lorne to Macdonald, 10 April 1884.
28    Helen Merrell Lynd, *England in the Eighteen-Eighties: Toward a Social Basis for Freedom* (London: Oxford, 1945), pp. 129-34; John W. Mason, "The Duke of Argyll and the Land Question in Late Nineteenth-Century Britain," Victorian Studies, Winter 1978, pp. 149-70; James Hunter, "The Politics of Highland Land Reform, 1873-1895," *Scottish Historical Review*, 1974, pp. 45-68.
29    Bodleian, Harcourt Papers, Lorne to William Harcourt, 30 October 1884.
30    *Ibid.*, Harcourt to Lorne, 3 November 1884.
31    Balfour, *Lady Victoria Campbell*, p. 161.
32    PAC, Lorne Papers, Lorne to Eighth Duke of Argyll, 26 April 1881.
33    PAC, Bourinot Papers, Lorne to Bourinot, 18 January 1902.
34    PAC, Macdonald Papers, Lorne to Macdonald, 10 April 1884; Louise to Alfred Tennyson, 12 April 1884, in Hope Dyson and Charles Tennyson, editors, *Dear and Honoured Lady: The Correspondence Between Queen Victoria and Alfred Tennyson* (Rutherford, New Jersey: Fairleigh Dikinson University Press, 1971), p. 113.
35    *Truth*, 14 August 1884.
36    *Ibid.*, 28 August 1884.
37    Kensington Palace Archives, undated newspaper clippings, c. 1885-86.
38    *Truth*, 9 November 1882.
39    Epton, *Victoria and Her Daughters*, p. 233.
40    Fulford, *Beloved Mama*, p. 170.
41    *Truth*, 11 September, 6 November, and 27 November 1884.
42    Epton, *Victoria and Her Daughters*, p. 177.

## NOTES TO CHAPTER SEVENTEEN

1    Jeffrey L. Lant, *Insubstantial Pageant: Ceremony and Confusion at Queen Victoria's Court* (London: Hamish Hamilton, 1979), p. 3.
2    Princess Victoria of Prussia, *Queen Victoria at Windsor and Balmoral*, edited by James Pope-Hennessy (London: George Allen and Unwin, 1959), p. 33.

3    Marie Mallet, *Life With Queen Victoria: Marie Mallet's Letters From Court 1887-1901*, edited by Victor Mallet (London: John Murray, 1968, pp. 40, 50.

4    *Truth*, 23 September 1886.

5    *Ibid.*, 4 November 1886.

6    *Malta Times*, 5 February 1887.

7    *Truth*, 7 April 1887.

8    Bodleian, Harcourt Papers, Lorne to William Harcourt, 16 May 1900.

9    Ronald Gower, *Old Diaries* (New York: Scribner, 1902), pp. 111-13.

10   Paget, *Embassies of Other Days*, II, 483.

11   Constance Battersea, *Reminiscences* (London: Macmillan, 1922), pp. 378-79.

12   *Ibid.*, pp. 380, 383.

13   Richard Hough, editor, *Advice to a Grand-Daughter: Letters From Queen Victoria to Princess Victoria of Hesse* (London: Heinemann, 1975), p. 109.

14   Elizabeth Longford, *Pilgrimage of Passion: The Life of Wilfrid Scawen Blunt* (London: Weidenfeld and Nicolson, 1979), p. 376.

15   *Ibid.*

16   Hunt-Lewis, "The Art of Princess Louise," in Duff, *Princess Louise*, p. 341.

17   Estella Canziani, *Round About Three Palace Green* (London: Methuen, 1939), p. 82.

18   Gower, *Old Diaries*, p. 200; Hunt-Lewis, "The Art of Princess Louise," in Duff, *Princess Louise*, p. 340.

19   Raleigh Trevelyan, *Princes Under the Volcano* (London: Macmillan, 1972), pp. 280, 500n. Trevelyan attributes this to "information from the late Mr. Luke Fildes."

20   Gower, *Old Diaries*, pp. 173-360.

21   *Ibid.*, p. 196.

22   Rupert Croft-Cooke, *Feasting With Panthers* (London: W.H. Allen, 1967), p. 194.

23   Rowell, *Queen Victoria Goes to the Theatre*, p. 91; Frederick Ponsonby, *Recollections of Three Reigns* (London: Eyre & Spottiswoode, 1951), p. 51.

24   Ponsonby, *Recollections of Three Reigns*, p. 51.

25   James Pope-Hennessy, *Queen Mary 1867-1953* (London: George Allen and Unwin, 1959), p. 317.

26   BL, Gladstone Papers, Louise to Catherine Gladstone, 1 February 1896.

27   Michaela Reid, *Ask Sir James* (London: Hodder & Stoughton, 1987), p. 103.

28   *Truth*, 13 February 1896.

29   British Library, Bishop William Boyd Carpenter Papers [hereafter BL, Carpenter Papers], Lorne to Carpenter, 25 December 1896; Gower, *Old Diaries*, p. 322.

## NOTES TO CHAPTER EIGHTEEN

1    Bodleian, Harcourt Papers, Lorne to William Harcourt, 28 May and 13 June 1891, and William Harcourt to Lorne, 22 November 1892; Argyll, *Passages From the Past*, II, 591.

2    Argyll, *Passages From the Past*, II, 589.

3    *Ibid.*, II, 591; Marquis of Lorne, "The Partition of Africa," *North American Review*, December 1890, pp. 701-12; *The Times*, 11 October 1892 and 6 June 1894.

4    Roland Oliver and Gervase Mathew, *History of Africa* (Oxford: Clarendon Press, 1963), I, 393.

5    Argyll, *Passages From the Past*, II, 584; Marquis of Lorne, "East Africa," *Nineteenth Century*, September 1891, p. 341.

6    *Truth*, 9 April and 16 April 1891.

7    J.W. Mackail, *The Life of William Morris* (London: Longmans, Green, 1901), II, 288.

8    *Truth*, 23 July 1896.

9    *Ibid.*, 28 January and 25 March 1892.

10   Public Archives of Canada, George Stewart Papers [hereafter PAC, Stewart Papers], Lorne to Stewart, 25 June 1892; Argyll, *Passages From the Past*, II, 600.

11   Argyll, *Passages From the Past*, II, 589.

12   Marquis of Lorne, "A Suggestion for Emigrants," *Nineteenth Century*, April 1889, pp. 608-14; Marquis of Lorne, "Canada and the United States," *North American Review*, May 1891, pp. 557-66; Marquis of Lorne, "Some Thoughts on Canada," *North American Review*, June 1895, pp. 712-21.

13   Marquis of Lorne, "Five Years' Advocacy of Provincial Parliaments," *Fortnightly Review*, June 1889, pp. 809-18; Marquis of Lorne, "Provincial Home Rule," *Contemporary Review*, August 1892, pp. 258-62.

14   John Wilson, *CB: A Life of Sir Henry Campbell-Bannerman* (London: Constable, 1973), pp. 550-51.

15   PAC, Stewart Papers, Lorne to Stewart, 16 July 1895.

16   Great Britain. *Parliamentary Debates. Fourth Series.* XXXIX, 1046, 16 April 1896.

17   Manchester *Guardian*, 4 May 1914.

18   *Athanaeum*, 30 January 1892, p. 147; see also *The Spectator*, 12 March 1892, pp. 371-72.

19   *Athanaeum*, 26 March 1898, p. 402.

20   Marquis of Lorne, "Who Were They? A Maltese Apparition," *Blackwood's Magazine*, December 1887, pp. 794-804; An Electrician (pseud.), "The Double-Bedded Room," *Blackwood's Magazine*, September 1894, pp. 411-16.

21   Marquis of Lorne, "Hunting Life in the Rockies," *Harper's Weekly*, 8 April 1893, pp. 320-23.

22   *Catholic World*, August 1891, p. 773; *Athanaeum*, 14 September 1895, p. 357.

23   Marquis of Lorne, "Love and Peril," *Three Notable Stories* (London: Spencer Blackett, 1890), pp. 62-63; Marquis of Lorne, *From Shadow to Sunlight* (New York: Appleton, 1891), pp. 95-96, 103.

24   Quebec *Mercury*, 17 September 1898.

25   *Sunday Times*, 3 May 1914.

26   Battiscombe, *Queen Alexandra*, p. 226.

27   Lord Suffield, *My Memories 1830-1913* (London: Herbert Jenkins, 1913), p. 319.

28   Mallet, *Life With Queen Victoria*, p. 169.

29   Joyce Marlow, *The Oak and the Ivy: An Intimate Biography of William and Catherine Gladstone* (Garden City: Doubleday, 1977), p. 286.

30   Buckle, *Letters of Queen Victoria*. Third Series, II, 334; Ponsonby, *Recollections of Three Reigns*, p. 78.

31   Maurice V. Brett, editor, *Journals and Letters of Reginald Viscount Esher* (London: Ivor Nicholson & Watson, 1934), I, 206; Mallet, *Life With Queen Victoria*, p. 128.

32   Quebec *Mercury*, 20 March 1899.

33   Augustus Hare, *The Story of My Life* (London: George Allen, 1900), VI, 341.

34   Quebec *Mercury*, 20 March 1899.

35   PAC, Bourinot Papers, Lorne to Bourinot, 9 December 1899.

36   Carman Miller, *The Canadian Career of the Fourth Earl of Minto* (Waterloo: Wilfrid Laurier University Press, 1980), pp. 49, 52; Lorne and the Earl of Minto had known each other since student days at Cambridge; Louise and Lady Minto were childhood friends.

37   Buckle, *Letters of Queen Victoria*. Third Series, III, 467.

38   Marquis of Lorne, "Realities of the South African War," *North American Review*, March 1900, pp. 305-11; *The Times*, 21 November 1901.

39   Balfour, *Ne Obliviscaris*, II, 382; Gwyn, *The Private Capital*, p. 375.

40    PAC, Bourinot Papers, Lorne to Bourinot, 1 February 1900; Duke of Argyll, "Emigration," in Louis Creswicke, editor, *South Africa and Its Future* (London: T.C. & E.C. Jack, 1903), pp. 181-97; Marquis of Lorne, "Planting Out State Children in South Africa," *Nineteenth Century*, April 1900, pp. 609-11.

41    Argyll, "Emigration," in Creswicke, *South Africa and Its Future*, pp. 181-97.

42    Gillian Wagner, *Barnardo* (London: Weidenfeld and Nicolson, 1979), pp. 252-55.

43    Hunt-Lewis, "The Art of Princess Louise," in Duff, *Princess Louise*, p. 342.


## NOTES TO CHAPTER NINETEEN

1     Gower, *Old Diaries*, p. 379.

2     British Library, Henry Campbell-Bannerman Papers [hereafter BL, Campbell-Bannerman Papers], Argyll to Campbell-Bannerman, 26 April 1900.

3     Edith Lytton, *Lady Lytton's Court Diary 1895-1899*, edited by Mary Lutyens (London: Rupert Hart-Davis, 1961), p. 26.

4     BL, Mary Gladstone Papers, Argyll to Mary Gladstone Drew, 28 March 1902.

5     Duff, *Princess Louise*, p. 234.

6     H.C. Shelley, "The Home of a Highland Noble," *New England Magazine*, February 1898, pp. 683-87.

7     Eighth Duke of Argyll, *Autobiography and Memoirs*, II, 551; Duff, *Princess Louise*, p. 234.

8     Berkshire Record Office, Glyn Papers [hereafter BRO, Glyn Papers], Argyll to Richard Glyn, 4 November 1909; Duke of Argyll, "Fair Farms Versus Fancy Crofts," *Nineteenth Century and After*, October 1907, pp. 517-23; Manchester *Guardian*, 4 May 1914.

9     Bodleian, Harcourt Papers, Argyll to Lewis Harcourt, 7 September 1902.

10    *Ibid.*

11    BL, Mary Gladstone Papers, Argyll to Mary Gladstone Drew, 14 April 1903.

12    Bodleian, Harcourt Papers, Argyll to Lewis Harcourt, 7 September and 12 September 1902.

13    Balfour, *Ne Obliviscaris*, II, 341.

14    *Ibid.*, II, 342.

15    Ponsonby, *Recollections of Three Reigns*, p. 82.

16    Bodleian, Harcourt Papers, Argyll to Lewis Harcourt, 8 February 1901.

17    Reid, *Ask Sir James*, p. 206; Ponsonby, *Recollections of Three Reigns*, pp. 83-84.

18    Duff, *Princess Louise*, p. 238.

19    Philip Ziegler, *Diana Cooper* (London: Hamish Hamilton, 1981), p. 127.

20    Epton, *Victoria and Her Daughters*, p. 222.

21    Gower, *Old Diaries*, pp. 402-03; see also Balfour, *Ne Obliviscaris*, II, 342.

22    *Times Literary Supplement*, 31 January 1902.

23    Peter Fraser, *Lord Esher: A Political Biography* (London: Hart-Davis, MacGibbon, 1973), p. 84.

24    Epton, *Victoria and Her Daughters*, p. 226.

25    David Duff, *Whisper Louise: Edward VII and Mrs. Creswell* (London: Frederick Muller, 1974), p. 127.

26    Madame Klepac, "A Royal Rebel," *Saturday Evening Post*, 4 January 1930, p. 145.

27    Madame Klepac, "A Royal Rebel," as told to Helen Dunham and Margaret Norris, *Saturday Evening Post*, 28 December 1929, pp. 14-15, 77-78, and 4 January 1930, pp. 33, 135-45.

28    *Ibid.*, 28 December 1929, p. 15.

29    *Ibid.*

30 Sir Almeric Fitzroy, *Memoirs* (London: Hutchinson & Co., n.d.), I, 367; Klepac, "A Royal Rebel," 28 December 1929, p. 15.

31 Klepac, "A Royal Rebel," 28 December 1929, p. 77.

32 *Ibid*; Duff, *Princess Louise*, p. 305.

33 Klepac, "A Royal Rebel," 4 January 1930, p. 135.

34 Duff, *Princess Louise*, pp. 307-10.

35 *Ibid.*, p. 317; Balfour, *Ne Obliviscaris*, II, 414.

36 Klepac, "A Royal Rebel," 28 December 1929, p. 78.

37 Duff, *Princess Louise*, p. 300.

38 Rhondda *Leader*, 28 July 1909.

## NOTES TO CHAPTER TWENTY

1 Klepac, "A Royal Rebel," *Saturday Evening Post*, 28 December 1929, p. 77.

2 H. Montgomery Hyde, *The Love That Dared Not Speak Its Name* (Boston: Little, Brown, 1970), p. 156.

3 *Ibid.*, p. 156; see also Trevelyan, *Princes Under the Volcano*, pp. 337-39, and Charles Higham, *The Adventures of Conan Doyle: The Life of the Creator of Sherlock Holmes* (New York: W.W. Norton, 1976), pp. 204-06.

4 Trevelyan, *Princes Under the Volcano*, p. 339.

5 Klepac, "A Royal Rebel," *Saturday Evening Post*, 4 January 1930, p. 138.

6 BRO, Glyn Papers, Argyll to Ralph Glyn, 7 September 1902 and 18 June 1903.

7 Helensburgh *News*, 7 May 1914.

8 *The Scotsman*, 4 May 1914; Frances Warwick, *Afterthoughts* (London: Cassell, 1931), pp. 152-53.

9 *The Scotsman*, 4 May 1914.

10 Duke of Argyll, "The House of Lords," *The Living Age*, 25 April 1908, pp. 195-200.

11 BL, Campbell-Bannerman Papers, Argyll to Campbell-Bannerman, 5 December 1905.

12 Dundee *Advertiser*, 25 November 1909.

13 *The Times*, 27 November 1909.

14 *Ibid.*, 15 April and 20 May 1910.

15 Manchester *Guardian*, 4 May 1914.

16 Duke of Argyll, *A Gift Book for the Home* (London: Hodder and Stoughton, 1901); National Gallery of Scotland, *Portrait of the National Gallery of Scotland* (Edinburgh: Edward Arnold, 1903); J.H. Batt, *Dr. Barnardo: The Foster-Father of Nobody's Children* (London: S.W. Partridge, 1904); Ethel Hogg, *Quinton Hogg: An Appreciation* (London: Archibald Constable, 1904); Duke of Argyll, "The Half-Breed's Story," *The Canadian Magazine*, January 1905, pp. 219-23.

17 *Times Literary Supplement*, 7 November 1907, p. 337; *Punch*, 20 November 1907, p. 378; *Bookman*, December 1907, pp. 131-32.

18 *Times Literary Supplement*, 21 July 1910, p. 260; see also *Bookman*, August 1910, p. 188; *The Nation*, December 1910, p. 608.

19 Vincent Sheehan, *Oscar Hammerstein I: The Life and Exploits of an Impressario* (New York: Simon and Schuster, 1956), p. 321.

20 Glasgow *Herald*, 30 December 1911 and 2 December 1913.

21 Ross, *Getting Into Parliament and After*, p. 112.

22 J.S. Redmayne, *Fruit Farming on the "Dry Belt" in British Columbia* (London: Times Book Club, 1909); Duke of Argyll, *Yesterday & Today in Canada* (London: George Allen & Sons, 1910).

23     *Times Literary Supplement*, 10 November 1910, p. 439; *Bookman*, February 1911, p. 352; *The Nation*, March 1911, p. 323.

24     Franco-British Exhibition, London, 1908, *Official Guide* (London: Bemrose & Sons, 1908), p. 46.

25     *The Times*, 12 July 1906 and 2 May 1907.

26     Viscount Mersey, *A Picture of Life 1872-1940* (London: John Murray, 1941), p. 222; *The Times*, 17 October 1907.

27     *The Times*, 30 April 1910.

28     *Ibid.*, 15 January 1907, 4 February 1904, 1 May 1907.

29     *Ibid.*, 14 October 1904.

30     *The Car*, 16 December 1908.

31     *The Times*, 16 December 1909, 3 March 1910, 6 May 1913.

32     *The Car*, 16 December 1908; *The Automotor Journal*, 19 December 1908; *Motor*, 10 January 1909.

## NOTES TO CHAPTER TWENTY-ONE

1     Manchester *Guardian*, 4 May 1914.

2     *Sunday Times*, 3 May 1914.

3     Artemis Cooper, editor, *A Durable Fire: The Letters of Duff and Diana Cooper 1913-1950* (London: Collins, 1983), p. 8.

4     Balfour, *Ne Obliviscaris*, I, 111.

5     Glasgow *Daily Record*, 4 May 1914.

6     *Sunday Times*, 3 May 1914; Manchester *Guardian*, 4 May 1914.

7     Manchester *Guardian*, 4 May 1914.

8     Oban *Times*, 9 May 1914.

9     Balfour, *Ne Obliviscaris*, I, 87, 110.

10     Bodleian, Harcourt Papers, Louise to Lewis Harcourt, 11 December 1914; BL, Carpenter Papers, Louise to Bishop Boyd Carpenter, 25 September 1915; BL, Mary Gladstone Papers, Louise to Mary Gladstone Drew, 27 February 1918.

11     BRO, Glyn Papers, Louise to Ralph Glyn, 23 September 1915 and 14 April 1916.

12     *Ibid.*, 14 April 1916.

13     BL, Carpenter Papers, Louise to Bishop Boyd Carpenter, 26 February 1916.

14     Bodleian, Harcourt Papers, Louise to Lewis Harcourt, 11 December 1914.

15     BRO, Glyn Papers, Louise to Ralph Glyn, n.d. (c1917).

16     Duff, *Princess Louise*, p. 274.

17     Ponsonby, *Recollections of Three Reigns*, p. 112.

18     Duff, *Princess Louise*, p. 313.

19     Richard Hough, *Louis & Victoria: The First Mountbattens* (London: Hutchinson, 1974), p. 375.

20     Duff, *Princess Louise*, p. 5.

21     *The Times*, 4 December 1939.

22     Douglas How, *The 8th Hussars: A History of the Regiment* (Sussex, New Brunswick: Maritime Publishing, 1964), pp. 371-72.

# FOR FURTHER READING

Ashdown, Dulcie. *Queen Victoria's Family*. London: Robert Hale, 1975.

Balfour, Frances. *Ne Obliviscaris: Dinna Forget*. London: Hodder and Stoughton, 1930. Two volumes.

Bennett, Daphne. *Queen Victoria's Children*. London: Victor Gollancz, 1980.

Benson, E.F. *Daughters of Queen Victoria*. London: Cassell, 1939.

Campbell, George, 8th Duke of Argyll. *Autobiography and Memoirs*. London: John Murray, 1906. Two volumes.

Campbell, John, Marquis of Lorne. *The Canadian North West*. Ottawa: Department of Agriculture, 1881.

——————. *Canadian Pictures Drawn with Pen and Pencil*. London: Religious Tract Society, 1885.

——————. *Memories of Scotland and Canada: Speeches and Verses*. Montreal: Dawson Brothers, 1884.

——————. *A Trip to the Tropics and Home Through America*. London: Hurst and Blackett, 1867.

——————. [as 9th Duke of Argyll] *Passages From the Past*. London: Hutchinson, 1907. Two volumes.

——————. *Yesterday and Today in Canada*. London: George Allen, 1910.

Cartwright, Sir Richard. *Reminiscences*. Toronto: William Briggs, 1912.

Collins, J.E. *Canada Under the Administration of Lord Lorne*. Toronto: Rose, 1884.

Cowan, John. *Canada's Governors-General 1867-1952*. Toronto: York Publishing Company, 1952.

Creighton, Donald. *Sir John A. Macdonald*. Volume II: *The Old Chieftain*. Toronto: Macmillan, 1955.

Duff, David. *The Life Story of H.R.H. Princess Louise, Duchess of Argyll*. London: Stanley Paul, 1940. Second edition published by Cedric Chivers Ltd., Portway, Bath, 1971.

Epton, Nina. *Victoria and Her Daughters*. London: Weidenfeld and Nicolson, 1971.

Farr, David M.L. *The Colonial Office and Canada 1867-1887*. Toronto: University of Toronto Press, 1955.

Gower, Ronald. *My Reminiscences*. London: Kegan Paul, Trench, Trubner, 1895.

——————. *Old Diaries*. New York: Scribner, 1902.

Gwyn, Sandra. *The Private Capital: Ambition and Love in the Age of Macdonald and Laurier*. Toronto: McClelland and Stewart, 1984.

Hubbard, R.H. *Rideau Hall: An Illustrated History of Government House, Ottawa, in Victorian and Edwardian Times*. Ottawa: Queen's Printer, 1967.

Lemieux, L.-J. *The Governors-General of Canada 1608-1931*. London: Lake & Bell, 1931.

Longford, Elizabeth. *Victoria, R.I.* London: Weidenfeld and Nicolson, 1964.

MacNutt, W.S. *Days of Lorne: Impressions of a Governor General*. Fredericton: Brunswick Press, 1955.

Mallet, Victor, ed. *Life With Queen Victoria: Marie Mallet's Letters from Court 1887-1901*. London: John Murray, 1968.

Nevill, Barry St. John, ed. *Life at the Court of Queen Victoria 1861-1901*. London: Methuen, 1984.

Ponsonby, Arthur. *Henry Ponsonby, Queen Victoria's Private Secretary*. London: Macmillan, 1942.

Reid, Michaela. *Ask Sir James*. London: Hodder & Stoughton, 1987.

Sisler, Rebecca. *Passionate Spirits: A History of the Royal Canadian Academy of Arts, 1880-1980*. Toronto: Clarke, Irwin, 1980.

Stamp, Robert M. *Kings, Queens and Canadians: A Celebration of Canada's Infatuation with the British Royal Family*. Markham: Fitzhenry & Whiteside, 1987.

Tuttle, Charles. *Royalty in Canada: Embracing Sketches of the Marquis of Lorne, the Princess Louise, and the Members of the New Government*. Montreal: Tuttle & Simpson, 1878.

Waite, Peter B. *Canada 1874-1896: Arduous Destiny*. Toronto: McClelland and Stewart, 1971.

Weintraub, Stanley. *Victoria: An Intinmate Biography*. New York: E.P. Dutton, 1987.

# INDEX

If individuals have more than one title, they have been indexed under the most commonly used title. Page numbers in **bold** indicate an illustration. Since Lorne and Louise appear on almost every page, they have not been indexed except for their pictures.

318